AF896570

Financial Inclusion for Viksit Bharat

This timely and meticulously curated volume is a landmark contribution to the discourse on inclusive growth in India. By bringing together diverse perspectives on digital transformation, gender equity, disability rights, rural credit, and retirement security, the editors provide a holistic blueprint for financial inclusion in the run-up to Viksit Bharat 2047. The rigorous empirical evidence, grounded in both global frameworks and grassroots realities, offers actionable insights for policymakers, regulators, and development practitioners. This book not only documents India's achievements-particularly in building world-class Digital Public Infrastructure-but also confronts the persistent structural barriers that hinder equitable access to finance. A must-read for anyone committed to ensuring that no citizen is left behind in the financial journey of our nation.

—Harun R Khan, *Former Deputy Governor, Reserve Bank of India*

Vikas Dixit · Rilina Basu Banerjee ·
Nisar Ahmad Khan
Editors

Financial Inclusion for Viksit Bharat

Innovations, Evidence and Pathways Toward Equitable Development

palgrave
macmillan

Editors
Vikas Dixit
Economics
Jadavpur University
Kolkata, West Bengal, India

Rilina Basu Banerjee
Economics
Jadavpur University
Kolkata, West Bengal, India

Nisar Ahmad Khan
Economics
Aligarh Muslim University
Aligarh, Uttar Pradesh, India

ISBN 978-981-92-0806-7 ISBN 978-981-92-0807-4 (eBook)
https://doi.org/10.1007/978-981-92-0807-4

© The Editor(s) (if applicable) and The Author(s), under exclusive license to Springer Nature Singapore Pte Ltd. 2026

This work is subject to copyright. All rights are solely and exclusively licensed by the Publisher, whether the whole or part of the material is concerned, specifically the rights of translation, reprinting, reuse of illustrations, recitation, broadcasting, reproduction on microfilms or in any other physical way, and transmission or information storage and retrieval, electronic adaptation, computer software, or by similar or dissimilar methodology now known or hereafter developed. Unless otherwise expressly agreed by the Publisher in writing, the Publisher does not authorise use or reproduction of all or any part of this work in any manner for the purpose of training, fine-tuning, evaluating, or developing artificial intelligence models, technologies, or systems. In accordance with Article 4(3) of the EU Directive 2019/790 on copyright and related rights in the Digital Single Market, the Publisher expressly reserves all rights with respect to this work under the text and data mining exception of the directive.
The use of general descriptive names, registered names, trademarks, service marks, etc. in this publication does not imply, even in the absence of a specific statement, that such names are exempt from the relevant protective laws and regulations and therefore free for general use.
The publisher, the authors and the editors are safe to assume that the advice and information in this book are believed to be true and accurate at the date of publication. Neither the publisher nor the authors or the editors give a warranty, expressed or implied, with respect to the material contained herein or for any errors or omissions that may have been made. The publisher remains neutral with regard to jurisdictional claims in published maps and institutional affiliations.

This Palgrave Macmillan imprint is published by the registered company Springer Nature Singapore Pte Ltd.
The registered company address is: 152 Beach Road, #21-01/04 Gateway East, Singapore 189721, Singapore

If disposing of this product, please recycle the paper.

Preface

The vision of a Viksit Bharat—a developed India by 2047—demands not only economic expansion but inclusive participation across all sections of society. At the heart of this vision lies financial inclusion: the ability of every citizen to access, use, and benefit from formal financial services in a meaningful and secure manner.

This volume took shape following deliberations during a national conference on financial inclusion held in early 2025 under the aegis of the Indian Council of Social Science Research (ICSSR). The gathering witnessed critical dialogues among scholars, practitioners, and policymakers from across India, each recognizing that the conversation on inclusion must move beyond access and account ownership toward trust, sustained use, and dignity.

In response to this need, this book brings together eleven rigorously researched chapters that cut across themes of digital transformation, global benchmarks, regional disparities, gender gaps, inclusion of persons with disabilities, retirement security, financial innovation, and rural credit-linked insurance. From global forums like the G20 to village-level banking correspondents, the authors explore many dimensions of financial empowerment.

This edited volume is the result of collective intellectual efforts and generous institutional support. The editors of this volume are deeply grateful to the Indian Council of Social Science Research (ICSSR) for sponsoring the national conference that laid the foundation for this book, and for their continued encouragement throughout the publication process. A sincere thank is to all the contributing authors for their timely submissions, thoughtful revisions, and scholarly engagement. The valuable inputs of the anonymous reviewers are also gratefully acknowledged whose constructive feedback helped strengthen the quality and relevance of the chapters. Special thanks are due to the team at Palgrave Macmillan for their professional guidance and support at every stage of this project. Lastly, a personal thank goes to our hosting institution and to our colleagues, research staff, and well-wishers whose support, patience, and encouragement made this academic journey both meaningful and rewarding. It is our hope that this volume will serve as a key resource for those working at the intersection of policy, finance, technology, and social inclusion. More importantly, we hope it contributes—however modestly—to building a financial ecosystem that genuinely leaves no one behind.

Kolkata, India — Vikas Dixit
Kolkata, India — Rilina Basu Banerjee
Aligarh, India — Nisar Ahmad Khan

About the Edited Volume

India's aspiration to become a Viksit Bharat (Developed India) by 2047 hinges on ensuring that every citizen is meaningfully integrated into the financial system. This edited volume offers a timely, multidimensional, and empirically grounded exploration of financial inclusion as both a developmental imperative and a strategic policy tool. It brings together eleven scholarly chapters authored by leading academicians, policymakers, and field researchers, combining global and national perspectives, theoretical frameworks, and real-world evidence.

The volume distinguishes itself through its interdisciplinary approach, methodological diversity, and equity-centred lens. It expands the conventional understanding of financial inclusion by foregrounding marginalised groups—persons with disabilities (PwDs), rural women, smallholder farmers, the elderly, and informal workers—as central stakeholders. Drawing on macroeconomic models, digital infrastructure assessments, and grassroots-level studies, the book blends conceptual clarity with actionable insights.

Organised into three thematic sections, the volume strategically progresses from global frameworks and national strategies to life-stage specific needs, institutional mechanisms, and place-based empirical analyses:

I. **Global and Strategic Perspectives on Financial Inclusion**

This section situates India's financial inclusion journey within the global discourse, especially under its G20 Presidency. It highlights India's leadership in developing scalable Digital Public Infrastructure (DPI) through initiatives like Aadhaar, UPI, PMJDY, and DBT. Chapters draw on datasets such as Global Findex and offer cross-country analyses to identify persistent inclusion gaps, proposing policy responses to address digital divides, financial literacy deficits, and climate-induced vulnerabilities.

II. **Inclusive Policies and Frameworks for Viksit Bharat**

Transitioning to national strategies, this section emphasizes life-long financial literacy, trust-building, and sustained access—particularly for underserved populations. It introduces innovative concepts like the Disability Financial Inclusion Index, provides evidence-based analysis of financial inclusion of PwDs and explores sector-specific strategies including retirement planning and gender-responsive digital finance. Empirical studies from Uttar Pradesh and Fairlie decomposition analyses reveal structural determinants of exclusion and the fragility of inclusion gains post-pandemic.

III. **Sectoral and Regional Pathways to Deepen Inclusion**

The final section delves into institutional and technological mechanisms, as well as regionally differentiated strategies. It includes theoretical models on FinTech's role in informal credit markets, subnational studies linking industrialization to digital financial access, and case-based insights from backward regions like the Sundarbans. Topics such as crop insurance access, microfinance outreach, and climate resilience are explored using large-scale surveys and econometric techniques.

Distinctive Features of the Volume

- Bridges policy and practice by featuring voices from both government institutions and academia.
- Integrates vulnerable groups as central to the financial inclusion discourse.

- Employs methodological diversity, including qualitative analysis, primary surveys, and advanced econometric models.
- Captures real-world evidence from backward regions alongside national and international trends.
- Offers policy-relevant recommendations grounded in data and theory.
- Aligns with India's National Strategy for Financial Inclusion (NSFI 2025–30).

This volume is an indispensable resource for scholars and students of economics, development studies, public policy, and finance; policymakers and regulators designing inclusive frameworks; practitioners in banking and digital governance; international development agencies; and civil society organisations advocating for rights-based financial inclusion. By weaving together conceptual, empirical, and policy dimensions, the book not only documents India's progress but also offers a globally relevant roadmap for inclusive development—anchored in equity, empowerment, and sustainability.

Contents

Editors and Contributors

About the Editors

Dr. Vikas Dixit is a Professor of Economics at Jadavpur University, Kolkata. He has earned his B.Sc. (hons.) in Statistics, M.A. in Economics, and Ph.D. in Public Expenditure, all from Aligarh Muslim University, Aligarh. With over 17 years of teaching and research experience, his academic work spans public finance, development economics, fiscal policy, and inclusive growth. He has published widely in peer-reviewed journals (including Foreign Trade Review, the Indian Economic Journal and Journal of Public Affairs) and edited volumes from Springer Regal, etc., with a particular focus on the efficiency and equity of public expenditure, intergovernmental fiscal transfers, and financial inclusion—especially for marginalized groups including persons with disabilities. He has led and collaborated on research projects funded by the ICSSR and NITI Aayog, and is currently the Principal Investigator of a major ICSSR-funded project on promoting financial inclusion of persons with disabilities in India. He has also co-organised national conferences and regularly contributes to curriculum development and doctoral supervision. Dr. Dixit is a life member of the Indian Economic Association, The Indian Econometric Society, and the Bengal Economic Association.

Rilina Basu Banerjee is a Professor of Economics at Jadavpur University, Kolkata. With over 15 years of teaching and research experience across premier institutions, her expertise lies in open economy macroeconomics, financial structures, and development economics. She earned her Ph.D. from Jadavpur University for her thesis on "Financial Structure and the Macroeconomy: Theory and Empirics." Dr. Basu has published widely in leading journals such as the Foreign Trade Review, Journal of Developing Areas, and The Pakistan Development Review. Her recent research includes empirical and theoretical studies on financial innovation, macroeconomic volatility, and educational mobility. She has supervised doctoral and M.Phil. research in these areas and has presented extensively at national and international academic forums. She is collaborating with Dr. Vikas Dixit and others in the ongoing ICSSR-funded major research project on Promoting Financial Inclusion for Persons with Disabilities in India. In addition to her academic contributions, she has co-organized major conferences and workshops on development economics and applied econometrics.

Nisar Ahmad Khan is a Professor of Economics at Aligarh Muslim University (AMU), Aligarh, where he has taught since 1983. A distinguished scholar in the fields of monetary economics and development economics, he earned his B.A., M.A., M.Phil., and Ph.D. from AMU, and was awarded the prestigious Cambridge Commonwealth Scholarship to pursue a Diploma in Development Studies at the University of Cambridge, UK. He also served as a UNDP-appointed Professor of Economics at the Ethiopian Civil Service College, Addis Ababa (2004–2007).

Prof. Khan has held several senior academic leadership roles, including Chairperson of the Department of Economics and Dean of the Faculty of Social Sciences at AMU. He has published extensively in national and international journals—many of them Scopus-indexed—and has completed several research projects focusing on banking efficiency, financial regulation, and development finance. He has also supervised numerous Ph.D. scholars and delivered invited lectures at prominent institutions across India. His teaching portfolio spans macroeconomics, monetary theory, international economics, and financial markets at both undergraduate and postgraduate levels.

Contributors

Dr. Syed Afzal Ahmad is an Assistant Professor in the Department of Business Management at Integral Business School, Integral University, Lucknow, with over a decade of academic and industry experience. He holds a Ph.D. in Management, with research centered on investor perception towards corporate reporting practices, along with an MBA in International Business and Finance. His teaching and research interests include financial management, security and investment analysis, banking, corporate responsibility, and business ethics. He has published 22 research papers in International and National journal indexed in prominent database like Scopus, ABDC and authored three books. He also holds three patents in emerging areas such as online fraud prevention, customer monitoring systems, and blockchain applications in banking. Dr. Ahmad is currently the Program Coordinator of the Doctoral Program in Management at Integral Business School and actively contributes to academic administration, research supervision, and university committees.

Ms. Shilpi Mayank Awasthi is a disability rights advocate, social entrepreneur, and consultant. She holds an M.Sc. in Microbiology and a PG Diploma in Computer Applications. She is the Founder & Managing Director of Yuvaan Research Foundation–Specialsaathi, and Founder of Bounce & Bloom Inclusive Preschool and SpecialSaathi Computer Code-Labs. She is also Co-Founder of Bounce & Bound Inclusive Fitness Studio for Kids. Her work spans inclusive education, skill development, digital literacy, adaptive sports, and vocational training for persons with disabilities. As a blogger and trainer, she focuses on building practical, community-rooted inclusion across schools, families, and workplaces. As a neurodivergent advocate and parent to a neurodivergent child, Shilpi brings both professional expertise and lived experience to her advocacy, consulting, and writing.

Dr. Moumita Basu is an Assistant Professor of Economics at Aliah University, Kolkata. She holds an M.Sc. from the University of Calcutta, an M.Phil. from Jadavpur University, and a Ph.D. from the University of Calcutta, where her research focused on macroeconomic adjustment in developing countries. With over 15 years of teaching experience, she has previously served at Bidhannagar College and Krishnagar Government College. Her research expertise lies in open economy macroeconomics, monetary economics, and international finance. She has published extensively in reputed journals such as Macroeconomics and Finance in Emerging Market Economies, Foreign Trade Review, South Asian Journal of Macroeconomics and Public Finance, Indian Economic Review, and Journal of Economic Studies. She has also actively participated in numerous national and international conferences.

Dr. Rilina Basu Banerjee is a Professor of Economics at Jadavpur University, Kolkata, with over 15 years of teaching and research experience. Her expertise lies in open economy macroeconomics, financial structures, and development economics. She holds a Ph.D. from Jadavpur University and has published in leading journals such as Foreign Trade Review, Journal of Developing Areas, and The Pakistan Development Review. Her research focuses on financial innovation, macroeconomic dynamics, and development issues. She is actively engaged in doctoral supervision and is a collaborator in an ICSSR-funded project on financial inclusion of persons with disabilities in India.

Dr. Trisha Bhattacharya is an Assistant Mistress (Gazetted 'A' rank) under the West Bengal Subordinate Education Service. She holds a Ph.D. in Economics from Rabindra Bharati University, Kolkata. With prior experience as a Lecturer at Techno India Group and as a Research Assistant at ICRA, she has contributed to macroeconomic research, policy analysis, and editorial work for publications such as ICRA Bulletin: Money & Finance. Her academic background includes an M.Sc. in Economics and a Master's degree in Human Resource and Organisational Management from the University of Calcutta. Her research interests include macroeconomics, labour and industrial economics, and economic policy analysis.

Shri. Harsha Bhowmik is currently working as Director (Digital Economy and Fintech) in the Ministry of Finance, Government of India, selected through UPSC lateral entry in 2021. With over 23 years of experience across industry and government, he specialises at the intersection of finance and technology. He has played a key role in national policy initiatives on fintech, digital payments, financial inclusion, and digital public infrastructure, including contributions to India's G20 Presidency 2023. He has represented India in G20 GPFI forums and led multiple international fintech collaborations. His expertise spans banking, payments, digital transformation, and emerging technologies such as AI, blockchain, and cybersecurity.

Dr. Amrita Chatterjee is an Associate Professor at Madras School of Economics, Chennai, India. She has got her PhD degree in Economics from Jadavpur University, Kolkata with a focus on Impact of Agricultural Biotechnology on Indian Economy. Her major research interests are Financial Inclusion, Development Economics and Gender Issues. She has published her research work in National and International journals.

Dr. Nilendu Chatterjee is an Assistant Professor in the Department of Economics at Bankim Sardar College, West Bengal, India. He holds a Ph.D. in Economics and specialises in resource economics, general equilibrium, and development economics. He has published research in journals such as International Journal of Sustainable Economies Management, Economic Affairs, and Foreign Trade Review. In addition, he has edited six books with reputed national and international publishers, including Routledge and Emerald.

Dr. Rimita Hom Chaudhury is an Assistant Professor in the Department of Economics at Nalanda University, Rajgir. She holds a Ph.D. in Economics from West Bengal State University and has several years of undergraduate teaching experience, specialising in microeconomics, statistics, and econometrics. Her research focuses on financial inclusion, microfinance, digital finance, and gender-related issues. She has published in reputed journals such as International Journal of Finance & Economics, Millennial Asia, Innovation and Development, Strategic Change, and Economics Bulletin.

Dr. Simontini Das is a Professor of Economics at Jadavpur University, Kolkata. She holds a Ph.D. in Economics from Jadavpur University and has extensive teaching and research experience in international trade, development economics, and econometrics. Her research focuses on trade, labour markets, financial inclusion, and digital finance, with publications in leading journals such as Information Technology for Development, Journal of Developing Areas, and South Asia Economic Journal. She has served as Principal Investigator on multiple research projects and has contributed to policy-oriented work on exports and economic development. She is also actively engaged in doctoral supervision and academic research guidance.

Dr. Vikas Dixit is a Professor of Economics at Jadavpur University, Kolkata. He holds a Ph.D in Public Finance from Aligarh Muslim University. With over 17 years of teaching and research experience, his work focuses on public finance, fiscal policy, social sector and financial inclusion. He has published in leading journals such as Foreign Trade Review, Journal of Public Affairs, The Indian Economic Journal, etc. He has also contributed in edited volumes published from Springer, Regal, etc. He is currently the Principal Investigator of an ICSSR-funded major project on financial inclusion of persons with disabilities in India. He has been actively involved in research, doctoral supervision, and academic collaborations.

Prof. Pami Dua is a Senior Professor of Economics and former Director of the Delhi School of Economics, University of Delhi, and currently serves as a Part-Time Member of the Economic Advisory Council to the Prime Minister. She has held several distinguished positions, including membership of the first Monetary Policy Committee of the Reserve Bank of India (2016–2020) and Co-Chair of the Think20 (T20)/G20 Task Force on Macroeconomics, Trade and Livelihoods (2023). Prof. Dua is a Distinguished Fellow at the Research and Information System for Developing Countries (RIS) and has been associated with leading institutions such as CAFRAL, IGIDR, and ECRI, New York. With over four decades of teaching and research experience, her work spans macroeconometrics, forecasting, monetary policy, and business cycle analysis. She has published extensively and served as Editor of the Indian Economic Review for nearly two decades. She holds a B.A. (Hons.) from Lady Shri Ram College and a Master's (with distinction) and Ph.D. in Economics from the London School of Economics. She is a recipient of several honours, including the Nishtha Dhriti Satyam Samman (University of Delhi) and the National Systems Gold Medal.

Ms. Aarti Garg is currently working as a Deputy Director in the Digital Economy and Fintech Division of Department of Economic Affairs, Ministry of Finance, Government of India. An officer of the Indian Economic Service (2022 batch, AIR 3), she has previously served as Assistant Director in International Economic Relations (IER) Division of Department of Economic Affairs, Ministry of Finance, Government of India. She has contributed to India 2023 G20 Presidency and represented India in SAARC Development Fund (SDF). Her professional areas of work include International cooperation, financial inclusion, Digital Public

Infrastructure, KYC, Digital Economy and Fintech. She holds a Master's degree in Economics from the Delhi School of Economics and a Bachelor's degree in Economics from Ramjas College, University of Delhi. Her research interests areas include international economic relations, trade policy analysis, MSMEs financing and development economics.

Dr. Chandralekha Ghosh is a Professor of Economics at West Bengal State University. Prior to her present affiliation, she served as a guest faculty member at Presidency College, Kolkata, and in the Department of Economics at the University of Calcutta. She holds a Ph.D. in Economics from Jadavpur University. Her research interests include agricultural economics, productivity and efficiency analysis, microfinance, financial inclusion, digital finance, green finance, and gender-related issues. With nearly two decades of teaching and research experience spanning econometrics, microeconomics and Indian economy, she has published extensively in reputed journals such as Applied Economics, International Journal of Finance and Economics, Economics Bulletin, Innovation and Development, Millennial Asia, Strategic Change, Economic and Political Weekly, and Gender in Management. She has also contributed to edited volumes by leading publishers. Dr. Ghosh has been actively involved in research projects funded by UGC and ICSSR, focusing on self-help groups, rural credit, and financial behaviour. She has also supervised doctoral and M.Phil. research and served as Head of the Department of Economics at West Bengal State University.

Ms. Depannita Ghosh is a Senior Research Analyst at NCAER in the Investor Education and Protection Fund (IEPF) Chair Unit, set up under an MoU between NCAER and IEPFA, Ministry of Corporate Affairs. She completed her M. Sc. in Economics from University of Calcutta and B. Sc. in Economics from Women's Christian College, Kolkata. Currently, she is pursuing PhD in Economics at CHRIST (Deemed to be University). Proficient in software applications like SPSS, Python and Stata, her areas of interest and expertise include Financial Education and Investor Education and Protection, Public Finance, Advanced Macroeconomics and Development Economics.

Dr. Deepika Goel is a Professor of Economics at Aryabhatta College, University of Delhi. She holds a Ph.D. and M.Phil. in Economics from the Delhi School of Economics. With extensive experience in higher education, she has previously served as Associate Professor at

Aryabhatta College and Assistant Professor at Shri Ram College of Commerce, University of Delhi. Her academic work focuses on teaching, research, and student development in economics with particular interest on macroeconomics, time series econometrics, forecasting, and financial inclusion. She completed her Bachelor's degree in Economics from Hansraj College, University of Delhi.

Mr. Adil Kamal is a Research Scholar at Integral Business School, Integral University, Lucknow. He holds a postgraduate degree in Finance (Master of Finance and Control) and brings over a decade of industry experience as a financial services professional, having served in leadership roles as Cluster Manager and Regional Manager. He is also associated with the Management & Technology Institute as Industry Faculty for BBA (IIFSB) and MBA (Finance) programmes. His research interests lie in Finance, Economics, and the application of Statistics and Econometrics to empirical research.

Shri. Prashant Kumar is currently working as Deputy Director in the Digital Economy and Fintech Division, Department of Economic Affairs (DEA), Ministry of Finance, Government of India. An officer of the Indian Economic Service (2020), he has previously served as Deputy Director in International Economic Relations (IER) Division, DEA, Ministry of Finance and Assistant Director in the IER Division during India's G20 Presidency and at the Commission for Agricultural Costs and Prices (CACP) under the Ministry of Agriculture and Farmers Welfare. He has represented India in the GPFI Working Group (G20) for the South Africa presidency His professional work spans international economic cooperation, financial inclusion, and agricultural policy. He holds a Master's degree in Economics from the Delhi School of Economics and a Bachelor's degree in Economics from St. Stephen's College, University of Delhi. His research interests include economic policy, global financial governance, and development economics.

Dr. Neeraj Kumar is Director at the Ministry of Finance, Government of India, where he works on bilateral economic cooperation, development finance, and global debt issues, including India's engagement with the G20 Common Framework and Paris Club processes. He has been involved in key economic and financial dialogues with partner countries and oversees development partnerships. His policy experience also includes financial market reforms, particularly in securities markets, stamp duty rationalisation, and FDI policy for stock exchanges. He holds an M.Phil. and Ph.D. in Economics from the Delhi School of Economics, with research interests in macroeconomics, financial markets, econometrics, and global debt dynamics.

Dr. Dipak Kundu is an Assistant Professor in the Department of Commerce at Bankim Sardar College, West Bengal, India. He holds a Ph.D. in Commerce and has published research in UGC-recognised journals such as Anveshak, Asian Journal of Banking and Finance, and SCMS Journal of Management. He has also contributed to edited volumes published by reputed academic publishers. His academic work focuses on contemporary issues in commerce and finance.

Dr. Arindam Laha is a Professor in the Department of Commerce at the University of Burdwan, West Bengal. He holds a Ph.D. in Economics from the University of Burdwan and has extensive teaching and research experience in agribusiness, sustainable business practices, financial inclusion, and social and solidarity economy. He has published widely in Scopus- and Web of Science-indexed journals and contributed to edited volumes by leading publishers such as Routledge, Emerald, and Palgrave Macmillan. Dr. Laha has led and participated in research projects funded by UGC and ICSSR, and his work has been recognised by institutions such as UNRISD and UNTFSSE. He has successfully supervised several doctoral and M.Phil. scholars and contributed to policy-oriented reports including the District Human Development Report and Sustainability Report. He is a recipient of the ILO's South-South Triangular Cooperation scholarship and a member of the UNRISD Working Group on Transforming Economies and Societies.

Ms. Joan Maria E. I. is a Ph.D. scholar in the Department of English at Sree Sankaracharya University of Sanskrit, Kalady. She holds an M.Phil. in English from the same university and completed her undergraduate and postgraduate studies at Maharaja's College, Ernakulam. She qualified the UGC NET in English in 2020 and is a recipient of the UGC National Fellowship for Persons with Disabilities. She has previously served as a Guest Lecturer at the College of Applied Science, Puthenvelikkara. Her research interests focus on Disability Studies.

Dr. C. S. Mohapatra is the IEPF Chair Professor at the National Council of Applied Economic Research (NCAER), where he leads the IEPF Chair Unit, established under an MoU between NCAER and the Investor

Education and Protection Fund Authority (IEPFA), Ministry of Corporate Affairs. He pursues advocacy, information dissemination, research, and policy initiatives aimed at promoting financial literacy, investor education and protection. A former Indian Economic Service officer (1986 batch), he brings over three and a half decades of experience in financial sector policy, economic administration, and institutional reforms. He served in senior positions in the Ministry of Finance, Government of India, retiring as Principal Adviser in the rank of Secretary, and played a key role in financial stability, regulatory reforms, GST and international economic engagement, including with the RBI, IMF, World Bank, G20, and BRICS. Dr. Mohapatra has contributed extensively to capital market development, financial sector legislation, and financial literacy initiatives, including the National Strategy on Financial Education. He holds a Ph.D. from Jawaharlal Nehru University and an MSc in Economics from the London School of Economics. He is a recipient of the Investor Education & Awareness Award (2024) by SEBI-AMFI and Bharat Vikas Award (2025) by Institute of Self-Reliance. He writes Op-Eds in national dailies, has published research articles and has edited two books.

Mr. Saurav Priyotosh Munshi is a Ph.D. scholar in the Department of Commerce at the University of Burdwan, West Bengal. He holds an M.Com. in Accounting and Finance from the University of Calcutta and an M.Phil. from the University of Burdwan, and is a recipient of the UGC-NET Junior Research Fellowship in Commerce. His research interests lie in credit and insurance markets. He has presented his work at institutions such as Krea University, IDS-Udaipur, IIT Kanpur, and Jadavpur University, and has published in journals including Agricultural Finance Review, International Journal of Banking, Risk and Insurance, and Journal of Income and Wealth.

Dr. Ranjanendra Narayan Nag is an Associate Professor of Economics at St. Xavier's College (Autonomous), Kolkata. He holds an M.Sc. (First Class First Rank) and a Ph.D. in Economics from the University of Calcutta. With extensive teaching and research experience, he specialises in open economy macroeconomics, general equilibrium, international trade theory, and micro-theoretic modelling. Dr. Nag has published widely in leading national and international journals, including Macroeconomics and Finance in Emerging Market Economies, Foreign Trade Review, South Asian Journal of Macroeconomics and Public Finance, Indian Economic Review, and Journal of Economic Studies, among others. He has also contributed to several edited volumes published by reputed academic publishers. He has supervised multiple doctoral and M.Phil. dissertations and has actively contributed to academic teaching, curriculum development, and research training across institutions.

Mr. Pratim Saha has done his Masters in Actuarial Economics from Madras School of Economics, Chennai. The chapter is part of his Masters Thesis. He is currently part of Financial Services, Risk & Regulatory team at PWC in Kolkata.

Shri Chanchal C. Sarkar is currently working as an Adviser, Economic Division, Department of Economic Affairs, Ministry of Finance, Govt. of India. He was elected as the Co-Chair the G20 financial inclusion Group for 2024–26 and also Co-Chaired the group under G20 Presidency of both Brazil and South Africa in 2024 and 2025 respectively.

He has over 25 years of experience working at various capacities in the Government of India in the country and abroad on bilateral, multilateral, regional trade and economic cooperation issues. Prior to his current assignment, Mr. Sarkar represented India at the South Asian Association for Regional Cooperation (SAARC) Secretariat, Kathmandu during 2018-2021 and dealt with region's Economy, Trade and Finance related issues.

Also, he has served as Director in the Ministry of Finance and was responsible for negotiating all International Bilateral Investment Treaties (BITs) and related disputes out of the BITs on behalf of India.

He holds M.A and M Phil in Economics from Jawaharlal Nehru University (JNU), New Delhi, India besides M. Sc in Public Management and Governance from the London School of Economics and Political Science (LSE), London. He is graduated from Jadavpur University in 1992.

Dr. Tanwi Shams is an Assistant Professor of Law at National Law University Odisha and the Director of the Centre for Disability Law and Advocacy. She holds a Ph.D. in Law from North- Eastern Hill University, Shillong, and an LL.M. in Intellectual Property and Technology Law from the National University of Singapore. She also brings prior professional experience from the banking sector. Her academic interests lie in Intellectual Property & Technology Law, Disability Law and Human Rights Law. She is actively engaged in research and is also a recipient of an ICSSR Special Project. Dr. Shams has contributed significantly to legal scholarship through her writings and research initiatives. She is the author of Disability and Inclusion: A Socio-Legal Exploration in Assam and has served as the editor of the book Prison Reform in India. Through her academic and institutional roles, she continues to promote inclusive legal education and advocacy.

Dr. Neha Verma is an Associate Professor of Economics at Kirori Mal College, University of Delhi. She holds a Ph.D. and M.A. in Economics from the Delhi School of Economics. With over a decade of teaching experience, she has previously served at Sri Guru Gobind Singh College of Commerce. Her research spans international economics, financial stability, gender economics, and development, with publications in leading journals such as Journal of Emerging Market Finance, SN Business and Economics, and South Asia Economic Journal. She has actively contributed to G20 policy briefs and presented her work at major international conferences. She is a recipient of the KMC Research Excellence Award and has also been recognised by EXIM Bank for her doctoral research.

List of Figures

Chapter 1

Chapter 2

Chapter 4

Chapter 6

Chapter 8

Chapter 9

Chapter 10

List of Tables

Chapter 5

Chapter 6

Chapter 7

Chapter 9

Chapter 10

Chapter 11

PART I

Global and Strategic Perspectives on Financial Inclusion

CHAPTER 1

Addressing Financial Inclusion Challenges Through Collaborative Efforts: India and G20

Chanchal C. Sarkar, Harsha Bhowmik, Prashant Kumar, and Aarti Garg

1 Background

Advancing financial inclusion has emerged as one of the most critical challenges and at the same time, an opportunity to improve the lives of billions of people worldwide. It represents the quest to provide equitable access to useful and affordable formal financial products and services to

Disclaimer: The views and opinions expressed in this paper are those of the author(s) and do not reflect the official position or policy of the Government of India.

C. C. Sarkar (✉) · H. Bhowmik · P. Kumar · A. Garg
Ministry of Finance, Government of India, New Delhi, India
e-mail: cc.sarkar@nic.in

H. Bhowmik
e-mail: harsha.bhowmik@gov.in

© The Author(s), under exclusive license to Springer Nature Singapore Pte Ltd. 2026
V. Dixit et al. (eds.), *Financial Inclusion for Viksit Bharat*,
https://doi.org/10.1007/978-981-92-0807-4_1

all individuals and businesses, mainly the marginalised and disadvantaged groups who are either outside of the formal financial system or barely into it. Ensuring such access to financial services has profound implications on the economic growth, social development and poverty reduction.

Therefore, the outcome of financial inclusion goes far beyond an individual's access to banking services. It also serves as a cornerstone for achieving broader developmental goals, including the United Nations Sustainable Development Goals (SDGs). Financial inclusion plays a vital role in advancing the Sustainable Development Goals (SDGs), particularly by promoting economic empowerment, reducing inequalities, and improving access to essential services. As per the G20 2023 Financial Inclusion Action Plan (FIAP), financial inclusion contributes towards achieving at least 7 out of 17 SDGs[1] as highlighted in Fig. 1 and outlined in the 2030 Agenda for Sustainable Development.

With various initiatives, including under G20, significant development has taken place, however, despite decades of efforts by governments, international organizations, and the private sector, the global financial inclusion landscape remains marked by significant disparities. According to recent data, approximately 1.4 billion adults worldwide[2] remain unbanked, lacking access to basic financial services. This exclusion disproportionately affects vulnerable populations, including women, rural communities, and low-income households, perpetuating cycles of poverty and limiting economic opportunities.

India's journey toward advancing financial inclusion represents one of the most remarkable transformation stories in recent history. A country where only 35% of adults had bank accounts in 2011, India has successfully elevated this figure to 80% by 2017, higher than the global average

---

P. Kumar
e-mail: prashant.kumar10@gov.in

A. Garg
e-mail: aarti.garg22@gov.in

[1] Global Partnership for Financial Inclusion (GPFI). *G20 2023 financial inclusion action plan*. Published September 19, 2023, on the GPFI website. https://www.gpfi.org/publications/g20-2023-financial-inclusion-action-plan.

[2] The Global Findex Database. (2021). *Financial inclusion, digital payments, and resilience in the age of COVID-19*.

Fig. 1 Sustainable development goals (*Source* THE 17 GOALS | Sustainable Development. https://sdgs.un.org/goals)

of 69%.[3] Today, about 96% of India's population are covered under the formal banking system.[4] This dramatic improvement, achieved in just a decade, offers valuable lessons for other emerging economies grappling with similar challenges.

Central to India's success has been its innovative approach to Digital Public Infrastructure (DPI), which gained global prominence during

[3] The Global Findex Database. (2017). *Measuring financial inclusion and opportunities to expand access to and use of financial services.*

[4] Reserve Bank of India. (2025). National Strategy for Financial Inclusion 2025-30

India's G20 Presidency in 2023.[5] The DPI framework represents a paradigm shift in how countries can leverage innovative technology to deliver public services at scale, fostering innovation while ensuring inclusivity and sustainability. This approach has not only transformed India's domestic financial landscape but also has influenced global policy attention and discussions initiatives worldwide.

The collaborative efforts between India and the other G20 nations have also been instrumental in advancing the global financial inclusion agenda. Through forums like the G20 Global Partnership for Financial Inclusion (GPFI), countries have shared experiences, developed common frameworks, and worked together to address the challenges in fostering financial inclusion. These collaborative efforts have resulted in policy recommendations, knowledge sharing initiatives, and the development of international standards that benefit G20 economies and beyond.

This chapter intends to explore the digital transformation journey for advancing financial inclusion, examining both India's domestic initiatives and its role in shaping global discourse. It delves into the conceptual understanding of financial inclusion globally, traces India's remarkable progress in advancing financial inclusion through various government initiatives, analyzes the significant impact of DPI, assesses the collaborative efforts with G20 partners and provides a perspective of other emerging issues and concerns introduced by advanced economies on the subject. Lastly, the chapter provides an update and analysis of emerging technologies and innovations that may hold promise to further advance financial inclusion while acknowledging the significant challenges that they may impose.

2 Understanding Financial Inclusion: Dimensions and Perspective

2.1 Global Understanding

While the concept of financial inclusion is well recognized as an important policy intervention, there doesn't exist any globally negotiated definition of financial inclusion. However, different countries and international organizations have attempted to articulate their own understanding of financial inclusion. For instance, the World Bank defines financial

[5] G20 Policy Recommendations for Advancing Financial Inclusion and Productivity Gains through DPI 2023.

inclusion as "*Individuals and businesses have access to useful and affordable financial products and services that meet their needs – transactions, payments, savings, credit and insurance – delivered in a responsible and sustainable way*".[6] This definition emphasizes the broad nature of financial inclusion, extending beyond mere account ownership to encompass the full spectrum of financial services.

The G20 Global Partnership for Financial Inclusion (GPFI), a working group under the G20 Finance Track aimed at advancing financial inclusion globally, offers a comprehensive understanding of financial inclusion that "*All working-age adults (persons at the age of 15+) have effective and quality access to and usage of — at a cost affordable to the Customers and sustainable for the providers—financial services provided by formal institutions.*"[7] This definition introduces critical concepts of effectiveness, quality, affordability, and sustainability, highlighting the multidimensional nature of financial inclusion.

National and regional perspectives add further nuance to the financial inclusion definition. South Africa, from the developing world's perspective, understands financial inclusion as "*A state in which all individuals and SMMEs have access to and can effectively use a range of quality products and services provided by the regulated financial sector*".[8] This definition emphasizes the importance of including both individuals and small businesses in the financial inclusion ecosystem and the role of regulation in ensuring quality and safety in the financial sector.

The United States, defines financial inclusion as "starting with equitable access to a range of financial products and services that are fair, safe, and useful in meeting individuals' and households' financial needs and goals, and also encompasses access to clear and trustworthy information that supports informed financial decision-making".[9] This definition places strong emphasis on financial literacy along with equitable access to services which are fair, safe and transparent.

[6] World Bank. (2018a). *Financial inclusion overview*. World Bank, Washington, DC. https://www.worldbank.org/en/topic/financialinclusion/overview#1.

[7] GPFI White Paper. (2016). *Global standard-setting bodies and financial inclusion: The evolving landscape publication*.

[8] FSCA Financial Inclusion Strategy (FSCA, 2024).

[9] U.S. Department of the Treasury. (2024, October 29). *Fact sheet: National strategy for financial inclusion in the United States* [Press release]. https://home.treasury.gov/news/press-releases/jy2692.

2.2 India's Perspective

In India, the RBI has been the nodal body to work and steer the work of Financial Inclusion. The concept of financial inclusion in India has also evolved over time as has been indicated at various times in multiple documents by the Central Bank. Financial inclusion has been defined as "*the process of ensuring access to financial services, timely and adequate credit for vulnerable groups such as weaker sections and low-income groups at an affordable cost*" by the Committee on Financial Inclusion—Chairman: Dr C Rangarajan, Reserve Bank of India (RBI), 2008. While the Committee on Medium-Term Path to Financial Inclusion (Chairman: Shri Deepak Mohanty, RBI, 2015) set up by RBI has explained financial inclusion as, "*convenient access to a basket of basic formal financial products and services that should include savings, remittance, credit, government-supported insurance and pension products to small and marginal farmers and low income households at reasonable cost with adequate protection progressively supplemented by social cash transfers, besides increasing the access of small and marginal enterprises to formal finance with a greater reliance on technology to cut costs and improve service delivery, ...*"

So, from the various definitions, it is seen that despite varied understandings of financial inclusion, all of them converge to the core attributes or dimensions of financial inclusion which are to ensure *access*, *usage* and *quality* of financial products and services. India's basic understanding on financial inclusion also closely aligns with the global understanding focusing on these three core dimensions.

2.3 The Three Dimensions of Financial Inclusion

1. **Access to Financial Services:** Access represents the foundational dimension of financial inclusion, referring to the banking, availability of financial products and services. This requires physical and digital infrastructure to deliver financial services, such as bank branches, ATMs, and digital payment systems, digital platforms etc. However, barriers such as high cost, discriminatory practices, excessive documentation requirements, and geographical constraints etc, may prevent the individuals and businesses to have access to formal financial systems and products and services and therefore, these barriers have to be adequately addressed to bring people under the formal financial system.

2. **Usage of Financial Services:** Usage is the second dimension that goes beyond mere access to examine how effectively and regularly people use the available financial services like savings, investments, insurance etc. This dimension recognizes that having an account or access to credit is not sufficient if these services are not actively used to meet financial needs. Barriers such as lack of funds, financial literacy, trust or high cost etc, may prevent individuals from using these services.
3. **Quality of Financial Services:** Quality being the third dimension encompasses the characteristics or attributes of design and delivery of financial products and services. This includes affordability, appropriateness to user needs, consumer safety and financial literacy and security, transparency in terms and conditions, convenience and the overall user experience. Quality also involves the responsiveness of service providers to customer needs and complaints, the reliability of service delivery, and the alignment of products with the specific requirements of different user segments. Quality is usually recognized as the function of access and usage dimension of financial inclusion.

2.4 Enablers of Financial Inclusion

In addition to the three core dimensions of financial inclusion, *financial literacy* and *consumer protection* are recognized as key enablers of financial inclusion. Financial literacy empowers individuals and businesses to make informed decisions regarding financial products and services, fostering responsible usage. Consumer protection, on the other hand, builds trust and ensures transparency, encouraging greater engagement with the formal financial system. As per India's National Strategy for Financial Inclusion (2019–2024), financial inclusion policies, financial literacy initiatives and customer grievance redressal framework forms the financial inclusion triad.

3 India's Financial Inclusion Journey: From Exclusion to Digital Leadership

3.1 Individuals

After the 2008 global financial crisis, financial inclusion gained global attention as a tool for promoting economic resilience, financial stability, and inclusive growth. Policymakers in India have also recognized the importance of bringing underserved populations into the formal financial system to cushion against future economic shocks and to promote growth and development. However, India started with very low levels of financial inclusion. In 2009, India's financial inclusion metrics reflected a picture of modest inclusion of formal financial services. Only 17% of adults had bank accounts, which placed India well below the global average, with just 15% of the population having unique identification documents and only 37% owning mobile phones. These statistics reflected millions of individuals and families living outside the formal financial system, relying on informal lending sources, cash transactions, and traditional savings methods. Thus, these indicated the enormous challenge that India faced and the long road that it had to travel towards achieving financial inclusion.

Driven by the digital transformation, particularly through Digital Public Infrastructure (DPI) as will be discussed later, India's financial inclusion initiatives made remarkable strides and achieved in 6 years what would have otherwise taken 47 years[10] (35% in 2011 to 80% in 2017). As shown in Fig. 2, today over 96% of the adult population have bank accounts, more than 1.4 billion unique Aadhaar generated and 73% of the population owns mobile phones.[11]

3.2 The MSME Credit Gap

India's micro, small, and medium enterprises (MSMEs) like all emerging economies forms the backbone of the nation's economy, contributing approximately 30% to the GDP and employing 62% of the business sector

[10] G20 Global Partnership for Financial Inclusion. G20 Policy Recommendations for Advancing Financial Inclusion and Productivity Gains through Digital Public Infrastructure. Ministry of Finance (India), published under the G20 India Presidency. Available from the Department of Economic Affairs website: "G20 Policy Recommendations for Advancing Financial Inclusion and Productivity Gains through DPI".

[11] Results of Comprehensive Modular Survey: Telecom, 2025.

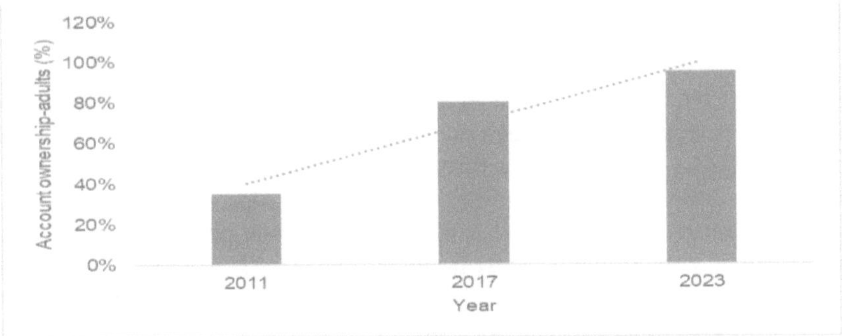

Fig. 2 Bank account ownership (*Source* World Bank Global Findex Database 2017; Results of Comprehensive Annual Modular Survey [July 2022–June 2023], MoSPI, Government of India)

workforce. Despite their crucial role in economic development and their significant contribution of 45.79% to India's total exports, MSMEs face persistent challenges in accessing credit that threatens their growth and sustainability.[12] The MSME financing was very low to start with, in 2007–08, the MSME segment in India accounted for only 6.6% of Net Bank Credit (NBC) from Scheduled Commercial Banks.[13] Ghatak (2009)[14] found that banks are reluctant to extend credit to small enterprises for several reasons, such as high administrative costs of small-scale lending, asymmetric information, high risk perception and lack of collateral etc.

By leveraging innovative digital technologies, India has increased the credit penetration which now stands at 9% for medium enterprises and 20% for micro and small enterprises. However, these figures remain considerably lower than developing economies like China (37%) and developed countries like the United States (50%). India continues to have an estimated ₹20–₹25 lakh crore unmet credit[15] for MSMEs.

[12] PIB. https://www.pib.gov.in/PressNoteDetails.aspx?id=154772&NoteId=154772&ModuleId=3.

[13] The Challenge of Employment in India An Informal Economy Perspective (2009). *National Council for Enterprises in the Unorganised Sector (NCEUS)*. https://dcmsme.gov.in/The_Challenge_of_employment_in_India.pdf.

[14] Ghatak, S. (2009). *Micro, Small and Medium Enterprises (MSME) in India: An Appraisal*. http://www.geasiapacifico.com/documents/MiPymes%20en%20la%20India.pdf.

[15] Understanding Indian Msme Sector. (2025). *SIDBI*. https://www.sidbi.in/uploads/Understanding_Indian_MSME_sector_Progress_and_Challenges_13_05_25_Final.pdf.

3.3 *ICT Infrastructure: Prerequisite for Digital Financial Inclusion*

Over the years, India has witnessed remarkable growth in digital connectivity and access to digital devices, creating the foundation necessary for digital financial inclusion. Telephone subscribers have surged from 346 million in 2008 to an astounding 1.2 billion in March 2025[16] (Fig. 3), reflecting more than threefold expansion in mobile penetration that has transformed how Indians access financial services. This growth has been particularly significant for reaching previously unbanked populations, as mobile phones have become the gateway through which people in rural and semi-urban areas engage with formal financial systems.

The expansion of low cost broadband connectivity portrays an equally compelling story of digital transformation. Mobile broadband, which had very few subscribers in 2008, reached its first major milestone with 40

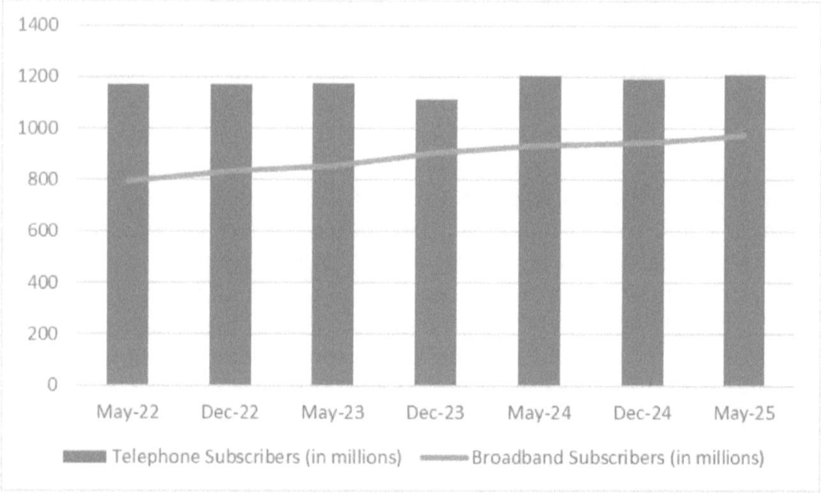

Fig. 3 Telephone subscribers and broadband subscribers (*Source* Telecom subscriptions Reports | Telecom Regulatory Authority of India. [2025, July 10])

[16] Highlights of Telecom Subscription Data as on 31st March, 2025. (n.d.-b). *PIB.* https://www.pib.gov.in/PressReleasePage.aspx?PRID=2127534#:~:text=Wireless%20(Mobile)%20subscription%20in%20urban,million%20during%20the%20same%20period.

million users by 2013 and now stands at an impressive 897 million in March 2025 (Fig. 3). Similarly, wired broadband has grown significantly, rising from 5.5 million subscribers in 2008 to 41.3 million in 2025.[17] This remarkable growth in mobile subscribers and broadband services has laid a strong foundation for initiatives like Aadhaar, enabling India to leapfrog its journey towards financial inclusion by providing the technological infrastructure.

3.4 *Building the Foundation: The Aadhaar Revolution (2010)*

Recognizing the importance of identifying each individual for bringing them under the formal financial system, the Indian government launched Aadhaar in 2010, a unique digital identification system aimed at providing every citizen with a verifiable identity. Unlike existing identity documents that often-required documentation that excluded marginalized populations, Aadhaar was designed to be truly universal, with minimum eligibility criteria.

The Aadhaar system represented a paradigm shift in identity management. Figure 4 shows that more than 1.44 billion Aadhaar IDs had been issued, covering more than 99% of the adult population.[18] This achievement created the foundation for all subsequent financial inclusion initiatives, as identity verification became quick, reliable, scalable and cost-effective for providing services by both government and private agencies alike.

The positive impacts of Aadhaar on efficiency, including real savings cannot be overstated. The introduction of electronic-Know Your Customer (e-KYC) processes reduced the cost of customer verification from INR 500–700 (approximately $6–9) per person to as low as INR 3

[17] Highlights of Telecom Subscription Data as on 31st March, 2025. (n.d.-b). *PIB.* https://www.pib.gov.in/PressReleasePage.aspx?PRID=2127534#:~:text=Wireless%20(Mobile)%20subscription%20in%20urban,million%20during%20the%20same%20period.

[18] Aadhaar dashboard. (n.d.). https://www.uidai.gov.in/aadhaar_dashboard/india.php#:~:text=*%20272%2C790%20Total%20Registered.%20*%20216%2C701%20Total%20Certified.%20*%201%2C383%2C454%2C546%20Total%20Aadhaar.

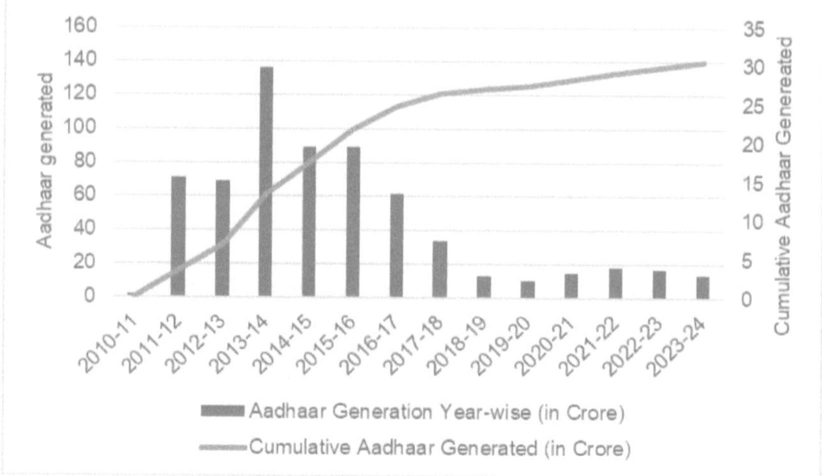

Fig. 4 Aadhaar (Digital Identity) (*Source* Annual Report of UIDAI for 2023–24)

(approximately $0.04).[19] This dramatic cost reduction made it economically viable for financial institutions to serve low-income customers, fundamentally altering the economics of financial inclusion.

3.5 *The Mass Banking Initiative: PMJDY and DBT (2014–2015)*

Building on the Aadhaar foundation, the government launched several flagship initiatives in 2014–2015 that transformed India's financial landscape. The most significant of these was the Pradhan Mantri Jan Dhan Yojana (PMJDY), launched in 2014 as a National Mission on Financial Inclusion.

PMJDY represented an integrated approach to financial inclusion, envisaging universal access to banking facilities with at least one basic banking account for every household. The program included financial literacy components, access to credit, insurance, and pension facilities.

[19] *Aadhaar brought down KYC cost to ₹3 from as high as ₹700, says Nirmala Sitharaman*. (2023, April 15). Business Line. https://www.thehindubusinessline.com/economy/aadhaar-brought-down-kyc-cost-to-3-from-as-high-as-700-says-nirmala-sitharaman/article66740192.ece.

Beneficiaries received RuPay Debit cards with built-in accident insurance coverage of INR 1 lakh (approximately $1,200).

The results of PMJDY have been extraordinary. By January 2025, approximately 545 million accounts had been opened under the program, with more than 55% held by women and 66% opened in rural and semi-urban areas.[20] The average deposit per account increased fourfold from INR 1,065 in 2015 to INR 4,352 in 2024, indicating that these accounts were not merely symbolic but were being actively used for savings[21] as shown in Fig. 5.

Complementing PMJDY was the Direct Benefit Transfer (DBT) scheme, which channeled government benefits directly into beneficiaries' bank accounts. This initiative served a dual purpose: improving the

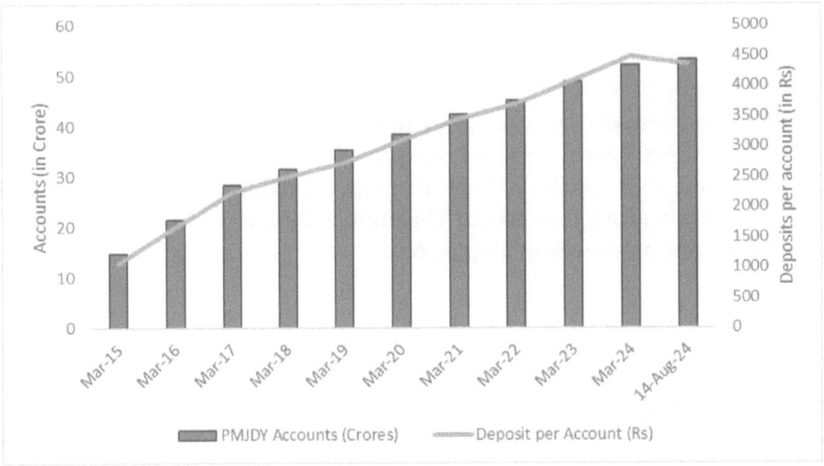

Fig. 5 Pradhan Mantri Jan Dhan Yojana (PMJDY) Bank Accounts (*Source* Pradhan Mantri Jan Dhan Yojana (PMJDY) press release)

[20] *Special campaigns have been launched for enrolling individuals under various financial inclusion Schemes.* (n.d.). https://www.pib.gov.in/PressReleaseIframePage.aspx?PRID=2101428.

[21] *Pradhan Mantri Jan Dhan Yojana (PMJDY)—National Mission for Financial Inclusion—completes a decade of successful implementation.* (n.d.). https://www.pib.gov.in/PressReleasePage.aspx?PRID=2049231.

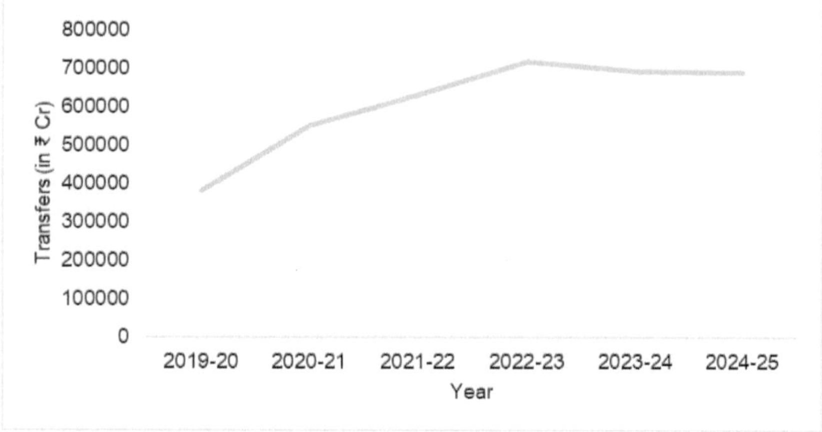

Fig. 6 Direct Benefit Transfer (DBT) (*Source* https://dbtbharat.gov.in/)

efficiency and transparency of government benefit delivery while encouraging the use of formal banking services. By 2024, total transfers under DBT reached INR 40.91 lakh crore (approximately $512 billion), with INR 6.89 lakh crore transferred through 9.3 billion transactions in FY 2024–25 alone as shown in Figure 6.[22]

3.6 *Social Protection Through Financial Inclusion: Jan Suraksha Schemes*

Recognizing that true financial inclusion must extend beyond basic banking to comprehensive financial security, the government launched three Jan Suraksha schemes in 2015. These initiatives, Pradhan Mantri Suraksha Bima Yojana (PMSBY), Pradhan Mantri Jeevan Jyoti Bima Yojana (PMJJBY), and Atal Pension Yojana (APY), aimed to provide insurance and pension coverage to previously excluded populations.

As of April 2025, PMSBY, providing accidental insurance coverage, enrolled over 510 million people and disbursed approximately INR 3121 crore in claims. PMJJBY, offering life insurance, achieved cumulative enrollment of 236.3 million people with 919896 claims disbursed

[22] Direct Benefit Transfer Government of India. (n.d.). https://dbtbharat.gov.in/.

totaling INR 18397 crore. APY, focused on pension security for unorganized sector workers, enrolled 76.6 million subscribers, with 47% being women.[23]

These schemes demonstrated that social protection could be delivered at scale through the formal financial system, providing security to millions of families while deepening financial inclusion.

3.7 The Digital Payments Revolution: UPI (2016)

The launch of the Unified Payments Interface (UPI) in 2016 marked a revolutionary moment in India's financial inclusion journey. UPI created a real-time fast payment system that enabled instant money transfers between bank accounts using mobile phones. The system's key innovation was its interoperability and scalability, linking multiple banks and allowing transactions across various digital platforms and applications, both in public and private sector domains.

UPI's growth has been phenomenal. From modest beginnings with around 10 million transactions worth INR 2800 crore in May 2017, it has become the backbone of India's digital payment ecosystem by recording 18.67 billion transactions worth INR 25.14 lakh crore (approximately $289.7 billion) by May 2025 as shown in Figure 7.[24] This growth was driven by UPI's key features: interoperability, scalability, ease of use along with zero cost, and the ability for private sector companies to build innovative fintech solutions on the platform. The low or zero transaction costs have helped retaining all in the business.

According to a recent IMF paper titled 'Growing Retail Digital Payments: The Value of Interoperability'[25] UPI is cited as a strong example where interoperability has indeed supported adoption. The study

[23] *Press Information Bureau, Government of India. Three Jan Suraksha Schemes—Pradhan Mantri Suraksha Bima Yojana (PMSBY), Pradhan Mantri Jeevan Jyoti Bima Yojana (PMJJBY) and Atal Pension Yojana (APY) complete 10 years of providing social security cover.* May 9, 2025. Available at: https://www.pib.gov.in/PressReleasePage.aspx?PRID=2127981.

[24] *Unified Payments Interface (UPI) Product Statistics | NPCI*. (n.d.). https://www.npci.org.in/what-we-do/upi/product-statistics.

[25] Peria, A. C. K. S. M. (2025, June 25). *Growing retail digital payments: The value of interoperability*. IMF. https://www.imf.org/en/Publications/fintech-notes/Issues/2025/06/25/Growing-Retail-Digital-Payments-The-Value-of-Interoperability-567814.

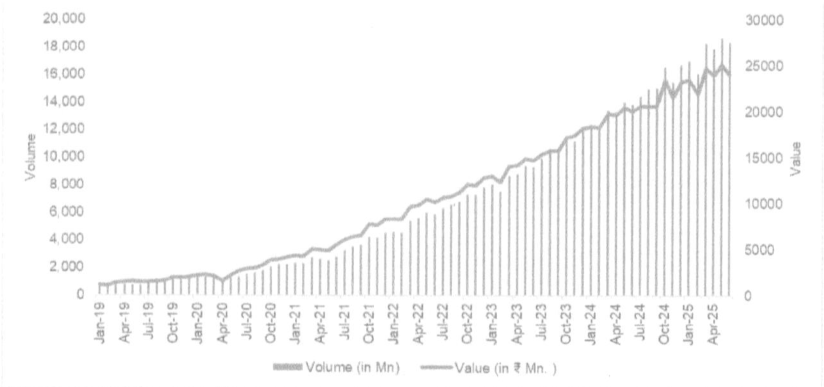

Fig. 7 UPI transactions (*Source* https://www.npci.org.in/what-we-do/upi/product-statistics)

further suggests that promoting interoperability could be a promising policy lever for countries seeking to transition away from cash.

3.8 Account Aggregator (AA) Framework (2021)

The post-COVID era brought new opportunities and challenges for financial inclusion. The surge in digital transactions created significant digital footprints, but this data remained fragmented across different financial institutions. India introduced the Account Aggregator (AA) framework in 2021 by covering such divergent and fragmented digital footprints.

The AA framework enables secure, consent-based data sharing between financial institutions, allowing individuals and small businesses to leverage their financial data to access credit and other services. Figure 8 shows that by March 2025, the cumulative number of accounts enabled on the AA platform reached 2.1 billion, with 179 million consents successfully fulfilled.[26]

[26] Sahamati—Collective of Account Aggregator Ecosystem. (2025, May 13). *AA Dashboard|Account aggregator industry dashboard—sahamati*. https://sahamati.org.in/aa-dashboard/.

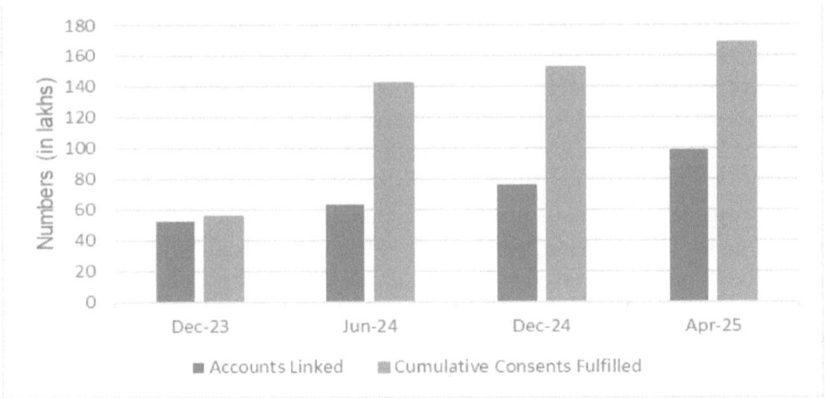

Fig. 8 Account aggregator framework (*Source* https://sahamati.org.in/aa-dashboard/)

This framework represents a shift toward data-driven financial inclusion, enabling lenders to make credit decisions based on cash flow and transaction history rather than traditional collateral requirements. The year-on-year growth in the value of loans from FY22 has witnessed a CAGR of 170% with Rs 129 billion disbursed in H1 FY24. Similarly, the volume of loans have steadily increased with more than 1.35 million loans disbursed in H1 FY24. The average ticket size of loans were Rs. 67,802 in FY22, Rs. 1,14,882 in FY23, and Rs. 95,348 in H1 FY24.[27]

3.9 Unified Lending Interface (ULI)

The RBI, in collaboration with Reserve Bank Innovation Hub (RBIH) has developed a platform called Unified Lending Interface (ULI). The platform enables the delivery of frictionless credit by facilitating seamless access and flow of digital information available across the financial ecosystem from various sources to lenders. ULI has made credit more accessible to the underserved populations such as small businesses by reducing documentation requirements and simplifying loan application processes. Operating on a plug-and-play model, ULI eliminates the need for complex one-to-one integrations between lenders and data providers,

[27] https://sahamati.org.in/wp-content/uploads/2024/02/Lending-through-AA-Dec23-Sahamati-Report.pdf.

enabling lenders to connect to the Platform once and access a broad array of data necessary for efficient credit assessments and decision-making. This streamlined process ultimately benefits consumers by providing tailored credit options without the need for paper-based documentation or physical visits to bank branches, reducing both cost and time.

Since the launch of the pilot in August 2023, ULI has achieved encouraging progress in terms of onboarded lenders, data services and value and volume of loans disbursed. As on date, 44 lenders, including various banks and NBFCs are utilising over 61 plus data services through ULI.[28] These services include digital land records of 8 states, GSTN data, Account Aggregation by Account Aggregators, house/property search data, Credit Guarantee through CGTMSE etc. These data sources facilitate twelve digital loan journeys, including Kisan Credit Card, Digital Cattle, MSME (unsecured), Housing, Personal, Tractor, Micro Business, Vehicle, Digital Gold, E-Mudra, Pension and Dairy Maintenance loans. Additionally, through the integration of the e-KCC portal of National Bank for Agriculture and Rural Development (NABARD) with ULI has enabled the inclusion of Regional Rural Banks (RRBs) and District Central Cooperative Banks (DCCBs) to the Platform addressing the challenges posed by the varying/ inadequate technical capabilities and infrastructure of these banks. The universe of lenders and data/service providers, including state governments for digital land records are continuously being scaled up progressively.

3.10 Financial Education and Consumer Protection Initiatives

As has already been indicated, the pursuit of comprehensive financial inclusion goes beyond merely providing access to banking and financial products and services. In order to make effective financial inclusion, it should comprehensively cover and improve all the dimensions: Access, Usage, and Quality. While infrastructure development and product availability facilitate access, the effective and rational utilization of financial services depends on individuals' financial education and awareness.RBI as a regulator of Banks and Non-Banking Financial Institutions, have taken numerous initiatives to strengthen financial literacy across the country.

[28] Bera, A. (2025, April 22). *ULI facilitated over 1.4 million loans worth Rs 65K crore, says RBI*. Financial Express. https://www.financialexpress.com/business/banking-finance/uli-facilitated-over-1-4-million-loans-worth-rs-65k-crore-says-rbi/3818576/.

To enhance grassroots financial education, particularly digital financial literacy, various Centers for Financial Literacy (CFL) and Financial Literacy Centers (FLCs) have been established nationwide. These centers serve as crucial touchpoints for community-based financial education. The institutional framework was further strengthened in 2013 with the establishment of the National Centre for Financial Education (NCFE), created with support from all major financial sector regulators including RBI, Securities and Exchange Board of India (SEBI), Insurance Regulatory and Development Authority (IRDAI), and Pension Fund Regulatory and Development Authority (PFRDA). NCFE implements the National Strategy for Financial Education (NSFE) and conducts comprehensive financial awareness and empowerment campaigns.

The central bank also released the Financial Awareness Messages (FAME) booklet, designed to provide essential financial literacy content for public education. Since 2016, RBI has annually observed Financial Literacy Week (FLW), with the 2024 edition focusing on the theme "Make a Right Start – Become Financially Smart," demonstrating sustained commitment to promoting financial awareness.

Further, the G20/OECD High-Level Principles on Financial Consumer Protection (Fig. 9), guides the creation of effective consumer protection frameworks globally. This comprehensive approach ensures a secure, transparent, and inclusive financial ecosystem that serves all stakeholders effectively.

India has also developed a robust legal and regulatory framework for consumer protection that addresses the evolving needs of the digital economy. The Consumer Protection Act of 2019, the Information Technology Act of 2000, and the Digital Personal Data Protection Act of 2023 collectively emphasize consent-based data processing and comprehensive consumer rights protection. The RBI has also implemented essential consumer protection mechanisms including the Banking Ombudsman Scheme, comprehensive Customer Protection Guidelines, and the Charter of Customer Rights, ensuring transparency, privacy, and fair treatment across all banking interactions. Complementing these efforts, the Securities and Exchange Board of India (SEBI) actively promotes investor protection through initiatives such as the Investor Protection and Education Fund and the SEBI Complaints Redress System. Thus, India's initiatives closely align with the G20/OECD High level principles recommended for effective consumer protection framework (Fig. 9).

Fig. 9 G20/OECD High-Level Principles on Financial Consumer Protection (*Source* G20/OECD. (2022). G20/OECD High-Level Principles on Financial Consumer Protection. https://web-archive.oecd.org/2022-12-12/648348-G20_OECD%20FCP%20Principles.pdf)

3.11 MSME Formalization and Financing

The foundational step is to integrate the vast informal MSME sector into the mainstream financial system. In this direction, the government launched the Udyam Assist Platform (UAP) to register Informal Micro Enterprises through a streamlined assistance process in 2023. This platform serves multiple strategic objectives: creating a credible repository for enterprises, providing priority sector status for MSME credit applications, establishing digital identities that enable access to emerging digital ecosystems encompassing financial services, skill development, government benefits, and e-commerce platforms.

The achievements so far through the UAP have been remarkable. As of December 2024, a total of 5.70 crore MSMEs have registered on the platform, demonstrating significant outreach and active participation of small businesses in formal economy. These registered enterprises collectively provide employment to the tune of 24.14 crore individuals.[29] Efforts are ongoing to focus on registering beneficiaries of the National Rural Livelihoods Mission (NRLM) and National Urban Livelihoods Mission (NULM), so as to include marginalized groups in the formal financial sector.

The integration process has been further enhanced through data contributions from Microfinance Institutions (MFIs) and Non-Banking Financial Companies (NBFCs), promoting greater transparency and integration within the MSME ecosystem. The initiative aims to register over 5 crores additional MSMEs within the next two years, reflecting a comprehensive plan to expand formalization and support mechanisms for small enterprises nationwide.

3.12 Credit Access and Financing Solutions

Addressing the substantial financing gap within the MSME sector requires targeted credit initiatives that overcome traditional barriers to formal lending. The Credit Guarantee Scheme for Micro and Small Enterprises (CGSMSE), launched in 2000, provides collateral-free loans up to ₹500 lakh with guarantee coverage reaching 85% for various enterprise categories. This scheme has significantly enhanced lending confidence among financial institutions, covering an impressive ₹6.78 lakh crore till June 2024.[30]

The Pradhan Mantri Mudra Yojana (PMMY), launched in 2015, extends collateral-free credit to small businesses through a structured approach. The scheme categorizes loans under three segments: Shishu, Kishore, and Tarun, each addressing different stages of enterprise development. Figure 10 shows that the credit sanctioned under PMMY has increased from 40 million in 2016–17 to 67 million in 2023–24 and 55 million in 2024–25.[31] Since inception, PMMY has sanctioned

[29] Press Information Bureau, Government of India, 'Year End Review—2024'–Ministry of Micro, Small and Medium Enterprises, January 1, 2025, https://www.pib.gov.in/PressReleasePage.aspx?PRID=2089308.

[30] CREDIT ACCESS AND FINANCE FOR MSMEs. https://www.pib.gov.in/PressReleseDetailm.aspx?PRID=2041684.

[31] https://www.mudra.org.in/.

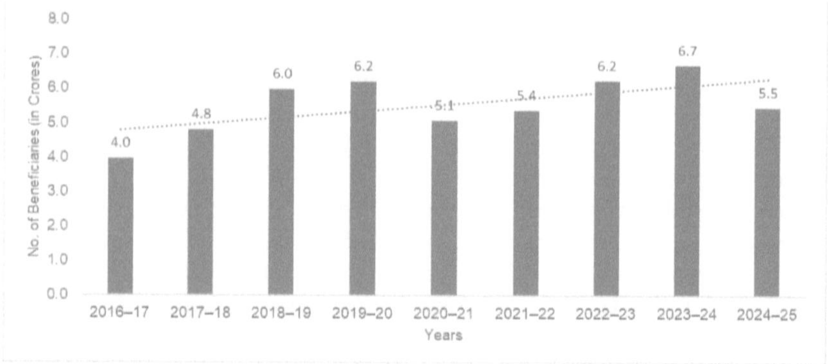

Fig. 10 Credit sanctioned under Mudra scheme (*Source* https://www.mudra.org.in/)

over 52 crore loans totaling ₹32.67 lakh crore, empowering countless micro-entrepreneurs across diverse sectors.[32]

The Stand-Up India Scheme, implemented in 2016, specifically targets vulnerable groups including Scheduled Caste/Scheduled Tribe and women entrepreneurs. The scheme facilitates loans ranging from ₹10 lakh to ₹1 crore, with a mandate requiring at least one loan for SC/ST beneficiaries and one for women entrepreneurs per bank branch. Remarkably, 84% of scheme accounts belong to women beneficiaries, highlighting its significant role in fostering inclusive entrepreneurship and gender-balanced economic participation.[33]

3.13 Technology-Enabled Credit Solutions

The evolution of digital infrastructure has enabled innovative credit delivery mechanisms that leverage technology for enhanced efficiency and reach. Small Industries Development Bank of India (SIDBI), in collaboration with Online PSB Loans Ltd (OPL) and Indian Software Product Industry RoundTable (iSPIRT), has developed the GST Sahay Application utilizing the Open Credit Enablement Network (OCEN) and

[32] A Decade of Growth with PM Mudra Yojana. https://www.pib.gov.in/PressReleasePage.aspx?PRID=2119781.

[33] 69% of the total 44.46 crore loans sanctioned under Pradhan Mantri Mudra Yojana, have been sanctioned to women.. https://www.pib.gov.in/PressReleasePage.aspx?PRID=1987773.

Account Aggregator (AA) frameworks. This application provides 'on-tap' invoice-based financing, delivering cash flow-based credit solutions for small-value loans to micro enterprises.

The important aspect is that the application journey is entirely paperless, covering the complete credit lifecycle from origination through repayment. The system integrates trade information from the Goods and Services Tax Network (GSTN), banking information through Account Aggregators, credit bureau data, and various components of India Stack including e-sign, e-stamping, and e-NACH mandate functionality to achieve seamless digital processing.

These collateral-free, unsecured small-value loans, based on GST invoices, create strong incentives for micro enterprises to join the formal GST framework. This approach not only facilitates credit access but also promotes broader formalization of the economy, contributing to growth and enhanced transparency in business operations.

One of the major initiatives taken by the government to address the working capital requirements of MSMEs was the setting up of the Trade Receivables Discounting System (TReDS). TReDS is an online platform that facilitates the financing of trade receivables for MSMEs from corporate buyers. It allows MSMEs to sell their unpaid invoices (receivables) to banks and financial institutions at a discounted rate, providing them with immediate liquidity. The process involves three parties: the MSME supplier, the buyer (corporate or government), and the financier (bank or NBFC). Additionally, insurance companies or credit guarantee funds can participate to hedge default risk. The transactions processed are "without recourse" to MSME sellers, i.e., they are not liable if the buyer does not pay. TReDS ensures transparency, competitive rates, and faster access to working capital, thereby reducing the credit risk and easing cash flow challenges faced by MSMEs. The system is regulated by the Reserve Bank of India (RBI).

As on date, five entities have been authorised by RBI to operate TReDS. These entities have collectively financed 41.58 Lakh invoices in FY 2023–24 totaling ₹1,38,241 Cr. Success ratio i.e., number of invoices uploaded to invoices financed on TReDS platform averaged 94%.[34]

[34] Soni, S. (2024b, November 8). TReDS: Govt reduces turnover threshold to Rs 250 cr to get more companies on invoice discounting platform. *Financial Express*. https://www.financialexpress.com/business/sme-treds-govt-reduces-turnover-threshold-to-rs-250-cr-to-get-more-companies-on-rbi-invoice-discounting-platform-3659670/.

To support India's traditional MSMEs such as artisans and crafts-people, who work with their hands and tools, the government launched the PM Vishwakarma Scheme in 2023. The scheme recognizes them as "Vishwakarmas" and extends end-to-end support. This includes formal recognition through an ID and certificate, skill upgradation through basic and advanced training (with a daily stipend), and a toolkit incentive of up to ₹15,000. It also provides credit support in two tranches—₹1 lakh and ₹2 lakh—at a highly concessional 5% interest rate, helping artisans expand their businesses without collateral. Beyond skill and credit support, the scheme also incentivizes digital transactions and strengthens market access for artisans by offering quality certification, branding, support for e-commerce onboarding (like GeM), and promotional assistance.[35]

As of 29.07.2024, loan sanctions have been granted to 56,526 applications, totaling Rs. 551.80 crore, and loan disbursements have been made to 15,878 applications, totaling Rs. 132.49 crore across the country under the credit component of the scheme and 9,05,328 applicants have opted for marketing support, out of total 14.38 lakh successfully registered eligible beneficiaries.[36] By institutionalizing these support mechanisms, this scheme aspires to enhance the dignity, income, and resilience of India's traditional artisan workforce.

The comprehensive framework of formalization initiatives, targeted credit schemes, and technology-enabled solutions collectively drives India's MSME sector toward enhanced financial inclusion, sustainable growth, and integration with the formal economy. These interconnected programs demonstrate the government's commitment to addressing the multifaceted challenges faced by small enterprises while leveraging technological innovations to create scalable, efficient solutions for inclusive economic development.

[35] Salient features and Guidelines of PM Vishwakarma Scheme. (n.d.). https://www.pib.gov.in/PressReleasePage.aspx?PRID=1959098.

[36] *PM Vishwakarma Scheme provides end-to-end support to artisans and craftspeople of 18 trades who work with their hands and tools.* (n.d.). https://www.pib.gov.in/PressReleasePage.aspx?PRID=2041501.

4 India and G20 Collaboration for Advancing Financial Inclusion

4.1 *The Global Imperative for Financial Inclusion*

In 2011, the World Bank's Global Financial Inclusion (Global Findex) Database revealed a startling statistic: 2 billion adults globally, roughly half of the total adult population then lacked access to formal financial sector as they did not have bank accounts. While account penetration was nearly universal in high-income economies, with 94% of adults having an account at a formal financial institution, the figure was only 54% in developing economies. This was a significant barrier to economic growth and poverty reduction.[37]

Recognizing its importance, G20 leaders identified financial inclusion as a key pillar of the global development agenda during the 2010 G20 Summit in Seoul which led to the establishment of the Global Partnership for Financial Inclusion (GPFI) under G20 Finance Track. The objective of this partnership is to advance financial inclusion within and beyond G20 countries.

4.1.1 GPFI: The Financial Inclusion Group of G20

The Group of Twenty (G20) is an international forum of both developing and developed countries which seeks to find solutions to global economic and financial issues. It has two tracks: Finance Track and Sherpa Track. Within the two tracks, there are thematically oriented working groups in which representatives from the Finance ministries and central banks of the members as well as various international organizations participate. These working groups meet regularly to carry out the task given by G20 leaders.

The GPFI, one of the G20 working groups of Finance track, is an inclusive platform comprising G20 countries, interested and invited non-G20 nations, and international organizations, aimed at advancing the global financial inclusion agenda. GPFI operates through a three-year Financial Inclusion Action Plan (FIAP), which outlines its objectives, priorities, and action areas annually. The group is led by two Co-Chairs—one representing developed countries and the other from developing

[37] Global Partnership for Financial Inclusion (GPFI). *Why Financial Inclusion*. Accessed July 3, 2025. Available at: https://www.gpfi.org/why-financial-inclusion.

countries—who oversee its functioning and provide guidance and support to the presidency each year. The Co-Chairs are appointed for a three-year term.

The G20 FIAP, under Saudi Presidency in 2020, defined the two key priorities of GPFI which were Digital Financial Inclusion and MSME Financing. These were taken forward in G20 2023 FIAP developed under India's Presidency. In addition, the FIAP outlines the three continuing areas of GPFI which are: reducing remittance costs to below 3% by 2030, aligning with the Sustainable Development Goals (SDGs); engagement with Standard-Setting Bodies (SSBs) and strengthening relationships with non-G20 countries, particularly these from the Global South. It also reflects on cross-cutting issues such as promoting consumer protection, digital and financial literacy, accessible and affordable financial services for women, underserved and vulnerable groups and liaising with other relevant groups and organizations on the issues related to financial inclusion.

In addition to the G20 countries, the GPFI membership includes the Honorary Patron, Queen Máxima of the Netherlands—who also serves as the UN Secretary-General's Special Advocate initially for inclusive finance and subsequently 2024 onward for Financial Health (UNSGSA). It also comprises eight Implementing Partners such as the World Bank, Consultative Group to Assist the Poor (CGAP), Alliance for Financial Inclusion (AFI), Better Than Cash Alliance (BTCA), Organization for Economic Co-operation and Development (OECD), International Finance Corporation (IFC), International Fund for Agricultural Development (IFAD), and Small and Medium Enterprises Finance Forum (SMEFF), as well as Affiliated Partners like the Bill & Melinda Gates Foundation, Women's World Banking (WWB), Access to Insurance Initiative (A2ii), etc. These members actively support GPFI in drafting documents and contribute to its discussions and deliberations.

4.1.2 *Notable Work Under GPFI*

GPFI introduced High-Level Principles (HLP) for digital financial inclusion, marking a significant step towards harnessing technology to empower underserved populations globally under the Chinese Presidency. In 2014–15, the G20 leaders identified the facilitation of remittance flows and the reduction of remittance costs to below 3% as key priorities, in line with the SDGs. Consequently, to move towards the goals, it was agreed that countries would submit their National Remittance Plans (NRPs) every two years and provide annual updates on their progress on targets. Since then, both the updated NRPs and annual progress reports have been developed as part of GPFI's ongoing areas of work. In 2020 under Saudi Arabia's presidency, the G20 2020 FIAP identified Digital Financial Inclusion and MSME Financing as the two key priorities of GPFI. The G20 High-Level Policy Guidelines on Digital Financial Inclusion for Youth, Women and SMEs were also produced in 2020. Under the Indonesian presidency in 2022, GPFI delivered a Regulatory Toolkit for enhanced Digital financial Inclusion of MSMEs and G20/OECD High Level Principles on Financial Consumer Protection. Complete list of deliverable produced in the last decade under GPFI is provided in the table below.

Year	*G20 Presidency*	*G20 GPFI Deliverables*
2025	South Africa (In-progress)	1. Moving from Access to Usage of financial Products and Services. (Presidency priority) 2. New and innovative technology and solutions for financial inclusion and for advancing the quality of inclusion for individuals and MSMEs. 3. An Implementation Framework for the 2024 G20 GPFI Action Plan for MSME Financing

(continued)

(continued)

Year	*G20 Presidency*	*G20 GPFI Deliverables*
2024	Brazil	1. Policy options for improving "last mile" access and quality inclusion for individuals and MSMEs through digital infrastructure, including Digital Public Infrastructure, consumer protection and other FIAP objectives; 2. A New Action Plan for MSME Financing (multi-year project) to identify crucial action areas and concrete initiatives/actions for countries to fill the gaps in MSME financing and improve access, also with a focus on utilizing innovative digital infrastructures, including Digital Public Infrastructure (DPI), for removing various traditional barriers in order to enhance financial inclusion; 3. Propose a conceptual framework and measurement tools of financial well-being (Presidency priority).
2023	India	1. G20 Policy Recommendations for Advancing Financial Inclusion and Productivity Gains through Digital Public Infrastructure (Presidency priority). 2. Regulatory Toolkit for Enhanced Digital Financial Inclusion of Micro, Small and Medium Enterprises (MSMEs) 3.Report on MSME best practices and innovative instruments to overcome common constraints in MSME financing
2022	Indonesia	1.Financial Inclusion Framework in Harnessing Digitalization to Increase Productivity, Sustainable and Inclusive Economy of Women, Youth and MSME (Presidency priority). 2.Implementation Framework for the G20 High-Level Principles (HLPs) on digital financial inclusion (DFI).

(continued)

(continued)

Year	*G20 Presidency*	*G20 GPFI Deliverables*
2021	Italy	1. G20 Menu of Policy Options for digital financial literacy and financial consumer and MSME protection MSME Digital Finance: Resilience and Innovation during COVID-19 2. Supporting Financial Resilience and Transformation through Digital Financial Literacy 3. Navigating the Storm: MSMEs' Financial and Digital Competences in Covid-19 Time 4. Lessons Learnt and Effective Approaches to Protect Consumers and Support Financial Inclusion in the Context of COVID-19 5. Resilience in the market for international remittances during the Covid-19 crisis
2020	Saudi Arabia	1. G20 High-Level Policy Guidelines on Digital Financial Inclusion for Youth, Women and SMEs 2. G-20: Data enhancement and Coordination in SME Finance Report 3. Unlocking Finance for Youth Entrepreneurs: Evidence from a Global Stocktaking
2019	Japan	1.G20 Fukuoka Policy Priorities on Aging and Financial Inclusion 2. G20 GPFI Indicators updated!
2018	Argentina	1. Regulatory approaches to enhance financial inclusion through digitisation (digital onboarding). 2. Development of digital payments infrastructure and incentives to accept digital payments.
2017	South Korea	1. Implementation of the G20 High-Level Principles for Digital Financial Inclusion. 2. Implementation of the G20 Action Plan on SME Financing. 3. Increased focus, underpinned by policy work, on the financial inclusion of vulnerable groups: forcibly displaced persons.

(continued)

(continued)

Year	*G20 Presidency*	*G20 GPFI Deliverables*
2016	China	1. G20 High-Level Principles for Digital Financial Inclusion 2. G20/OECD INFE Ensuring Financial Education and Consumer Protection for All in the Digital Age 3. G20 Action Plan on SME Financing Implementation Framework 4. G20 Financial Inclusion Indicators (2016 Update) 5. Global Standard-Setting Bodies and Financial Inclusion: The Evolving Landscape

4.2 Measuring Financial Inclusion

In 2012, the basic set of indicators to measure financial inclusion across access and usage dimensions were decided. These indicators are based on the three dimensions of financial inclusion, i.e., access, usage and quality and cover metrics such as account ownership, access to internet, enterprise loans, financial literacy among others. The World Bank's Global Findex Database has long served as the leading source of data on global access to financial services, covering areas such as payments, savings, and borrowing, and is typically released every four years. Another key data source is the IMF's Financial Access Survey (FAS), which provides supply-side data to assess access to and usage of financial products and services. To strengthen and update the indicators used for measuring financial inclusion, the FAS Advisory Group was recently established in 2023, with GPFI Co-Chairs also serving as members of the Advisory Group.

These basic sets of indicators were then expanded in 2013 as G20 Financial Inclusion Indicators, providing further insight into access and usage aspects, including indicators on the emerging mobile financial services space. Under the Chinese G20 Presidency in 2016, new indicators were added to the G20 Financial Inclusion Indicators to measure the use, availability, and quality of digital financial services. The expansion and revision of the existing set of indicators was driven by the development of new digital models, as well as the availability of new data on both the demand for and supply of digital financial services. The updated and new indicators measured both use of digital payments and access to digital infrastructure.

Measuring Financial Inclusion in India[38]

In India, RBI also measures the performance of financial inclusion using the *Financial Inclusion (FI) Index*. The Index is based on the three dimensions of financial inclusion, viz., 'Access', 'Usage' and 'Quality' with weights as 35, 45 and 20 per cent respectively. The weights were determined to make the index forward-looking with higher weights to the deepening aspect of financial inclusion ('Usage' and 'Quality'). Broadly, one-third of total weight has been assigned to 'Access' where most of the initiatives in the past have been undertaken and which reflects the extent of supply side financial infrastructure made available. Two-thirds of the weight has been assigned to the deepening aspect of financial inclusion, i.e., 'Usage' and 'Quality'. Each of these three sub-indices are further composed of a distinct set of dimensions computed based on a non-overlapping set of indicators.

'Access' sub-index which is further divided into four dimensions, viz., 'Banking', 'Digital', 'Pension', and 'Insurance', reflects the efforts made on the supply side of financial inclusion, such as availability of physical and digital infrastructure and measures for making basic products and services available for the excluded segments.

'Usage' sub-index is divided into five dimensions, viz., 'Savings & Investment', 'Credit', 'Digital', 'Insurance' and 'Pension'. It is more of a demand side measure and reflects the extent of active usage of financial infrastructure by way of savings, investment, insurance, availing of credit and remittance facilities, etc. The indicators are designed to reflect savings and investment habits, availability of credit from banks and non-banks, use of retail digital payments, penetration of insurance both life and non-life, and contribution to various pension schemes.

'Quality' sub-index has three dimensions, viz., 'Financial Literacy', 'Consumer Protection', and 'Inequality' in the distribution of financial infrastructure with 19 indicators. These indicators capture the efforts undertaken by the stakeholders to make citizens aware of the appropriate

[38] *Reserve Bank of India, Financial Inclusion Index—A Comprehensive Measure for Access, Usage and Quality, RBI Bulletin*, September 16, 2021. Available at: https://rbi.org.in/scripts/BS_ViewBulletin.aspx?Id=20502.

financial services available, safe ways of using them, and making them aware of their rights such as to overcome the psychological barriers. They also reflect effectiveness of the grievance redress mechanism and account for uneven distribution of certain indicators of financial access and usage.

4.3 *Work Under India G20 Presidency*

Despite the numerous initiatives undertaken and progress made both domestically and internationally, significant challenges still remained in advancing financial inclusion. These challenges existed on both the demand and supply sides such as limited access to essential enablers such as identification, documentation, mobile connectivity, and the internet; physical distance from and lack of trust in financial institutions; sociocultural norms that discriminate against or unintentionally bias certain groups; infrastructure gaps and geographical remoteness; insufficient financial education and literacy; low population density and high operating costs; poor infrastructure and high customer service fees; asymmetric information and high barriers to entry.

To address these challenges at the national level, India adopted the approach of Digital Public Infrastructure (DPI). Aiming to showcase its successful digital transformation journey, India made its G20 priority to work on "Leveraging Digital Public Infrastructure for advancing financial inclusion and productivity gains". This marked the first time the term "DPI" was formally introduced and conceptualized, leading to its global recognition and acceptance.

DPI represents an infrastructure-based approach in achieving societal goals by leveraging technology within a robust ecosystem that includes markets, governance, and technology. Designed in the public interest, it fosters innovation by encouraging competitive private sector solutions while operating within strong and yet supportive regulatory frameworks. By utilizing open technology standards and enabling policies, DPI brings out the best of market capabilities to deliver inclusive, scalable, and efficient financial inclusion.

A DPI approach is essentially built on three interconnected layers. The **Market layer** drives innovation and competition, enabling both public and private players to design inclusive products for all. The **Governance layer** provides the legal and institutional frameworks necessary to ensure accountability and fairness while promoting public program adoption. Finally, the **Technology layer** underpins this system with shared specifications and systems for identifiers, data sharing, digital credentials, payments, and more.

Together, these layers create a powerful, integrated infrastructure that accelerates progress toward a digitally inclusive society, transforming lives and economies alike. DPI also consists of various building blocks or layers. In general, we can categorize them in three layers as—Digital Identity, Digital Payment systems and data sharing platforms, each of which plays a crucial role in ensuring equitable access and efficient delivery of services.

The digital identity layer focuses on establishing a secure, verifiable, and universally accessible digital identity system. A robust digital identity is foundational for enabling access to a range of services, including financial, government, and healthcare services. For example—Aadhaar, e-KYC, e-sign and GSTN.

The payments layer enables the digital transfer of money, ensuring that people can make transactions quickly, securely, and at low cost. This layer is vital for driving financial inclusion by providing individuals and businesses with access to formal payment systems. For example—Unified Payments Interface (UPI), Aadhaar Enabled Payment System, Aadhaar Payment Bridge, Bharat Bill Payment System.

The data sharing layer focuses on consent-based data sharing between different stakeholders (financial institutions, users and service providers) to enable easy access to credit. For example—Account Aggregator Framework.

The building blocks of DPI together play a pivotal role in creating an inclusive, equitable, scalable and sustainable financial system. DPI plays a transformative role in modern economies by breaking traditional barriers to access, improving transparency and information, thereby fostering inclusivity. It is open, scalable, and interoperable, enabling systems to integrate seamlessly and expand as needed. It serves as a foundation for innovation, enabling the creation of digital ecosystems that further support entrepreneurship and innovation. Furthermore, DPI has quicker adaptability to change, allowing it to respond swiftly to change and technological advancements. It improves productivity while reducing inefficiencies such as leakages and unnecessary costs. As highlighted in the UNDP Report 2023, DPI has the potential to accelerate economic growth by an impressive 20–33% by 2030.[39] This demonstrates the immense promise of DPI as a catalyst for sustainable development, innovation, and prosperity, underscoring its importance in shaping the future of our global economy.

4.4 Achievements Under India's G20 Presidency

In accordance with the presidency priority on "***leveraging DPI for advancing financial inclusion and productivity gains***", GPFI produced a G20 deliverable in the form of a report on "***G20 Policy recommendations for advancing financial inclusion and Productivity Gains through DPI***"[40] under the G20 India Presidency, in collaboration with the World Bank in 2023. These DPI policy recommendations were unanimously endorsed by all G20 leaders in the 2023 Delhi Declaration. It offers an in-depth understanding of the concept of Digital Public Infrastructure (DPI), explores its use cases, and provides policy recommendations for the development of the DPI ecosystem to accelerate financial inclusion and productivity gains which are as follows: develop well-designed DPIs and the broader enabling environment through a widely accepted set of good practices; encourage appropriate risk-based regulation, supervision, and oversight arrangements for financial-sector use of DPIs; promote sound internal governance arrangements and enable DPIs to offer products and services in a way that no one is left behind and the interests of the consumer are safeguarded.

Additionally, the new G20 2023 Financial Inclusion Action Plan (FIAP) was developed, setting out the priorities, action areas, and deliverables for the period 2024–2026. The 2023 FIAP retained the core priorities identified in the 2020 FIAP—Digital Financial Inclusion and MSME Financing. Moreover, it introduced a significant new action area: "Promoting open, interoperable, reliable, inclusive, and secure digital

[39] UNDP (2023). *The human and economic impact of digital public infrastructure*. United Nations Development Programme. https://www.undp.org/sites/g/files/zskgke326/files/2023-07/undp-the-human-and-economic-impact-of-digital-public-infrastructure-final.pdf.

[40] Government of India, Department of Economic Affairs, G20 Policy Recommendations for Advancing Financial Inclusion and Productivity Gains through Digital Public Infrastructure. (2023). https://dea.gov.in/sites/default/files/G20%20Policy%20Recommendations%20for%20Advancing%20Financial%20Inlcusion%20and%20Productivity%20Gains%20through%20DPI.pdf.

infrastructures (including internet, mobile connectivity, DPIs, and ICT) to accelerate the delivery of digital financial services for the financial inclusion of individuals and MSMEs."

Furthermore, India conducted several knowledge-sharing and experience exchange initiatives—such as the Voice of Global South initiative—to actively engage with non-G20 countries, especially those in the Global South. These efforts, undertaken as part of GPFI's ongoing work, aimed to share insights and lessons from India's digital transformation journey in advancing financial inclusion.

Notably, under the Indian Presidency in 2023, Digital Economy Working Group (DEWG) together with contribution from GPFI, could achieve a consensus for the first time on a framework of DPI and it was formally accepted by countries on any international forum.

In addition, the 'India's G20 Task Force on Digital Public Infrastructure for Economic Transformation, Financial Inclusion, and Development' under the Co-Chairs—Shri Amitabh Kant, the then G20 Sherpa of India, and Shri Nandan Nilekani, Co-founder and Chairman of Infosys, as well as the Founding Chairman of UIDAI (Aadhaar) was established in January 2023 to oversee and support the implementation of India's G20 Presidency agenda and priorities related to Digital Public Infrastructure (DPI) and Financial Inclusion. The 'Report of India's G20 Task Force on Digital Public Infrastructure'[41] was published in July 2024.[42] This Report highlights the DPI Approach as a transformative paradigm that effectively addresses global challenges through innovative technological solutions. It presents a range of policy recommendations with the objective of strengthening the foundations of DPI worldwide. It also underscores the critical need for countries to make their existing DPI universally applicable, emphasizing the dissemination of pertinent protocols and standards and the development of comprehensive packages that could be utilized by other countries particularly Global South in establishing their own DPIs. Additionally, it offers insights into financing and

[41] Government of India, Department of Economic Affairs, Report of India's G20 Task Force on Digital Public Infrastructure, July 15, 2024, https://www.dea.gov.in/sites/default/files/Report%20of%20Indias%20G20%20Task%20Force%20On%20Digital%20Public%20Infrastructure.pdf.

[42] https://dea.gov.in/sites/default/files/Report%20of%20Indias%20G20%20Task%20Force%20On%20Digital%20Public%20Infrastructure.pdf.

the implementation of DPIs while addressing the elements of skilling and monitoring the progress of DPI deployment and adoption.

Further, IMF in its 2023 working paper titled "*Stacking up the Benefits: Lessons from India's Digital Journey*", also recognised that India's journey in developing a world-class DPI highlights powerful lessons for other countries embarking on their own digital transformation, in particular a design approach that focuses on shared building blocks and supporting innovation across the ecosystem.[43]

Lastly, India was nominated as the Co-Chair of the G20 GPFI Working Group for the 2024–2026 term, alongside Italy. This role provides India with a wider scope and broad platform to advance its priorities, as well as those of emerging economies, particularly the Global South, within the multilateral forum.

4.5 *Legacy of Continuing Impact: Outcomes Under India's Co-Chairship (2024–25)*

The G20 2023 FIAP, endorsed under India's presidency, is set to be implemented over the next three years (2024–2026), continuing through the presidencies of Brazil and South Africa.

As a result of implementation of 2023 FIAP, during India's Co-Chairship in 2024, under Brazil's G20 Presidency, the GPFI released a report titled "Policy Options for Last Mile Access and Quality Inclusion through Digital Infrastructure, including Digital Public Infrastructure (DPI), Consumer Protection, and Other FIAP Objectives."[44] The report underscores DPI as a key enabler for advancing financial inclusion at the last mile. Additionally, the GPFI developed the "2024 G20 GPFI Action Plan for MSME Financing",[45] which recognized DPI as a critical policy support mechanism for fostering FinTech solutions to enhance MSME

[43] Alonso, C., Bhojwani, T., Hanedar, E., Prihardini, D., Uña, G., & Zhabska, K. (2023, March 31). *Stacking up the benefits: Lessons from India's digital journey* (IMF Working Paper No. 23/78). Washington, DC: International Monetary Fund.

[44] Global Partnership for Financial Inclusion (GPFI). (2024, December 6). *G20 Policy options to improve last mile access and quality of inclusion*. https://www.gpfi.org/news/g20-policy-options-improve-last-mile-access-and-quality-inclusion.

[45] Global Partnership for Financial Inclusion (2024). *GPFI MSME finance action plan*. February 3, 2025, https://www.gpfi.org/news/2024-gpfi-msme-finance-action-plan-0.

access to finance. Through these efforts, India continued to advance its core priority of leveraging DPI to promote financial inclusion.

Similarly, under South Africa's G20 Presidency in 2025, the GPFI continues to emphasize the role of digital infrastructure in enhancing the usage of financial services across various products and segments, as outlined in South Africa's priority paper, "*Moving from Access to Usage*." DPI, comprising digital identity, payment systems, and data exchange—is also set to be recognized as an innovative technological solution for advancing the quality of financial inclusion in one of the FIAP deliverables.

Furthermore, as part of the Implementation Framework of the G20 GPFI Action Plan for MSME Financing, India underscored the importance of DPI during a webinar organized by the World Bank Group on 29th May 2025, which will be documented in the framework's summary report.

4.6 'DPI Goes Global': G20 as Catalyst for Inter-nationalisation

As a result of India's G20 Presidency, the concept of DPI gained global recognition and traction. Interoperable cross-border payment systems are becoming a cornerstone of global economic integration and financial inclusion. By enabling seamless, efficient, and cost-effective transactions across countries, these systems benefit businesses, individuals, and governments alike. They foster international trade and investment, improve transparency, and enhance security in financial ecosystems. Such interoperability ensures that money moves faster and cheaper across borders, unlocking opportunities for economic growth and making financial services accessible to the underserved.

Particularly, India has emerged as a significant global player in the payment domain, with 49% of the world's real-time transactions recorded in 2023, according to the ACI Worldwide Report 2024.[46]

The Unified Payments Interface (UPI), India's fast payment system, now lives in seven countries, including the UAE, Singapore, Bhutan, and France, allowing seamless cross-border transactions for Indians abroad. NPCI International has extended its outreach to 80+ countries, with

[46] Press Information Bureau, Government of India. (2024, August 12). *India's G20 financial inclusion policy recommendations launched*. https://www.pib.gov.in/PressReleasePage.aspx?PRID=2079544.

active partnerships across 30+ nations. In 2024, UPI QR acceptance was operationalized in France, Sri Lanka, Mauritius, and Nepal. Notably, Mauritius became the first non-Asian country to issue RuPay cards, enabling their use locally and in India.

5 Global Deliberations on Financial Inclusion: Issues and Concerns

5.1 *Financial Well-being*

Under Brazil's G20 Presidency in 2024, the concept of "Financial Well-being," closely aligned with the notion of financial health, was introduced as a key priority in GPFI discussions with strong support from OECD and Queen Maxima (UNSGSA). The primary objective was to develop a comprehensive definition and a measurement framework for financial well-being, recognizing that mere access to and usage of financial services do not always lead to financial wellbeing of people. While developed nations like the G7 have achieved universal financial inclusion, they are now grappling with emerging challenges such as over-indebtedness and irresponsible consumer behavior, which negatively impact overall well-being. As a result, there is a tendency to shift towards an outcome-based approach to ensure that financial inclusion policies positively affect individuals' financial health and well-being.

This new approach is a problematic one at least on two accounts, one it goes beyond the scope of financial inclusion, two strong chances of bringing climate related issues within the discourse of GPFI underlying the developmental needs of global south.

India, thus have expressed reservations regarding the adoption of this new approach/concept. It emphasized that financial well-being is highly subjective, varying significantly across individuals and national contexts. It is a very broad concept and depends upon various macro-economic, socio-economic, cultural factors etc and therefore, goes beyond the scope of financial inclusion. Moreover, its direct link to financial inclusion is not well-established and unsubstantiated by empirical evidence. Representing the voice of emerging economies, India cautioned that introduction of such an advanced concept as can divert global attention from the more pressing challenge of ensuring basic access to and usage of financial products and services for excluded and underserved populations.

Despite strong support from G7 countries, India continued to uphold its position on financial well-being. Through sustained negotiations and constructive dialogue and deliberations, India eventually worked on the "*G20 Policy Note on Financial Well-being*" and brought important qualifications to reflect the concerns of emerging economies. It is mainly because of India's insistence that disclaimer was included as: "*Under the Brazilian Presidency's initiative, for the purpose of understanding, we recognise financial well-being as a new, voluntary, evolving, and customisable concept, which may differ based on individual, household, societal, and national needs, development priorities, and contextual circumstances, and can generally be described as*..." Additionally, India advocated for including the phrase "*keeping in mind country-specific circumstances*" within the working definition of financial well-being, thereby ensuring that the concept remains flexible and adaptable to diverse developmental contexts.

So, clearly countries are free to interpret the concept of FWB and get suitable flexibility to factor their needs and circumstances.

5.2 Contextualizing Climate Finance in MSME Discussions

An additional issue was proposed to be introduced by developed countries during Brazil's G20 Presidency was the integration of climate finance considerations into financial inclusion discussions. Specifically, within the 2024 G20 GPFI Action Plan for MSME Financing, a proposal was made to include a dedicated box highlighting climate-related transition and mitigation risks as emerging challenges for MSMEs.

India expressed strong reservations regarding this inclusion, emphasizing that climate finance falls within the mandate of other G20 groups—particularly the Sustainable Finance Working Group—which are specifically tasked with addressing such matters. Moreover, India argued that the proposed content extended beyond the scope of the 2023 Financial Inclusion Action Plan (FIAP), which had clearly defined focus areas for GPFI deliverables.

Finally, India agreed for the inclusion of box only after a suitable disclaimer was inserted stating that discussions and policy developments concerning climate finance falls under the purview of other specialized streams and working groups within the G20, particularly those focused on climate and energy, and GPFI focus should remain on financial inclusion.

5.3 *Continued Push of Financial Well-being/Health*

The agenda of integrating *Financial Well-being* or *Financial Health* into global financial inclusion discourse did not conclude with Brazil's G20 Presidency in 2024. The intent was to introduce the concept in 2024 and institutionalize it more comprehensively in 2025 across all major global platforms discussing financial inclusion. This agenda championed by Queen Máxima of the Netherlands, the UN Secretary-General's Special Advocate (UNSGSA), who notably updated her own designation title from "*Special Advocate for Inclusive Finance*" to "*Special Advocate for Financial Health*" to reflect this evolving priority.

Under South Africa's G20 Presidency in 2025, efforts are underway to embed financial health across key deliverables. This includes integrating the concept into the Presidency's priority—"*Moving from Access to Usage*"—and into the FIAP deliverable on "*New and Innovative Technology Solutions for Quality Financial Inclusion*," with the aim of keeping the narrative alive and forward-moving.

India again maintained a consistent position on this issue, reiterating its earlier stance during the Brazil Presidency. It continues to highlight the need for foundational access and usage in developing economies, and the limited empirical evidence linking financial health to financial inclusion

Despite any evidence of link between financial inclusion and financial well-being, discussions on financial health are now expanding beyond the GPFI platform. The IMF's Financial Access Survey (FAS) is exploring the inclusion of supply-side financial health indicators. Similarly, the World Bank's Global Findex Database 2025 will feature a dedicated chapter on demand-side financial health indicators. In addition, the Bank for International Settlements (BIS) is planning a dedicated workshop on financial health in November 2025—reflecting the growing global momentum around this evolving concept. Furthermore, the Fourth International Conference on Financing for Development (FFD4) also underscored the pivotal role of digital technology in advancing both financial inclusion and financial health in its final outcome document.

5.4 *Emerging Opportunities with Regard to Evolving Digital Financial Landscape*

One of the most significant developments is the growing adoption of Central Bank Digital Currencies (CBDCs)—digital forms of money issued by central banks. Following the launch of several pilot programs in India between 2022 and 2023 for both wholesale and retail use, CBDCs aim to reduce reliance on physical cash, lower transaction costs, and expand access to formal financial systems. These innovations have the potential to fundamentally transform financial ecosystems, enhancing efficiency and inclusivity.

Another promising advancement is the convergence of Artificial Intelligence (AI) with Digital Public Infrastructure (DPI)—a fusion increasingly referred to as "Digital Public Intelligence". In India, for instance, AI-driven tools such as Natural Language Processing and Bhashini AI are breaking down linguistic barriers, making digital financial services more inclusive and accessible to diverse population segments.

At the same time, the rapid pace of digitalisation has elevated the importance of cybersecurity. The proliferation of threats—including attacks on critical infrastructure, mobile malware, and data privacy concerns—demands a proactive response. India is addressing these risks through initiatives such as the National Cyber Security Strategy 2020 and the work of CERT-In, underpinned by legal frameworks like the Information Technology Act, 2000.

To sustain this momentum, investments in industry-academia collaboration and cybersecurity capacity are essential. These efforts are laying the groundwork for a secure, inclusive, and resilient digital financial future.

5.5 *Gaps in Financial Inclusion*

Despite significant progress in advancing financial inclusion, several critical gaps continue to hinder the full realization of inclusive financial systems globally and within India. 1.5 billion adults worldwide—nearly 24% of the global adult population—still remain unbanked,[47] lacking access to even basic financial services. In India, 5% of the adult population is still unbanked, particularly in rural and remote regions, underscoring the need for last mile outreach and inclusion.[48] The global credit gap

[47] World Bank Group. (2024). *The global findex database 2021.* World Bank. https://www.worldbank.org/en/publication/globalfindex.

[48] *Results of Comprehensive Annual Modular Survey, July 2022–June 2023.* (n.d.). https://www.pib.gov.in/PressReleasePage.aspx?PRID=2063571#:~:text=(viii)%20A round%2094.6%25%20persons,institution%20at%20all%20India%20level.&text=As%20a%20part%20of%20the,%2C%202022%20to%20June%2C%202023.

for SMEs is estimated at a staggering $5.2 trillion,[49] posing a serious constraint to have inclusive financial sector and growth.

In developing countries, about 41% of MSMEs face unmet financing needs,[50] limiting their ability to scale, create jobs, and contribute to economic development. In India, the MSME credit gap is estimated at ₹20–25 lakh crore, reflecting the systemic challenges small businesses face in accessing formal credit.[51] This shortfall impedes MSMEs' ability to grow, innovate, and drive employment and economic activity. Over 50% of the global unbanked population are women,[52] pointing to a significant gender disparity in financial inclusion. Women are often disproportionately excluded due to socio-cultural norms, lower financial literacy, and restrictive regulatory environments. In India, while there is no significant gender gap in account ownership, there exists a 13-percentage points gender gap in usage,[53] indicating that women are less likely to engage in active financial transactions. This highlights the need for targeted efforts to enhance financial literacy, confidence, and usage among women.

The average global cost of remittances for India remains high at 6.25%, far exceeding the SDG target of 3% by 2024. This continues to be a substantial burden on low-income household's dependent on cross-border transfers. In the case of India, the cost of sending remittances remains above 5%, affecting millions of migrant workers and their families,

[49] Bruhn, M., Hommes, M., Khanna, M., Singh, S., Sorokina, A., & Wimpey, J. S. (2017). Assessment of the shortfalls and opportunities in financing micro, small and medium enterprises in emerging markets. In *MSME finance gap*. International Finance Corporation. https://documents1.worldbank.org/curated/en/653831510568517947/pdf/121264-WP-PUBLIC-MSMEReportFINAL.pdf.

[50] *Bridging the MSME financing gap for sustainable development | ITC*. (n.d.). ITC. https://www.intracen.org/news-and-events/news/bridging-the-msme-financing-gap-for-sustainable-development.

[51] Understanding Indian MSME Sector. (2025). SIDBI. https://www.sidbi.in/uploads/Understanding_Indian_MSME_sector_Progress_and_Challenges_13_05_25_Final.pdf

[52] World Bank Group. (2024). *The global findex database 2021. World Bank*. https://www.worldbank.org/en/publication/globalfindex.

[53] Ibid.

and indicating an area where further cost-reduction strategies are urgently needed.[54]

6 Way Forward

To address and remove the persistent gaps in financial inclusion, a comprehensive approach is required, one that combines both domestic and international efforts, strategically and operationally. At the domestic strategic level, each country's National Financial Inclusion Strategy should focus on last-mile inclusion and a multi-stakeholder approach that also integrates consumer protection, financial literacy, livelihood promotion and skill development. Creating an enabling environment that incentivizes private sector participation, fosters innovation, and enhances market competition will be critical. While DPI has demonstrated strong positive results, integrating emerging technologies such as Artificial Intelligence (AI) and Central Bank Digital Currencies (CBDCs) can further augment the reach, efficiency and customization of financial services. Additionally, innovative investment in research and development, along with strengthened collaborations, will foster innovation and facilitate sharing of best practices and successful models.

On the operational front, there is a pressing need to expand digital infrastructure to ensure complete coverage, particularly in underserved regions. With basic access to bank accounts largely achieved, the next phase should prioritize deeper financial engagement through more complex products like insurance, pensions, and investment instruments. Regulatory frameworks must strike a balance between promoting innovation and ensuring consumer protection, making a proportionate, cross-regulatory approach vital. Addressing the credit gap in the MSME sector will require scaling up of innovative lending models, such as those based on trade receivables and cash flows, to reach even the smallest enterprises at the grassroots level.

Domestically, India also now needs to place greater emphasis on the usage and quality dimensions of financial inclusion. While access has improved significantly, various studies have consistently shown that actual

[54] World Bank. (2024). *2024 Update to leaders on progress towards the G20 remittance target* [Report]. https://www.gpfi.org/sites/default/files/NEW%202024%20Update%20to%20Leaders%20on%20Progress%20Towards%20the%20G20%20Remittance%20Target.pdf.

usage remains notably low. Without targeted and comprehensive policy interventions and active collaboration between the government and the private sector, progress on the usage dimension may remain limited. Enhanced and intended work on this dimension will contribute towards our developmental journey.

Internationally, emerging economies must assertively contribute to shaping the global financial inclusion agenda in such a manner so that their legitimate developmental initiatives are not compromised with excessive and disproportionate commitments on issues beyond financial inclusion. Engaging in meaningful collaborations with other nations and international institutions for research, policy development, and implementation will be vital. India's leadership in financial inclusion provides a valuable blueprint for other countries. Documenting and disseminating India's innovative approaches can serve as an example to the global audience. It is equally important for developing countries to collaborate collectively and advocate for their priorities and challenge global narratives that may not reflect their specific needs. Emerging economies should seek further work to link financial inclusion before working on the latter as the same may dilute the core development objectives and priorities of the developing world. On the international operational side, the growing importance of interoperable cross-border digital payment systems should be recognized and encouraged. These systems offer opportunities to enhance financial inclusion and economic integration globally. India should continue to promote the internationalization of DPI by fostering knowledge exchange, formalizing cooperation through Memoranda of Understanding (MoUs), and hosting global seminars and workshops to showcase its successful model. Ongoing research across various dimensions of financial inclusion will further strengthen global understanding and policymaking. The announcement of the Hon'ble Prime Minister to establish the Social Impact Fund (SIF) with the initial provision of $25 million in 2023 in the G20 Summit in this regard is an important step. The Global South Centre at Research and Information System for Developing Countries (RIS) may also expand its efforts on financial inclusion by sharing knowledge, building capacities, and supporting locally relevant and inclusive solutions..

References

Comprehensive Annual Modular Survey, 2022–23. (2023). *MOSPI*. https://www.mospi.gov.in/sites/default/files/publication_reports/CAMS%20Report_October_N.pdf

Copestake, A., Kirti, D., & Peria, M. S. M. (2025). Growing retail digital payments: The value of interoperability. *Fintech Notes*. Accessed July 11, 2025. https://doi.org/10.5089/9798229014250.063

Entrepreneurs and Survey Participants, Department of Financial Services, MoF, Credit Guarantee Fund Trust for Micro and Small Enterprises (CGTMSE), Banking Sector Experts, ONDC, Research Partner, & Mittal, M. (2025). *Understanding Indian MSME sector progress and challenges*. https://www.sidbi.in/uploads/Understanding_Indian_MSME_sector_Progress_and_Challenges_13_05_25_Final.pdf

FACT SHEET: National Strategy for Financial Inclusion in the United States. (2025, February 8). *U.S. Department of The Treasury*. https://home.treasury.gov/news/press-releases/jy2692

Global Financial Inclusion (Global FINDEX) Database. (2011). https://microdata.worldbank.org/index.php/catalog/1102/related-publications

GPFI. (2023). *G20 2023 financial inclusion action plan*. https://www.gpfi.org/publications/g20-2023-financial-inclusion-action-plan

GPFI. (n.d.). *Global Standard-Setting Bodies and Financial Inclusion: The evolving landscape*. https://www.gpfi.org/publications/global-standard-setting-bodies-and-financial-inclusion-evolving-landscape

National Strategy for Financial Inclusion. (2019). In *National Strategy for Financial Inclusion* (p. 1). https://www.rbi.org.in/commonman/Upload/English/Content/PDFs/English_16042021.pdf

OECD. (2022). *G20/OECD high-level principles on financial consumer protection 2022*. OECD. https://doi.org/10.1787/48cc3df0-en

RBI Bulletin—Reserve Bank of India. (2021). https://rbi.org.in/scripts/BS_ViewBulletin.aspx?Id=20502

Report of India's G20 Task Force on Digital Public Infrastructure. (2024). *India's G20 Task force on digital public infrastructure for economic transformation*. Financial Inclusion and Development. https://dea.gov.in/sites/default/files/Report%20of%20Indias%20G20%20Task%20Force%20On%20Digital%20Public%20Infrastructure.pdf

Sahamati—Collective of Account Aggregator Ecosystem. (2025, May 13). *AA dashboard | account aggregator industry dashboard—Sahamati*. https://sahamati.org.in/aa-dashboard/

Sarkar, C. C., Sengupta, M. S., Ardic, O., Rabadan, G. G., Marin, G., Natarajan, H., Piveteau, T., Ramteke, N., Sarkar, A., Desai, V., Marskell, J., Clark, J., Staschen, S., Teima, G., Gelb, A., Pesme,

J., Qiang, C. Z., & Hagner, C. (2023). *G20 Policy recommendations for advancing financial inclusion and productivity gains through digital public infrastructures: Global partnership for financial inclusion.* World Bank. https://documents1.worldbank.org/curated/en/099092023121016458/pdf/P178703046f82d07c0bbc60b5e474ea7841.pdf

The Global Findex Database. (2017). *Measuring financial inclusion and the Fintech revolution.* World Bank. https://documents.worldbank.org/pt/publication/documents-reports/documentdetail/332881525873182837/the-global-findex-database-2017-measuring-financial-inclusion-and-the-fintech-revolution

World Bank. (2024). *2024 update to leaders on progress towards the G20 remittance target* [Report]. https://www.gpfi.org/sites/default/files/NEW%202024%20Update%20to%20Leaders%20on%20Progress%20Towards%20the%20G20%20Remittance%20Target.pdf

World Bank Group. (2025). *The global findex database 2021.* World Bank. https://www.worldbank.org/en/publication/globalfindex

Zhabska, C. A. B. H. P. U. (2023, March 31). *Stacking up the benefits: Lessons from India's digital journey.* IMF. https://www.imf.org/en/Publications/WP/Issues/2023/03/31/Stacking-up-the-Benefits-Lessons-from-Indias-Digital-Journey-531692

CHAPTER 2

Enhancing Financial Inclusion in Developing Countries: Addressing the Gaps

Pami Dua, Deepika Goel, Neha Verma, and Neeraj Kumar

1 Introduction

Financial inclusion refers to ensuring individuals and businesses have access to appropriate financial products and services in an affordable, transparent, and sustainable manner. The last two decades have witnessed rapid development in financial inclusion initiatives in many emerging

This paper is an extended version of the earlier open-source publication T20, India (2023) policy brief titled 'Reducing the Financial Inclusion Gaps: A Policy Roadmap for Developing Economies', authored by Pami Dua, Deepika Goel, Neeraj Kumar, and Neha Verma in August 2023; original at https://t20ind.org/research/reducing-financial-inclusion-gaps/ .

P. Dua (✉)
Delhi School of Economics, University of Delhi, Delhi, India
e-mail: dua@econdse.org

Economic Advisory Council to the Prime Minister, Government of India, Delhi, India

© The Author(s), under exclusive license to Springer Nature Singapore Pte Ltd. 2026

V. Dixit et al. (eds.), *Financial Inclusion for Viksit Bharat*,
https://doi.org/10.1007/978-981-92-0807-4_2

and developing economies. Financial inclusion can be incorporated into the broad macroeconomic framework across its three dimensions, access, usage, and quality, through various payment channels, insurance and pension-related instruments, transaction banking, digital ecosystem, financial literacy, and consumer protection.

The efficient allocation of funds facilitated by financial inclusion policies promotes economic growth (Ozili, 2020). In contrast, economic growth enhances liquidity and increases the availability of funds, thereby expanding access to and use of financial services by all sections of society (Dua et al., 2023a). However, the theoretical linkages between financial inclusion and credit creation, digitalization, tax compliance, macroeconomic stability, and inclusive growth are contingent on the inclusivity of all sections of the population within the country's financial ecosystem.

The *gaps in financial inclusion* denote a state in which certain individuals or groups lack universal access to essential financial services, such as savings accounts and credit, primarily due to socioeconomic and individual factors. This issue is particularly prominent among certain demographics in developing economies, including those defined by gender, age, income, education, and occupation. These gaps limit the economic opportunities and participation of certain groups in society, thereby exacerbating poverty and inequality (Park & Mercado, 2015). It also diminishes the resilience of poor and vulnerable groups to financial and economic shocks. Universal financial inclusion can provide mechanisms to cope with such shocks.

Research and Information System for Developing Countries (RIS), New Delhi, India

D. Goel
Aryabhatta College, University of Delhi, Delhi, India
e-mail: deepika@aryabhattacollege.ac.in

N. Verma
Kirori Mal College, University of Delhi, Delhi, India
e-mail: nverma@kmc.du.ac.in

N. Kumar
Department of Economic Affairs, Ministry of Finance, Government of India, Delhi, India
e-mail: neeraj@econdse.org

Global Findex 2025 indicates that approximately 2.1 billion adults worldwide remain unbanked or underbanked, meaning that they lack an account with any financial institution or lack access to a mobile money provider. Moreover, the data suggest gaps in financial inclusion across demographic groups, which are more pronounced in developing economies than in advanced economies. Financial exclusion driven by factors such as geographical location, financial literacy, education, income, age, ethnicity, and gender can also impede the effectiveness of government initiatives aimed at promoting financial inclusion.

Individual characteristics play a critical role in the financial exclusion narrative for certain groups in the population. For example, women are more likely to be unbanked than men due to limitations in mobility, societal norms, non-participation in the labour force, and a lack of official identification. Similarly, younger cohorts, particularly in low-income countries, are more likely to be unbanked than adults because of their lower asset accumulation, fewer opportunities for economic advancement, and greater risk of disengagement from or dropout from formal education.

This chapter uses data from the Global Findex Database for 2021 and 2025 (Demirguc-Kunt et al., 2022) to identify gaps in access, usage, and quality of financial inclusion in developing countries, compare their performance with that of developed countries, and propose policy solutions to address the financial exclusion of specific groups.

The chapter is organized into six sections. Section 2 discusses the dimensions of financial inclusion and how gaps across these dimensions can hamper people's social and economic well-being. Section 3 discusses the literature review of the issue. Section 4 presents the results of the data analysis using the Global Findex Database for 2021. Section 5 summarises the trends emerging from Global Findex 2025 and the limitations of the analysis. Section 6 suggests the policy prescriptions, and Sect. 7 concludes the chapter.

2 Understanding the Gaps in Financial Inclusion

Information collected on financial inclusion can be broadly categorized into three key dimensions: access, usage, and quality. Each dimension offers a distinct perspective on the state of financial inclusion, and the collective data across dimensions offers a comprehensive view of a nation's progress in expanding financial services to marginalized and underserved segments of society. **Access** represents the extent to which financial services reach underserved areas, such as the availability of bank branches or point-of-sale (POS) devices[1] in rural regions. It also considers demand-side obstacles that customers encounter when seeking to access financial institutions, including high costs and limited information. **Usage** refers to the actual use of financial services by individuals and businesses. Its key indicators include regularity and frequency of financial transactions, depth of usage, such as having multiple financial products or services (e.g., savings, credit, insurance), affordability and convenience of services, ensuring that they meet the needs of users, e.g., average savings balances, number of transactions per account, number of electronic payments made. **Quality** encompasses the design, efficiency, and relevance of financial services to users' needs. The main aspects include the suitability of financial products for diverse customer segments (e.g., low-income groups or small businesses), financial literacy, and consumer protection to ensure informed use, reliability, and trust in financial services, thereby fostering users' confidence in their financial dealings.

Addressing gaps in financial inclusion along these three dimensions with strategic policy interventions is crucial, as they hinder financial and social well-being at the individual, household, and macroeconomic levels.

- Women's exclusion from the financial ecosystem compromises their empowerment and equality of opportunity.
- Financial exclusion affects the underserved, particularly in low-income countries, impacting their educational investment, earning potential, and economic mobility. The income-based exclusion from financial services can impede medium and small enterprises' access to credit and insurance, potentially harming start-ups and increasing unemployment.
- The gap in financial inclusion among younger and older adults restricts the ability of younger adults to benefit from government aid during financial distress. It complicates decisions regarding further education, employment opportunities, and business establishment.

[1] A POS (Point-of-Sale) system enables businesses to process customer payments and track sales. Traditionally, a POS system referred to a store's cash register. However, modern POS systems are fully digital, allowing them to serve customers and complete transactions from anywhere. All that's required is a POS app and an internet-connected device, like a tablet or smartphone.

- Less-educated adults, often from rural areas or the informal sector, face challenges in accessing credit and insurance services or saving for financial uncertainties due to their exclusion from the formal financial system.
- The exclusion of some voluntarily or involuntarily unemployed adults adds to their vulnerability and impedes future income and job creation opportunities.

Thus, exclusion based on any individual characteristic, such as age, gender, or income, has cascading effects, compounding the vulnerabilities of those with low income, low resilience, inequality of opportunity, and heightened financial stress. This undermines the objective of financial inclusion.

At the macroeconomic level, gaps in financial inclusion can impede economic and political participation, thereby exacerbating inequality, poverty, and gender disparities. Those who are financially underserved are particularly vulnerable to financial stress caused by climate change-related disasters (IPCC, 2023; Sirtaine & McKay, 2022). Therefore, it is crucial to address financial exclusion at national and global levels to adapt better and mitigate climate risks (Dua et al., 2023b). These risks are intensified in low-income countries due to inadequate physical and financial infrastructure and weak regulatory structures.

Growing evidence suggests that climate change can exacerbate the financial stress and vulnerability of adults in developing countries to economic shocks, thereby widening the gaps in financial access and usage. This creates a cycle that further makes it increasingly difficult for low-income countries to adapt to a warmer world. Consequently, integrating financial inclusion and climate action within the policy frameworks of the G20 countries is imperative.

Thus, to maximise the impact of financial inclusion initiatives and achieve universal access to and use of financial services, it is essential to bridge existing gaps across geography, financial literacy, and individual characteristics, including age, income, education level, gender, and ethnicity.

3 Literature Review

The existence of gaps in financial inclusion across various population groups is well-documented in the Empirical literature. Individual-level survey data have been used to examine the reasons for these gaps and the inherent interlinkages among them.

The empirical findings for India suggest that women are less likely than men to be financially included with respect to account ownership and formal savings and borrowing, largely due to their lower labour force participation (Ghosh & Chaudhury, 2019). Thus, the gender gap and occupation gap collectively undermine the financial inclusion of women in India. In the context of usage, the credit received by women in India is significantly lower than that received by men (Chavan, 2020). The increase in women's deposits in India is not matched by a comparable increase in the use of financial services, such as access to credit, which remains lagging. Thus, the financial inclusion gaps, disaggregated by access and usage, require examination to address financial exclusion.

Low income and lower educational attainment among women (Girón et al., 2021; Ndoya & Tsala, 2021) are often cited as crucial reasons for their limited access to formal bank accounts and lower use of digital financial services. This underscores the importance of the intersection between gender, income, and education gaps in financial inclusion. Abdu and Buba (2015) find, in the context of Nigeria, that young age, better income, and higher education can help close the financial inclusion gap among households. Sharif et al. (2023) also find that educational attainment can help bridge the gender gap in financial inclusion for low-income countries. Moreover, financial literacy and proximity to financial institutions have been found to positively affect the gender gap in Namibia (Mukong et al., 2020).

The transition from traditional banking to the provision and use of digital financial products and services has also affected the gaps. Evidence from African countries suggests that innovations in financial services, such as mobile banking, have improved overall financial access for the population by overcoming infrastructure constraints (Allen et al., 2014). Moreover, the provision of fintech credit can fill the credit gap in low-income countries (IMF, 2020).

However, using a household survey from Kenya, Johnen and Mußhoff (2023) find that the gender gap in financial inclusion has widened with the expansion of formal digital credit. There is also evidence that the increased digitalization of financial services can exacerbate financial stress and increase the likelihood of households falling into debt traps (Yue et al., 2022). This can create a vicious circle of income gaps in financial inclusion.

Closing these gaps would facilitate smooth adaptation and mitigation of climate change-related risks in low-income economies that face heightened financial stress and vulnerability to climate shocks. Financial inclusion is considerably effective in addressing climate resilience. Financial inclusion helps people adapt to climate change and disasters by investing in physical assets, education, and businesses (Calderone et al., 2019). Several studies highlight the impact of climate risk on income insecurity among low-income households. Areas particularly sensitive to climate threats should be the focus of policies and programs, with priority given to impoverished individuals for financial inclusion. Since urbanization contributes to climate change, fostering resilience among the urban poor, particularly in developing nations, should be emphasized in both rural and urban contexts (Castells-Quintana et al., 2018).

4 Disparities in Financial Inclusion: Stylised Facts

The share of adults with a financial account in the world increased from 51% in 2011 (Klapper et al., 2022) to 79% in 2024 (Global Findex Database, 2025), thus giving people a safe and convenient way to make payments, save money, and borrow in the form of loans. This not only facilitates investments in education and health but also increases resilience to financial shocks. In this section, trends in various indicators for all three dimensions of financial inclusion are presented. Further, gaps about gender, income, age, education, and occupation are analysed.[2]

[2] Rural–urban gap is not included due to the unavailability of data for all countries. However, where data are available, this is noted in the text.

4.1 Access to Financial Services

In developing economies[3] account ownership has increased by 33 percentage points, bringing the total account ownership for adults in developing countries up to 75% over 2011–2024 (Fig. 1). However, disparities persist in access to, use of, and quality of financial products and services across income, region, gender, education level, and age.

Disparities exist between developed and developing economies, as well as among developing economies. Some Asian countries like Malaysia and Mongolia are at the forefront of financial inclusion, where most households actively use banking services for savings and payments along with

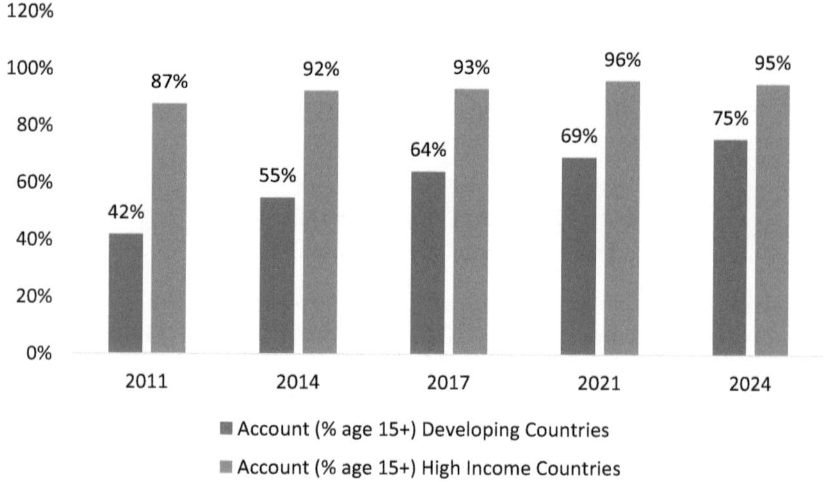

Fig. 1 Account (%) all adults (Age 15+) (*Note* The data in the figure refers to the percentage of respondents who report having an account (by themselves or together with someone else) at a bank or another type of financial institution or report personally using a mobile money service in the past year. *Source* Authors' compilation using Global Findex Database, 2025)

[3] For the current 2024 fiscal year, as per the income classification by the World Bank, low-income economies are defined as those with a GNI per capita of $1,135 or less in 2022; lower-middle-income economies are those with a GNI per capita between $1,136 and $4,465; upper-middle-income economies are those with a GNI per capita between $4,466 and $13,845; high-income economies are those with a GNI per capita of $13,846 or more. Low- and Middle-Income countries are referred to as developing economies.

mobile banking, but in countries like Myanmar and Nepal, informal banking channels are still prevalent, and less than 40% of the households have a bank account (Loukoianova et al., 2018). However, a large proportion of the population in developing countries still lacks an account. Some reasons for not owning an account are shown in Fig. 2. The affordability of accounts is a major constraint, as individuals who engage in small transactions may find it costly to bear even minimal transaction costs. The requirement to submit documents for account opening may exclude workers in rural areas, women, informal-sector workers, or migrants, as they may lack proof of residence or other official documents to substantiate their claims. A lack of financial literacy or knowledge may also lead individuals to place less trust in financial institutions.

Approximately 9% of adults in developing countries have inactive accounts, compared with 1% in high-income countries (Global Findex Database, 2021). In 2024, 6% adults in developing countries have inactive accounts (Global Findex Database, 2025). The most common reasons for not using their inactive accounts are that the financial institution is too distant or that they require assistance to access the accounts. Quite often, people do not have enough money to put into an account, lack trust in banks or financial institutions, or simply do not understand the need for a financial account.

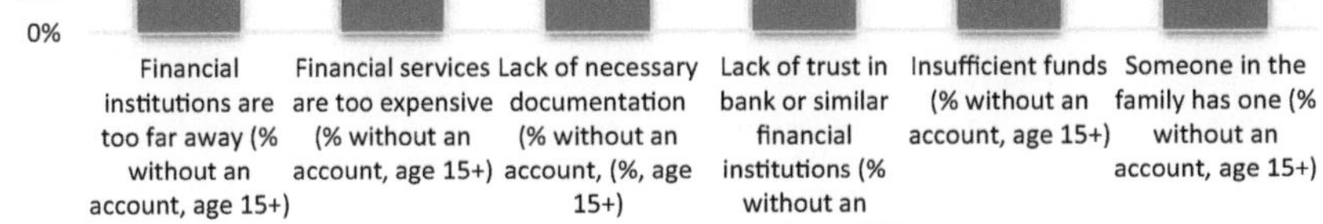

Fig. 2 Reasons for no account ownership in developing countries (2024) (*Note* The data in the figure refers to the percentage of respondents who report not having a financial account because of the stated reasons. *Source* Authors' compilation using Global Findex Database, 2025)

Financial inclusion gaps are estimated by gender, age, education, income, and occupation. These gaps are explained in Table 1.

Figure 3 reveals that these gaps are larger in developing countries than in high-income countries.

- In developing economies, 68% of women, compared to 74% of men, own an account.
- Sixty-five percent of adults with primary education or less own an account, compared with 75% of adults with secondary education or higher in developing economies.
- In developing economies, there is an income gap of approximately 8 percentage points in account ownership between the poorest 40% and the richest 60% of adults.
- In developing economies, account ownership among adults who are not in the labour force is substantially lower than among those who are in the labour force, and this disparity is larger than that observed in high-income economies.

Table 1 Definition of Financial Inclusion Gaps

Gaps	*Definition (Adults are defined as the percentage of the population who are 15+ years old)*
Gender Gap	Percentage difference between female and male adults in access, usage, and quality of financial services
Age Gap	Percentage difference between young (age 15–24) and older (age 25+) adults in access, usage, and quality of financial services
Education Gap	Percentage difference between adults with primary education or less and adults with secondary education or more in access, usage, and quality of financial services
Income Gap	Percentage difference between the poorest 40% of adults and the richest 60% of adults in access, usage, and quality of financial services-
Occupation Gap	Percentage difference between adults out of the labour force and those in the labour force in access, usage, and quality of financial services
Location Gap	Percentage difference between adults in rural areas and those in the urban areas in access, usage, and quality of financial services

Source Authors' contribution

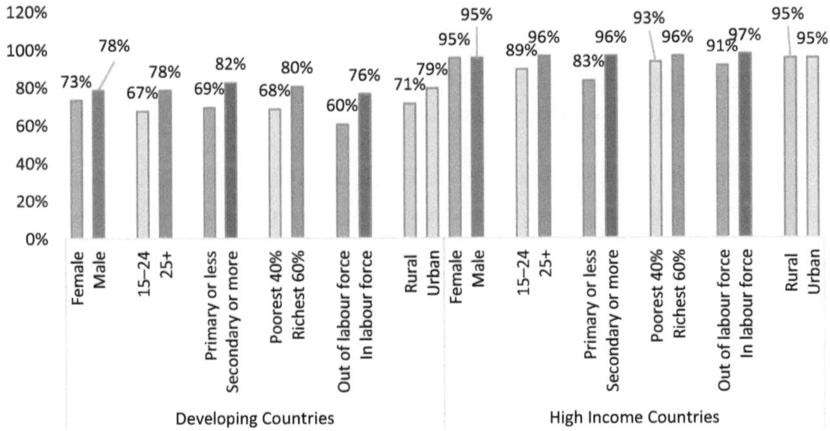

Fig. 3 Gaps in account ownership among adults (%) by different categories—2024 (*Note* The data in the figure refers to the percentage of respondents who report having an account (by themselves or together with someone else) at a bank or another type of financial institution or report personally using a mobile money service in the past year. *Source* Authors' compilation using Global Findex Database, 2024)

Digital financial services, such as mobile money, cards, e-wallets, and direct account-to-account payments, have driven substantial growth in account ownership and usage worldwide, particularly in developing countries. Mobile money accounts have been the most important enablers of account access and usage in developing countries, with the share of mobile money accounts increasing from 5% in 2017 to 13% in 2021 and to 18 percent in 2024 (Global Findex Database, 2025). However, demographic gaps are evident in mobile money account ownership. For example, only 15% of women in developing countries hold such an account, compared with 22% of men. Based on education attainment, only 10% of adults with primary education or less hold a mobile money account, compared with 27% of adults with secondary education or higher.

Large variations in financial inclusion by gender, age, education, income, and occupation exist across advanced and developing countries.

This is analysed by calculating gaps in financial inclusion across G20 countries based on these individual characteristics, as shown inTable 2.[4] The following results emerge from Table 2[5]:

Gender gap (% female–% male)

- The gender gap is closed in most advanced economies, except Saudi Arabia, indicating that men and women have equal levels of account ownership.
- The gap is zero in India, implying equal account ownership among men and women. In contrast, the gap is 2 percentage points in the USA, indicating higher account ownership among women than men.
- Türkiye, Bangladesh, Nigeria, Saudi Arabia, and Mexico exhibit large negative gender gaps in financial access, with men being more likely than women to own an account in these countries.

Age gap (% young–% old)

- The age gap in India is −13 percentage points, indicating that account ownership among young adults is substantially lower than among older adults.
- In the USA, the age gap is relatively small at −1 percentage point, suggesting near parity in account ownership between younger and older adults.

Education gap (% primary education–% secondary education)

- Education-based gaps in account ownership are observed in both advanced and emerging economies. Substantial gaps persist in Australia, Canada, the United States, South Africa, Argentina, China, Indonesia, Türkiye, and Mexico, indicating lower account ownership among adults with only primary education.
- In India, the education gap is −5 percentage points, implying that adults with at most primary education are less likely to own an account than those with secondary education or higher.

[4] Highlighted cells with different colours represent the different financial inclusion gaps.

[5] Evaluation of the reasons for the country-specific gaps is beyond the scope of the present work.

Table 2 Account ownership variations between advanced and developing economies—Year 2021

Countries/Region	Gender gap	Age gap	Education gap	Income gap	Occupation gap
Advanced Economies					
High income (Aggregate)	1%	−4%	−7%	−4%	−2%
Euro area	−1%	−4%	−2%	−2%	−1%
Australia	1%	1%	−14%	−2%	−2%
Canada	0%	0%	−10%	−1%	−1%
France	2%	0%	−4%	−2%	−1%
Germany	0%	0%	0%	0%	0%
Italy	0%	−16%	0%	−4%	−3%
Japan	1%	−9%	−5%	−1%	−1%
Korea, Rep.	0%	0%	−3%	−3%	−4%
Saudi Arabia	−19%	−4%	3%	−12%	−31%
Singapore	−1%	−4%	−7%	−3%	−5%
Spain	−2%	−1%	−3%	−1%	3%
United Arab Emirates	0%	0%	−2%	0%	−1%
United Kingdom	4%	−1%	−38%	−6%	0%
United States	2%	−8%	−10%	−4%	2%
Developing Economies					
Developing (Aggregate)	−6%	−12%	−14%	−8%	−14%
Argentina	4%	4%	−23%	−11%	1%
Bangladesh	−20%	−7%	−10%	−7%	−15%
China	−3%	−1%	−14%	−9%	−14%
Egypt, Arab Rep.	−7%	−24%	−5%	−12%	−7%
India	0%	−13%	−5%	1%	−8%
Indonesia	1%	4%	−22%	−8%	−19%
Mauritius	−3%	−8%	−9%	0%	−11%
Mexico	−14%	1%	−24%	−28%	−22%
Netherlands	−1%	−2%	0%	−1%	−1%
Nigeria	−20%	−16%	−39%	−21%	−25%
Russian Federation	1%	4%	−8%	−6%	−7%
South Africa	1%	−8%	−13%	−12%	−12%
Turkey	−22%	−1%	−20%	−22%	−20%

Source Authors' calculations from the Global Findex Database, 2021

- The education gap is particularly large in the USA at −38 percentage points, indicating a pronounced disparity in account ownership between adults with only primary education and those with at least secondary education.

Income gap (% poorest 40%–% richest 60%)

- In India, the income gap has turned positive, with the poorest 40% of adults exhibiting account ownership that is 1 percentage point higher than that of the richest 60%.
- In the USA, the income gap in account ownership is −6 percentage points, indicating that account ownership among poorer adults is lower than among richer adults.
- In most developed economies, account ownership is lower among the poorest 40% of adults, with the notable exceptions of Germany and the UAE.

Occupation gap (% out of labour force—% in labour force)

- The occupation gap is zero in the USA, indicating no difference in account ownership between adults inside and outside the labour force. In contrast, India exhibits an occupation gap of −8 percentage points, indicating lower account ownership among adults not in the labour force.
- Most developing economies display substantial disparities in account ownership between adults who are out of the labour force and those who are in the labour force, with Argentina being a notable exception. This indicates systematically lower account ownership among adults outside the labour force.

The COVID-19 pandemic accelerated efforts to promote financial inclusion worldwide through various means, including government-distributed emergency payments sent to bank accounts and debit cards. Studies have shown that during the pandemic, there was a rise in the use of internet banking, mobile banking, and ATMs for making payments and receiving transfers.

Digital payments are financial transactions conducted using a mobile money account, a debit or credit card, or a mobile phone or internet connection. These payments can involve making purchases from an account, sending money to friends or family, or paying bills. They also encompass in-store and online purchases, utility bill payments, domestic money transfers, payments for agricultural goods, and the receipt of wages, government assistance, or pensions directly into or from a financial account.

In many high-income countries, digital payments are primarily processed via debit and credit cards. According to Global Findex data for 2021, 57% of adults in high-income countries own a credit card, whereas 86% own a debit card. However, in developing nations, a smaller proportion of adults, that is, 17% and 45% respectively, own these types of cards. Furthermore, significant gaps exist in the ownership of debit and credit cards across developing and advanced countries. According to Global Findex 2025, credit and debit card ownership in developing countries has improved, with 20% of adults owning credit cards and 52% owning debit cards.

Table 3 Variation in ownership of debit and credit cards between advanced and developing economies—Year 2021

Countries/ Region	Gender Gap		Age Gap		Education Gap		Income Gap		Occupation Gap	
	Debit Card	Credit Card	Debit Card	Credit Card	Debit Card	Credit Card	Debit Card	Credit Card	Debit Card	Credit Card
Advanced Economies										
High income (Aggregate)	1%	1%	−6%	−23%	−16%	−21%	−7%	−17%	−10%	−11%
Euro area	−3%	−1%	−3%	−8%	−8%	−1%	−3%	−6%	−6%	−5%
Australia	2%	6%	2%	−43%	−30%	−30%	−5%	−15%	−9%	4%
Canada	0%	1%	−4%	−7%	−17%	−45%	−4%	−13%	−5%	−9%
France	−1%	−5%	−4%	12%	−6%	−23%	1%	4%	−8%	−17%
Germany	−2%	9%	4%	−11%	5%	6%	−1%	−11%	−2%	1%
Italy	−3%	4%	−9%	−7%	−5%	3%	−10%	−3%	−6%	0%
Japan	1%	1%	−29%	−38%	−25%	−40%	−7%	−11%	−10%	−22%
Korea, Rep.	−3%	−3%	16%	−56%	−26%	−17%	−18%	−18%	−8%	−38%
Saudi Arabia	−17%	2%	−7%	6%	−1%	−25%	−12%	−14%	−31%	−15%
Singapore	−1%	−6%	−6%	−31%	−16%	−48%	−4%	−26%	−10%	−40%
Spain	−9%	−3%	−3%	10%	−10%	4%	3%	−4%	−4%	2%
United Arab Emirates	1%	4%	3%	−9%	−2%	−4%	1%	−4%	−3%	−5%
United Kingdom	7%	2%	−7%	−35%	−40%	−54%	−8%	−34%	−17%	−5%
United States	6%	−1%	−7%	4%	−15%	−7%	−4%	0%	3%	0%
Developing Economies										
Developing (Aggregate)	−9%	−3%	−11%	−11%	−23%	−12%	−15%	−8%	−15%	−6%
Argentina	−4%	−11%	−9%	−13%	−26%	−23%	−18%	−13%	−7%	−10%
Bangladesh	−6%	−1%	−2%	0%	−5%	−1%	−2%	−1%	−5%	−1%
China	−2%	4%	3%	−18%	−21%	−22%	−18%	−14%	−20%	−13%
Egypt, Arab Rep.	−6%	−2%	−19%	−4%	−5%	−4%	−10%	−2%	−7%	−2%
India	−16%	−5%	−3%	−1%	−24%	−8%	−19%	−4%	−13%	−3%
Indonesia	2%	1%	0%	0%	−25%	−3%	−15%	−1%	−13%	−1%
Mauritius	−5%	−7%	−13%	−8%	−15%	−18%	−1%	−10%	−23%	−13%
Mexico	−16%	−7%	−9%	5%	−25%	−10%	−29%	−13%	−23%	−7%
Netherlands	0%	−9%	0%	−33%	1%	−26%	0%	−22%	−2%	−21%
Nigeria	−19%	0%	−14%	−1%	−37%	1%	−19%	−1%	−24%	−2%
Russian Federation	−9%	−2%	15%	−19%	−16%	−11%	−14%	−7%	−13%	−10%
South Africa	−9%	−2%	−21%	−1%	−17%	−9%	−18%	−9%	−18%	−10%
Turkey	−29%	−27%	−4%	−12%	−27%	−18%	−21%	−19%	−24%	−21%

Source Authors' compilation using Global Findex Database, 2021

According to the 2021 data, Table 3 suggests the following[6]:
Gender gap (% female–% male)

- For debit card ownership, the gender gap is closed in most advanced economies; however, in Saudi Arabia, Korea, and Spain, the gap is negative, indicating lower debit card ownership among women than men.
- Credit card ownership is lower among women than men in Singapore, Spain, Korea, and Saudi Arabia.
- Overall, debit and credit card ownership is higher among men than women in most countries, with the exceptions of the Netherlands and Indonesia for debit cards, and China, Indonesia, and Nigeria for credit cards, where women exhibit higher ownership rates.

Age gap (% young–% old)

- In India, the age gap is −3 percentage points for debit cards and −1 percentage point for credit cards, indicating lower card ownership among young adults relative to older adults.
- Substantial age-related disparities in both debit and credit card ownership are observed in the UK, China, the Netherlands, and Australia, with older adults being more likely to own cards than younger adults.

Education gap (% primary education–% secondary education)

- Education-based gaps in debit and credit card ownership are present in both advanced and emerging economies, with the exceptions of Germany, Italy, Spain, and the Netherlands. In most countries, adults with at most primary education are less likely to have debit or credit cards than those with at least secondary education.
- In India, the education gap is −28 percentage points for debit cards and −8 percentage points for credit cards, indicating substantially lower card ownership among adults with only primary education than those with secondary education.

[6] Evaluation of the reasons for country-specific gaps is beyond the scope of the present work.

Income gap (% poorest 40%–% richest 60%)

- In France, Spain, and the UAE, the income gap is positive, indicating that a higher proportion of adults in the poorest 40% own debit and credit cards compared to adults in the richest 60%.

Occupation gap (% out of labour force–% in labour force)

- The occupation gap is zero in the USA, indicating no difference in account ownership between adults inside and outside the labour force. In contrast, India exhibits an occupation gap of −8 percentage points, indicating lower account ownership among adults not in the labour force.
- Most developing economies display substantial disparities in credit and debit card ownership between adults who are out of the labour force and those who are in the labour force, with Argentina being a notable exception.

Disparities in credit and debit card ownership among vulnerable groups limit their participation in the digital financial ecosystem.

Ownership of a mobile or access to an internet connection is the basic prerequisite for making digital payments through a bank or via mobile money accounts. Figure 4 shows that the percentage of adults owning a mobile phone or having internet access is relatively high in advanced economies. Developing countries, on the other hand, show a lower proportion of adults having an internet connection.

Summary: Analysis of the indicators of the access dimension of financial inclusion suggests the following:

- ***According to the Global Findex Database, 2021, access to financial services has improved over the past decade; however, disparities by gender, age, education, income, and occupation persist.***
- ***The gender gap in account ownership has largely closed in most developed and developing economies; however, it remains significant in countries such as Saudi Arabia, Bangladesh, Mexico, and Türkiye. Other demographic gaps continue to persist across both advanced and developing economies.***

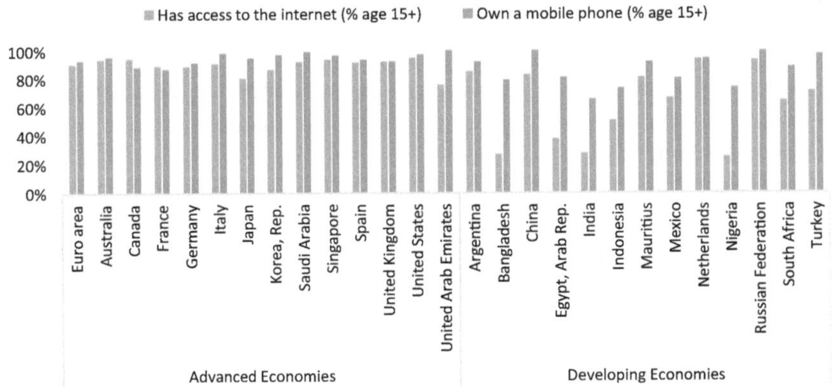

Fig. 4 Adults (age 15+) with access to internet and mobile phones (%)—2021 (*Note* The data in the figure refers to the percentage of respondents who report having access to the internet and owning a mobile phone. *Source* Authors' compilation using Global Findex Database, 2021)

- ***Similarly, the gender gap in debit and credit card ownership has narrowed in most economies, although other demographic gaps remain substantial.***
- ***Financial inclusion can serve as a tool for inclusive growth. However, exclusion of the vulnerable groups, such as women, the poor, the unemployed, the young, and the less educated, in financial access undermines broader objectives of inclusivity, growth, and development. Such exclusion prevents them from participating in the formal financial system and deprives them of access to government transfers, savings for future needs, credit, or loans in times of need, thereby reducing their resilience to unpredictable financial shocks.***

4.2 *Usage of Financial Services*

Among financial services, digital payments are among the most popular. The use of digital payments increased significantly during the pandemic, as digitalisation enabled governments to transfer funds to those in need and supported many small businesses. The share of adults making or receiving digital payments in developing countries increased by 22 percentage points from 2014 to 2021 (See Fig. 5). This increase outpaced the increase in account ownership during the same period. However, substantial variation exists across gender, age, income, education, and occupation within developing economies, as well as between the two sets of countries (Fig. 6).

Significant variations in the individual characteristics of financial inclusion, with respect to the usage dimension, were calculated (Table 4). Calculating these gaps for financial use facilitates cross-country comparisons and guides policy interventions.

Table 4 shows the following[7]:

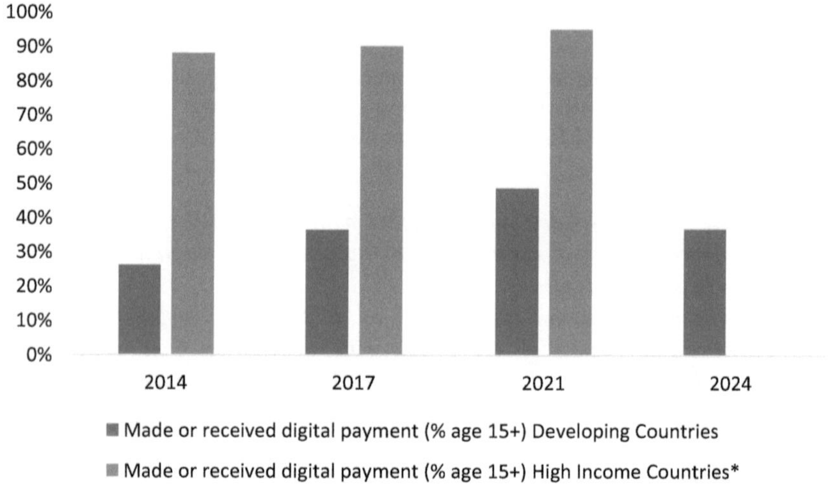

Fig. 5 Adults who made or received a digital payment (%) (*Note* The data in the figure refers to the percentage of respondents who report using mobile money, a debit or credit card, or a mobile phone to make a payment from an account or report using the internet to pay bills or to buy something online or in a store-in the past year. *Global Findex 2025 does not report usage indicators for high-income countries. *Source* Authors' compilation using Global Findex Database, 2025)

[7] Evaluation of reasons for country-specific gaps is beyond the scope of the present work.

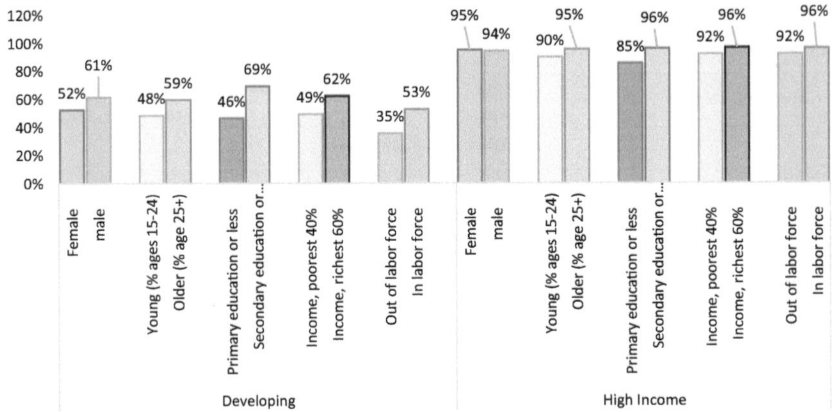

Fig. 6 Adults who made or received a digital payment (%) by different categories—2021 (*Note* Proportion of adults who report using mobile money, a debit or credit card, or a mobile phone to make a payment from an account or report using the internet to pay bills or to buy something online or in a store in the past year. *Source* Authors' compilation using Global Findex Database, 2021)

- Saudi Arabia exhibits the largest financial usage gap among advanced economies, while among emerging economies, Argentina, Türkiye, and Mexico display substantial gaps.
- India and Türkiye also exhibit large gender gaps in making or receiving digital payments, indicating that fewer women than men make or receive digital payments in these economies.
- Education and occupation-based disparities in digital payments are evident in both advanced and developing economies, with lower usage among adults with only primary education and among those who are out of the labour force.
- Income-based gaps in digital payment remain pronounced in developing economies. In 2021, the income gap narrowed to 9 percentage points, down from 13 percentage points in 2017, indicating an increase in the use of digital payments among adults in the poorest 40% during 2017–2021. However, the gap remained negative, implying that adults in the richest 60% continue to make or receive digital payments more frequently.
- In developing economies, exclusion of certain sections of the population from the formal financial system is also accentuated by digital

Table 4 Variations in made or received digital payments between advanced and developing economies—year 2021

Countries/ Region	Gender Gap	Age Gap	Education Gap	Income Gap	Occupation Gap
Advanced Economies					
Euro area	−1%	−5%	−4%	−2%	−3%
Australia	2%	1%	−14%	−2%	−3%
Canada	0%	0%	−9%	−2%	−2%
France	1%	1%	−5%	−2%	−3%
Germany	−1%	−3%	1%	1%	1%
Italy	−1%	−19%	−3%	−5%	−6%
Japan	0%	−18%	−15%	−3%	−6%
Korea, Rep.	0%	−2%	−6%	−5%	−5%
Saudi Arabia	−18%	−3%	4%	−14%	−33%
United Kingdom	0%	1%	−2%	0%	0%
United States	6%	−3%	−40%	−7%	−3%
Singapore	−4%	−1%	−12%	−5%	−12%
Spain	−3%	−1%	−3%	1%	3%
United Arab Emirates	0%	−3%	−20%	−5%	−1%
Developing Economies					
Argentina	−2%	13%	−31%	−10%	−11%
Brazil	−7%	1%	−7%	−7%	−14%
China	−2%	2%	−17%	−12%	0%
India	−13%	−7%	−19%	−15%	−11%
Indonesia	3%	11%	−24%	−7%	−10%
Russian Federation	1%	7%	−7%	−7%	−7%
South Africa	3%	−13%	−12%	−18%	−17%
Türkiye	−25%	−1%	−23%	−23%	−23%
Mexico	−8%	−2%	−18%	−19%	−20%
Bangladesh	−24%	−6%	−7%	−7%	−21%
Egypt	−8%	−18%	−7%	−12%	−7%
Mauritius	−11%	−9%	−18%	−10%	−21%
Netherlands	0%	−2%	1%	−3%	−3%
Nigeria	−22%	−13%	−36%	−23%	−20%

Source Author's Calculations from the Global Findex Database, 2021

exclusion, whereby some adults are excluded from financial services due to the rapid shift toward digital delivery channels.

Findex data, 2021 suggests the following regarding financial usage:

- Adults in high-income countries received wages mainly into their accounts or onto a card. This is true for both public- and private-sector wages. Only 5% of adults receive wages in cash. However, in developing countries, 26% of individuals receive wages in cash.
- A significantly higher proportion of adults, that is, 52%, receive government payments in high-income countries, compared to 22% in developing countries.
- In high-income economies, the majority of recipients receive government payments directly into a bank account. An additional 13% receive them through other non-cash methods, likely including checks or vouchers. Similarly, in developing economies, most adults (67%) also receive government payments into an account. A similar trend is observed for private-sector payments, transfers, and pensions.
- The share of adults making utility payments from an account in high-income countries is 76%, whereas in developing economies it is only 40%. Developing countries experienced a sharp increase in digital payments since the onset of the COVID-19 pandemic, with most adults making such payments for the first time.

A digital payment can be made straight from an account without the need to withdraw cash, typically through the use of a credit or debit card, or by using a mobile phone or internet connection. In high-income countries, 90% of adults used at least one of these methods to make a payment. In contrast, in developing countries, 45% of adults did so.

Table 5 Demographic gaps in saving any money between advanced and developing economies—year 2021

Country/ Region	Gender Gap	Age Gap	Education Gap	Income Gap	Occupation Gap
Advanced Economies					
High income (aggregate)	−3%	1%	−16%	−15%	−11%
Euro area	−3%	6%	−10%	−8%	−5%
Australia	2%	8%	−34%	−16%	−21%
Canada	−4%	14%	−21%	−14%	−15%
France	0%	−6%	−7%	−8%	−2%
Germany	0%	9%	−4%	2%	−3%
Italy	−9%	10%	−8%	−8%	2%
Japan	−2%	−2%	−21%	−13%	−13%
Korea, Rep.	2%	−2%	−31%	−30%	−17%
Saudi Arabia	−2%	−1%	−44%	−15%	−19%
Singapore	1%	−24%	−17%	−13%	−16%
Spain	−7%	10%	−6%	−7%	−8%
United Arab Emirates	2%	5%	−6%	0%	−8%
United Kingdom	−5%	−1%	−19%	−28%	−14%
United States	−16%	−2%	−5%	3%	−18%
Developing Economies					
Developing (aggregate)	−3%	−2%	−18%	−17%	−15%
Argentina	−23%	29%	−26%	−23%	−23%
Bangladesh	−5%	−1%	−5%	−9%	−11%
China	2%	−1%	−22%	−21%	−23%
Egypt, Arab Rep.	−3%	−12%	−6%	−10%	−9%
India	−3%	−3%	−14%	−14%	−8%
Indonesia	6%	15%	−36%	−15%	−11%
Mauritius	−4%	19%	−32%	−9%	−17%
Mexico	−8%	7%	−27%	−19%	−22%
Netherlands	−3%	13%	−37%	−15%	−18%
Nigeria	−3%	−9%	−19%	−14%	−23%
Russian Federation	−8%	24%	−11%	−22%	−11%
South Africa	3%	−23%	−1%	−17%	−20%
Turkey	−7%	18%	−17%	−20%	−10%

Source Author's Calculations from the Global Findex Database, 2021

Another important use of financial services is saving to meet future expenses, such as education, health care, or other emergencies. In high-income countries, 76% of adults saved, according to the 2021 Findex report, while 42% of adults in developing economies did so. Gaps in saving behaviour among high-income and advanced economies are reported in Table 5. The trends suggest the following[8]:

- Significant gender gaps are observed in self-reported saving behaviour in both high-income and developing economies, with men being more likely than women to report saving or setting aside money for any reason.
- The United States and Argentina exhibit particularly large gender gaps, reflecting substantially lower saving rates among women in these countries.
- Both high-income and developing economies display education, income, and occupation-based disparities in saving behaviour. Adults with only primary education, those in lower-income groups, and those who are out of the labour force are less likely to save than adults with secondary education or higher, higher incomes, and employment.
- A pronounced disparity in saving behaviour between richer and poorer adults is also evident, especially in Singapore, South Africa, and Nigeria.

According to the Findex survey, globally, 26% of adults reported saving for old age, with the proportion at 53% in high-income countries and 19% in developing countries. Among those saving, approximately two-thirds in developing economies and over three-quarters in high-income economies reported saving through formal financial channels.

The percentage of adults using formal borrowing methods in developing economies remains relatively low but has grown over the past decade, from roughly 16% in both 2014 and 2017 to 23% in 2021. In contrast, in high-income countries, the rate of formal borrowing has remained stable at approximately 56%. Significant gender, education, occupation, and income gaps existed in 2021 among high-income countries. Developing economies exhibit pronounced gender, age, and occupation gaps, whereas education and income gaps are less pronounced.

Summary: Analysis of the indicators of the usage dimension of financial inclusion suggests the following:

[8] Evaluation of the reasons for country-specific gaps are beyond the scope of the present work.

- *According to the Global Findex Database, 2021, the use of financial services has increased over the period 2011–2021; however, disparities by gender, age, education, income, and occupation persist.*
- *Gender gaps in digital payment usage are more pronounced in developing economies than in advanced economies, with women being less likely than men to make or receive digital payments. Similarly, young adults, individuals with only primary education, those from poorer households, and the unemployed are less likely to use digital payments in both advanced and developing economies, with these disparities sharper in developing economies.*
- *Across the sample, women are less likely than men to save, while age-related gaps in saving behaviour have narrowed in most countries. In contrast, disparities by education, income, and occupation remain substantial.*
- *Data suggest that although access to formal financial services has improved in most developing economies, usage remains significantly lower than in advanced economies. This indicates a breakdown in the link between access and usage in developing countries. While account ownership is a necessary prerequisite for financial inclusion, it is not sufficient for effective financial use. Although a large share of adults now hold accounts, a substantial proportion of these accounts remain inactive or are used for limited purposes, such as receiving government transfers. Several factors weaken the translation of access into usage, including insufficient funds, high costs of financial services, and a lack of trust in formal financial institutions. In addition, dynamics within a demographic group also matter. For example, in some households, if a male member holds an account, women may not perceive a need to open one themselves. Low digital literacy, connectivity constraints, and limited acceptance of digital cards, particularly in rural areas, further restrict the use of digital financial services. In contrast, advanced economies benefit from stronger institutions, more stable income patterns, and broader digital infrastructure, which facilitate a closer alignment between financial access and effective usage.*
- *Digitalisation fosters financial inclusion, growth, and development. It facilitates outreach to previously excluded groups through digital channels. Significant demographic gaps in the use of financial services indicate that financial systems are not inclusive and*

that the infrastructure designed to strengthen payment systems is underutilised.

An overall analysis of gaps in financial access and usage indicates that some countries exhibit significant demographic gaps, whereas others experienced a reversal of these gaps in 2021. Improvement in financial inclusion gaps across countries may be driven by factors such as strengthened digital infrastructure, the adoption of improved or AI-driven technologies, targeted financial literacy initiatives, and simplified regulatory and consumer protection measures. For instance, the government's concentrated efforts through digitalisation and financial literacy measures to close the last-mile gap in India have triggered a trickle-down effect of reforms across broader areas and individuals (Chauhan, 2022; Dua et al., 2023a, 2025). This government initiative may be responsible for greater inclusion of the poor in India's formal financial system. Similarly, in Argentina, financial inclusion is expanded through a combination of market development, digital infrastructure, and appropriate regulation. The country has implemented an interoperable instant payment system, primarily for retail transactions, which encourages broader participation in formal financial services. This is further facilitated by robust digital infrastructure, such as the internet, identification systems, and appropriate regulatory measures (Trujillo & Brandon, 2023). According to the IMF (2020), technological change is also reshaping Indonesia's financial system through two parallel developments: the digitalisation of services in payments, digital banking, and peer-to-peer lending by established financial institutions and the entry of fintech firms into core financial activities. The UAE has also moved beyond the initial "bank the unbanked" phase into a deeper stage of inclusion, in which digital fintech platforms, regulatory frameworks, and literacy programmes work in tandem (Arab Monetary Fund, 2021). Likewise, most European economies benefit from advanced financial technologies that enable the provision of innovative financial services to populations that are otherwise difficult to serve. Rather than displacing traditional institutions, fintech-driven disruption has encouraged cooperative arrangements between fintech firms and established financial intermediaries. These partnerships have expanded the reach of basic financial services, particularly in locations where maintaining physical bank branches is not viable, thereby supporting greater financial access (Ozili, 2021). More specifically, the reversal of the age gap may be due to increased saving among young people in advanced economies, as economic uncertainty, weak employment growth, and rising costs have shifted behavior from post-pandemic spending toward prioritizing savings and emergency funds.[9] The reversal of the occupation gap in account ownership in some countries, such as Australia, may be due to increased mobile internet access.[10]

4.3 *Financial Well-Being*

Financial well-being extends beyond the access and usage dimensions of financial inclusion and encompasses the quality dimension, as reflected in individuals perceived financial security and their capacity to withstand economic shocks. In this study, financial well-being is conceptualized in two aspects: financial health, which captures concerns about meeting future expenses, and financial resilience, which reflects the ability to mobilize emergency funds within a short time horizon.

The Global Findex database (2021) shows that adults in developing countries find it very difficult to access emergency funds. Approximately 35% of women and 42% of the poor are most likely to be least resilient to economic shocks, as they find it difficult to raise emergency funds within 30 days. In developing economies, 55% of adults report being able to access emergency funds within 30 days without significant difficulty. Data also suggest that, for 30% of adults in developing countries, the most common source of emergency funds is family and friends, rather than savings. However, in advanced economies, 49% of adults depend on savings for emergency funds (See Fig. 7).

Figure 8 suggests that 8% of women in high-income countries report that it is not possible to raise emergency funds within 30 days, compared with 6% of men. However, in developing countries, these percentages are 15% and 11%, respectively. Only 25% of women in developing countries, compared with 50% in high-income countries, report that it is easy to access emergency funds within 30 days. Hence, with respect to financial resilience, there is also a significant gender gap. Such gaps are also evident

[9] Gen Z Achieving Success in Saving, Showing Interest in CDs to Accelerate Growth, Santander Bank Survey Finds—Santander US https://share.google/QA6Y7MMAD5io1Ghyj.

[10] https://www.rba.gov.au/publications/bulletin/2023/jun/cash-use-and-attitudes-in-australia.html.

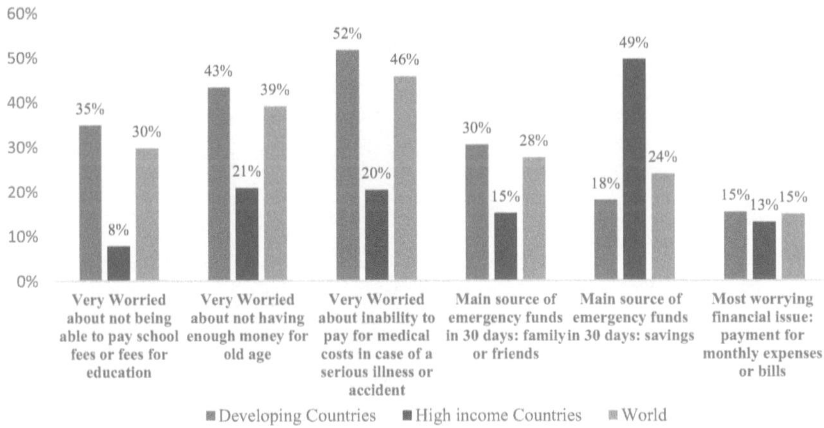

Fig. 7 Quality indicators of financial inclusion—2021 (*Note* The data in the figure refer to the percentage of respondents who reported their primary financial worry regarding different expenses and their source of emergency funds. *Source*: Authors' compilation using Global Findex Database, 2021)

in income, where the poor find it difficult to secure emergency funds within 30 days.[11]

The inability to gather funds during emergencies contributes to financial insecurity among adults in developing countries. This often leads them to experience financial stress from medical bills, monthly expenses, education fees, and, most importantly, the need to arrange funds for old age. Common sources of financial stress among adults in developing countries in 2024 are listed in Table 6. Although sources of financial stress declined in 2024, concern about paying monthly expenses and educational fees increased across all demographic groups.

Summary: Analysis of the indicators of the usage dimension of financial inclusion suggests the following:

- ***Developing countries tend to have lower financial resilience than advanced countries.***

[11] The findings are not shown here for the sake of brevity and can be made available upon request.

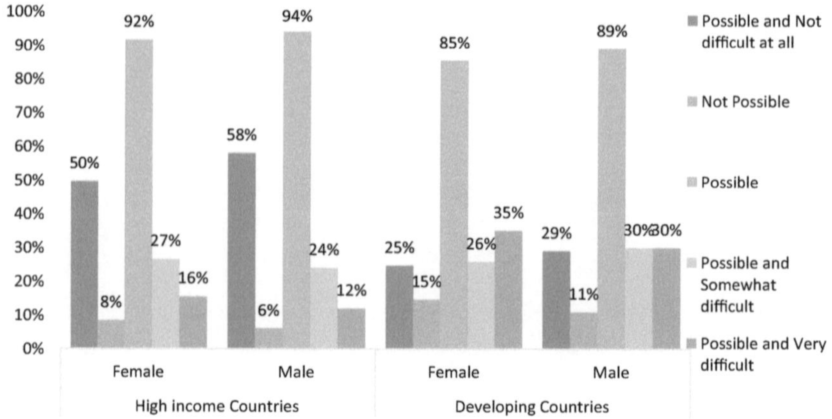

Fig. 8 Coming up with emergency funds in 30 days (age 15+ years)–2021 (*Note* The data in the figure represent the percentage of respondents who reported whether it is possible to raise emergency funds within 30 days. *Source* Authors' compilation using Global Findex Database, 2021)

- ***In developing countries, women are less resilient than men. A higher proportion of men can arrange emergency funds within a given period than women.***
- ***Women worry more about education and daily expenses, while men worry more about old-age expenses.***
- ***Young adults worry more about monthly expenses and education fees, while older adults worry more about old-age expenses.***
- ***Adults with primary education worry more about old age, monthly expenses, and education fees.***
- ***Poor adults worry about money for old-age monthly expenses and education fees.***
- ***These trends have important implications, as the expansion of formal financial inclusion has not translated into improved financial resilience and well-being across all demographic groups. As a result, significant segments of the population remain financially vulnerable and less able to cope with economic and financial shocks.***

Developing countries also face larger risks of rising food and fuel prices and more frequent and intense climate shocks. The Notre Dame Global

Table 6 Sources of financial stress for adults in developing countries—year 2024

Characteristics	*Adults (age 15+)*	*Money for old age*	*Paying for Medical costs in case of a serious illness*	*Paying for monthly expenses*	*Paying for school or education fees*
Gender	Female	14%	27%	30%	16%
	Male	14%	25%	31%	13%
Age	Young (% ages 15–24)	5%	21%	33%	25%
	Older (% age 25+)	17%	28%	30%	12%
Education	Primary education or less	16%	24%	32%	14%
	Secondary education or more	12%	28%	29%	15%
Income	Income, poorest 40%	13%	26%	33%	16%
	Income, richest 60%	14%	27%	29%	14%
Location	Rural	13%	25%	31%	17%
	Urban	14%	27%	30%	13%
Occupation	Out of labour force	12%	22%	35%	19%
	In the labour force	13%	23%	35%	15%

Note The data in the table represent the percentage of respondents who reported their primary financial worry for each expense category. *Source* Authors' compilation using Global Findex Database, 2025

Adaptation Initiative (ND-GAIN)[12] provides data on countries' vulnerability and readiness to adapt to climate change.

The ND-GAIN values for the G20 countries exhibit significant disparities that can be interpreted in the context of their economic development. Developed economies, such as Germany, the United Kingdom, Australia,

[12] ND-GAIN is a program of the University of Notre Dame's Environmental Change Initiative. This Country Index uses two decades of data across 45 indicators to rank 181 countries annually based upon their vulnerability and their readiness to successfully adapt. High values of this index represent high degree of readiness of a country to improve resilience and hence lesser vulnerability to climate change and vice versa.

Canada, France, the United States, Japan, and the Republic of Korea, all have high ND-GAIN values. This suggests that these countries are highly prepared to enhance resilience and are less vulnerable to climate change, likely due to their robust infrastructure, resources, and technologies for adapting to climate-related risks. However, they are among the largest greenhouse gas emitters, highlighting their responsibility for climate mitigation.

Emerging economies, such as India, Indonesia, Mexico, South Africa, Brazil, and Argentina, have lower ND-GAIN scores, indicating higher vulnerability and lower readiness for climate resilience. These countries, despite contributing less to global emissions, are often the most affected by climate change because they rely on climate-sensitive sectors, such as agriculture, and have limited resources for adaptation.

These disparities underscore the importance of tailoring climate-resilience strategies according to the specific circumstances of each country. In this regard, financial inclusion can play a crucial role in equipping vulnerable populations, particularly in lower-scoring countries, with the resources needed to mitigate climate risks. Additionally, it emphasises the responsibility of higher-scoring, more developed countries to support global climate resilience efforts, considering their significant contribution to global emissions.

Role of G20s

The financial inclusion and climate change agenda has implications for the G20 in two significant ways, both as an agent and as a recipient. Developing and emerging economies in the G20, such as India, Brazil, and Mexico, with large low-income vulnerable groups, can undertake various policy actions to mitigate the numerous impacts that climate instability inflicts on their poor. Financial inclusion, specifically the incorporation of poor communities into the existing financial framework (while expanding certain aspects to meet their specific needs), can help build resilience and aid adaptation.

India's financial inclusion initiatives, notably the Pradhan Mantri Jan-Dhan Yojana (PMJDY), Stand-up India Scheme, Kisan Credit Card (KCC) scheme, and Unified Payments Interface (UPI), are crucial in bolstering climate resilience among the economically disadvantaged. With increased access and enhanced digital payment infrastructure, economically disadvantaged individuals in India have been enabled to accumulate savings, access credit, and invest in a range of climate-adaptive measures, such as improved irrigation systems, high-yielding seeds, sustainable farming practices, and weather-resistant infrastructure, thereby enhancing their resilience to climate-related uncertainties and shocks. Together, these programs, along with successes such as Mozambique's 2013 flood-aid mobile cash transfers, illustrate the transformative role of financial inclusion in facilitating risk-reduction measures.

Government initiatives, such as crop insurance and pooled-livelihood insurance schemes, have become pivotal, as they provide an effective mechanism for integrating vulnerable communities into formal financial frameworks, thereby strengthening their resilience to economic and climate shocks. A compelling example of this approach is the Caribbean Catastrophe Risk Insurance Facility (CCRIF), the world's first multi-country multiperil risk pool based on parametric insurance. Comprising 22 Caribbean and Central American governments, the CCRIF aims to protect the economically disadvantaged from climate risk. This model offers valuable insights for the G20 nations by illustrating the potential of innovative financial inclusion strategies to empower vulnerable populations and foster climate resilience.

Members of the G20 can consider implementing similar frameworks for vulnerable populations. These institutions can be established by agent nations (the developed, high-income members of the G20) in favour of recipient nations. With the development of widespread digital networks, the use of mobile cash transfers, e-cash, and digital instruments can also help sustain the demand for cash during disasters. Governments focused on digital expansion can adapt their existing frameworks to make them climate-sensitive and inclusive (Mhlanga, 2022).

By fulfilling these responsibilities, G20 nations can drive a globally inclusive financial system that concurrently addresses the pressing challenge of climate change and moves toward a sustainable and equitable future.

5 Global Findex 2025: Main Trends and Limitations of the Study

The World Bank released the updated version of the Global Findex database for 2025 in August 2025, which provided financial inclusion indicators for 2024 and for 2011–2021. However, this edition of Findex prioritized low- and middle-income countries and did not survey consumers in advanced economies regarding financial use and well-being.

Hence, a comparison between developing and advanced countries is not possible using the latest study, which also becomes a limitation of the study. Nevertheless, we note gaps in financial access and usage among developing countries for 2024. These gaps are presented in Table 7.

Table 7 Demographic gaps in financial access and usage indicators in developing economies—Year 2024 (Adults, %age 15+)

	Account Ownership	*Owns a Debit card*	*Owns a Credit card*	*Made or Received Digital Payment*	*Saved any money*
Gender Gap	−5%	−8%	−3%	−13%	−5%
Income Gap	−12%	−16%	−10%	−21%	−19%
Age Gap	−11%	−17%	−13%	2%	−3%
Location Gap	−8%	−20%	−15%	−12%	−14%
Occupation Gap	−16%	−16%	−6%	−21%	−20%
Education Gap	−13%	−25%	−10%	−34%	−19%

Source Authors' compilation using Global Findex Database 2025

The main trends emerging from Findex 2025 with respect to developing countries are as follows:

- According to Global Findex 2025, the gaps in account ownership, debit, and credit card ownership have improved substantially, which suggests an enhanced focus on improving financial access within different demographic groups. This implies that, in 2024, a greater number of women, the poor, young adults, adults with primary education, those in rural areas, and those out of the labour force had access to an account than in 2021 (Dua et al., 2025).
- Account ownership has increased for developing as well as advanced countries.
- Although gender gaps have narrowed across developing countries, significant income, occupation, and education gaps still persist. A reduction in gender gaps signifies financial empowerment of women across developing countries.
- Greater access implies that a larger number of individuals can now save, take credit/loans, and receive government transfers in the form of wages, payments, and pensions.

- A larger proportion of adults in all demographic groups now own a debit and credit card. This implies that more adults can now use cards to make payments and receive wages or transfers to their cards. Hence, individuals' participation in the formal digital economy is higher.
- However, demographic gaps still persist. Table 7 shows that fewer women, low-income adults, those in rural areas, and those out of the labour force don't make or receive digital payments. Since digital inclusion provides a pathway to greater financial inclusion, excluding certain segments of the population would undermine the objective of inclusive growth.
- Income, education, and occupation-based gaps are larger among the usage indicators of digital payment usage and savings. This implies that economic and human capital are significant barriers to effective financial inclusion.
- In terms of financial well-being, only 7% adults in developing countries say that it is not possible to come up with emergency funds in 30 days. 89% of women, 86% poor adults, 91% young adults, 91% of rural residents, 85% of adults who are out of the labour force, and 91% adults with primary education report that it is possible to come up with emergency funds in 30 days. This implies greater resilience among the vulnerable groups in developing countries during 2024.
- The main source of emergency funds for 21% women and 22% men during 2024 is savings. These percentages were 17% and 18%, respectively, in 2021. This implies that adults rely more on formal financial sources than on family or friends for emergency funds. This also indicates greater trust among individuals in the formal financial system.
- During 2024, financial stress of individuals regarding monthly expenses and school fees payment has increased across all demographic groups (Table 6). However, concern about money for old age has declined considerably across all groups. This indicates a shift in the source of financial worry among individuals in developing countries. The reasons for this shift and the mechanisms to address this concern warrant evaluation in future research.

6 Policy Recommendations

To address persistent financial exclusion among certain demographic groups and to bolster resilience to climate change-related risks in developing economies, a multifaceted approach is needed. Our analysis suggests that this should involve strengthening digital infrastructure, enhancing financial literacy, refining institutional structures, and introducing innovative, custom-made financial products and services tailored to the specific needs of these marginalised groups (See Dua et al., 2023a, 2025).

1. **Strengthening Digital Financial Infrastructure**
    - **Democratising financial access is viable through digitalisation,** which enhances transaction ease, deepens service reach, and reduces providers' physical barriers. For example, India has prioritised digital infrastructure as a public good, with biometric identity systems, a real-time small-transaction payment platform, interoperability, and a robust regulatory framework.
    - **Addressing the digital divide** in developing economies is critical for curbing financial exclusion **among vulnerable groups.** For instance, Singapore runs targeted programs such as the 'Go Digital Campaign', 'Hawkers Go Digital', and 'Seniors Go Digital Campaign' to incentivise specific demographics.
    - **Promoting competition in the telecom and Internet industries** can effectively extend the reach of low-cost digital infrastructure.
    - **Ensuring a responsible digital ecosystem is essential.** This entails developing technical standards and protocols for high-quality financial service delivery, implementing robust cybersecurity measures, and supporting R&D in digital solutions to mitigate financial exclusion and enhance cost-effective access to services.

2. **Better Institutional Setup**
    - Boosting **public sector bank (PSBs) efficiency** is crucial, as it preserves consumer confidence during economic distress and strengthens the banking system.

- Collaboration with **private banks, non-profit organisations, and bilateral and multilateral partners** can expedite financial inclusion. Leveraging CSR initiatives can enhance private banks' focus on this agenda, as seen in Cambodia's surge in mobile payments.
- **Better data collection** is required for effective policy design, monitoring, and coordination among agencies. This involves sharing credit information, promoting automation, maintaining regular data updates, and disaggregating data.
- Addressing the issue of documentation shortage, a **digital national identity** such as Aadhaar in India, MyInfo in Singapore, or UAE Pass can serve as a bedrock for digital finance.
- A **financial data protection framework** is indispensable for fostering trust in financial institutions and ensuring consumer protection.
- An efficient, **stable political and legal system** is key to financial development and citizen participation in the formal financial system, as seen in developed European countries.
- It is important to **strengthen coordination** at regional, national, and international levels, acknowledging financial exclusion's impacts on financial stability and economic growth.

3. **Fostering Innovation in Financial Products and Services**

- The promotion **of tailor-made innovative financial products** is crucial to ensure financial inclusivity. Such initiatives should be aligned with community needs, demographics, and regional specificities. For example, gender-sensitive financial services, such as savings accounts designed for women's needs, can prove effective.
- **The integration of financial inclusion programs** with health and education priorities can help reduce group disparities.
- Utilising innovative practices for **branchless banking** can provide doorstep delivery of financial services to excluded groups. Models such as banking correspondent networks, which employ female agents to serve the unbanked population, have proven successful in Brazil and India.
- Transitioning from traditional banking to innovative methods such as **basic cellular and** telecommunication **technology** for mobile payment applications can help bridge the digital divide,

eliminating the need for internet connections or sophisticated smartphones.

4. **Enhancing Financial Literacy**

   - **Digital media** such as mobile apps, online courses, and virtual reality should be utilised alongside traditional methods such as print media and radio for more effective financial education programs. These can be designed specifically for targeted groups to address gaps in financial inclusion.
   - **Information-Education-Communication campaigns** should be implemented to spread awareness of government schemes aimed at financial inclusion, inform about their benefits, and establish channels for grievance redressal and feedback.
   - **Public Education Infrastructure** can significantly contribute to promoting financial inclusion. Volunteers can assist targeted groups in understanding the importance of savings and available products.
   - To advocate for insurance services, the community should be educated about the necessity of insurance and the availability of **customised financial products** tailored to the specific risks faced by the underserved population.

5. **Affordability and Implementation Issues**

   - To combat **financial exclusion among women due to affordability issues**, initiatives should aim to increase their income generation capacities. These could include efforts to increase the female labour force participation rate and to promote financial independence and formal credit access. Additionally, microfinance initiatives have demonstrated potential to foster income generation and entrepreneurship among women, thereby helping to bridge the gender gap in financial inclusion.
   - Public **investment** in providing basic infrastructure in underserved areas can foster private investments that are critical for promoting digital finance.

6. **Financial inclusion as a tool to mitigate climate change risks**

   - Tailored **financial services and enhanced access** to these services can enable the vulnerable to adopt environment-friendly practices. This could encompass mechanisms like green finance for MSMEs and small farmers, regulatory enablers for Pay-as-you-go solar and water models[13] (as adopted in Sub-Saharan Africa), and incentives for inclusive green FinTech innovation.

- **Access to affordable** insurance **products for farmers and MSMEs** can equip farmers to cope with income shocks caused by extreme weather conditions.

7 Conclusion

This paper shows that, while financial inclusion has improved considerably over 2011–24 in terms of access and usage, substantial gaps remain between advanced and developing economies and across developing economies. These gaps reflect barriers associated with demographic characteristics such as gender, age, income, and occupation. According to the World Bank's Global Findex Database (2021), account ownership has significantly improved across developing countries, but disparities persist among marginalized and vulnerable groups. Access gaps in digital financial services, such as mobile money and digital payment platforms, have substantially narrowed across advanced and developing countries. Still, significant differences in usage and trust persist, particularly among the poor, the less educated, and women.

The COVID-19 pandemic accelerated the adoption of digital payment methods and the use of digital channels for the receipt of emergency payments and social assistance from governments, particularly in developing countries. However, the reach of such measures was constrained by the limited availability of mobile phones and internet access for all. There exist significant gaps in the proportion of adults who make or receive digital payments across developed and developing economies. The persistence of gender, income, age, education, and occupation gaps leads to the exclusion of these groups from accessing the social and other benefits of digitalisation.

The research underscores that financial inclusion is a developmental objective, and it promotes financial resilience and social protection.

[13] Pay as you go (PAYGO) services give customers access to environmentally friendly technologies such as solar and other alternative power sources, where they can take a small loan to buy power from an off-grid solar panel, and then pay it off in instalments through mobile money accounts.

Formal savings and borrowing enhance household financial planning and act as buffers against climate shocks and emergencies. In areas susceptible to climate-induced disasters, financial services such as insurance, green credit, and digital cash transfers can greatly enhance adaptive capacity and lower vulnerability.

Furthermore, the examination of G20 nations reveals inequalities in financial inclusion. This indicates that the objective of universal financial inclusion is insufficient without appropriate policy frameworks. Rich nations need first to address inclusion gaps within their jurisdictions and second to support developing countries through knowledge sharing, investment in inclusive fintech, and climate-resilient financial solutions.

A comprehensive and inclusive policy approach is essential to bridge the financial inclusion divide. This encompasses bolstering digital financial infrastructure, advocating for innovative and customized financial products, improving institutional capabilities, and nurturing financial literacy among all demographic segments. Policymakers need to focus on the challenges of inclusion and prioritize the inclusion of women, young adults, people living in rural areas, and informal-sector workers within the formal financial system.

References

Abdu, M., Buba, A., Adamu, I., & Muhammad, T. (2015). Drivers of financial inclusion and gender gap in Nigeria. *The Empirical Econometrics and Quantitative Economics Letters (EEQEL), 4*(4), 186–199.

Allen, F., Carletti, E., Cull, R., Qian, J. Q., Senbet, L., & Valenzuela, P. (2014). The African financial development and financial inclusion gaps. *Journal of African Economies, 23*(5), 614–642.

Arab Monetary Fund. (2021). *Innovative methods for increasing responsible financial inclusion, financial inclusion task force in the Arab countries*, Arab Monetary Fund.

Calderone, M., Weingartner, L., & Kroessin, M. R. (2019). *Investing in financial inclusion for climate resilience and adaptation: The role of Islamic financial services*. ODI.

Castells-Quintana, D., Lopez-Uribe, M. D. P., & McDermott, T. K. J. (2018). Adaptation to climate change: A review through a development economics lens. *World Development, 104*, 183–196.

Chauhan, S. (2022). *Financial inclusion in India inching close to the last Mile* (EAC-PM Working Paper Series EAC-PM/WP/03/2022). https://eacpm.gov.in/wp-content/uploads/2023/07/3-Financial-Inclusion-Srishti-Chauhan.pdf

Chavan, P. (2020). Women's access to banking in India: Policy context, trends, and predictors. *Review of Agrarian Studies, 10*(1), 7–36.

Demirguc-Kunt, A., Klapper, L., Singer, D., & Ansar, S. (2022). *The Global Findex database 2021.* World Bank Publications-Books.

Dua, P., Goel, D., Kumar, N., & Verma, N. (2023a). Financial inclusion, economic growth, and taxes: An overview. In P. Dua (Ed.), *Financial inclusion: Perspectives and recent initiatives.* National Book Trust.

Dua, P., Goel, D., Kumar, N., & Verma, N. (2023b). *Reducing financial inclusion gaps: A policy roadmap for developing economies.* G20 Policy Briefs.

Dua, P., Goel, D., Kumar, N., & Verma, N. (2025). *Financial inclusion in India—Progress, issues, and policy options* (RIS Discussion Paper, 313). DP#313-2025.

Ghosh, C., & Chaudhury, R. H. (2019). Gender gap in case of financial inclusion: An empirical analysis in Indian context. *Economics Bulletin, 39*(4), 2615–2630.

Girón, A., Kazemikhasragh, A., Cicchiello, A. F., & Panetti, E. (2021). Financial inclusion measurement in the least developed countries in Asia and Africa. *Journal of the Knowledge Economy, 13*(2), 1–14.

IMF. (2020). *Filling the gap: Digital credit and financial inclusion* (IMF Working Paper No. 20/2015). International Monetary Fund.

IPCC. (2023). *Climate change 2023: Synthesis report*. A Report of the Intergovernmental Panel on Climate Change. IPCC, Geneva, Switzerland.

Johnen, C., & Mußhoff, O. (2023). Digital credit and the gender gap in financial inclusion: Empirical evidence from Kenya. *Journal of International Development, 35*(2), 272–295.

Klapper, L., Singer, D., & Ansar, S. (2022). *The little data book on financial inclusion 2022* (Vol. 4). World Bank Group.

Loukoianova, M. E., Yang, Y., Guo, M. S., Hunter, M. L., Jahan, M. S., Jamaludin, M. F., & Wu, M. Y. (2018). *Financial inclusion in Asia-Pacific.* International Monetary Fund.

Mhlanga, D. (2022). *The role of financial inclusion and FinTech in addressing climate-related challenges in the industry 4.0: Lessons for sustainable development goals*. Frontiers in Climate. https://doi.org/10.3389/fclim.2022.949178

Mukong, A., Shiwayu, N., & Kaulihowa, T. (2020). A decomposition of the gender gap in financial inclusion: Evidence from Namibia. *African Journal of Business and Economic Research, 15*(4), 149.

Ndoya, H. H., & Tsala, C. O. (2021). What drive gender gap in financial inclusion? Evidence from Cameroon. *African Development Review, 33*(4), 674–687.

Ozili, P. K. (2020). Theories of financial inclusion. In *Uncertainty and challenges in contemporary economic behaviour* (pp. 89–115). Emerald Publishing Limited.

Ozili, P. K. (2021). Financial inclusion in Europe: What we know. *Expert White Paper Series, 1.*

Park, C.-Y., & Mercado, R. (2015). *Financial inclusion, poverty, and income inequality in developing Asia* (Asian Development Bank Economics Working Paper Series, 426).

Sharif, S., Naghavi, N., Waheed, H., & Ehigiamusoe, K. U. (2023). The role of education in filling the gender gap in financial inclusion in low-income economies. *International Journal of Emerging Markets, 18*(12), 5755–5777.

Sirtaine, S., & McKay, C. (2022). *In an era of urgent climate risk, does financial inclusion matter?* (CGAP Leadership Essay Series). https://www.cgap.org/blog/in-era-of-urgent-climate-risk-does-financial-inclusion-matter

Trujillo, V., Brandon, R, F. (2023, October 4). *How did Argentina increase the number of bank accounts by more than 100%?* World Bank Blogs.

Yue, P., Korkmaz, A. G., Yin, Z., & Zhou, H. (2022). The rise of digital finance: Financial inclusion or debt trap? *Finance Research Letters, 47*, Article 102604.

CHAPTER 3

Financial Innovation, Inclusion and Socio-Economic Development: An Experience from Cross Country Analysis

Simontini Das, Trisha Bhattacharya, and Rilina Basu Banerjee

1 Introduction

The relationship between financial innovation[1] and economic growth has received a great deal of attention in recent academic literature. Financial innovation is undoubtedly helpful in promoting financial sector development and economic growth (Beck et al., 2007; Demirguc-Kunt et al., 2018; Iman, 2014; Laeven et al., 2015; Levine, 2005; Michalopoulos

[1] As Defined by Frame and White (2004) financial innovation is the act of creating and then channelizing new financial instruments and technologies, institutions and markets.

S. Das (✉) · R. Basu Banerjee
Department of Economics, Jadavpur University, Kolkata, India
e-mail: simontini@gmail.com

T. Bhattacharya
Department of School Education, Government of West Bengal, South 24 Parganas, India

© The Author(s), under exclusive license to Springer Nature Singapore Pte Ltd. 2026
V. Dixit et al. (eds.), *Financial Inclusion for Viksit Bharat*,
https://doi.org/10.1007/978-981-92-0807-4_3

et al., 2009). However, the role of financial innovation in promoting world-wide socioeconomic development has not received much attention. Out of the different forms of financial innovation[2] dissemination of process innovation has relatively greater impact than the product innovation (Allen & Yago, 2010; Greenhalgh & Rogers, 2010; Oslo Manual, 2005; Pain, 2011). While process innovation is the intensive penetration of ICT infrastructure that boost up financial sector by continuous improvements in process of financial transactions at a reduced cost (Chatterjee & Das, 2021; Dan, 2013; Haftu, 2019; Majeed & Ayub, 2018; Michalopoulos et al., 2009; Ozili, 2018; Sassia & Goaied, 2012), product innovation is the introduction of new or significantly improved version of financial products to meet market needs, thus constituting a client-focused kind of financial innovation. In this paper we aim to bridge the caveat in the literature by investigating the association of process innovation on socio economic well-being of nations.

Process based innovation makes financial services more accessible to the society leading to the financial inclusion of the marginalised section of the society. It is complemented through diffusion of ICT and can contribute to economic growth by improving operational efficiency, reducing transaction cost, increasing volume of trade, bringing in innovation and development, promoting financial inclusion, increasing employment and demand, and developing the financial sector (Datta & Agarwal, 2004; Nasab & Aghaei, 2009; Pradhan et al., 2018a; Pradhan et al., 2014, 2015; Rohman & Bohlin, 2014; Vu, 2011). Automatically effective implementation of Information Communication Technology (ICT) becomes a bare necessity to facilitate financial process innovation across the countries (Chatterjee & Das, 2021). Productive usage of ICT indicators improves the productivity and efficiency of financial sector, which requires financial education and awareness among the common people. This kind of technology-led financial innovation not only reduces time and cost but positively influences banks' performances of countries. Bhattacharya et al. (2023) has shown how technology-led innovation improves overall Indian Scheduled Commercial banks' performances over the years. The causal relation between financial innovation, financial inclusion and ICT has got much attention in panel data set up (Chatterjee,

[2] Process based and product based innovations are two major forms of financial innovation (See Oslo Manual, 2005; Greenhalgh & Rogers, 2010; Allen & Yago, 2010; Pain, 2011).

2020). The effects of financial innovation have largely been observed to be limited to the developed world. The major reason behind it is the lagging ICT infrastructure, dependence on agriculture, low per capita income and low level of educational attainments in emerging economies due to poor policies and insufficient investments (Laryea, 1999; Niebel, 2018).

Like other innovations, financial innovation offers significant opportunities for economic growth and development. Financial innovation in terms of digital payment services, electronic banking, risk management, remittances, electronic business etc. has an extensive impact on economic growth and development of an economy (Lerner & Tufano, 2011; Oyelami et al., 2020). The Digital Payments Report observes that in 2020, the digital payments segment has a global transaction value projected to reach nearly US$5,000,000 in 2020. According to Bu et al. (2022) Financial Technology (Fin Tech) has a U-shaped relationship on the real economy. Initially innovation restrains economic growth then continuous improvement enhances economic growth. However, the betterment of a country remains under/over stated without the study of its social indicators (Anand & Sen, 1994; Sarma & Pais, 2011; Taghizadeh-Hesary et al., 2019; Ul. Haq, 1996; Yumashev et al., 2020). The recent financial crisis has raised debates about financial access to workers which can reduce poverty and positively affect the labour market (Bruhn & Love, 2014; Cull et al., 2014; Mol, 2014; Pagano & Pica, 2012; World Bank, 2014; Zulfiqar et al., 2016). An analysis by the World Bank (World Development Report, 2015–16) showed that financial inclusion has a positive impact on employment, new businesses, and GDP (Bruhn & Love, 2014). In this context, this paper intends to examine the different socio-economic consequences of process innovation in a cross-country framework.

While there are papers which investigate the association between financial innovation and economic growth,[3] there are very few studies which look into the channels through which digital innovation can help process innovation. Moreover, we have tried to construct a comprehensive index of process innovation and analyse its socio-economic impact in a cross country set up.

[3] See Levine (1997), Shiller (2008, 2018), Beck et al. (2016) etc.

The paper is organised as follows. Section 2 provides data description, empirical model specification and index construction. Section 3 undertakes econometric analysis and discussion while Sect. 4 concludes the paper along with relevant policy prescriptions.

2 Data Description, Model Specification and Index Construction

This section delineates the data description, model specification, discussion on estimation methodology and index construction.

2.1 Data Description

The data is taken from the Global Financial Inclusion (Global Findex) Database of World Bank, World Development Indicator (WDI) of World Bank, World Bank national accounts data, Organisation for Economic Co-operation (OECD) National Accounts data files, UNDP database, Financial Access Survey (FAS) of International Monetary Fund (IMF), Bank for International Settlements (BIS), Non-banking financial database of World Bank, Sigma Reports from Swiss Re and various banking reports database. One of the constraints of the research is the unavailability of consistent data for longer period. The information is available only for 2011, 2014 and 2017[4] and for limited countries. The research considers financial process innovation and estimates simultaneous equation system to analyse the impact of financial innovation on economic growth and development. For process innovation, total 95 countries[5] from different income groups are considered for the analysis. Financial innovation may have heterogeneous impacts on developmental process across different types of countries. To capture that heterogeneity a cross-section specific dummy is introduced to differentiate developmental status

[4] Data on use of credit card, debit card transaction, use of mobile phone to pay bills, digital payments etc. of the countries are not regular before 2011. Hence, we cannot extend our analysis before 2011. The dataset has been taken from World Bank (Global Findex) survey which is available for the year 2011, 2014 and 2017 only.

[5] Except some Middle East countries all eexhaustive set are taken depending on the availability of the data from World Bank Financial Development Database.

of the countries. The countries are classified into two groups[6] developed and developing. Out of 95, 35 countries are developed and rest 60 are developing countries.

2.2 Model Specification

2.2.1 Estimable Model and Method of Estimation

Process innovation has impact on financial development, which in turn improvises different macro-economic indicators through financial inclusion. Here three macro-economic variables are considered; human development index, per capita gross domestic product and unemployment. Developmental theory confirms that these three variables are interrelated. Anand and Sen (1994) and M. Ul. Haq (1996) establishes an interrelation between per capita income and human development. These two are expected to have a detrimental impact on unemployment. Hence the discussion on the impacts of different financial innovations on human developmental status, per capita GDP and unemployment demands a simultaneous equation system (SES) framework. We have constructed such a model consisting of per capita GDP, unemployment and human development as endogenous variables[7]. SES has been largely applied to explore such inter-linkages (Andrei et al., 2009a, 2009b; Bai & Wei, 2001; Kaufmann et al., 2002, 2003). The estimation method of instrumental variables is used to solve the endogeneity problem in SEM, which leads to biased and inconsistent estimation.

[6] For classification purpose we have followed World Bank classification (World Economic Situation and Prospects, 2021) of countries. The WESP (World Economic Situation and Prospects) classifies all countries of the world into one of three broad categories: developed economies, economies in transition and developing economies. In this paper among 95 countries only 4 countries are in economies in transition group. Hence, we have considered them as developing countries.

[7] See Yumashev et al. (2020), Murshed and Mredula (2018).

The structural equations of the Simultaneous Equation Model are given below:

$$
\begin{aligned}
&Lag(log\ Per\ Capita\ GDP)i \\
&\quad = \beta_1 0 + \beta_1 1(HDI)i \\
&\quad +\beta_1 2(Unemployment\ as\ percentage\ of\ total\ labour\ force)i \\
&\quad +\gamma_1 1(Trade\ openness\ as\ a\ share\ of\ GDP)i \\
&\quad +\gamma_1 2(Broad\ Money\ Growth,\ Annual)i \\
&\quad +\gamma_1 3(Official\ Exchange\ Rate\ Growth)i \\
&\quad +\gamma_1 4(Service\ Value\ Added\ as\ a\ share\ of\ GDP)i \\
&\quad +\gamma_1 5(Process\ Innovation\ Index)i \\
&\quad +\gamma_1 6(D * Process\ Innovation\ Index)i + u_1 i
\end{aligned}
\tag{2.1}
$$

Instruments: Industry Value Added and Secondary School Enrolment as a share of Gross Enrolment (Chatterjee, 2020; Chatterjee & Das, 2021; Sarma & Pais, 2011).

$$
\begin{aligned}
&(HDI)i \\
&= \beta_2 0 + \beta_2 2(Unemploymentaspercentageoftotallabourforce)i \\
&\quad +\beta_2 3Lag(LogPerCapitaGDP)i \\
&\quad +\gamma_2 1(GrossFixedExpenditureaspercentofGDP)i \\
&\quad +\gamma_2 2(UrbanPopulationasapercentageofTotalPopulation)i \\
&\quad +\gamma_2 3(ServiceValueAddedasashareofGDP)i \\
&\quad +\gamma_2 4(SecondarySchoolEnrollmentasashareofGrossEnrollment)i \\
&\quad +\gamma_2 6(OfficialExchangerateGrowth)i \\
&\quad +[\gamma]_2 7(ProcessInnovationIndex)i \\
&\quad +\gamma_2 8(D * ProcessInnovationIndex)i + u_2 i
\end{aligned}
\tag{2.2}
$$

Instruments: Industry Value Added and Inflation (Chatterjee, 2020; Chatterjee & Das, 2021; Sarma & Pais, 2011).

$$\begin{aligned}
&(Unemployment\ as\ percentage\ of\ total\ labour\ force)i \\
&= \beta_3 0 + \beta_3 1(HDI)i + \beta_3 2Lag(Log\ Per\ Capita\ GDP)i \\
&\quad +\gamma_3 1(Gross\ Fixed\ Capital\ Formation\ as\ share\ of\ GDP)i \\
&\quad +[\gamma_3 2(Broad\ Money\ Growth)i \\
&\quad +\gamma_3 3(ICT\ imports\ as\ proportion\ of\ total\ import)i \\
&\quad +\gamma_3 4(Secondary\ School\ Enrollment\ as\ a\ share\ of\ Gross\ Enrollment) \\
&\quad +\gamma_3 5(Official\ Exchange\ rate\ Growth)i \\
&\quad +\gamma_3 6(Urban\ Population\ as\ a\ percentage\ of\ Total\ Population)i \\
&\quad +\gamma_3 7(Process\ Innovation\ Index)i \\
&\quad +\gamma_3 8(D * Process\ Innovation\ Index)i \\
&\quad +u]_3 i
\end{aligned} \tag{2.3}$$

Instruments: Inflation and service Value Added as share of GDP (Chatterjee, 2020; Chatterjee & Das, 2021; Sarma & Pais, 2011).

i = 1 ... N and t = 2011, 2014, 2017;

N: the number of countries.

u_{1i}, $u_{2i} and u_{3i}$ are error terms corresponding to the first, second and third equation respectively. β_{10}, β_{20}, β_{30} are constants corresponding to the first, second and third equation respectively. Principal Component Analysis is used to construct process innovation index (detail description is available in methodology part).

The endogenous variables we have chosen are lag values of log of GDP (Gross Domestic Product) per capita and HDI (Human Development Index) and Unemployment. Economic condition or income level is measured by logarithm of GDP per capita. Aggregates are based on constant 2010 US dollars. In most cases it is evident that GDP is considered as a sole measure of economic performance, neglecting other important developmental issues. While researchers like Sarma and Pais (2011), Chatterjee, (2020); Baluch and Ariff, (2007) have considered GDP per capita as a measure of economic performance to capture income distributional characteristic of the society, Sarma and Pais (2011) has used

HDI (Human Development Index) to understand development. Details definitions of dependent and control variables used in our analysis along with their sources are given in Appendix (Tables 7–9). This SES satisfies order condition and rank condition for identification. To estimate endogenous explanatory variables in multiple regression model Simultaneous Equation Modelling (SEM) are used. Three Stage Least Square (3 SLS), introduced by Zellner and Theil (1962), has been used to estimate simultaneous equation system (SES) in this framework[8] (Cadoret et al., 2004). There are different approaches to solve the problem of endogeneity. Instrumental Variable (IV) methods is regarded as most effective approach than 2SLS and 3SLS methods. Instrumental Variable method solves the problem of time-varying omitted variables that are correlated with the explanatory variables. It is also used to solve the problems of error-in-variables. Instrumental variable method is used here for estimation to capture dynamic dimension of the model.

A cross-country specific dummy is introduced here. D = 0 for Developing countries; D = 1 for Developed Countries. This 'D' is interacted with innovation index to examine the impact of country-specific characteristics on the effect of innovation on socio-economic conditions of the nations.

2.3 *Index Construction*

ATMs, debit cards, credit cards, mobile money, different forms of digital payments are completely a new form of innovation that have revolutionised the business model of the financial industry. Plethora of research have been made on the use of electronic modes of payment or transaction services and its impact on socio-economic growth (Bacache et al., 2013; Bertschek et al., 2013; Bojnec & Ferto, 2012; Bouras et al., 2009; Crandall et al., 2007; Czernich et al., 2011). Hence in this current research we have taken some ICT enabled variables that represents a new process in the financial sector that revolutionized the mode of transactions with the use of digital platforms like plastic money, card-based transactions and of course cashless transactions via mobile or internet. These are essentially classified as process related innovation our current research.

[8] Simple OLS method cannot be applied here as the estimators suffer from endogeneity bias or simultaneous equation bias.

The present paper considers mainly financial process based innovations and its effects on growth, developmental process and labour market through financial inclusion. The research follows OECD and Cámara and Tuesta (2017) methodology for constructing a multidimensional index for Process Innovation (PII). The weights of the index are obtained from a two-stage Principal Component Analysis (PCA). PII are constructed for 95 countries for the period 2011, 2014 and 2017. PCA is the most the scientific methods of index construction in the presence of at least three variables (according to Steiger, 1979, PCA is preferred over Common Factor Analysis as an indexing strategy[9]). In the present research, the variables, considered for construction of indices, are correlated. Weights of the innovation variables are calculated during factor analysis. Endogenous weights are used to construct multi-dimensional financial innovation index.

According to The Global Findex Database 2017, World Bank, Payment cards such as debit or credit cards provide account owners a convenient way to make payments from their account without withdrawing cash. In 2017, 80 percent of adults of high-income economies reported using a debit or credit card to make at least one payment in the past 12 months, while in developing economies only 22 percent did so (World Bank Report, 2014). In high-income economies 55 percent of adults reported owning credit cards in 2017, whereas credit card ownership in developing economies remains low and unchanged around 10 percent in course of time.

Table 1 shows that usages of debit card, credit cards and digital payment mode of transactions have become most decisive components than the other variables across the developed and developing nations in 2017.Conversely payment of bills using mobile phone and number of ATMs per 100,000 adults are losing its importance over the years. Hence use of digital payments are no doubt becoming a dominant mode of transaction than others mode cross the countries.

The paper considers large number of countries with diversified developmental status, size, demographic profile, income profile, employment status etc. The paper constructs process innovation index to understand the impact of financial innovation in a composite manner in a cross

[9] Because it is not necessary to make assumptions on the raw data, such as selecting the underlying number of common factors. Particularly, PCA is better when set of variables are correlated but the level of adoption varies across the countries.

Table 1 Weights calculated for process innovation variables

Year	*Use of credit cards (V1)*	*Use of debit cards (V2)*	*Made digital payments in the past year (V3)*	*Paid utility bills: using a mobile phone (V4)*	*Number ATMs per 100,000 adults (V5)*
2011	0.21318	0.18471	0.23157	0.09673	0.16686
2014	0.22166	0.21801	0.23950	0.03762	0.01461
2017	0.23233	0.23060	0.25063	0.00403	0.00360

Source Authors' calculation

Table 2 Average values of process innovation

Average financial innovation index	*Developed countries*	*Developing countries*
Process innovation index	0.5000	0.1917

Source Author's calculation

country framework. In order to compare innovation between developed and developing countries mean values of the process innovation index are presented in a Table 2.

The average value of process innovation index of developed countries is 0.5000 and that for developing countries is 0.1917 respectively, that indicates that diffusion of process innovation is relatively more widespread in developed nations than in the developing countries. This difference in the average values of innovation index across developed and developing countries justifies the need of separate analysis for two set of countries.

3 Econometric Analysis

The present section undertakes a comparative analysis to understand the diverging impacts of different financial innovations on growth, development and labour market of an economy. Per capita income at constant price, Human Development Index and unemployment are considered to gauge the macroeconomic performances of the countries. Instrumental Variable estimation method is carried out considering 3 years to make a comparative analysis of financial innovation among developed, developing and overall countries.

Impact of process Innovation on Per Capita Income, Human Development and Unemployment:

It is important to investigate the impacts of financial innovations on country level economic performance which is expected to trickle down to the human development and unemployment status of the respective economy. Table 3, 4 and 5 summarise the influences of process innovation on per capita national income, human development and unemployment respectively across the developed and developing countries.

Table 3 describes the estimation results of process based financial innovation on the per capita income level among overall, developing and developed countries. Econometric analysis exhibits that process innovation has a significant positive impact on per capita GDP across countries throughout the time period. The interactive term between the developmental status of the country when considered, process innovation has significant effects on income levels, inferring that existing developmental status of the country does have an indirect effect on the consequences of process innovation on per capita income level. The same positive significance result prevails in the developing as well as the developed countries. It infers that ICT supported digitisation in financial sector helps in increasing access to institutional finance to the unbanked population of the society and promotes financial inclusion by reducing the time and monetary cost across the nations. This accelerates economic performances not only to the developed but to the developing nations. This finding is in line with Hassan (2005) and Sassia and Goaied (2012) who show that ICT is an essential part of economy's growth process; it improves the productive capacity and competitiveness by improving efficiency. Cross-country comparison elucidates that the positive effect of process innovation on per capita GDP is stronger for developing countries (the estimated coefficient is 1.14) than developed countries (the coefficient is 0.816). As the dissemination of ICT baked process innovation in the developed countries has already reached a saturation level, hence its effects on economic growth may less than that of on developing countries. On the other hand, developing countries are either at their early stage or at middle stage of process innovation dissemination trajectory, so there is more opportunity of improvement. Increase in bank credit through process innovation affects aggregate demand and will definitely raise economic activities of the nations.

Table 3 Impact of Process innovation on per capita income for overall, developing and developed countries

Endogenous dependent variable: Lag (Log GDP)	*Process innovation overall* *Coeff*	*Process innovation developing* *Coeff*	*Process innovation developed* *Coeff*
HDI	7.983*** (0.000)	8.78*** (0.000)	0.795 (0.798)
Unemployment, total (% of total labour force)	–0.018 (0.226)	–0.118** (0.016)	0.19 (0.92)
Trade openness (Sum of exports and imports of goods and services measured as a share of gross domestic product	0.215 (0.205)	–0.786 (0.123)	–0.167 (0.584)
Broad Money Growth (Annual)	–0.002 (0.018)	–0.015** (0.015)	–0.004 (0.061)
Services Value Added	–	–	0.611(0.120)
Official exchange rate Growth	–0.209*** (0.000)	0.656 (0.334)	0.22 (0.207)
Innovation Index	**0.394* (0.078)**	**1.41* (0.079)**	**0.816* (0.066)**
D*Innovation Index	**0.423** (0.018)**	–	–
Number of Observations	282	177	105
R-sq	Within = 0.5945, between = 0.919, Overall = 0.917	Within = 0.59, between = 0.79, Overall = 0.58	Within = 0.04, between = 0.74, Overall = 0.69
Instrumented	HDI, Unemployment	HDI, Unemployment	HDI, Unemployment
Instruments	Industry Value Added and Secondary School Enrolment as a share of Gross Enrolment	Industry Value Added and Secondary School Enrolment as a share of Gross Enrolment	Industry Value Added and Secondary School Enrolment as a share of Gross Enrolment

Source Authors calculation
* *indicates 10% level of significance,* ** *indicates 5% level of significance,* *** *indicates 1% level of significance*

HDI has consistent significant positive effect on per capita income level during the last decades. Higher HDI implies better quality of life enhanced productivity, skill-formation, and health condition of the labour force. This further increases the per capita income. Broad Money Growth has a significant negative impact on countries GDP per capita. Growth

Table 4 Impacts of Process innovation on human development index for overall, developing and developed countries

Endogenous Dependent Variable: HDI	*Process innovation overall* Coeff	*Process innovation developing* Coeff	*Process innovation developed* Coeff
Lag log GDP	0.0213 (0.584)	0.041** (0.057)	0.085 (0.563)
Unemployment, total (% of total labour force)	–0.002 (0.486)	0.004 (0.311)	–0.005 (0.135)
Trade openness (Sum of exports and imports of goods and services measured as a share of gross domestic product	0.030 (0.231)	–	0.062 (0.102)
Official Exchange Rate Growth	0.019** (0.008)	0.050 (0.5)	0.89 (0.667)
Secondary School Enrolment as a share of Gross Enrolment	–	0.235*** (0.009)	0.051** (0.037)
Services Value added	0.0327 (0.447)	–	–
Urban Population out of total population	0.160 (0.101)	–	–
Innovation Index	**0.135** (0.074)**	**0.151** (0.060)**	0.0679 (0.122)
D*Innovation Index	0.085 (0.112)	–	–
Number of Observations	282	177	105
R-sq	Within = 0.511, between = 0.809, Overall = 0.805	Within = 0.35, between = 0.84, Overall = 0.83	Within = 0.34, between = 0.54, Overall = 0.47
Instrumented	GDP, Unemployment	GDP, Unemployment	GDP, Unemployment
Instruments	Industry Value Added and Inflation	Industry Value Added and Inflation	Industry Value Added and Annual broad money growth

Source Authors' calculation
* *indicates 10% level of significance,* ** *indicates 5% level of significance,* *** *indicates 1% level of significance*

of local currency also has a significant positive impact on GDP. If the currency appreciates, it may reduce export valuation thereby negatively impact countries GDP. Unemployment rate has a significant negative

Table 5 Impacts of process innovation on unemployment for overall, developing and developed countries

Endogenous dependent variable: unemployment rate	*Process innovation in overall* Coeff	*Process innovation in developing* Coeff	*Process innovation in developed* Coeff
HDI	47.06 (0.698)	21.336 (0.339)	−11.933 (0.903)
Lag Log per capita GDP	−0.868 (0.942)	−0.77(0.556)	−0.92 (0.767)
Gross Fixed Capital Formation as Share of GDP	−6.665*** (0.001)	−2.513 (0.170)	−12.454 (0.101)
ICT Imports to Total Goods Imports	−1.975(0.634)	–	–
Urban Population out of Total Population	–	−1.137 (0.881)	−4.238 (0.661)
Broad Money Growth (Annual)	−0.035** (0.008)	−0.008 (0.549)	−0.041 (0.134)
Official Exchange Rate Growth	0.697 (0.789)	0.212(0.977)	
Innovation Index	**−9.667** (0.082)**	**−8.029* (0.090)**	−2.509 (0.839)
D*Innovation Index	−2.626 (0.614)	–	–
Number of Observations	282	177	105
R-sq	Within = 0.035, between = 0.0755, Overall = 0.0724	Within = 0.014, between = 0.037, Overall = 0.036	Within = 0.349, between = 0.403, Overall = 0.377
Instrumented	HDI, Lag log GDP	HDI, Lag Log GDP	HDI, Lag Log GDP
Instruments	Inflation and Service Value Added	Industry Value Added and Secondary School Enrolment as a share of Gross Enrolment	Industry Value Added and Secondary School Enrolment as a share of Gross Enrolment

Source Authors' calculation
* *indicates 10% level of significance,* ** *indicates 5% level of significance,* *** *indicates 1% level of significance*

effect on the per capita GDP only for the developing countries. for developed countries this effect is insignificant.

Table 4 describes the results of impacts of process based financial innovations on human development index over the time. Human development index is a more comprehensive indicator to gauge the different developmental dimensions of the economy.

During the last decades digital finance supported by ICT enabled device gains its popularity. It is inferred from the result that process based transactions enhances human development along with economic wellbeing of nations. Economic impact percolates down to the society that improves human development simultaneously. In this way, ICT supported process innovation helps in financial inclusion and leads to overall developments. The coefficients of interactive term of process innovation however remain statistically insignificant, implying that existing development status of a country does not have any indirect influence on human development. Apparently, it is found that process innovation has positive significance on HDI in developing countries but not for the developed countries. That implies that after reaching a threshold level of development, counties overall human development is not affected by additional level of financial innovation.

Other control variables like Secondary school education, trade openness have significant positive impact on human development index. Increase in the quality of life in terms of higher educational attainment and good quality health facility enhance the developmental status of the countries. This affirms the capability approach of Prof. A. Sen (Anand & Sen, 1994; Ul. Haq, 1990). Educational attainment definitely improves the comprehensive development of the economy. It leads to infrastructural development of countries which in turn improves overall developmental status of nations. On the other hand, local currency growth has negative impact on HDI. A depreciating official exchange rate negatively impacts HDI by reducing purchasing power of the economy which increases import costs and can also stimulate exports. However, the overall impact on HDI is complex and depends on various factors.

Therefore, Cross country analysis confirms that from the very beginning of the last decade, process innovation in financial sector raises the per capita income as well as human development status of the individual countries. Process innovation definitely a growth enabler for both developing and developed nations, however it only improves human development of developing ones.

The third endogenous variable is the unemployment rate of the economy. Table 5 describes the impacts of process innovation on the unemployment status of the economy.

The multi-country analysis confirms that process innovation has significantly negative impact on unemployment. This infers that process innovation is reducing unemployment rates along with the rise in per capita income level and improvement in human development status of countries. In case of developed versus developing countries analysis process innovation helps to reduce unemployment problem only in case of developing countries, not for the developed countries, inferring that the innovative financial process fails to create additional job opportunities after reaching a threshold level of development attained by the developed countries. By increasing access of financial services along with the capability to use those services effectively, people can invest in their education to improve their potential to become employed. If financially excluded sections (MSMEs, agricultural and others), start borrowing from formal financial institutions due to the rise in access to financial services, more job opportunities will be created resulting in the decline in unemployment rates. This finding is in line with Mol (2014), Sykes et al. (2016), Mugo and Kilonzo (2017); and Blancher (2019), who argue that financial inclusion reduces unemployment. Process innovation, here reduces unemployment rate of the country through financial inclusion of the unbanked section of the society. Similarly other studies done by Bruhn and Love (2014) find that financial inclusion increases employment. Thus, financial innovation definitely increases financial access and usage thereby creating more start-ups and new job opportunities which leads to rise in per capita income level and eventually overall human development of the countries. In the first half of the last decade, dissemination of process innovation in financial sector remains restricted mainly within the developed world, and developing countries have very little access to these services due to lack of infrastructural facilities, awareness and financial literacy (World Bank Report, 2012). ICT diffusion in financial sector though has been started, but its penetration was insignificant. Over the time adoption of process innovation gains momentum and consequently its affirmative impact on the socio-economic factors becomes more perceivable.

Among the control variables, gross fixed capital formation shows negative significant impact on unemployment. Improvement in fixed capital creates employment opportunities within the economy that helps to reduce unemployment. Broad money growth is negatively significant with unemployment which affirms Philip's curve approach i.e., inflation or broad money growth is inversely related with unemployment.

The above analysis infers that process innovation has significant impacts on per capita income, human development and unemployment only for the developing countries. After achieving a critical level of development, it fails to influence the human development status and unemployment in the developed countries. At that time it can have affirmative impact only on per capita economy, in case of developed country.

The comprehensive investigation confirms that the rate of dissemination of process innovation is much faster among developed and developing nations. Hence it is found that the process innovation has the more extensive consequences on different macroeconomic parameters of an economy. The process innovation in financial sector has strong affirmative impacts on per capita income and human development status of the economy along with a positive impact on job creating opportunity. In most of the cases, the nature of these impacts is independent of the existing developmental status of the countries. The present paper is distinctive in a sense that it first undertakes a comprehensive analysis on the developmental consequences of financial process innovations.

4 Concluding Remarks

The paper comprehensively explains the socio-economic impact of different types of financial innovation. The result clearly suggests that there is significant positive impact of process innovation on income level as well as human development for all years. Widespread ICT based process innovation helps in increase in formal sector finance within the economy that reduces time cost, monetary cost and in turn increases transparency of the banking system. As a consequence, this immediately raises per capita income and human developments of the economy along with a sharp reduction in unemployment rate. The research suggests that process innovation if properly implemented within the financial institutions, and then it will be a job creating innovation.

The paper suggests the policy of continuous financial process innovation to accelerate economic performance and comprehensive development along with employment opportunities of the countries irrespective of their initial status. Proper expansion of ICT infrastructure within and between the countries is a necessary pre-condition to accelerate the diffusion of process innovation in organised financial sector. Along with this, proper awareness build-up, spread of financial literacy along with general education, adequate vigilance to restrict financial fraud are also required to perceive the affirmative effect of process innovation. In the conclusion, the research comes up with an interesting finding that process related innovation is gaining its importance over last few years and also facilitates socio-economic perspective of nations. Finally, the paper indicates a strong interlink between digitalised financial system and economic performance which lead us to the further analysis at country-specific level in future.

Though Rapid growth of Information and Communication Technologies (ICT) plays a crucial role behind all types of financial innovations, the paper needs to consider the impacts of financial product innovation on growth and development. Moreover, it is agreed by many researchers that product and process innovations affect each other and they need to be adopted together (Buzzachi et al., 1995; Damanpour & Gopalakrishnan, 2001). In particular the study needs to consider the issue of financial innovation in a holistic way taking both new financial products and innovative process and its socio-economic impact. One big limitation of this kind of research is limitation of data especially for product innovation data in a cross country set up. However, the study can be extended by concentrating on both process and product innovations where more developing countries can be taken for analysis and interaction between developed and developing can be studied. Countries efficiency levels can be measured in respect to both types of innovations.

Disclosure Statement No potential conflict of interest was reported by the author(s).

Appendix

Definition of Dependent Variables

See Table 6.

Table 6 List of dependent variables, definitions and sources

Logarithm of GDP per capita (in 2010 constant USD)	Logarithm of GDP per capita (in 2000 constant USD) is gross domestic product divided by midyear population. GDP is the sum of gross value added by all resident producers in the economy plus any product taxes and minus any subsidies not included in the value of the products. It is calculated without making deductions for depreciation of fabricated assets or for depletion and degradation of natural resources. Data are in constant 2010 U.S. dollars
HDI	Human Development Index (HDI): A composite index measuring average achievement in three basic dimensions of human development—a long and healthy life, knowledge and a decent standard of living. See Technical note 1 at http://hdr.undp.org/sites/default/files/hdr2019_technical_notes.pdf for details on how the HDI is calculated

Description of Control Variables

See Tables 7 and 8.

Table 7 List of control variables, definitions, and sources

Gross Fixed capital Formation (percent of GDP)	Gross fixed capital formation (formerly gross domestic fixed investment) includes land improvements (fences, ditches, drains, and so on); plant, machinery, and equipment purchases; and the construction of roads, railways, and the like, including schools, offices, hospitals, private residential dwellings, and commercial and industrial buildings. According to the 1993 SNA, net acquisitions of valuables are also considered capital formation
Trade openness (percent of GDP)	Trade is the sum of exports and imports of goods and services measured as a share of gross domestic product
Gross enr. ratio (secondary)	Gross enrollment ratio is the ratio of total enrollment, regardless of age, to the population of the age group that officially corresponds to the level of education shown. Secondary education completes the provision of basic education that began at the primary level and aims at laying the foundations for lifelong learning and human development, by offering more subject- or skill-oriented instruction using more specialized teachers
Stocks traded, total value (% of GDP)	The value of shares traded is the total number of shares traded, both domestic and foreign, multiplied by their respective matching prices. Figures are single counted (only one side of the transaction is considered). Companies admitted to listing and admitted to trading are included in the data. Data are end of year values

(continued)

Table 7 (continued)

Industry (including construction) value added of GDP	Industry corresponds to ISIC divisions 10–45 and includes manufacturing (ISIC divisions 15–37). It comprises value added in mining, manufacturing (also reported as a separate subgroup), construction, electricity, water, and gas. Value added is the net output of a sector after adding up all outputs and subtracting intermediate inputs. It is calculated without making deductions for depreciation of fabricated assets or depletion and degradation of natural resources
Services value added as a percentage of GDP	Services correspond to ISIC divisions 50–99 and they include value added in wholesale and retail trade (including hotels and restaurants), transport, and government, financial, professional, and personal services such as education, health care, and real estate services. Also included are imputed bank service charges, import duties, and any statistical discrepancies noted by national compilers as well as discrepancies arising from rescaling. Value added is the net output of a sector after adding up all outputs and subtracting intermediate inputs. It is calculated without making deductions for depreciation of fabricated assets or depletion and degradation of natural resources
Population growth rate	Annual population growth rate for year t is the exponential rate of growth of midyear population from year t – 1 to t, expressed as a percentage. Population is based on the de facto definition of population, which counts all residents regardless of legal status or citizenship
Urban population as percentage of total population	Urban population refers to people living in urban areas as defined by national statistical offices. The data are collected and smoothed by United Nations Population Division

(continued)

Table 7 (continued)

Broad money growth (annual %)	Broad money is the sum of currency outside banks; demand deposits other than those of the central government; the time, savings, and foreign currency deposits of resident sectors other than the central government; bank and traveler's checks; and other securities such as certificates of deposit and commercial paper
Domestic credit to private sector (% of GDP)	Domestic credit to private sector refers to financial resources provided to the private sector by financial corporations, such as through loans, purchases of nonequity securities, and trade credits and other accounts receivable, that establish a claim for repayment. For some countries these claims include credit to public enterprises. The financial corporations include monetary authorities and deposit money banks, as well as other financial corporations where data are available (including corporations that do not accept transferable deposits but do incur such liabilities as time and savings deposits). Examples of other financial corporations are finance and leasing companies, money lenders, insurance corporations, pension funds, and foreign exchange companies
ICT goods imports (% total goods imports)	Information and communication technology goods imports include computers and peripheral equipment, communication equipment, consumer electronic equipment, electronic components, and other information and technology goods (miscellaneous)
Official exchange rate (LCU per US$, period average)	Official exchange rate refers to the exchange rate determined by national authorities or to the rate determined in the legally sanctioned exchange market. This indicator represents the ratio of Local Currency Units relative to United States dollars. This indicator is derived as an average over the reference period

Table 8 List of financial innovation variables, definitions, and sources

Total Debit card ownership (% age 15+)	The percentage of respondents who report having a debit card
Total Credit card ownership (% age 15+)	The percentage of respondents who report having a Credit card
Made digital payments in the past year (% age 15+)	The percentage of respondents who report using mobile money, a debit or credit card, or a mobile phone to make a payment from an account, or report using the internet to pay bills or to buy something online, in the past 12 months. It also includes respondents who report paying bills or sending remittances directly from a financial institution account or through a mobile money account in the past 12 months
Paid utility bills: using a mobile phone	The percentage of respondents who report personally making regular payments for water, electricity, or trash collection in the past 12 months through a mobile phone
Number ATMs per 100,000 adults	For each country calculated as: 100,000*Number of ATMs/adult population in the reporting country

References

Alexey, Y., Sergey, K., Alexey, M., & Ślusarczyk, B. (2020). Global indicators of sustainable development: Evaluation of the influence of the human development index on consumption and quality of energy. *Energies, 13*, 2768. https://doi.org/10.3390/en13112768

Allen, F., & Yago, G. (2010). *Financing the future: Market-based innovations for growth*. Pearson Education, Inc.

Alt, R., Beck, R., & Smits, M. T. (2018). FinTech and the transformation of the financial industry. *Electronic Markets, 28*, 235–243.

Anand, S., & Sen, A. K. (1994). *Human development index: Methodology and measurement* (Human Development Report Office Occasional Papers 12).

Andersen, T. (2006).*Global derivatives – A strategic risk management perspective*. Pearson Education Limited.

Andrei, T., Matei, A., & Oancea, B. (2009a). Simultaneous equations models used in the study of some issues related to the corruption and performance of services in the public health system. *Theoretical and Applied Economies, XVI*, 1(530), 3–18, Available at SSRN: http://ssrn.com/abstract=1 333 528

Andrei, T., Teodorescu, D., Bourbonnais, R., & Oancea, B. (2009b). A simultaneous equations model for estimating corruption in higher education. *Acta Oeconomica, 59*(4), 411–439. http://www.jstor.org/stable/40729920

Bai, C.-E., & Wei, S.-J. (2001). *The quality of bureaucracy and capital account policies. Policy* (Research Working paper). World Bank e library. https://doi.org/10.1596/1813-9450-2575

Baluch, A., & Ariff, M. (2007). Derivative markets and economic growth: Is there a relationship? Bond University. *Globalisation and Development Centre*, Working Paper Series No. 13, Gold Coast, Australia.

Beck, T., Demirgüç-Kunt, A., & Levine, R. (2007). Finance, inequality and the poor. *Journal of Economic Growth, Springer, 12*(1), 27–49.

Berger, A. N., Clarke, G. R., Cull, R., Klapper, L., & Udell, G. F. (2005). Corporate governance and bank performance: A joint analysis of the static, selection, and dynamic effects of domestic, foreign, and state ownership. *Journal of Banking and Finance, 29*(8–9), 2179–2221.

Bernanke, B. S. (2018). *The real effects of the financial crisis*. Manuscript, Brookings Institution; presented at the Fall 2018 Conference for the Brookings Papers on Economic Activity.

Bernanke, B. S., & Blinder, A. S. (1988). Credit, money, and aggregate demand. *American Economic Review, 78*, 435–439.

Bernanke, B., & Gertler, M. (1995). Inside the black box: The credit channel of monetary policy transmission. *Journal of Economic Perspective, 9*(4), 27–48.

Bhattacharya, T., Das, S., & Basu, R. (2023). Financial Innovation and bank performance: An empirical analysis of commercial banks. *International Journal of Business Innovation and Research (IJBIR), 31*(4). https://doi.org/10.1504/IJBIR.2023.134141

Bratta, B., Livio, R., Paolo, A., & Francesca, M. (2022). Assessing the impact of digital technology diffusion policies. Evidence from Italy. *Economics of Innovation and New Technology*. https://doi.org/10.1080/10438599.2022.2075357

Bruhn, M., & Love, I. (2014). The real impact of improved access to finance: Evidence from Mexico. *Journal of Finance, 69*, 1347–1376. https://doi.org/10.1111/jofi.12091

Buzzacchi, L., Colombo, M. G., & Mariotti, S. (1995). Technological regimes and innovation in services: The case of the Italian banking industry. *Research Policy, 24*(1), 151–168. https://www.researchgate.net/publication/303574664_Interaction_effect_between_product_and_process_innovation_The_case_of_Tunisian_banks [accessed Aug 22 2022].

Cadoret-David, I., Martin, F., Herrard, N., Tanguy, S., & Benjamin, C. (2004). Econométrieappliquée.

Cecchetti, S. G., & Schoenholtz, K. L. (2015). *Money, banking, and financial markets* (4th ed.). McGraw-Hill Education.

Chatterjee, A. (2020). Financial inclusion, information and communication technology diffusion, and economic growth: A panel data analysis. *Information Technology for Development*. https://doi.org/10.1080/02681102.2020.1734770

Chatterjee, A., & Das, S. (2021). Information communication technology diffusion and financial inclusion: An inter-state analysis for India. *Innovation and Development, 11*(1), 1–23.

Cull, R., Demirgüç-Kunt, A., & Morduch, J. (2014). Banks and Microbanks. *Journal of Financial Services, 46*, 1–53. https://doi.org/10.1007/s10693-013-0177-z

Damanpour, F., & Gopalakrishnan, S. (2001). The dynamics of the adoption of product and process innovations in organizations. *Journal of Management Studies, 38*, 45–65. https://doi.org/10.1111/1467-6486.00227

Dan, A. (2013). Toward a supply-side theory of financial innovation. *Journal of Comparative Economics, 41*(2).

Demirguc-Kunt A., Klapper, L., Singer, D., Ansar, S., & Hess, J. (2018). *The Global Findex Database 2017: Measuring Financial Inclusion and the Fintech Revolution*. World Bank. https://doi.org/10.1596/978-1-4648-1259-0

Deutsche Borse Group report. (2008, April). *The global derivative market: An introduction*. Deutsche Börse AG.

Frame, S. W., & White, L. J. (2004). Empirical studies of financial innovation: Lots of talk, little action? *Journal of Economic Literature, American Economic Association (AWAweb), 42*(1), 116–144.

Friedman, M., & Schwartz, A. (1963). *A monetary history of the United States, 1867–1960*. Princeton University Press.

Giudici, P. (2018). Fintech risk management: A research challenge for artificial intelligence in finance. *Frontiers in Artificial. Intelligence, 1*, 1.

Greenhalgh, C., & Rogers, M. (2010). *Innovation, intellectual property, and economic growth*. Princeton University Press.

Greenwood, J., & Jovanovic, B. (1990). Financial development, growth and distribution of income. *Journal of Political Economy, 98*, 1076–1107.

Haftu, G. G. (2019). Information communications technology and economic growth in Sub-Saharan Africa: A panel data approach. *Telecommunications Policy, 43*(1), 88–99.

Haq, Mahbub. Ul. (1996). *Reflections on human development*. Oxford University Press. 288 pages. ISBN 0-19-510193-6.

Hassan, M. K. (2005). *FDI, information technology and economic growth in the MENA region* (10th ERF paper).

Iman, N. (2014). Innovation in financial services: A tale from e-banking development in Indonesia. *International Journal of Business Innovation and Research, Inderscience Enterprises Ltd., 8*(5), 498–522.

Ishida, J. (2015). Hierarchies versus committees: Communication and information acquisition in organizations. *The Japanese Economic Review, 66*(1), 62–88.

Jbili, A., Enders, K., & Trichel, V. (1997). *Financial reforms in Algeria, Moroccop and Tunisia: A preliminary assessment* (International Monetary Fund Working Paper).

Jord'a, O., Schularick, M., & Taylor, A. M. (2013). When credit bites back. *Journal of Money, Credit and Banking, 45*(s2), 3–28.

Jord'a, O., Schularick, M., & Taylor, A. M. (2016). Macro financial history and the new business cycle facts. *NBER Macroeconomics Annual, 31*(1), 213–263.

Kaufmann, D., & Kraay, A. (2002). *Growth without governance* (Policy Research Working Paper Series 2928). The World Bank.

Laeven, L., Levine, R., & Michalopoulos, S. (2015). Financial innovation and endogenous growth. *Journal of Financial Intermediation, Elsevier, 24*(1), 1–24.

Laryea, E. T. (1999). The technological challenges facing developing countries in the move to paperless international trade. *Bond Law Review, 11*(2), 274–286.

Lazový, J., & Sipko, J. (2014). Impact of financial derivatives on the real economy. *International Journal of Management Excellence, 4*(1).

Lee, J. W., & Brahmasrene, T. (2014). ICT, CO2 emissions and economic growth: Evidence from a panel of ASEAN. *Global Economic Review: Perspectives on East Asian Economies and Industries, 432*, 93–109.

Lerner, J., & Tufano, P. (2011). The consequences of financial innovation: A counterfactual research agenda. *Annual Review of Financial Economics, 3*(1), 41–85.

Levine, R. (2005). Finance and growth: Theory and evidence. In P. Aghion & S. Durlauf (Ed.), *Handbook of economic growth* (edition 1, vol. 1, chapter 12, pp. 865–934). Elsevier.

Llewellyn, D. T. (2009). Financial innovation and the economics of banking and the financial system. In L. Anderloni, D. T. Llewellyn, & R. H. Schmidt (Eds.), *Financial innovation in retail and corporate banking*. Edward Elgar.

Majeed, M. T., & Ayub, T. (2018). Information and Communication Technology (ICT) and Economic Growth Nexus: A comparative global analysis. *Pakistan Journal of Commerce and Social Sciences, 12*(2), 443–476.

Manual, O. (2005). *The measurement of scientific and technological activities: Proposed guideliness for collecting and interpreting technological innovation data (Oslo Manual)*. Organisation for Economic Co-operation and Development.

Merton, R. C. & Bodie. (1995). A conceptual framework for analyzing the financial environment. Chap. 1 in *The Global Financial System: A Functional Perspective*, by D. B. Crane, K. A. Froot, Scott P. Mason, André Perold, R. C.

Merton, Z. Bodie, E. R. Sirri, and P. Tufano, 3–31. Harvard Business School Press.

Michalopoulos, S., Leaven, L., Levine, R. (2009). Financial innovation and endogenous growth. *National Bureau of Economic Research*, Working Paper 15356, Cambridge, September, pp. 1–33.

MOL, Mitsui O.S.K. Lines, Ltd: Financial Highlights (Fiscal Year, 2014 Ended March 31, 2015).

Mugo & Kilonzo. (2017). *Community level impacts of financial inclusion in Kenya with particular focus on poverty eradication and employment creation.* Central Bank of Kenya.

Nasab, E., & Aghaei, M. (2009). The effect of ICT on economic growth: Further evidence. *International Bulletin of Business Administration, 10*, 5.

Niebel, T. (2018). ICT and economic growth–Comparing developing, emerging and developed countries. *World Development, 104*(C), 197–211.

Oyelami, L. O., Adebiyi, S. O., & Adekunle, B. S. (2020). Electronic payment adoption and consumers' spending growth: Empirical evidence from Nigeria. *Future Business Journal, 6*, 1–14.

Ozili, P. K. (2018). Impact of digital finance on financial inclusion and stability. *BorsaIstanbul Review, 18*, 329–340.

Pagano, M., & Pica, G. (2012). Finance and employment. *Economic Policy, 27*(69), 5–55. https://EconPapers.repec.org/RePEc:oup:ecpoli:v:27:y:2012:i:69:p:5-55

Pain, D. (2011). *Product innovation in non-life insurance markets: Where little "i" meets big "I". Sigma No. 4.* Swiss Reinsurance Company.

Partnoy, F. (2001). The shifting contours of global derivatives regulation. University of Pennsylvania. *Journal of International Economic Law.*

Prabha, A., Savard, K., & Wickramarachi, H. (2014). *Deriving the economic impact of derivatives, growth through risk management* (Working paper). Milken Institute.

Pradhan, R. P., Arvin, M. B., Norman, N. R., & Bele, S. K. (2014). Economic growth and the development of telecommunications infrastructure in the G-20 countries: A panel-VAR approach. *Telecommunications Policy, 38*(7), 634–649.

Pradhan, R. P., Arvin, M. B., & Norman, B. M. (2015). The dynamics of information and communications technologies infrastructure, economic growth, and financial development: Evidence from Asian countries. *Technology in Society (Elsevier), 42*(42), 135–149.

Pradhan, R. P., Arvin, M. B., Hall, J. H., & Bennett, S. E. 2018a. Mobile telephony, economic growth, financial development, foreign direct investment, and imports of ICT goods: The case of the G-20 countries. *Economia e PoliticaIndustriale: Journal of Industrial and Business Economics*, Springer; Associazione Amici di Economia e PoliticaIndustriale, *45*(2), 279–310.

Pradhan, R. P., Arvin, M. B., Nair, M., Mittal, J., & Norman, N. R. (2017b). Telecommunications infrastructure and usage and the FDI–growth nexus: Evidence from Asian-21 countries. *Information Technology for Development, 23*(2), 235–260. https://doi.org/10.1080/02681102.2016.1217822 (Accessed on 23 January 2021).

Pradhan, R. P., Mallik, G., & Bagchi, T. P. (2018b). Information communication technology (ICT) infrastructure and economic growth: A causality evinced by cross-country panel data. *Indian Institute of Management Bangalore (IIMB) Management Review*, (30), 91–103.

Pradhan, R., Arvin, M., Nair, M., Bennett, S., & Bahmani, S. (2017a). ICT-finance-growth nexus: Empirical evidence from the next-11 countries. *Cuadernos de Economía, 40*, 115–134.

Pradhan, R., Mallik, G., & Bagchi, T. P. (2018). Information communication technology (ICT) infrastructure and economic growth: A causality evinced by cross-country panel data. *IIMB Management Review, 30*(1): 91–103, ISSN 0970-3896, https://doi.org/10.1016/j.iimb.2018.01.001

Re, S. (2015). *Global insurance review 2015 and outlook 2016/17*. Economic Research and Consulting, November 2015. *Website of Global Data Insurance*.

Rohman, I. K., & Bohlin, E. (2014). Decomposition analysis of the telecommunications sector in Indonesia: What does the cellular era shed light on? *Telecommunications Policy, 38*(3), 248–263.

Sarma, M., & Pais, J. (2011). Financial inclusion and development. *Journal of International Development, 23*, 613–628.

Sassia, S., & Goaied, M. (2012). Financial development, ICT diffusion and economic growth: Lessons from MENA region. *Telecommunications Policy, 37*(2013), 252–261.

Sepehrdoust, H. (2018). Impact of information and communication technology and financial development on economic growth of OPEC developing economies. *Kasetsart Journal of Social Sciences*. https://doi.org/10.1016/j.kjss.2018.01.008

Shahiduzzaman, M., & Alam, K. (2014). The long-run impact of information and communication technology on economic output: The case of Australia. *Telecommunications Policy, 38*(7), 623–633.

Shleifer & Summers. (1988). Breach of Trust in hostile takeovers. In A. Auerbach (Ed.), *Corporate takeovers: Causes and consequences* (pp. 33–56). University of Chicago Press.

Statista. Digital Payments Report 2020. Available online: https://www.statista.com/study/41122/fintech-report digital payments/ (accessed on 1 January, 2022).

Steiger, J. H. (1979). Factor indeterminacy in the 1930s and the 1970s: Some interesting parallels. *Psychometrika, 44*, 157–167.

Stiglitz, J. (1993). Short-term contracts as a monitoring device. *NBER: National Bureau of Economic Research*. Retrieved from https://policycommons.net/artifacts/1381638/short-term-contracts-as-a-monitoring-device/1995902/ on 10 Aug 2022. CID: 20.500.12592/dzfgch.

Taghizadeh-Hesary, F., Phi, N. T. M., Hong, H. H. T., & Chu, V. T. (2019). Does financial integration matter for financial development? Evidence from the East Asian and Pacific Region. *Journal of Economic Integration, 34*(4), 591–618. https://www.jstor.org/stable/26820388

Vu, K. M. (2011). ICT as a source of economic growth in the information age: Empirical evidence from the 1996–2005 period. *Telecommunications Policy, 35*(4), 357–372.

World Trade Organisation. (2008). *World Trade report: Trade in globalizing world.*

World Bank. (2019a). *World development indicators*. World Bank Publications. Retrieved from https://data.worldbank.org/datacatalog/world-development-indicators

World Bank. (2019b). *World governance indicators*. World Bank Publications. Retrieved from http://info.worldbank.org/governance/wgi/#home

World Bank. (2012). *The annual report*. World Bank.

World Development Report, 2014.

Ya, B., Xinghui, Y., & Li, H. (2022). The nonlinear impact of FinTech on the real economic growth: Evidence from China. *Economics of Innovation and New Technology*. https://doi.org/10.1080/10438599.2022.2095512

Yorulmazer, T. (2013). *Has financial innovation made the world riskier? CDS, regulatory arbitrage and systemic risk*. Available at SSRN: https://ssrn.com/abstract=2176493 or https://doi.org/10.2139/ssrn.2176493 (Accessed on 14 February 2021).

Zellner, A., & Theil, H. (1962). Three-stage least squares: simultaneous estimation of simultaneous equations. *Econometrica, 30*(1), 54–78. https://doi.org/10.2307/1911287

Zulfiqar, K., Chaudhary, M. A., & Aslam, A. (2016). Financial inclusion and its implications for inclusive growth in Pakistan. *Pakistan Economic and Social Review, 54*(2), 297–325. https://www.jstor.org/stable/26616711

PART II

Inclusive Policies and Frameworks for Viksit Bharat

CHAPTER 4

Financial Inclusion for Viksit Bharat: Sustained Literacy, Trust, and Access for All

C. S. Mohapatra and Depannita Ghosh

1 Introduction

1.1 Rethinking Financial Inclusion for Viksit Bharat

The vision of Viksit Bharat@2047, India's aspiration to become a developed nation by its centenary, places financial inclusion at its very core. Financial inclusion is widely recognized as a "key enabler to reducing poverty and boosting prosperity" (World Bank, 2021). For India, the world's largest democracy, this imperative is not merely economic but a profound social commitment. The Economic Survey (2024) observes that, "the government has achieved significant progress in financial inclusion, with the Financial Inclusion Index of the Reserve Bank of India (RBI) increasing from 53.9 in March 2021 to 64.2 at the end of March 2024." Yet, as India's financial landscape becomes more digital and

C. S. Mohapatra (✉) · D. Ghosh
National Council of Applied Economic Research (NCAER), New Delhi, India
e-mail: csmohapatra@ncaer.org

D. Ghosh
e-mail: dghosh@ncaer.org

© The Author(s), under exclusive license to Springer Nature Singapore Pte Ltd. 2026

V. Dixit et al. (eds.), *Financial Inclusion for Viksit Bharat*,
https://doi.org/10.1007/978-981-92-0807-4_4

complex, the challenge is to ensure that every citizen enjoys not just access, but also sustained literacy, trust, and universal access of financial services.

India has indeed made remarkable progress. The Pradhan Mantri Jan Dhan Yojana (PMJDY) has resulted in over 54.58 crore bank accounts, while the Unified Payments Interface (UPI) processed more than Rs. 199.9 lakh crore in FY 2023–24. Yet, inclusion gaps persist rooted in gender, geography, disability, literacy, and digital access. For the vision of Viksit Bharat to materialize, financial inclusion needs to evolve into a rights-based, technology driven, and lifetime framework. As India approaches its centenary of independence in 2047, the aspiration for a "Viksit Bharat"—a developed, equitable, and digitally empowered nation—demands a fundamental rethinking of financial inclusion. No longer can success be measured solely by number of bank accounts or mobile wallets. True inclusion requires to encompass effective usage, institutional trust, sustained financial literacy, digital security, and adaptive outreach. Financial systems must serve not just channels for savings and credit but as enablers of human dignity, agency, and participation, particularly for the historically excluded population.

This chapter proposes a multidimensional model for long-term financial inclusion—combining sustained financial literacy, institutional trust, and universal access, with a focus on marginalized groups. Drawing from Indian and global evidence, it offers actionable insights and policy blueprints aligned with equity and resilience.

1.2 Reframing Financial Inclusion for the 2047 Vision

The roots of financial exclusion in India runs deep. Post-independence, the financial sector was largely urban-centric to start with. Nationalization of banks in 1969 was a pivotal moment, compelling commercial banks to extend their reach to rural areas and prioritize agricultural lending. The creation of Regional Rural Banks (RRBs) and cooperative banks in the 1970s and 1980s further advanced this agenda. As the Economic Survey (2024) highlights, "Rural Financial Institutions (RFIs) have been an important player in facilitating India's financial inclusion journey." The 1990s and 2000s witnessed the rise of microfinance institutions (MFIs) and the Self-Help Group (SHG) movement. By 2024, over 12 million SHGs had been formed, with 88% of them comprising women, collectively managing savings worth over Rs. 47,000 crore and accessing Rs.

1.2 lakh crore in credit annually (NABARD, 2024). This movement democratized access to finance and empowered women and marginalized communities.

In the past two decades, India's financial inclusion narrative has been dominated by measurable milestones—bank accounts opened, ATMs installed, and mobile wallet registrations recorded. PMJDY, launched in 2014, was a watershed moment. By January 2025, PMJDY had enabled the opening of over 54.58 crore accounts, with cumulative deposits exceeding Rs. 2.46 lakh crore. Notably, 68% of Mudra loans have benefited women and 50% have gone to SC/ST/OBC categories, reflecting a deliberate focus on equity (SIDBI, 2024). As the Government notes, "the motto, 'From Jan Dhan to Jan Suraksha,' encapsulates the vision of financial security and inclusive growth for all." The Atal Pension Yojana (APY) has seen impressive growth, reaching 7.33 crore by January 2025, with more than 89.95 lakh new participants in FY 2024–25. The Pradhan Mantri Jeevan Jyoti Bima Yojana (PMJJBY) and Pradhan Mantri Suraksha Bima Yojana (PMSBY) have enrolled 22.52 crore and 49.12 crore individuals respectively, disbursing over Rs.20,000 crore in claims. These initiatives are instrumental in promoting financial empowerment and inclusive growth. The Pradhan Mantri Mudra Yojana (PMMY) has sanctioned Rs. 32.36 lakh crore for 51.41 crore loans, focusing on women and marginalized groups. The Stand-Up India Scheme has sanctioned Rs. 53,609 crore for 2.36 lakh entrepreneurs, particularly SC/ST and women. The Union Budget 2025 introduced "customised credit cards with a limit of INR 0.5 million for micro enterprises registered on the Udyam portal, with plans to issue one million such cards in the first year." (PIB, 2025). Rural Financial Institutions (RFIs), including Regional Rural Banks (RRBs) and cooperative banks, are essential in bridging the urban–rural divide. As of March 2024, RRBs reported a consolidated net profit of Rs. 7,571 crore, with a credit-to-deposit ratio of 71.2%. Rural Financial Institutions also show lower NPAs and better credit off-take (PIB, 2025).

India's digital revolution has further transformed its financial landscape. The UPI processed over 13,116 crore transactions worth Rs. 199.9 lakh crore in FY 2023–24 (NPCI, 2024). Aadhaar-enabled Payment System (AePS) and mobile wallets have democratized access, even for those without smartphones. Fintech startups have introduced micro-savings, micro-insurance, and digital lending tailored to low-income and informal sector workers. Digital KYC, e-signatures, and paperless onboarding have reduced barriers, while AI-driven credit scoring models have expanded credit access for "thin-file" customers (Startup India, 2024).

The KCC scheme has provided timely and affordable credit to farmers. By FY 2023–24, over 7.92 crore active KCC accounts had been opened, with credit disbursements increasing from Rs. 8.45 lakh crore in FY 2014–15 to Rs. 24.30 lakh crore in FY 2023–24 (Ministry of Agriculture and Farmers Welfare, 2024). However, small holder and marginalized farmers continue to face documentation and awareness challenges. The State Bank of India's "Digital Village" initiative has trained over 1.2 million villagers in digital banking (State Bank of India, 2024). Fintech startups like PayNearby have deployed micro-ATMs and literacy kiosks in urban slums, offering IVR tutorials in 22 languages (PayNearby, 2024). Inclusive design is critical for Persons with Disabilities (PwDs). While some banks have adopted assistive features like sign language videos, audio modules, tactile materials, adoption remains limited (Centre for Internet and Society, 2023).

However, these advances do not necessarily equate to meaningful universal financial inclusion. Access alone does not ensure empowerment. Mere presence of financial instruments does not guarantee usage, comprehension, or trust. In fact, inclusion that stops at access can mark deeper exclusions—what can be termed "exclusion in disguise." Individuals may hold a bank account yet remain financially disengaged due to fear, lack of understanding, systemic discrimination, or practical barriers to utilization. This paradox is reflected in the Reserve Bank of India's Financial Inclusion Index (FI-Index) which rose from 53.9 in March 2021 to 64.2 by March 2024. As the Economic Survey (2024) cautions, "while these developments herald a new era for the financial sector, they also introduce potential risks from a regulatory standpoint." The rise in consumer debt, expansion of unsecured lending, and growing number of young investors highlight the need for balance between growth and stability.

Despite near-universal account penetration, usage gaps persist. Approximately 42% of female account owners were found to have inactive accounts compared to 30% among men. Men hold 50% more bank accounts than women" as per Data for India (2025). Even in developed states like Gujarat and Maharashtra, the share of women with a bank account lags behind men. While this upward trend signifies commendable institutional efforts, disaggregated metrics reveal worrying gaps. Many beneficiaries of Government welfare continue to withdraw transfers in full upon receipt reflecting financial insecurity and limited saving capacity. The World Bank's Global Findex Database (2021) reports that "account ownership has more than doubled in the past decade, rising from 35% in 2011 to 78% in 2021." Yet, the challenge of account dormancy and gender gaps remains pressing issues which is observed in other regions like sub-Saharan Africa, wherein 57% of adults have accounts, but only 36% use them actively (World Bank, 2021). Kenya's M-Pesa, often cited as a model, has achieved near-universal usage but still faces challenges in reaching women and rural populations.

The financial ecosystem of the twenty-first century is fundamentally different from that of previous generations. It is increasingly digital, data-driven, and governed by complex algorithms. From microloans to pensions, from mobile wallets to cryptocurrency, financial decisions today often depend on digital platforms, AI-powered systems, and predictive analytics. While this evolution holds immense promise in terms of scalability and cost-efficiency, it also introduces a host of risks—technological exclusion, privacy breaches, algorithmic bias, and consumer disempowerment.

2 Challenges and Dimensions of Exclusion in the Digital Age

2.1 Multidimensional Vulnerabilities: Gender, Disability, Geography, Digital Divide

India's financial system, though rapidly expanding, remains unevenly accessible to many of its most vulnerable citizens. The reality of financial exclusion is not monolithic; it is layered and intersectional—shaped by gender, disability, caste, religion, geography, and literacy levels. These dimensions of vulnerability compound each other creating significant barriers to full participation in the economy.

2.1.1 Gendered Constraints

While PMJDY has ensured over 24 crore women have bank accounts, studies show that less than half of these accounts are actively used, especially in rural areas. Women often lack control over their accounts, have limited mobility, or face social norms that discourage engagement with banks or digital platforms.

The gender gap in financial literacy mirrors broader social inequalities. Female account owners have more inactive accounts, as compared to that of men. "Indian men hold 50% more bank accounts than women". Only 48% of rural women actively use formal financial services, compared to 72% of men (World Bank, 2023). The barriers include lack of documentation, limited digital access and social norms. Moreover, women's access to formal credit remains constrained by lack of collateral due to male-dominated property regimes, informal sector employment without documentation or lack of tailored products that reflect women's income patterns. Solutions include gender-sensitive credit scoring, joint liability models, and women-led SHGs acting as both users and facilitators. Empowering women as financial literacy ambassadors has also proven effective in increasing trust and uptake.

2.1.2 Disability and Design Exclusion

PwDs, constituting 2.2% of India's population, face compounded challenges from inaccessible banking infrastructure and a lack of tailored educational resources (NSO, 2018). Only 12% of public banks offer braille-enabled ATMs or sign language support (Centre for Internet and Society, 2023). The systemic barriers include inaccessible ATMs and bank branches, apps incompatible with screen-readers and lack of sign language, braille, or audio-visual materials. (Box 1).

Despite mandates under the Rights of Persons with Disabilities Act (2016), only 12% of public sector bank branches offer assistive technologies. Solutions include audio modules, tactile cards, voice navigation, inclusive training, financial literacy material in Indian Sign Language (ISL) and Easy-to-Read (E2R) formats etc.

2.1.3 Geographic Exclusion and Infrastructure Gaps

Rural India, home to nearly 65% of the population, continues to face patchy digital infrastructure, unreliable internet, and device scarcity. While over 80% of households have at least one bank account, only 34% digital modes for transactions (Ministry of Rural Development, 2024) primarily due to fear of fraud lack of nearby grievance redress options or absence of digital training in local languages. Tribal communities and remote regions like the Northeast face even greater challenges including distance from branch networks and language mismatches.

2.1.4 *The Digital Divide*

India's digital revolution has outpaced its financial literacy revolution. However, only 34% of rural residents use digital wallets, compared to 78% in urban areas (The Economic Times, 2024). Women, older adults, and PwDs face additional barriers of device affordability, connectivity, and digital literacy. Rapid digital financial services expansion without parallel user education—has led to a new form of exclusion, functional incapability. This is especially worrisome as more and more welfare benefits, loans, and subsidies are disbursed through digital channels. Populations lacking smartphones or stable internet, awareness of fraud prevention and sound knowledge of available redress mechanisms, all these are increasing their vulnerability to scams, over-indebtedness, and misinformation which are interconnected and reinforcing.

Global best practices offer valuable lessons in this regard. Kenya's M-Pesa and Bangladesh's bKash provide scalable, inclusive models. M-Pesa, launched in 2007, serves over 90% of Kenyan adults and handles transactions equivalent to 50% of the nation's GDP. Bangladesh's bKash, with 70 million users, has seen 40% of new users being women due to targeted literacy drives and rural agent networks. Brazil's National Strategy for Financial Education (ENEF) demonstrates integrated policy can incorporate financial literacy into school curricula and adult education. ENEF's multi-stakeholder approach—engaging government, regulators, and civil society—has significantly enhanced financial capability and reduced account dormancy.

India's UPI, praised for its open architecture and interoperability, is emerging as a global model of digital financial inclusion. India can draw on global best practices to ensure its digital financial architecture is supported by robust, inclusive, and context-sensitive education and outreach frameworks that leave no one behind. Inclusion policies need to move from a one-size-fits-all model to differentiated, context-sensitive strategies.

2.2 *Institutional Framework, Trust and Grievance Redress Mechanisms*

2.2.1 *Institutional Framework*

India's financial sector features a diverse array of regulatory institutions, each with distinct mandates and jurisdictions. The Reserve Bank of India (RBI), Securities and Exchange Board of India (SEBI), Insurance Regulatory and Development Authority of India (IRDAI), Pension Fund Regulatory and Development Authority (PFRDA), and Investor Education and Protection Fund Authority (IEPFA) play significant roles in promoting financial inclusion. Financial sector Market Infrastructure Institutions (MIIs) such as stock exchanges, depositories, financial intermediaries and corporate sector associations etc. also play their part in building financial awareness. However, fragmented oversight can result in duplicated efforts, inconsistent outreach strategies, and missed opportunities for collective impact. A coordinated, harmonized, and user-centric governance framework is essential for financial inclusion in the context of Viksit Bharat.

Each regulator has, over the past decade, made meaningful strides in expanding financial access and awareness. RBI's Financial Literacy Centres (FLCs), for example, have helped disseminate financial education through structured modules, particularly in rural districts. SEBI has focused on investor awareness and grievance redress, while IRDAI has promoted insurance literacy through the Insurance Awareness Campaign. PFRDA has made notable progress in onboarding informal sector workers to pension products like the Atal Pension Yojana. The IEPFA, under the Ministry of Corporate Affairs, has been pivotal in driving fraud awareness and promoting safe financial behavior through mass outreach initiatives. While India's regulatory ecosystem has individually achieved commendable progress, its true potential for transformative inclusion lies in coming together to deliver unified, inclusive, and participatory financial education and protection systems. The goal is not merely harmonization for efficiency but synergy for equity.

2.2.2 Trust

India recorded 1.39 million cyberattacks in 2022, with phishing and identity theft on the rise (Business Standard, 2023). Vulnerable populations are particularly at risk due to low digital literacy. "The rapid adoption of digital payments has heightened exposure to cyber fraud" (Economic Survey, 2024). Strengthening cybersecurity awareness and providing accessible reporting channels hence, are essential. Ministry of Electronics and Information Technology (MeitY), Government of India has taken a number of legal, technical and administrative policy measures for addressing cyber security challenges. This includes National Cyber Security Policy (2013), Guidelines on Information Security Practices for

Government Entities (2023), enactment of Information Technology (IT) Act, 2000 and setting-up of Indian Computer Emergency Response Team (CERT-In) for 24 × 7 cyber incident response under the IT Act, 2000, Cyber Security R&D and Capacity Building in Cyber Security. Recognizing the criticality of cyber security for safeguarding the integrity and stability of the financial sector, Union Budget 2017–18 had announced for setting up a dedicated Indian Computer Emergency Response Team for Financial Sector (Cert-Fin). Subsequently, Computer Security Incident Response Team- Finance (CSIRT-Fin) was set up under CERT-In as the incident response force which focuses on mitigation processes, providing on-site awareness, expertise, and recovery oversight for the financial sector and has been assigned the responsibility for coordinating and supporting the response to a computer security event or incident within the financial sector constituency (MeITY, 2025).

At the heart of sustained financial inclusion lies an intangible yet indispensable asset of trust. Trust in financial institutions, fairness of systems, and reliability of grievance redress channels determines whether individuals simply open accounts or actively engage with the formal financial sector over time. For historically excluded populations including women, persons with disabilities, and rural communities—trust is built not solely through infrastructure but through responsive systems, respectful service delivery, and effective consumer protection. The journey toward trust begins with transparency. Many first-time users, particularly from low-literacy or marginalized backgrounds, struggle to comprehend terms and conditions of loans, insurance, or investments. Complex documentation, opaque charges, and sudden penalties can create a perception of risk and suspicion. Beneficiaries have reported signing documents without full comprehension, often coerced or misled by intermediaries. Such experiences erode faith in the system and increase dependence on informal lenders, despite the higher costs or difficult terms they impose.

To counter the erosion of trust, India's financial institutions should prioritize linguistically inclusive and culturally sensitive communication. Product information, rights, and redressal mechanisms are required to be available in multiple languages, simplified and accessible modes including audio-visual materials and sign language. Central to building and sustaining trust is the presence of robust accessible grievance redress systems. RBI has taken a series of steps for promoting financial inclusion through its Financial Literacy Centres and has been quite active in developing awareness and taking protection measures for early detection and prevention of frauds and scams. SEBI Complaint Redress System (SCORES) platform is a notable example of institutional effort to improve investor redressal (SEBI, 2023). Its upgraded version, SCORES 2.0, introduced in 2024, offers several user-friendly features such as shortened complaint resolution timelines, automated routing of complaints, and integration with the KYC Registration Agency database (SEBI, 2024). This represents a significant step toward improving user experience and accountability in the securities market. The Investor Education and Protection Fund Authority (IEPFA) has played a vital role in safeguarding users, particularly those vulnerable to financial fraud through its awareness programs. Through partnerships with financial institutions, academic institutions, private banks and fintech platforms, IEPFA has deployed outreach campaigns, digital content, and fraud alerts across digital and physical channels. IRDAI and PFRDA also have their grievance redressal systems in place and strive to attend to grievances expeditiously as also promote awareness in the related fields of insurance and pensions sector respectively. These initiatives not only enhance awareness and demystify the complex landscape of financial grievance processes.

The long-term vision for financial inclusion ought to, therefore, rest on the dual pillars of transparent service delivery and effective consumer protection. Trust is not incidental—it is the outcome of systems that are just, responsive, and rooted in the lived realities of users.

2.2.3 Grievance Redressal

Access to redress remains limited for many. Rural residents, urban slum dwellers, and persons with disabilities often lack digital access, procedural knowledge, or confidence to file complaints. Banking staff may also lack the training to assist users in navigating grievance channels, particularly when dealing with cyber fraud or digital errors. To address this gap, it is imperative that grievance redress platforms be integrated with accessible technologies including voice-command interfaces, regional language support, and screen reader compatibility. Establishing physical grievance kiosks at the district or block levels staffed by trained facilitators can help users log and track their complaints. The proposed Financial Redress Agency (FRA), a unified redress mechanism suggested by the Financial Sector Legislative Reforms Commission (FSLRC) is a good idea to work upon in this area of consumer protection (FSLRC Report, 2013). In this era of rapid digitalization, where scams and frauds are rising at an alarming rate, a unified grievance redress mechanism is the need of the hour. Such a system would allow complaints lodged in one sector to be seamlessly referred to the appropriate authority, minimizing the burden on users and a wholistic monitoring can help detect problem areas for better and efficient delivery across the entire financial sector.

Box 1: Case Study: Banking with Eyes Closed, but Vision Intact

Dr. Vikas Dixit, a highly educated economist and Associate Professor at a leading Indian university. With a Ph.D. from a reputed University and a deep understanding of economic systems, Dr. Dixit should, in theory, have no trouble navigating India's financial ecosystem. But there's one factor that continues to shadow his journey: his visual impairment.

From his student days in Aligarh to his current professional life in Kolkata, Dr. Dixit's attempts to access basic banking services have often been fraught with indignity and inefficiency. In one instance, while trying to open a bank account, he was asked to bring two witnesses from the same branch—a discriminatory hurdle rarely applied to others. Once, a bank even insisted he open a joint account with a family member. Another time, a teller loudly announced the cash handed over to him, asking someone else in the queue to verify it—undermining his independence and privacy.

Despite these challenges, Dr. Dixit did not relent. He embraced digital banking as a lifeline. With tools like JAWS screen reader on his computer and TalkBack on his Android phone, he began independently using internet banking and UPI apps like Google Pay and WhatsApp Pay. But even in the digital world, accessibility isn't guaranteed. Some buttons are visually rendered without labels, and QR code scanners don't guide the user on camera positioning. Worse, swipe machines in stores remain inaccessible, with no tactile feedback or screen-reader support, exposing his PIN entry to onlookers. Security, surprisingly, has never been an issue. But lack of accessible financial literacy has. While he has managed to stay informed through self-research, watching CNBC Awaaz, and reading official websites, Dr. Dixit notes that structured financial literacy programs for visually impaired people are rare or non-existent.

When asked about government initiatives, he refers to a scheme under the National Divyangjan Finance and Development Corporation, but also laments the poor outreach and lack of awareness among bank staff.

His suggestions are clear, practical, and urgent: make accessibility audits mandatory for bank apps and branches, train staff to understand the needs of persons with disabilities (PwDs), and embed inclusive education from an early age. He advocates for a world where visually impaired individuals can manage their finances without apologies, assistance, or extra effort—a world where independence is the default, not the exception.

"Digital banking has brought convenience, but we need to ensure it doesn't become yet another space where we're left behind," Dr. Dixit reflects

His story is not one of despair, but of resilience—and it highlights the systemic changes needed to ensure that financial inclusion in India is not just policy-deep, but practice-deep.

The increasing use of AI in financial services requires nuanced understanding of its implications, ensuring its responsible and transparent usage (Mohapatra & Ghosh, 2023). In an increasingly automated financial landscape, algorithms determine eligibility, pricing, and even dispute outcomes. Without transparency and accountability, users may feel alienated or unfairly treated.

3 Building an Inclusive and Empowering Financial Ecosystems

3.1 The Four-Pillar Framework for Functional and Resilient Financial Inclusion

As India positions itself to achieve the vision of Viksit Bharat@2047, inclusion requires to be reconceptualized not only as a matter of access and infrastructure, but as an issue of functional, resilient, and equitable participation in the financial ecosystem. Reframing financial inclusion for the digital age requires probing deeper qualitative questions such as:

- Can the user access financial services confidently and securely? Do they have updated knowledge and expertise to navigate through their financial journey?
- Do they understand their rights and obligations, and the risks and benefits of financial products?
- Do they have mechanisms to seek recourse when something goes wrong?
- Are the services physically, linguistically, and culturally accessible to them?

Inclusion is no longer just about enrollment—it's about capability, confidence, and continuity. This necessitates a paradigm shift—from access to what the authors call as "functional and resilient inclusion." This shift, requires a fundamental reordering of institutional priorities and policy design. Functional inclusion focuses on meaningful engagement while resilient inclusion equips individuals to withstand financial shocks. Figure 1 shows that achieving this transformation involves embedding four key principles into the design and delivery of financial services:

- **Sustained Digital and Financial Literacy:** Education cannot be a one-time awareness campaign. Users need to be equipped with

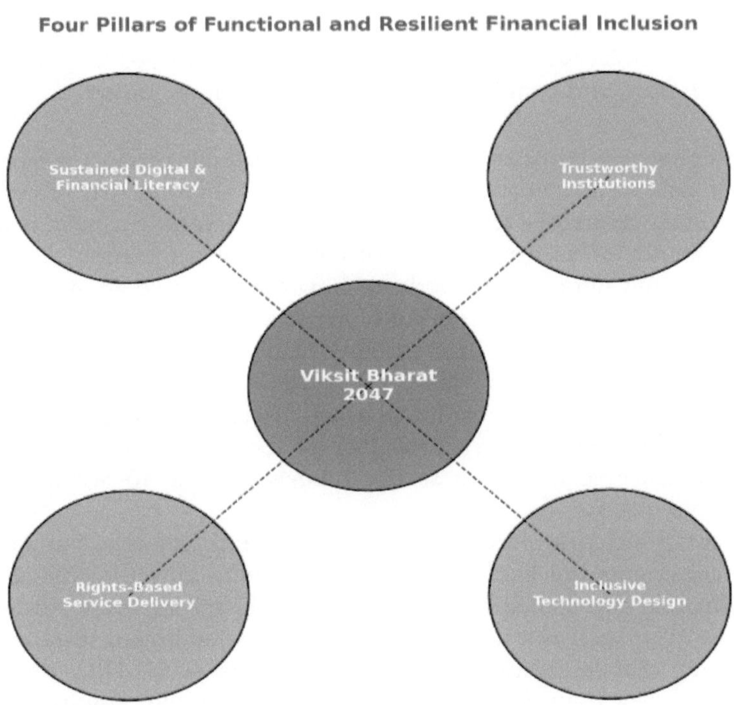

Fig. 1 Four pillars of functional and resilient financial inclusion (*Source* Authors' own)

continuous, context-sensitive learning opportunities that evolve with technological and economic change.

- **Trustworthy Institutions:** Trust is the cornerstone of any financial relationship. This includes not only financial institutions but also intermediaries, agents, and digital platforms which would demonstrate transparency, fairness, and cultural sensitivity.
- **Transparent, Rights-Based Service Delivery for all:** Services need to be designed for all including the vulnerable communities with clarity, simplicity, and accountability. This includes clear communication of terms, simplified grievance redress mechanisms, and legal protections for vulnerable users.
- **Inclusive Technology Design:** Digital financial products may be fully accessible to vulnerable groups such as persons with disabilities, elderly users, linguistic minorities, and people with low literacy levels. Universal design principles need to be embedded into apps, interfaces, and communication materials from the outset.

This proposed framework demands more than just product diversification. It calls for imaginative and inclusive policy-making that recognizes the systemic nature of exclusion. Financial illiteracy, for example, is often the result not of user apathy but of educational deprivation, linguistic mismatch, and information overload. Low credit uptake among women is not a reflection of disinterest but of gendered norms, asset inequalities, and mobility constraints. Inaccessibility of digital platforms to persons with disabilities reflects a failure of institutional empathy rather than technical inevitability. In many rural and tribal areas, digital adoption is stunted by poor infrastructure, lack of local-language support, and the dominance of top-down service models that fail to accommodate community needs.

Financial inclusion needs to be reimagined and redesigned to address these constraints holistically in collaboration with Government, regulators, financial intermediaries, civil society, and the private sector. Inclusion requires to be seen as a normative mission—a commitment to economic citizenship that is inclusive, adaptive, and rights-based. Only then can India's journey toward Viksit Bharat become a journey toward a truly participatory financial democracy.

3.2 The Digital Public Infrastructure

Technology has emerged as the single most transformative force in India's financial inclusion journey. With the expansion of mobile networks, the rollout of Aadhaar-enabled systems, and the explosion of fintech startups, digital innovation has broken several traditional barriers—distance, documentation, and physical infrastructure. However, technology is not neutral. Its benefits depend on who can access it, understand it, and use it safely. In the absence of a careful design and inclusive deployment, technology can also deepen exclusion, especially among rural populations, persons with disabilities, the elderly, and digitally illiterate citizens.

India's digital public infrastructure—known as India Stack—offers a strong foundation for universal financial services. Components such as Aadhaar for biometric identification, the UPI for real-time digital payments, DigiLocker for document storage, and the Account Aggregator framework for consent-based data sharing have transformed financial engagement. These platforms offer remarkable scalability and cost-efficiency.

3.3 Bridging the Digital Divide

Digital adoption is not universal. Many citizens—especially those at the margins—face structural hurdles to participating in this digital transformation. These include poor internet connectivity, unaffordable smartphones, lack of digital literacy, and fear of cyber fraud. UPI 123PAY, launched to enable feature phone transactions without internet is a positive step towards bridging this divide. But its reach and awareness remain limited. Similarly, several financial apps are not compatible with screen readers, and most interfaces do not support vernacular languages or tactile feedback, making them inaccessible to persons with visual, cognitive, or motor impairments.

To address these challenges, technology needs to be guided by the principles of universal design, participatory development, and adaptive learning. Banks and fintech firms ought to prioritize accessibility features in their apps and devices. This includes voice-based navigation, adjustable text size, high-contrast themes, audio instructions, and compatibility with assistive devices. Developers may consult with disability rights groups during the design phase to ensure real-world usability. Government regulations should require that all public-facing financial apps meet minimum accessibility standards, akin to physical accessibility mandates for buildings.

Artificial intelligence (AI) and machine learning (ML) are reshaping financial service delivery. AI-powered chatbots now offer 24 × 7 customer assistance in multiple Indian languages, and ML algorithms are being used to assess creditworthiness based on alternative data—such as mobile usage patterns, transaction behavior, and SMS trails. These innovations are particularly useful for informal workers and micro-entrepreneurs who lack formal documentation but demonstrate strong digital behavior. However, these algorithms are essential to be deployed with caution. Without transparency and accountability, automated systems can reinforce existing biases and deny services unfairly. For example, women entrepreneurs may receive lower credit scores simply because their business-related digital activity appears under-represented. Thus, algorithmic fairness and explainability needs to become central to digital financial governance. Regulators should require periodic audits of AI systems to ensure they do not disproportionately exclude certain groups.

Blockchain technology holds promise for inclusion, particularly in areas like land records, digital identity, and transparent disbursement of welfare funds. States like Telangana have already piloted blockchain-based land titling systems to secure farmer assets and improve credit linkage. In the insurance sector, blockchain-based smart contracts can automate claims processing and reduce disputes, especially in weather-indexed crop insurance. Assistive fintech, thus, represents a new frontier in inclusive technology. Startups such as Trestle Labs, provide real-time audio support for banking documents, SignAble, offers live Indian Sign Language interpreters for digital consultations, have showcased how niche innovations can bridge massive gaps in access. The challenge lies in scaling such models through public–private partnerships and ensuring that they are integrated into mainstream financial service platforms.

While technology holds immense potential to accelerate financial inclusion, it requires to be shaped by ethical, inclusive, and participatory frameworks. Innovation should not be confined to urban fintech hubs but requires to be localized, context-aware, and grounded in the lived realities of India's underserved citizens. Technology is essential to serve as a bridge towards achieving the goal of Viksit Bharat.

3.4 *Financial Literacy as a Lifelong Public Good*

Financial literacy is the foundation of meaningful financial inclusion. The National Centre for Financial Education (NCFE, 2023) reports that only 27% of Indian adults possess basic financial literacy, with particularly low rates among women, rural residents, and marginalized groups. These gaps are not just a result of educational deprivation; they reflect socio-cultural norms, gendered mobility constraints, language mismatches, and institutional biases that make financial systems alien or intimidating. "Financial literacy is not a one-time intervention but a lifelong process," argues the Economic Survey (2024).

Financial literacy stands as both a foundation and a safeguard. It is the bridge between access and empowerment, between possession of a bank account and effective participation in the financial system. Without the ability to understand, evaluate, and confidently use financial products, citizens—especially those from vulnerable backgrounds—remain exposed to exploitation, errors, and exclusion, even when formal financial channels are nominally available to them.

Financial literacy in India has traditionally been approached as a one-time intervention, typically through standalone workshops, awareness campaigns, or printed pamphlets. While such initiatives are welcome, they are inadequate for navigating today's complex, fast-changing financial environment. With the rise of digital platforms, algorithmic lending, mobile apps, and a proliferation of financial products—from buy-now-pay-later (BNPL) schemes to micro-insurance and investment portals—the cognitive demands on users have increased dramatically. As such, financial literacy needs to be reframed as a dynamic, continuous, and adaptive process—much like health literacy or digital competence.

A reimagined approach is essential to integrate tiered financial education across life stages. In schools, financial concepts such as savings, budgeting, responsible borrowing, and digital safety must be woven into age-appropriate curricula. Adolescents need to learn not only how to calculate interest but also how to detect phishing, compare loan products, and use digital wallets safely. Under the National Education Policy (NEP) 2020, there is now an opening to embed such content in secondary and vocational education streams. In higher education institutions, especially in fields like agriculture, nursing, trade skills, and small business management, financial training tailored to specific occupational contexts can yield immense returns. For working adults, periodic refresher modules—delivered through workplaces, SHGs, cooperatives, or Panchayat-based sessions—are essential. These should be built into government schemes such as MGNREGA, PMJDY, or Atal Pension Yojana, ensuring that financial literacy becomes a habitual part of state-citizen interaction. For example, when a woman receives a micro loan through a SHG, she could simultaneously be enrolled in a three-month audio-visual training on managing debt and understanding repayment schedules. Such "just-in-time" literacy models, closely tied to product uptake, have been found to significantly improve comprehension and reduce defaults.

Currently, training modules differ across sectors, leading to fragmented knowledge transfer. Synergy may extend to capacity-building for financial educators and frontline personnel. National Institute of Securities Market (NISM) has enrolled 3,31,962 of participants under their Certification programs as on March 2024 (NISM, 2024). A cross-sectoral certification program—perhaps under NISM's oversight—can help create a cadre of multipurpose financial educators equipped to guide users through the entire spectrum of financial services, from savings to pensions to fraud redress. Synergy thrives when rooted in inclusivity. All collaborative programs should account for the needs of digitally excluded individuals, persons with disabilities, and linguistic minorities. Standardized modules can be developed in screen-reader friendly formats, Indian Sign Language, braille, and audio modes. Public-facing digital platforms can incorporate these accessibility features as a regulatory mandate, not a discretionary add-on.

Equally important is vernacularisation and localisation. Financial literacy cannot be effective if it speaks in jargon or is confined to dominant languages. India's linguistic diversity requires that all materials be available in local languages and dialects, with cultural metaphors and examples that resonate. In tribal regions, audio tools, storytelling formats, and community radio can be powerful mediums. Among the elderly, in-person group sessions and one-on-one assistance by trained local youth can enhance comprehension and trust.

The Pradhan Mantri Gramin Digital Saksharta Abhiyan (PMGDISHA) is a promising model that aims to make rural households digitally literate, with modules specifically tailored to digital banking, mobile transactions, and cyber safety (PMGDSA, 2024). According to SME Times, as of 2024, it had trained over 6.39 crore individuals. However, the program can be complemented by ongoing reinforcement, periodic updates, and linkages with grievance redress systems so that users feel empowered to act when confronted with anomalies or fraud.

Furthermore, the content of financial literacy needs to evolve with time. It may now include awareness of data privacy rights, understanding of credit scoring mechanisms, digital loan risks, and even emerging areas such as carbon credits, green finance, and crypto-related scams. As users move beyond basic transactions toward savings, investments, and pensions, their knowledge needs become more sophisticated. The state, in collaboration with educational institutions, fintech platforms, and civil society, has to develop tiered content frameworks to serve these needs.

Financial literacy, thus, is not a narrow economic skill but a citizenship competency—a tool that enables individuals to engage with the state, the market, and their communities on equitable terms. Just as universal education is a right, so too universal, adaptive financial education. It should be recognized as a public good, supported by sustained investment and inter-ministerial coordination.

3.5 Community-Centric Models and Local Literacy Multipliers

In a vast and socio-culturally diverse country like India, centralized interventions alone cannot ensure universal financial inclusion. Policies designed in national capitals must resonate in remote hamlets, forested tribal belts, urban slums, and flood-prone delta regions. Inclusion requires to be built from within the communities through community-based delivery models, local representation, and trust networks that bring abstract systems to life in practical and culturally relevant ways.

SHGs, cooperatives, Anganwadi centers, and Panchayat-level bodies have played a critical role in connecting state policies with grassroots communities (Ministry of WCD, 2024). Over the past two decades, the National Rural Livelihoods Mission (NRLM) has mobilized more than 1.2 crore SHG members, many of whom have become significant economic contributors (Ministry of Rural Development, 2024). Through the NRLM's Financial Literacy Ambassador program, these women now also function as peer educators, conducting informal financial literacy workshops in vernacular languages. These sessions are tailored to local contexts, helping to demystify financial concepts and promote inclusion through community-based, culturally relevant learning.

Community-Centric Models succeed because they are built on peer trust, shared lived experiences, and community validation. When village woman explains UPI transactions to her neighbors, her words carry more weight than a bank official conducting a one-time training. Moreover, such peer educators can address culturally specific doubts, counter myths, and provide ongoing support. Peer educators also act as local watchdogs, alerting authorities to patterns of fraud, misinformation, or institutional neglect.

In densely populated informal urban settlements, grassroot NGOs and social enterprises have deployed financial literacy kiosks powered by micro-ATMs, interactive voice response (IVR) tools, and multilingual digital assistants. Startups like PayNearby have partnered with state governments to set up over 50,000 such micro-outlets, which double as education points and transaction hubs. These are staffed by local youth trained in basic digital and financial literacy, thus generating employment while enhancing community capacity. However, such models require sustained support, both financial and institutional. Peer educators need to be formally recognized, trained, and compensated, not merely expected to function as unpaid volunteers. Similarly, grassroots literacy hubs need digital infrastructure, periodic content updates, and strong linkages to nearby financial institutions. Block and district-level Financial Inclusion Resource Centres, managed by consortia of public and private stakeholders, can serve as backbones for such local efforts—offering advanced training, grievance redress pathways, and contextual curriculum development.

Community radio remains an underused yet highly effective medium. With its deep reach and linguistic adaptability, it can disseminate not only awareness but real-time updates—such as phishing scams, changes in policy, or new financial entitlements. Drama-based segments, folk songs, and interview formats can turn abstract financial ideas into relatable narratives, particularly in tribal and semi-literate contexts.

Importantly, persons with disabilities must not be left out of these community-led efforts. Inclusion is not just about inviting participation—it is about restructuring environments to make participation possible. SHGs and training hubs have to proactively include PwDs as both learners and leaders. This requires inclusive pedagogy, accessible training material, and representation of persons with disabilities as trainers, not merely as beneficiaries.

Finally, private sector actors should be engaged not just as financiers through Corporate Social Responsibility (CSR), but as active co-creators of locally relevant financial solutions. CSR initiatives have already played a significant role in expanding financial literacy programs, with banks and fintech companies offering workshops, webinars, and digital resources. These institutions can further collaborate with SHGs, NGOs, and municipal bodies to design need-specific financial tools—such as loan products for seasonal migrant workers, insurance schemes for transgender street vendors, or savings apps tailored for elderly pensioners with low digital literacy. Drawing inspiration from global best practices, such as the UK's Money Advice Service—which offers free, impartial financial guidance via digital platforms, call centers, and community outreach to ensure accessibility for all, including persons with disabilities—India can enhance its financial inclusion efforts through similarly integrated, accessible, and context-sensitive approaches.

In essence, a community-centric model of financial inclusion does not merely extend the reach of formal institutions—it rebuilds those institutions in the image of the communities they serve, embedding participation, trust, and adaptability into the very fabric of service delivery. These models will be critical in ensuring that inclusion becomes an enduring feature of Indian society, rather than a temporary policy success.

4 A Resilient Financial Ecosystem for Viksit Bharat: The Roadmap

4.1 Policy Architecture for Inclusive and Integrated Strategy

For financial inclusion in India to move from episodic programs to embedded structures, it requires to be supported by a robust, coherent, and future-facing policy architecture. This architecture should be informed by the dynamic realities of users, grounded in constitutional values of equality and participation, and structured to withstand economic, climatic, and technological shocks. In other words, inclusion must be institutionalised, not improvised.

At the heart of this architecture lies the need for unified strategy documents with measurable goals and inter-agency ownership. India already has foundational blueprints such as the National Strategy for Financial Inclusion (NSFI) and the National Strategy for Financial Education (NSFE), developed under the guidance of the Government (RBI, 2020, 2021). However, these strategies now need to be modernised to address emerging challenges such as algorithmic finance, climate-linked risks, cross-border digital flows, and evolving data sovereignty regimes. The revised strategies must also reflect the demographic transition, incorporating the needs of an aging population, the growing gig economy, and digitally native youth.

There is a growing case for a National Disability Financial Inclusion Strategy (NDFIS). This would set time-bound targets, define accessibility standards, and allocate dedicated funds for innovation in assistive fintech. The strategy requires to include the development of a Disability Financial Inclusion Index, similar to the RBI's FI-Index, which tracks progress not merely in access but also in usability, satisfaction, and systemic accommodation of diverse needs.

A key aspect of the policy architecture calls for the integration of financial education into mainstream curricula and institutional frameworks. This goes beyond including a few textbook chapters on budgeting or savings. Financial education requires to be treated at par with digital literacy and civics—delivered across life stages, integrated into skilling programs, and embedded into government schemes. For example, skill development centers under Skill India can incorporate modules on loan evaluation, digital wallet safety, and income tax basics. Similarly, Anganwadi centres and Panchayat Bhawans can serve as nodes for localized outreach on government insurance or pension schemes.

Digital inclusion policy requires to evolve beyond device provisioning or connectivity. It requires to encompass device usability, secure interfaces, accessible design, and post-access support. Providing a smartphone to a rural household is only the beginning. True digital inclusion occurs when that device becomes a tool for economic decision-making, rights assertion, and resilience against exploitation. To this end, the Digital India program should adopt a financial inclusion lens—ensuring that digital public goods are designed to serve vulnerable users first.

At the operational level, India needs to strengthen and professionalise the last-mile banking infrastructure. Business Correspondents (BCs), India Post agents, bank mitras, and micro-ATM operators are often the first and only interface citizens have with the financial system. These actors need to be trained not just in transactions but also in ethics, empathy, and user education. They must be equipped to detect fraud, guide users in grievance redressal, and offer tailored advice. A National Business Correspondents (BC) Accreditation Framework, with incentives for inclusive performance and community engagement, can help formalize and empower this ecosystem.

Additionally, India needs a Unified Financial Inclusion Dashboard (UFID), aggregating data from banks, NBFCs, insurance firms, pensions, and fintechs. This dashboard should be disaggregated by gender, disability, geography, and income status, allowing for real-time policy feedback loops. Such a data system is essential to be designed with robust privacy safeguards and governed by consent frameworks, especially as personal financial data becomes increasingly central to service delivery.

Importantly, the inclusion framework ought to be anchored in legal and rights-based approaches. Just as the Right to Education or Right to Information have transformed their respective domains, financial inclusion should be viewed as a public entitlement—subject to grievance processes, audit trails, and judicial oversight. Legal mechanisms need to be developed to address digital fraud, denial of access, algorithmic bias, and systemic discrimination within financial services.

Finally, India ought to invest more in inclusive innovation ecosystems. Programs like Startup India, Atal Innovation Mission, and SIDBI's MUDRA initiatives may provide incentives for startups working in assistive fintech, rural credit scoring, gamified learning, and ethical AI for finance. These platforms should host inclusive design challenges, support incubation of women- and disability-led fintechs, and ensure market access for solutions that address real-world inclusion gaps.

4.2 Need for a National Financial Literacy Integration Mission (NFLIM)

The absence of a unified financial literacy framework often results in overlapping content, divergent messaging, and a lack of clarity for end-users. This disjointed experience is particularly confusing for individuals with low literacy or digital exposure. For instance, a rural woman may receive investment-related advice from an SHG group trained under SEBI programs, pension enrollment information from PFRDA outreach, and a loan under a PM scheme linked to RBI's BC network—each offering its own financial education module, potentially with thrust on different content delivery styles.

A National Financial Literacy Integration Mission (NFLIM) could bring together all financial regulators and other intermediaries to co-create inclusive, adaptive, and standardized literacy materials. The proposed NFLIM will dovetail and periodically modernize the National Strategies for Financial Inclusion and literacy efforts, i.e., NSFI and

NSFE, suited to the dynamically evolving digitalized financial world. Such a mission would not only promote efficiency and coherence but also enable resource sharing, mutual training, and cross-regulatory innovation. The NCFE, has been constituted to act as the nodal coordinating body, setting curriculum guidelines, ensuring linguistic and cultural adaptability, and monitoring impact at the ground level. Besides, regulators require to integrate shared data systems, particularly for tracking literacy progress, identifying underserved geographies, and mapping digital fraud patterns. Joint dashboards reflecting inclusion metrics across banking, insurance, pensions, and capital markets would help policymakers make informed, timely interventions. NCFE can act as the Secretariat for the National Mission.

Thus, the future of India's financial inclusion will not be secured by isolated schemes or pilot projects. It will depend on the architecture of rules, incentives, institutions, and infrastructures that together shape the daily economic lives of over a billion citizens. To build a resilient and inclusive Bharat, this architecture should be anticipatory, adaptive, and accountable.

4.3 A Participatory and Rights-Based Financial Future for All by 2047

As India envisions itself as a developed and inclusive nation by 2047—Viksit Bharat—it is essential to recognize that financial inclusion is not simply a policy outcome or an economic indicator. It is a democratic promise. A promise that every individual, regardless of income, caste, gender, geography, or disability, has the right to access, understand, and benefit from the formal financial system without fear, friction, or exclusion. This transformation requires not only expanded infrastructure but also reoriented institutions, localized strategies, and a culture of economic dignity. The successes of recent years are undeniable. Over 54 crore Jan Dhan accounts opened, trillions of rupees transacted through UPI, millions of citizens enrolled in pension and insurance schemes—these are remarkable achievements. But the vision of Viksit Bharat demands a deeper transformation. One where every account is used meaningfully, where every user feels safe and informed, and where the system responds with fairness, accessibility, and respect. This future needs to be shaped by foundational principles of four 'P's.

Participation. Financial inclusion can be co-created with the people it seeks to serve. From policy design to product development, the lived experiences of rural women, disabled youth, tribal entrepreneurs, migrant laborers, and gig workers may inform every stage. Community institutions need to be empowered not just as delivery agents but as partners in governance. Financial educators, SHG leaders, disability advocates, and Panchayat members can have a seat at the policymaking table.

Protection. As digital systems proliferate, the risks of surveillance, fraud, algorithmic exclusion, and data misuse intensify. Citizens can be equipped with knowledge, tools, and legal remedies to protect their financial lives. Data protection laws, cybercrime hotlines, grievance redress portals, and AI audit mechanisms need to be strengthened to uphold digital dignity and safety.

Provisioning. Inclusion cannot depend solely on market dynamics. The state requires to play a proactive role in provisioning for universal access—through financial education in schools, rural digital infrastructure, subsidies for assistive devices, and support for inclusive fintech startups. Public investment needs to prioritize the underserved, ensuring that no region or demographic is left behind due to lack of profitability.

Permanence. Financial literacy should be continuous. Grievance systems must be permanent and visible. Inclusion should be embedded in the mandates of regulators, banks, educational institutions, and local governments—not left to the volatility of elections or donor cycles. Inclusion must move from the margins of policy to the mainstream of governance.

4.4 Conclusion

The year 2047 marks more than just 100 years of political independence. It is a moment to reflect on what kind of economic freedom we have built—who has access, who has agency, and who is still waiting at the margins. The road to that future will not be paved by technology or regulation alone. It will be paved by trust, participation, and a shared commitment to equity.

If India is to fulfill its promise of inclusive prosperity, then financial inclusion needs to become more than a metric. It must become a moral and social compact—a living expression of democracy in the economic realm. This will help us achieve the dream of Viksit Bharat through a universally financially included India.

References

Business Standard. (2023, November 15). 1.39 million cyberattacks handled in 2022, phishing attacks rise. *Business Standard*. https://www.business-standard.com/india-news/1-39-million-cyberattacks-handled-in-2022-phishing-attacks-rise-cert-in-123111500614_1.html

Centre for Internet and Society. (2023). *Accessibility of digital banking in India*. https://cis-india.org

Ministry of Agriculture and Farmers Welfare. (2024). *Kisan Credit Card (KCC) scheme: Progress report. Government of India*. https://agricoop.nic.in/en/kisan-credit-card

Ministry of Electronics and Information Technology. (2024, December). *Annual Report of MEITY 2024–25*. Government of India. https://www.meity.gov.in/static/uploads/2024/12/10fcadec462c330211502fed3d24ea83.pdf

Ministry of Finance, Government of India. (2024). *Economic Survey 2023–2024*. Government of India. https://www.indiabudget.gov.in/economicsurvey/

Ministry of Finance, Government of India. (2013). *Report of the financial sector legislative reforms commission, March 2013*. Government of India. https://dea.gov.in/files/other_reports_documents/FSLRCReportVol1.pdf

Ministry of Finance, Government of India. (2025). *Union Budget 2025–2026*. Government of India. https://www.indiabudget.gov.in/

Ministry of Rural Development. (2024). *National Rural Livelihoods Mission: Annual report 2023–2024*. Government of India. FSLRC. https://aajeevika.gov.in/sites/default/files/nrlp_repository/NRLM_Annual_Report_2023-24.pdf

Ministry of Women and Child Development. (2024). *Annual report 2023–2024*. Government of India. https://www.spniwcd.wcd.gov.in/reports/archive/annual-reports

Mohapatra, C. S. & Ghosh, D. (2024). Investor protection paradigm in India: Mounting criticality of digitalisation. *Margin: The Journal of Applied Economic Research, 17*(3–4), 251–278. https://doi.org/10.1177/00252921241262674

National Bank for Agriculture and Rural Development. (2024). *Annual report 2023–2024*. NABARD. https://nsearchives.nseindia.com/content/debt/WDM/Debt_31072024132522_NAR24EWebVersion.pdf

National Centre for Financial Education. (2023). *Status of financial education in India*. NCFE. https://ncfe.org.in/

National Institute of Securities Markets. (2024). *Annual report 2023–2024*. NISM. https://www.nism.ac.in/wp-content/uploads/2024/08/annual-report.pdf

National Payments Corporation of India. (2024). *UPI annual report FY24*. NPCI. https://www.npci.org.in/what-we-do/upi/product-statistics

National Statistical Office. (2018). *Persons with Disabilities in India. Ministry of Statistics and Programme Implementation.* https://www.mospi.gov.in/sites/default/files/publication_reports/Report_583_Final_0.pdf

PayNearby. (2024). *Micro-ATM and financial literacy kiosk initiative.* Nearby Technologies Pvt. Ltd. https://paynearby.in/news/micro-atm-financial-literacy

Press Information Bureau. (2025, February 1). *Driving financial empowerment.* Ministry of Finance. https://www.pib.gov.in/PressReleasePage.aspx?PRID=2098435

Press Information Bureau. (2025, February 4). Budget 2025–26: *Fuelling MSME expansion. Ministry of Micro, Small and Medium Enterprises.* https://www.pib.gov.in/PressReleasePage.aspx?PRID=2099687

Press Information Bureau. (2025, March 7). Jan Dhan Yojana: Progress report. *Press Information Bureau.* https://pib.gov.in/PressReleasePage.aspx?PRID=2112321

Press Information Bureau. (2024, December 26). Ministry of Finance Year Ender 2024: Department of Financial Services. *Press Information Bureau.* https://www.pib.gov.in/PressReleaseIframePage.aspx?PRID=2088182

Pradhan Mantri Gramin Digital Saksharta Abhiyan. (2024). *Progress dashboard.* Government of India. https://www.pmgdisha.in/

Reserve Bank of India. (2020). *National strategy for financial education: 2020–2025.* RBI. https://ncfe.org.in/nsfe/

Reserve Bank of India. (2021). N*ational strategy for financial inclusion: 2019–2024.* RBI. https://www.rbi.org.in/FinancialEducation/content/English_16042021.PDF

Reserve Bank of India. (2024). *Financial Inclusion Index for March 2024.* RBI. https://avantiscdnprodstorage.blob.core.windows.net/legalupdatedocs/33335/RBI_notified_regarding_the_Financial_Inclusion_Index_for_March_2024_July092024.pdf

Securities and Exchange Board of India. (2023, July 31). SEBI SCORES—Securities market investment—SEBI investor. *SEBI*. https://investor.sebi.gov.in/sebi_scores.html

Securities and Exchange Board of India. (2024, April 1). SCORES 2.0 platform launch notification. *SEBI*. SEBI | SCORES 2.0 New Technology to strengthen SEBI Complaint Redressal System for Investors.

Small Industries Development Bank of India. (2024). *MUDRA Yojana annual report 2023–2024.* SIDBI. https://www.sidbi.in/en/reports

SME Times. (2024, December 5). 6.39 crore people in rural India trained in digital literacy: Centre. *SME Times.* https://www.smetimes.in/smetimes/in-depth/2024/Dec/05/digital-literacy-india.html

Startup India. (2024). *Fintech for inclusion: Case studies*. Invest India. https://www.startupindia.gov.in/content/sih/en/startupgov/regulatory_updates.html

State Bank of India. (2024). *Digital village project report*. SBI. https://bank.sbi/web/corporate-governance/csr/digital-village

Waghmare, A. (2025, February 5). *Access to banking. Data For India*. https://www.dataforindia.com/access-to-banking/

World Bank. (2021). *Global Findex Database: India country profile*. https://globalfindex.worldbank.org/country/india

CHAPTER 5

Retirement Planning as a Pillar of Financial Inclusion: Securing the Golden Years in Viksit Bharat

Adil Kamal, Syed Afzal Ahmad, and Vikas Dixit

1 Introduction

India stands at the cusp of a demographic transformation: while it currently enjoys a large youth population, the cohort of senior citizens is expanding rapidly. The World Population Ageing 2017 UN report (United Nations, 2017) predicts that by 2030, the number of people aged 60 or older will exceed the number of children under 10. Two-thirds of

A. Kamal (✉) · S. A. Ahmad
Department of Business Management, Integral Business School, Integral University, Lucknow, India
e-mail: kamaladil@gmail.com

S. A. Ahmad
e-mail: safzal@iul.ac.in

V. Dixit
Department of Economics, Jadavpur University, Kolkata, India
e-mail: vikas.dixit@jadavpuruniversity.in

© The Author(s), under exclusive license to Springer Nature Singapore Pte Ltd. 2026

V. Dixit et al. (eds.), *Financial Inclusion for Viksit Bharat*,
https://doi.org/10.1007/978-981-92-0807-4_5

these older people are expected to live in developing regions, and this phenomenon is also being experienced in India. The report highlights the need for focused planning to address the changing population structure. A recent report of the NITI Aayog (NITI Aayog, 2024) projects that India currently comprises a little over 10% of the population, translating to about 104 million, and is projected to reach 19.5 per cent of the total population by 2050. This report (NITI Aayog, 2024) further cites a Longitudinal Ageing Study of India (LASI) 2021 report (a full-scale national survey) on the status and determinants of the ageing population in India by the Ministry of Health & Family Welfare. This cited report found that, in terms of social protection, only 18 per cent reported being covered by any health insurance, 28 per cent were aware of any concession for senior citizens, and 24 per cent reported problems in providing documents to avail services. As much as 70 per cent of the elderly population was dependent for everyday maintenance, and 78 per cent was living without any pension cover. A rising trend of nuclear families, inadequate financial security nets, and deficient financial planning for senior citizens were identified as being among some major areas of concerns. This greying of India brings into sharp focus the urgency of retirement planning. Adequate financial preparation for old age is not only a personal necessity but a societal imperative—without it, the burden on families and public resources grows, and the well-being of the elderly is jeopardized. Today, many of India's elderly already face financial insecurity: roughly 40 per cent of senior citizens are in the poorest wealth quintile and about one-fifth have no personal income.[1]

Such statistics underscore that financial inclusion must extend beyond basic banking to encompass old-age security. Financial inclusion generally refers to ensuring access to useful and affordable financial services—savings, credit, insurance, etc.—for all individuals, especially the underserved. In the Indian context, massive strides have been made in recent years (for example, hundreds of millions of bank accounts opened under the Jan Dhan Yojana). However, retirement planning remains a relatively under-emphasized pillar of financial inclusion. True financial inclusion implies not just access to money today, but the ability to sustain oneself financially throughout one's life cycle, including the non-earning post-retirement years. Viksit Bharat 2047, the Indian government's vision for

[1] Accessed at https://india.unfpa.org/en/news/india-ageing-elderly-make-20-population-2050-unfpa-report on May 30, 2025.

a developed India by the 100th anniversary of independence, highlights inclusive growth and prosperity. A crucial component of this vision is ensuring that every citizen can age with financial security and dignity. Retirement planning, therefore, is a pillar of inclusive finance—it "secures the golden years" and prevents the excluded elderly from slipping into poverty. A financially secure retired population also contributes to the economy by sustaining consumption and reducing dependency burdens. In short, robust retirement planning supports the broader goals of Viksit Bharat 2047 by fostering an inclusive, financially resilient society. Paradoxically, although Indians acknowledge the importance of retirement saving, actual preparedness is lagging. A Retirement Readiness Survey, conducted in 2020 by PGIM India Mutual Fund in partnership with Nielsen India reveals three striking findings: (a) that Indians are focusing more on current expenses than future planning; (b) Indians plan for retirement when they have surplus money, and can save without sacrificing current comforts; and (c) Indians have also tended to rely heavily on their children, likened to a reverse mortgage, promising to leave their wealth to children in return for care and financial support in old age.[2]

Although new initiatives in the last decade (discussed in Sect. 3 of this chapter) have begun to improve coverage, the majority of Indians in the unorganised sector still lack access to structured retirement income. This gap between aspiration and action—people want a secure retirement but most do not adequately plan or invest for it—is a central development challenge. Against this backdrop, this chapter examines how retirement planning can serve as a key pillar of financial inclusion in India, with a special focus on evidence from a primary survey of employees in higher education institutions in Uttar Pradesh. The choice of this demographic is deliberate: higher education sector employees are typically literate, employed in formal or semi-formal jobs, and presumably aware of financial matters to some extent—in other words, one might expect relatively better retirement planning in this group. Yet, understanding their behaviour and attitudes can shed light on the facilitators and barriers to retirement planning even among the educated middle-class. If even in this segment we find gaps in planning, the situation may be more acute in less advantaged populations.

[2] The report is accessed on January 1, 2025 at https://www.pgimindia.com/mutual-funds/assets/images/retirement/surveyInsights/Retirement%20Readiness%20Survey%202020.pdf.

This chapter builds on both international and Indian literature, reviewed in the next section, to provide a balanced view of theoretical frameworks and empirical findings related to retirement planning and financial inclusion. This is followed by an overview of the retirement-savings landscape in India in Sect. 3 that includes government-backed schemes and private market products which together form the toolkit for any aspiring retiree. Section 4 provides methodological details and outlines the empirical strategy followed for conducting the primary survey. The results of the empirical exercise are discussed in Sect. 5, while Sect. 6 concludes the chapter and presents some forward-looking policy recommendations aligned with the Viksit Bharat 2047 agenda.

2 Literature Review

2.1 *Theoretical Perspectives on Retirement Planning*

Retirement planning encompasses a multifaceted array of theories spanning economics, psychology, sociology, and behavioural finance. This section delves into foundational models and contemporary frameworks, critically evaluating their strengths and limitations.

The early theoretical contributions having their implications for retirement planning seem to owe their origin in the works of Franco Modigliani and Richard Brumberg in the early 1950s (Modigliani & Brumberg, 1954, 1980). They posited a theory of spending based on the idea that people make intelligent choices about how much they want to spend at each age, limited only by the resources available over their lives. By building up and running down assets, working people can make provision for their retirement, and more generally, tailor their consumption patterns to their needs at different ages, independently of their incomes at each age. This theory popularly came to be known as the "life cycle hypothesis": people save during their working years to fund their retirement years when income ceases. This theory predicted that in countries with higher rates of economic growth, higher proportions of the working age population would tend to have higher saving rates (Modigliani, 1970). An important assumption of this theory is that the period of retirement is fixed: changes in wage rates, wealth or other variables may alter the allocation of lifetime consumption between working years and retirement years but they do not change the allocation of the years themselves between work and retirement. However, as noted in Feldstein (1976), the assumption of a fixed retirement period conflicts with observed behaviour and has unintentionally caused some important evidence to be incorrectly interpreted as conflicting with the basic notion of rational life cycle saving. Moreover, it is interesting to note here that while the possible importance of social security was recognised in the original life cycle hypothesis of saving, it was not formally incorporated as a separate variable, neither in the original theory nor in subsequent theoretical or empirical analyses of this theory (see, for example, Friedman, 1957; Albert & Modigliani, 1963; Modigliani, 1970; Mayer, 1972, among others). The original theory considers the ordinary "fungible wealth" variable in the aggregate consumption function.

It was Feldstein (1974, 1976) who extended and generalised the original life cycle theory to include and analyse the impact of social security on the individual's simultaneous decision about retirement and saving.[3] Using the aggregate US time series data for the period from 1929 to 1971 (excluding 1941 to 1946), the author found that the social security substantially depressed personal savings by 30 per cent to 50 per cent. Considering the period of retirement as endogenous in his model, Feldstein (1976) notes that workers covered by pensions are incentivised to retire earlier than they otherwise would. The pensions would, therefore, have two effects on direct personal savings: (i) it reduces personal saving because it substitutes for household assets, but (ii) it also increases personal saving because it lengthens the period of retirement over which accumulated assets will be spread. Thus, the net effect of pensions depends upon the relative strength of these two forces.

In later years, there also emerged a set of positive theories of social security, grouped into two types—political theories and efficiency theories. According to the political theories of social security, which are further classified into voting models and pressure group models, social security is simply a redistribution of resources from the young generation to the old generation with the latter generation winning the political fight with other groups of citizens. On the other hand, the efficiency theories emphasise

[3] Miller and Charles (1974) presented an alternative extension of the life cycle hypothesis with very different implications about the impact of social security and of public debt from that of Feldstein. Miller and Charles' extended version considers planned bequests and assumes that each individual's utility depends not only on his own consumption but also on the utility of all future generations.

the role of government-administered social security programmes to alleviate market inefficiencies. According to these theories, markets cannot provide social security (such as a certain kind of insurance) efficiently, and thus, government needs to step-in. For a detailed review of these positive theories of social security, please see Mulligan and Martin (1999a, 1999b). Also, for a theoretical exposition of an overlapping-generations model of social security, see (Tabellini, 2000).

The issue of retirement planning has also been examined from psychological, sociological, and behavioural economics lenses. For example, Ajzen's (1991) Theory of Planned Behaviour (TPB) posits that intention is the strongest predictor of behaviour, including retirement planning. Intention, in turn, is influenced by attitude toward the behaviour (e.g., belief that planning improves post-retirement well-being); subjective norms (social pressures or expectations); and perceived behavioural control (one's confidence in the ability to plan). Hershey et al. (2007) validated TPB in predicting retirement savings intentions among Dutch employees. In another contribution, Hershey and Mowen (2000) linked planning activity to personality traits such as conscientiousness and future time perspective, underscoring the psychological basis of financial foresight. Cognitive resources and future orientation play critical roles in long-term planning. Individuals with higher executive function and future time perspective tend to engage more in retirement planning (Lusardi & Mitchell, 2011). Locke and Latham (2002) suggest that specific, challenging, and self-set goals improve task performance. Applied to retirement planning, individuals who set clear savings targets and monitor progress tend to achieve better retirement outcomes.

Among some sociological approaches having implications on retirement planning, Atchley's (1989) Continuity Theory extends role theory by proposing that individuals maintain consistent patterns of thinking and behaviour, including financial management, from mid-life into retirement. Role theory suggests that retirement is a process of role exit (from worker to retiree) and role redefinition. Preparations for retirement are shaped by how individuals view their future identity and roles. Sociological perspectives also highlight the role of social class, education, and occupation in retirement planning. It is argued that people from higher socioeconomic backgrounds are more likely to possess financial literacy, stable employment, and institutional access to retirement benefits (Lusardi & Mitchell, 2007). Studies have found that women, racial minorities, and informal workers are structurally disadvantaged in retirement preparedness due to social stratification (OECD, 2021).

Behavioural economics adds the concept of present bias—the tendency to prioritise current consumption over future needs. Drawing from Simon (1955), bounded rationality suggests individuals lack the cognitive resources or information to optimize retirement planning. Madrian and Shea (2001) found that automatic enrolment in retirement plans significantly increases participation, reflecting the importance of defaults and inertia in retirement decisions. Thaler (1999) proposed that individuals compartmentalise money into "mental accounts." Retirement savings may be underfunded if individuals fail to segregate long-term savings from other accounts or treat windfalls irrationally. The prospect Theory (Kahneman & Tversky, 1979) explains that individuals weigh losses more heavily than equivalent gains, which may lead to excessive risk aversion in retirement investment, especially among older populations. The financial capability model (Atkinson et al., 2006) combines psychological traits, social context, and institutional access to explain financial decision-making. It includes: financial knowledge and skills, motivation and confidence, and social support and contextual barriers. Shefrin and Thaler (1988) extended the traditional life-cycle model by incorporating behavioural elements such as self-control and framing, emphasising why individuals may deviate from optimal savings paths.

A comprehensive understanding of retirement planning must, therefore, account for not only economic principles but also psychological motivations, sociological structures, and behavioural biases. The interplay of individual traits, social influence, institutional settings, and cognitive limitations shapes the retirement decision-making process. Policymakers can design better financial inclusion strategies—like nudges, defaults, and targeted literacy campaigns—by drawing insights from these interdisciplinary theories.

2.2 *Review of Some Empirical Works*

This section reviews empirical studies that explore the determinants of retirement planning. The review covers a variety of studies, both from India and abroad, and explores both economic and non-economic factors affecting retirement planning.

Hershey et al. (2007) emphasized that psychological factors, such as future orientation and goal-setting, significantly influence saving behaviour. Procrastination, lack of self-control, and short-term thinking were identified as key barriers to effective planning. In their "Save More Tomorrow" program, Benartzi and Thaler (2013) highlighted how automatic enrollment and default contribution increases help employees overcome behavioural biases, encouraging consistent retirement savings. Guo et al. (2024) developed a model that combines social cognitive theory (SCT) and the theory of planned behaviour (TPB) to investigate the effect of attitude toward retirement planning, social group support, perceived financial knowledge, and future time perspective on retirement planning intention, as well as the mediating influence of retirement planning intention. Using data from 514 faculty members of public universities in China through an online questionnaire survey, The authors find that perceived financial knowledge demonstrated the strongest positive influence on retirement planning intention, followed by future time perspective and social group support, with retirement planning intention as a mediator. This research suggests that implementing financial education workshops and personalized planning services could promote retirement planning behaviour. Hassan et al. (2016) conducted a study in Malaysia to examine factors contributing to individual's retirement planning behaviour and the private pension system in private sector. Based on the survey of a total of 500 working individuals aged 40 years and above from the private sector, the study identified several significant variables in the prediction of retirement planning among working individuals in Malaysia, including individual who had higher levels of education, higher levels of income, financial literacy, retirement goal clarity and attitude towards retirement. The authors observed a correlation between retirement planning behaviour and saving for old aged.

Numerous studies have shown that financial literacy plays a vital role in determining when individuals start saving for retirement.[4] A higher level of understanding regarding compound interest, inflation, and pension instruments leads to earlier and more consistent saving behaviour. Lusardi and Mitchell (2017) conducted a global review and found that financial literacy is strongly correlated with early retirement saving across countries. Those who can correctly answer basic financial literacy questions are significantly more likely to have retirement savings. Lusardi

[4] See for example, Gallego-Losada et al. (2022) for a bibliometric analysis of retirement planning and financial literacy.

and Mitchell (2011) derived similar findings for United States: individuals with higher levels of financial literacy were more likely to engage in retirement planning activities. Bucher-Koenen et al. (2017) used longitudinal Dutch data and found that those with higher financial literacy were more likely to start saving early, and less likely to regret their past saving behaviour. Rooij et al. (2011) explored the relationship between financial literacy and retirement planning in the Netherlands. They found that financially literate individuals were more likely to invest in complex financial instruments, ensuring better preparedness for retirement. Kaur et al. (2021) studied Indian millennials and concluded that higher financial awareness leads to earlier initiation of retirement savings, especially when mediated by goal-setting and financial self-efficacy. Khan et al. (2022) examined Indian public sector employees and found that knowledge of NPS and EPFO increased early participation, controlling for income and age. Sane and Thomas (2018) investigated retirement savings behavior among formal and informal sector employees, noting that financial illiteracy and lack of awareness about retirement schemes like the National Pension System (NPS) and Atal Pension Yojana (APY) significantly hinder participation.

Behavioural economics literature emphasizes risk attitudes and income level as critical in explaining how much individuals allocate toward long-term financial instruments like pensions or NPS. Towards this end, Feldman and Beehr (2011) reported that risk-averse individuals tend to avoid long-term illiquid investments such as pensions, leading to lower allocation toward retirement-specific assets. Tan et al. (2017) analysed Malaysian workers and found that risk tolerance, measured via a psychometric scale, positively influenced retirement fund allocation, independent of age or education. Sivaramakrishnan et al. (2017) conducted a study among Indian urban employees and concluded that higher monthly income and long-term investment orientation significantly influence higher retirement corpus allocation. Duflo and Saez (2003) showed that even among people with similar income, those with more confidence in financial matters and higher risk tolerance were more likely to invest in employer pension schemes. Bhushan and Medury (2013) examined salaried individuals in India and found that people with higher income and greater financial risk appetite invested a larger share in NPS and PPF-type retirement instruments.

Retirement decisions are also increasingly being framed as social processes influenced by peer discussions, family conversations, and formal consultations. For instance, Clark et al. (2012) studied the impact of employer-led education initiatives in the U.S., concluding that tailored financial counselling sessions significantly improved employees' participation in retirement plans. Hershey et al. (2013) found that individuals who discussed retirement planning with family or advisors were more likely to have both early savings and higher allocations. Rooij et al. (2011) found that respondents who had formal financial plans were significantly more likely to allocate resources effectively toward retirement, even after controlling for financial literacy. Kaur and Arora (2020) highlighted that Indian employees who consulted with HR or financial advisors about NPS and EPFO benefits were more confident and proactive in allocating funds for retirement. Wiener and Doescher (2008) previously demonstrated that spousal encouragement and family discussions were strong predictors of the decision to begin planning early and to commit more to retirement accounts. Pandey and Gupta (2020) found that employees often rely on familial support during old age, diminishing the perceived need for formal retirement savings. This cultural reliance creates a barrier to adopting financial products designed for retirement.

Some recent Indian studies attempt to integrate multiple dimensions—literacy, income, gender, access to schemes—into unified models of retirement preparedness. For example, Chaurasia and Sahu (2020) used IHDS data to show that occupational status, financial literacy, and access to formal retirement schemes jointly influence retirement readiness among Indian households. Agarwalla et al. (2015) developed a financial capability index and used it to predict retirement planning behaviour among working professionals in India, showing strong links to both early start and higher allocations. Chatterjee and De (2021) highlighted that women are less likely to plan for retirement due to lower financial independence, limited access to financial resources, and traditional gender roles. The study emphasised the need for targeted financial education and gender-specific incentives to bridge this gap. Sane and Thomas (2018) revealed that irregular incomes and lack of access to formal financial products hinder informal workers' ability to save for retirement.

The empirical literature reviewed in this section offers useful insights on various economic as well as non-economic factors influencing individual's retirement planning. Although prior studies have examined financial literacy, income, and risk attitudes as determinants of retirement saving, few have simultaneously analysed both the timing and extent of retirement planning using primary data. There is especially a lack of context-specific research focusing on employees in Indian higher education institutions, particularly in Uttar Pradesh. Moreover, the role of social planning interactions—such as family discussions and professional consultations—remains empirically underexplored. By addressing these limitations, this study contributes original evidence toward a more comprehensive understanding of retirement preparedness in a critical yet understudied demographic segment. Before moving to the discussion of empirical design and results of empirical analysis, it is imperative to take a stock of the existing schemes of retirement planning in India with a critical lens.

3 Retirement Planning Schemes in India: A Critical Overview

India's retirement landscape has historically been dominated by publicly administered pension and provident fund systems for formal sector workers, but in recent years, it has expanded to include market-linked and voluntary options available to a wider population, including informal and gig economy workers. However, large sections of the workforce, especially in the unorganised sector, remain without sufficient retirement security. This section provides a critical appraisal of major public and private retirement schemes in India, their coverage, features, and challenges.

3.1 Public Retirement Schemes

There are a number of retirement schemes in the public sector, and interestingly most of these schemes are outside the control of Public Fund Regulatory and Development Authority (PFRDA).

3.1.1 Civil Servants' Pension (CSP)

The Civil Servants' Pension (CSP) is a traditional defined benefit scheme which runs on the basis of pay-as-you-go-system, for employees of Central Government who were recruited up to 31st December, 2003 and employees of State Governments recruited up to the effective date mentioned in notifications issued by those governments. CSP is an unfunded scheme and there has been no attempt at building up pension assets through contribution or any other provision. CSP scheme is indexed to wages and inflation. A modified one rank one-wage principle applies to it wherein all retired employees of a certain rank get the same pension. The main problem under CSP is that of fiscal stress. A brief description of CSP is given in Table 1.

State governments in India also have DB programmes substantially like the CSP at the Centre and have been under severe fiscal pressure given their large workforce. In addition, employees of organizations which are government undertakings are part of the "Central Provident Fund" or the "Government Provident Fund." Both these pay an administered rate of return on contributions and allow for early withdrawals. Even though they are called provident funds, there is no separate fund and benefits are paid out of the Consolidated Fund of India. These are thus PAYGo programmes, but are free of longevity risk. In addition, the size of the payments involved is small. Hence, these problems are of second order when compared with CSP (Sane & Shah, 2011).

The defined benefit (DB) PAYGo scheme financed by the Government of India also applies to armed forces personnels. Various types of military pensions are summarised in Table 2.

Table 1 Characteristics of CSP

Type	*Funding*	*Coverage*	*Contribution rate*	*Vesting*	*Benefit*
Defined Benefit	Unfunded, pay as you go (PAYGo)	Government employees	0	20 years or 10 years if at the end of service	Monthly pension Commutation provision Maximum benefit rate Survivor benefit Indexation arrangement Forgo 40% of the pension and take it as lump sum restored after 15 years of retirement 50% of wages in the last 10 months of employment 30% of the monthly pension Consumer price index

Source Sane and Shah (2011)

Table 2 Types of pension

Type of pension	*Details*
Service pension	Granted @ 50% of last drawn or average of last 10 months' emoluments, whichever is beneficial; min. Rs. 9000/month. Requires 20 years of service (Commissioned Officer) or 15 years (PBOR)
Family pension	Granted @ 30% of reckonable emoluments last drawn; minimum Rs. 9000/month (in case of natural death)
Special family pension	Granted @ 60% of reckonable emoluments last drawn (death attributable to or aggravated by military service)
Liberalized family pension	Equal to last drawn reckonable emoluments (death in war, war-like, counter-insurgency, or terrorist operations)
Disability pension	Granted in invalided out cases; includes Service Element (50%) and Disability Element (30% for 100% disability, proportionately reduced for less). Not payable if disability <20%
War injury pension	War Injury Element = 100% of last drawn emoluments (invalided out); 60% if discharged. Reduced proportionally for <100% disability
Invalid pension	Granted when invalided out due to disability not attributable to/ aggravated by service (NANA). Earlier 10-year service minimum now waived for personnel invalided on/after 04.01.2019
Reservist pension	Granted after completing 15 years combined Colour + Reserve service. Equals 2/3 of minimum pension for Sepoy
First appeal	Appeal against denial of entitlement may be submitted to Record Office/Service HQ within 6 months. Reviewed by First Appeal Committee under 2008 Entitlement Rules
Second appeal	Second appeal (if First Appeal is rejected) may be filed within 6 months to Second Appeal Committee under 2008 Entitlement Rules

Source https://desw.gov.in/en/pensions (accessed on May 30, 2025)

3.1.2 Employees' Provident Fund (EPF)

For the organised sector employees, the basic structure of pension and other retirement benefits have been outlined in the Employees Provident Funds (EPF) and Miscellaneous Provisions (MP) Act, 1952. The provisions of this Act are applicable to all defined establishments, employing more than 20 workers and cover over 11.8 crores EPF members and their families in the organized sector. This Act is administered by Employees Provident Fund Organisation (EPFO). The Employees Provident Fund (EPF) Scheme is an individual account defined contribution scheme (in operation since 1952) wherein both the employees and employer contribute to the fund at the rate of 12 per cent of the employee's pay. The EPF scheme enjoys an 'EEE' tax structure under the Old Tax Regime which constitutes a major tax based subsidy. This scheme is administered by Employees' Provident Fund Organisation (EPFO). There are number of provisions under the scheme for pre-mature withdrawal of accumulation. This pre-mature withdrawal provision is frequently used by the members of the scheme which leads to small balances at the time of their superannuation. Because of low balance in individual account, the members' old age income benefit is negligible. Thus, While EPF has ensured savings discipline, critics point to high withdrawal rates before retirement and limited portability across jobs.[5] Compliance gaps also exist in small and medium enterprises (SMEs) and contractual labour.

The EPF & MP Act, 1952 remained unquestioned and there were virtually no changes in the contribution, administration and benefits being provided under this Act for almost four decades. First major change occurred in 1995, with the conversion of part of defined contribution EPF Scheme to a defined benefit scheme in the form of Employees' Pension Scheme. This change in the EPF & MP Act, 1952 marked an important break from the then existing policy of the Employees Provident Fund Organisation in two ways:

a. With this amendment, the concept of a mandated annuity to the employees of private sector was introduced for the first time.
b. It added a new pension liability (since the scheme is not fully funded) to the existing liability with regard to the civil servants of Central and State Governments.

3.1.3 Employees' Pension Scheme (EPS)

The Employees' Pension Scheme (EPS), introduced in 1995, is a defined benefit scheme, based on a contribution rate of 8.33 per cent from the employee to which government makes an additional contribution of 1.16 per cent. EPS is applicable to the workers who entered into employment after 1995. This scheme provides defined benefit pension on retirement after 10 years of service. In case of death of a member, the scheme provides for a pension to the spouse for his/her remaining life. The pension formula is based on average salary and years of service. This scheme also suffers from issues of absence of portability as well

[5] https://www.goodreturns.in/news/epfo-grapples-with-surge-in-full-provident-fund-withdrawals-by-young-subscribers-1412691.html.

as inadequate and unsustainable retirement benefits, more especially for low-income workers. The impetus to pension sector reforms in India was provided by three reports, namely, the Project OASIS Committee Report 1999,[6] report by the Insurance Regulatory and Development Authority (IRDA) of 2001 on Pension Reforms in the Unorganised Sector, and report of the High Level Expert Group on New Pensions System by the Government of India (2002).[7]

3.1.4 National Pension System (NPS)

The New Pension System (NPS), which later came to be known as the National Pension System (NPS) was launched on January 1, 2004, mandatorily for all new entrants to Central Government service, except Armed Forces. State Governments adopted this system at different dates. As a regulatory framework of NPS, Government constituted an Interim Pension Fund Regulatory and Development Authority (IPFRDA) as a precursor to the statutory regulator, Pension Fund Regulatory and Development Authority (PFRDA), vide Pension Fund Regulatory and Development Authority Act, 2014. PFRDA thus regulates and administers NPS. NPS is a restructured defined contribution pension system which was extended on a voluntary basis to private sector employees and all other citizens of India (both resident and Non-resident) in the age group of 18–70 years. For Central Government employees, the employer contribution is 14 per cent, while for other employers, it is voluntary up to 10 per cent. NPS provides market-linked returns. Subscribers choose between equity, corporate debt, and G-sec options. On withdrawal at the time of retirement, the subscriber gets 60 per cent of the entire accumulated corpus, while a minimum of 40 per cent must be annuitised. NPS offers flexibility, portability, tax efficiency, and higher potential returns. However, issues include low voluntary participation, lack of awareness, and insufficient annuity market development (Basu, 2023).

3.1.5 Atal Pension Yojana (APY)

APY was launched on May 9, 2015 to create a universal social security system (with minimum guaranteed monthly pension ranging from

[6] The report can be accessed at https://www.pfrda.org.in/WriteReadData/Links/Rep2d5d02004-a7c9-4875-be6e-f8b92744e210.pdf.

[7] Pension Reforms in India—A Social Security Need by D. Swaroop; accessed in 2016 at https://www.licpensionfund.in/pdf/PensionReforms.pdf.

Rs.1000 to Rs.5000 after 60) for all Indians, especially the poor, the under-privileged and the workers in the unorganised sector. Administered by PFRDA, APY is open to all bank account holders in the age group of 18–40 years and the contributions differ (Re1-Rs.100, Rs.101-Rs.500, Rs.501-Rs.1000, etc.), based on pension amount chosen. The minimum pension would be guaranteed by the Government, i.e., if the accumulated corpus based on contributions earns a lower than estimated return on investment and is inadequate to provide the minimum guaranteed pension, the Central Government would fund such inadequacy. Alternatively, if the returns on investment are higher, the subscribers would get enhanced pensionary benefits. Subscribers can make contributions to APY on monthly/ quarterly / half-yearly basis. After the death of the subscriber, the monthly pension would be available to his/her spouse, and after the death of the spouse, the pension corpus, as accumulated at age 60 of the subscriber, would be returned to the nominee of the subscriber. In case of premature death of subscriber (death before 60 years of age), spouse of the subscriber can continue contribution to APY account of the subscriber, for the remaining vesting period, till the original subscriber would have attained the age of 60 years. Subscribers can voluntarily exit from APY subject to certain conditions, on deduction of Government co-contribution and return/interest thereon. From 1st October, 2022, any citizen who is or has been an income-tax payer, shall not be eligible to join APY. APY has improved retirement inclusion among informal workers. Yet, meagre coverage and the modest pension amount remains a critical issue.

3.2 *Voluntary and Private Retirement Products*

3.2.1 *Public Provident Fund (PPF)*

PPF is offered by post offices as well as by public and private banks. It is government-administered, tax-free offering higher rate of interest (7–8 per cent). The tenure of this scheme is for 15 years, extendable on maturity. The investment in this scheme during a financial year can be made of any amount ranging from Rs.500 to Rs.150000. PPF is highly popular among middle-class savers for tax exemption (EEE status). But the investment ceiling limits its utility as a primary retirement vehicle.

3.2.2 *Life Insurance Retirement Plans (Annuity and Pension Plans)*

These are pension plans managed by insurance companies (e.g., LIC and private insurers, like HDFC Life, ICICI Prudential) which may offer life insurance coverage along with the pension benefit. The investor can choose to pay either monthly or quarterly. Some companies may even offer yearly payments towards these plans. Under these plans the investor pays an amount regularly over a fixed period and enjoys the benefits after retirement. These may include Deferred Annuity Plans, Immediate Annuities, and Unit-Linked Pension Plans (ULPPs). LIC's Jeevan Shanti and Jeevan Akshay are among the most subscribed annuity products. Some mutual funds also offer SEBI-regulated annuity plans that provide regular income to investors. These plans are similar to pension plans and are designed for retirement planning. These include equity/debt-oriented retirement funds (e.g., HDFC Retirement Savings Fund). They provide tax benefits under Section 80C of the old tax regime with a 5-year lock-in. Despite being popular instruments of retirement planning, all these insurance and annuity-based plans yield low annuity returns (often 5–6 per cent annually). Their complex terms and high commission structures make them less attractive for informed investors (IRDAI, 2023). Annuity mutual funds provide market exposure and higher return potential, but uptake is limited by low investor awareness, risk aversion, and no annuity integration.

It is thus clear from the discussion of this section that despite the proliferation of various pension schemes, India still faces significant retirement preparedness challenges. Low funded schemes with meagre coverage of unorganised work force and lack of regulatory oversight are some major challenges on the supply-side of retirement planning. In the subsequent sections, an attempt is made to understand the demand-side perspective of retirement planning.

4 Empirical Approach and Methodology

4.1 *Objectives and Hypotheses*

The primary objective of this chapter's empirical investigation is to analyse retirement planning behaviour among employees in higher education institutions in Uttar Pradesh, India, and to identify key factors that promote or hinder effective retirement planning. Within this broad objective, we focus on two specific aspects of retirement planning as dependent variables in our analysis: (1) the age at which an individual begins investing or saving specifically for retirement (we term this early-age investment behaviour), and (2) the extent or proportion of an individual's current investments that are earmarked for retirement purposes (retirement investment allocation). By concentrating on these two outcomes, we maintain a clear narrative focus: the first captures when people start planning (timing), and the second captures how much priority they give to retirement in their financial planning. Both dimensions are crucial—starting early and allocating sufficiently are desirable behaviours for retirement security. Based on the literature review and practical considerations, we formulate the following testable hypotheses:

H1 (Early Start Hypothesis):	Financial literacy and awareness are positively associated with an early start to retirement investing.

Rationale: Individuals who possess greater knowledge of financial concepts and are aware of retirement planning benefits are expected to begin saving for retirement at a younger age than those with low financial literacy. In our context, we expect employees who score higher on a financial literacy index or who demonstrate awareness of retirement schemes to have started retirement investments earlier (for example, in their 20s) relative to less literate peers. This hypothesis will be tested by examining the relationship between a respondent's financial literacy (measured through survey questions) and the categorical age bracket when they first began retirement saving.

H2 (Allocation Priority Hypothesis):	Individuals with higher risk tolerance and income are more likely to allocate a larger share of their investments to retirement-specific instruments.

Rationale: Retirement planning often competes with other financial goals. We hypothesise that those who are more risk-tolerant may be more willing to invest in long-term growth-oriented retirement instruments (like equity funds or NPS), thus ending up with a higher proportion of their portfolio dedicated to retirement, since they are not overly fearful of short-term market fluctuations. Additionally, higher-income earners have more surplus funds to deploy and may be able to earmark a greater percentage toward retirement without compromising present needs. We will test this by seeing if respondents who indicate a higher risk tolerance level (e.g., willing to take investment risks for higher returns) and those in higher salary brackets have greater odds of being in the "high retirement investment allocation" category.

H3 (Support & Planning Hypothesis):	Those who have discussed or planned retirement with family or financial advisors are more likely to both start early and invest more for retirement.

Rationale: This hypothesis is exploratory and stems from the idea that planning is a social process as well—discussing with a spouse or seeking professional advice can encourage action. We suspect that respondents who have engaged in retirement planning discussions (an indicator of goal clarity and intent) will show better outcomes on both the above dimensions. This will be tested by looking at survey responses on whether the individual has a formal retirement plan or has consulted anyone regarding retirement, and how that correlates with early start and allocation.

All hypotheses will be examined while controlling for other relevant factors (covariates) to isolate the effect of the key independent variables. These controls include age (since older respondents by definition have had more years in which they could have started saving, though we interpret results cautiously for this due to the cohort effect), gender, marital status, number of dependents, and type of employment (permanent vs. contractual, which may influence access to schemes like EPF). The intent is to test whether the identified factors (literacy, risk tolerance, income, planning discussions) have a statistically significant impact on retirement planning behaviour, in line with our expectations.

4.2 *Survey Design and Sampling*

This study utilises primary data collected through a survey of employees working in higher education institutions in Uttar Pradesh (UP), India. Uttar Pradesh is India's third largest economy accounting for around 8 per cent of national output and is the most populated State as per the latest Census 2011. The survey was conducted in 2024 and covered teaching and non-teaching staff from a mix of Central universities/colleges, State universities/colleges, deemed/private universities and autonomous institutes across UP. We focused on higher education employees as they are generally salaried (hence likely to have some formal financial engagements like a bank account or provident fund) and literate, providing a relevant context to examine retirement planning behaviours. A stratified sampling approach was used to ensure representation from different types of institutions and locations. Responses have been collected from selected tier 2 and tier 3 cities of east and west zones of UP. The final sample consists of N = 356 respondents (after data cleaning for incomplete responses). Of these, about 58 per cent are male and 42 per cent female. The average age of respondents is 38 years, with a range from mid-20s (entry-level lecturers or staff) to early 60s (senior professors nearing retirement). Approximately 70 per cent are teaching faculty and 30 per cent are administrative or support staff. In terms of marital status, 65 per cent are married. The sample thus provides a diverse cross-section in terms of age and career stage: some are decades away from retirement, while others are close to it.

4.3 Questionnaire and Key Measures

The survey instrument included sections on personal and professional background, financial literacy and attitudes, current financial behaviour, and specific retirement planning questions. We highlight the key measures relevant to this chapter's analysis:

Dependent Variable 1—Early-age Investment Behaviour: Respondents were asked at what age they first started saving or investing specifically for retirement. To ensure clarity, examples were given (e.g., opening a pension account, buying a retirement policy, or earmarking a portion of savings for retirement counts, whereas general saving without a retirement goal doesn't count). Responses were captured in brackets: before 25 years of age, between 25 and 30 years, between 30 and 35 years, between 35 and 40 years, and after 40 years. For analysis, we treat this as an ordinal variable indicating the timeliness of starting retirement planning (with categories ordered from 1 = "before 25 years of age" up to 5 = "after 40 years of age"). In our sample, only 10 per cent reported starting before age 25, 14 per cent and 20 per cent reported between 25–30 and 30–35 respectively, 30% between 35–40 and 26 per cent started at 40 or later or not at all. We acknowledge a potential cohort effect here: older respondents who started at say 45 may reflect that options or awareness were lacking in their younger days. We account for age in the model to partially handle this.

Dependent Variable 2—Retirement Investment Allocation: We inquired what portion of the individual's current monthly savings/ investments is allocated toward retirement-specific instruments. This was phrased as: "Approximately what percentage of your total investments/ savings each month is dedicated to retirement (for example, contributions to NPS/EPF, retirement mutual funds, etc.) as opposed to other goals (children's education, house, etc.)?" Respondents chose among ranges: 0 per cent (none specifically for retirement), 1–10 per cent, 11–20per cent, 21–30 per cent, >30 per cent. This captures the priority given to retirement in their financial planning. We found a roughly bell-shaped distribution: about 20 per cent said 0 per cent (they save, but not earmarked for retirement yet), 35 per cent said up to 10 per cent, 25 per cent said 11–20 per cent, 15 per cent said 21–30 per cent, and only 5 per cent said more than 30 per cent. For analysis we created an ordinal variable for allocation (1 = no allocation (0 per cent), up to 5 = highest allocation (>30 per cent)). One could also treat it as continuous (mid-points of ranges), but ordinal logistic regression is suitable given the categorical nature of the survey response.

Independent Variables:

Financial Literacy Score: The survey included 5 basic financial literacy questions (covering concepts of compound interest, inflation, risk diversification, etc.) similar to those used in global studies (OECD, 2022). We computed a literacy score ranging from 1 to 5 based on correct answers. Additionally, respondents were asked to rate their own financial knowledge on a scale of 1 (very low) to 5 (very high). The mean score was 3.4 out of 5, with 28% getting all questions right and 15% scoring 1 or 0. We consider a respondent "high financial literacy" if score ≥ 4 and "low" if ≤ 2, for some analyses, but use the continuous score in regressions.

Risk Tolerance: We adapted a standard risk-aversion question: "Please indicate your level of agreement/disagreement with the following statement on a scale of 1 to 5, 1 being strongly disagree and 5 strongly agree" with the statement: "I am comfortable in taking financial risk". We also asked questions on investment instruments where they invest, including equities or equity funds (yes/no) as a behavioural indicator of risk tolerance. About 40 per cent of respondents fell in the high risk-tolerance category (they either ticked "strongly agree" or "agree" option that they are comfortable in taking financial risk), while 30% were very risk-averse.

Income Level: Monthly income was captured in brackets (<Rs.50,000, Rs.50,000–100,000, Rs.100,000–150,000, Rs.150,000–200,000, >Rs.200,000). We use income both as an ordinal bracket and log of midpoints in some regression specifications. Most respondents (being educators) earned between Rs.50000 and ₹150,000 per month. We expect income to influence how much one can save.

Retirement Scheme Participation: We recorded whether the individual is currently participating in any retirement scheme—e.g., contributing to EPF, NPS, APY, or having an insurance pension plan. 60 per cent reported EPF (mostly the permanent employees), 20 per cent had NPS (some had both EPF and NPS if they moved jobs), 10 per cent had voluntary NPS, 15 per cent had a life insurance pension or ULIP, and 20 per cent said none. We create a dummy for having at least one formal retirement product. This can affect both the likelihood of planning and the allocation (those who have no scheme might not be allocating anything specifically).

Retirement Planning Conscience and Communication: The survey asked if the respondent has ever calculated how much they might need in retirement, and if they have discussed retirement planning with family or a financial advisor. This is a proxy for goal clarity and planning intent. Roughly 30 per cent said they have made a rough calculation of retirement needs, and about 25 per cent have consulted someone or at least had a serious discussion with their spouse about it. We use this as a binary indicator in testing H3.

Demographics: Age Group (starting from 18 to 28 years up to 58 and above), Gender (Male = 1, Female = 0), Marital Status (married = 1, 0 otherwise), and Number of Dependents were recorded. Marital status could influence planning—for example, married individuals might feel more responsibility to plan. In our sample, married individuals indeed had a slightly higher likelihood of having started retirement saving (perhaps due to spousal encouragement or seeing family responsibilities). We include these variables mainly as controls.

Job-related: Whether the job is teaching or non-teaching, and whether the nature of job is permanent or other than permanent. For these two separate dummies have been created: JobType = 1 if teaching, 0 otherwise, and JobNature = 1 if permanent, 0 otherwise. Permanent staff often have EPF/NPS by default, which might spur or substitute additional planning. We control for this to isolate individual initiative beyond mandatory schemes.

4.4 Data Quality and Diagnostics

Before analysis, data were checked for consistency and missing values. We achieved a clean dataset of 356 as mentioned earlier. We also conducted reliability tests for any multi-item constructs. For instance, the 5-item financial literacy quiz has a Cronbach's alpha of 0.78, indicating acceptable internal consistency for a knowledge measure. We chose an ordered logistic regression (also known as ordinal logit or proportional odds model) for each of the two dependent variables, since they are ordinal categories. The proportional odds assumption (that the relationship between predictors and the log-odds of being in higher versus lower categories is constant across outcome thresholds) was tested using a Brant test. The tests did not reveal any significant violations for our main models ($p > 0.05$ for all variables, implying the proportional odds assumption holds). Where there was a slight indication of non-proportionality for a control variable (age in the DV1 model), we further scrutinised but it was marginal and we proceeded with the ordinal logit for simplicity. All analysis was conducted using Stata SE 16 software.

5 Discussion of Regression Results

5.1 Factors Affecting Early-Age Investment Behaviour

Table 3 summarises the ordered logit results for early-age investment behaviour (higher values = started earlier).

The regression results, presented in Table 3 strongly support H1 (Early Start Hypothesis): Financial literacy is a significant positive predictor of starting retirement planning at a younger age. The odds ratio for the financial literacy score is 1.52, meaning that for each unit increase in the literacy score, the odds of being in a higher "earlier start" category increase by about 52 per cent. In practical terms, a respondent who scored high on the literacy quiz (e.g., 5/5) was far more likely to have begun investing in their 20s compared to someone who scored low (0–1/5). This aligns with the literature that financial knowledge enables action: those who understand concepts like compounding clearly

Table 3 Ordered logistic regression results (dependent variable: early-age investment behaviour)

Predictor	*Odds ratio*	*Std. Error*	*z-stat*	p-*value*
Financial Literacy	1.52	0.46	3.3	0.018
Risk Tolerance Level	1.20	-0.71	-1.7	0.082
Monthly Income	1.33	0.64	2.1	0.047
Retirement Conscience and Communication	2.10	0.72	2.9	0.001
Age	0.96	-0.44	-2.2	0.045
Gender	0.78	-0.6	-1.3	0.268
Marital Status	1.15	-1.07	-1.07	0.337
Has Formal Retirement Scheme	1.05	-4.2	-0.25	0.556
Pseudo R^2	0.33			
χ^2	168.05 [0]			

Source Authors' computation using Stata

recognize the value of starting early, as echoed by Lusardi and Mitchell (2011). Risk tolerance (H2, part related to early start) shows a positive but only marginally significant effect (OR = 1.20, $p \approx 0.08$). The coefficient suggests that more risk-tolerant individuals tend to start somewhat earlier, but the evidence is not as strong as for literacy or income. It is quite possible that risk tolerance plays a bigger role in how they invest rather than when they start. Some risk-averse individuals might delay investing because they fear loss, but since even conservative products (like PPF or pension plans) exist, risk aversion alone might not prevent starting entirely—it may just channel people into safe options. Therefore, while the result supports the idea that comfort with financial risk can encourage early participation (perhaps because such individuals are not intimidated by investment products), we treat this evidence as suggestive. Income level shows a significant positive impact (OR = 1.30, $p < 0.05$). This indicates higher-income respondents were more likely to start earlier. One interpretation is that disposable income allows people to allocate money to long-term goals sooner. Also, higher income often correlates with better education or exposure, which could overlap with literacy. We did control for literacy, so income here captures perhaps the financial capacity aspect. The policy implication is that lower-income individuals may want to save for retirement but truly find it hard to spare the money until incomes rise—a case for perhaps matching contributions or government incentives to kickstart their saving earlier. Notably, having an explicit retirement discussion or calculation has a large and significant effect (OR = 2.10, $p < 0.01$). Those who had engaged in retirement planning discussions (with spouse or advisor) have more than double the odds of being early starters. This is a striking validation of H3 in terms of early start: talking about retirement likely reflects a proactive mindset and also may provide the encouragement or information needed to act. It underscores that when individuals take the step to plan or discuss, it often results in concrete early actions. It might be that causality works both ways (people who start early then discuss it), but the survey question was framed to capture if they had ever done it, so for younger people it usually meant they did it before or around the time they started saving. This finding resonates with the idea that goal clarity and family support matter.

Among control variables, Table 3 reveals that age shows a small coefficient (OR = 0.96, $p < 0.05$). This implies older respondents are (not surprisingly) less likely to belong to the "started early" group—essentially confirming that a lot of the older generation in our sample began later in life. This could be partially a cohort effect: financial planning awareness might have been lower 20 years ago, so many current 50-year-olds only started in their 40s. Meanwhile, younger people in their 20s today have more opportunities (NPS, mutual funds, etc.) and information to start in their 20s. Thus, the age effect is understood not as older people being negligent now, but reflecting their past context. We included age mainly to adjust for this in the literacy and income effects. Interestingly, gender was not significant—the OR < 1 suggests women were slightly less likely to start early, but it was not statistically significant. This is somewhat heartening: at least among these educated employees, women were not drastically behind men in terms of initiating retirement savings. It may reflect that female educators are relatively empowered or that many of them are part of the mandatory schemes (EPF) that essentially force a start. Marital status was positive but not significant when other factors were accounted for; being married alone didn't guarantee starting early—it likely interacts with whether the couple prioritises it (captured by the discussion variable perhaps). Having a formal pension scheme (like EPF/NPS) did not significantly predict early start in this model, which is interesting. One might expect if someone is in a job with EPF, that means they effectively started saving for retirement by default when they took the job. However, our definition of "started investing for retirement" was broad and some EPF members might not consider their EPF as a conscious "I started planning" since it's automatic—some indicated the age they personally started planning outside mandatory deductions. There is also overlap with age and job type here: younger individuals may not yet be in permanent jobs with EPF, etc. Essentially, the presence of a formal scheme by itself was not a big determinant once we control for personal attributes.

5.2 *Factors Influencing Retirement Investment Allocation*

We now turn to the second aspect: what determines how much priority (share of investments) individuals give to retirement saving. Table 4 presents the ordered logit results for retirement investment allocation. It is seen from this table that risk tolerance stands out as a significant factor: OR = 1.30 ($p < 0.05$). This supports H2 (for the allocation aspect)—individuals with higher risk tolerance allocate a higher share of their investments to retirement-specific vehicles. The interpretation is that those comfortable with risk likely invest in instruments like equities or long-term pension funds that are geared towards retirement, whereas risk-averse individuals might keep more money in safe short-term instruments (or even gold/FD) not specifically tagged for retirement. As a result, the proportion going into dedicated retirement saving (which often includes instruments that have some market risk or lock-in) is lower for them. One could also see it as risk-tolerant folks possibly target a larger retirement corpus (aiming higher, thus investing more aggressively for that goal). Income with OR = 1.18, $p = 0.10$, and financial literacy with OR = 1.20, $p = 0.09$, show a positive and marginally significant effect. Higher income individuals tend to allocate slightly more proportion to retirement, but the effect is not very strong once other factors (like having a scheme) are included. It is plausible that while higher earners put more absolute money, their proportion might not differ hugely if they also invest in other goals. Similarly, more literate respondents allocate more to retirement, which makes sense—they likely understand how much needs to be saved or appreciate the advantages of certain retirement products (tax benefits, compounding). However, its impact on allocation is not as pronounced as on the timing. This could be because once someone has started, how much they allocate may be more constrained by income or life stage. Nonetheless, a literate person might optimise his/her portfolio better. We consider this partial support for H1's broader implication—literacy does correlate with better retirement funding behaviour overall, not just early start. An interesting and somewhat unexpected finding emerging from Table 4 is that those who have a formal retirement scheme (EPF/NPS) show higher odds (OR = 1.45, $p < 0.05$) of allocating a greater share to retirement. One might have hypothesised the opposite—that if one already has EPF, they might feel that is enough and not save extra. But our result indicates having a formal scheme actually goes hand-in-hand with saving more for retirement, perhaps because it builds a habit or awareness. It could also be that those who are inclined to plan proactively ensure they take advantage of available schemes. On the other hand, those without any formal scheme may be ignoring retirement altogether (hence 0 per cent allocation for them). This suggests that expanding formal coverage (like bringing more employees under NPS or EPF) might not make people complacent as feared, but instead can integrate them into a retirement-saving mindset which they might even supplement. This is a positive sign for inclusion efforts like APY and NPS—getting someone into a scheme at least ensures they start allocating regularly to retirement, even if initially small. Another strong result relates to retirement conscience and communication. Those who have calculated their retirement needs (even roughly) have significantly higher allocation (OR = 1.60, $p < 0.01$). This again ties to H3 (planning mindset). In other words, someone having a clear estimation of his/her post-retirement requirements is likely to realise the need to invest more each month, thereby increasing his/her allocation. It shows the power of planning and setting targets—it translates into action.

Age appears with OR = 1.04 ($p < 0.05$), meaning older respondents tend to allocate a higher portion to retirement. This is understandable: as people get closer to retirement, they often ramp up their contributions or shift other savings into retirement accounts. Younger individuals might be juggling other goals (like saving for a home, wedding, etc.), whereas by mid-career or later, retirement looms larger. Additionally, older individuals might have finished some obligations (like children's education by 50s) and can devote more to retirement. This result is consistent with life-cycle behaviour—the only caution is it might also reflect that younger ones still have time to catch up and may do so later. Regardless, at any given time, age is a factor in the current allocation to retirement. One notable demographic effect is with regards to gender; it turns out to be significant here, with OR = 0.75 ($p < 0.05$) for females versus males, indicating that women in our sample allocate a

Table 4 Ordered logistic regression results (dependent variable: investment allocation for retirement)

Predictor	*Odds ratio*	*Std. Error*	*z-stat*	p-*value*
Risk Tolerance Level	1.30	0.59	2.2	0.043
Monthly Income	1.18	-0.72	-1.64	0.097
Financial Literacy	1.20	-0.73	-1.65	0.085
Has Formal Retirement Scheme	1.45	0.71	2.05	0.044
Retirement Conscience and Communication	1.60	0.59	2.7	0
Age	1.04	0.45	2.30	0.049
Gender	0.75	-0.38	-2.00	0.041
Marital Status	1.40	-0.84	-1.67	0.099
Pseudo R^2	0.29			
χ^2	211.13 [0]			

Source Authors' computation using Stata

lower proportion of their investments to retirement compared to men, even after controlling for income, literacy, etc. This could imply that female employees might prioritize other forms of saving (maybe more in gold, or saving for children, etc.) or possibly that some married women rely on their spouse's retirement planning to some extent. This is an interesting finding, because earlier we saw no strong gender difference in early-age investment behaviour, but in allocation, a gap emerges. It suggests that outreach to improve retirement investment among women is warranted—perhaps tailoring products that appeal to them or addressing specific concerns. It also might reflect lower risk tolerance on average among women; indeed, in our sample, women had slightly lower risk tolerance scores, which could mediate this result. When risk tolerance was included, the gender effect persisted, implying other factors (maybe cultural or confidence factors) at play. In any case, recognising this gap is important for inclusive policy—financial inclusion efforts must ensure women are equally securing their golden years. Marital status (married vs. singles) had a positive effect (OR = 1.40) with $p = 0.10$, suggesting married individuals might allocate more to retirement (perhaps because they are thinking as a family about the future). This was not strong evidence but in line with expectation that family responsibilities can cut both ways—they increase expenses but also the desire for future security. Here it leans towards the latter.

6 Discussion of Findings and Some Policy Recommendations

The empirical results of the preceding section offer important insights that bridge the gap between academic understanding of retirement behaviour and practical measures to enhance financial inclusion. Several discussion points emerge:

(1). Importance of Financial Literacy and Education: Our finding that financial literacy significantly influences the timing of retirement planning underscores the critical role of education in financial inclusion. Simply put, when people know better, they do better. The fact that many individuals in our sample delayed planning due to lack of awareness or misconceptions aligns with broader evidence that improving financial literacy can lead to better retirement outcomes. This suggests that initiatives like workplace financial education seminars, inclusion of basic personal finance in educational curricula, and public awareness campaigns could materially shift behaviours. For example, universities (including where our respondents work) could hold annual workshops on retirement planning for staff—this could cover how to estimate retirement needs, information on NPS/EPF nomination, etc. If such interventions move even a fraction of employees from a late start to an early start, the long-run impact is substantial. The Government and regulators are already aware of this; PFRDA has been conducting NPS awareness programs. Our research reinforces that these efforts must be sustained and scaled. Government could partner with fintech apps to include educational modules or nudges in their interfaces. Financial inclusion is not just about opening bank accounts; it is about imparting the knowledge to use financial tools effectively.

(2). Behavioural Nudges and Planning Mindset: The analysis highlighted the role of having discussions or calculations—essentially, a planning mindset—in driving retirement preparation. This is a nuanced but crucial aspect of inclusion: even if one has access to financial products, one might not use them without the right mindset. This indicates a need for behavioural nudges. For instance, employers can implement opt-out schemes: automatically enrol employees in NPS or voluntary provident fund contributions, which they can opt out of if they choose. Such default enrolment could address inertia. Another idea is providing retirement planning tools (e.g., easy online calculators) and encouraging employees to use them annually—our finding that those who made calculations invest more suggests that if we get people to confront the numbers (how much will I need? am I on track?), it might spur them to increase savings rate. Some companies abroad send out retirement readiness statements; Indian employers or pension providers could adopt similar practices. The influence of spousal/family discussion suggests that social support and norms are influential. Government and community programs could try to shift the social norm from "family will take care of elders" to "each individual/family should prepare for their old age." This is slowly happening as evidenced by APY's acceptance, but more effort is required on this front. The private financial industry should be encouraged (through regulatory support) to innovate products that can help individuals save for retirement conveniently and with appropriate risk management. For example, beyond APY, banks and fintechs could offer flexible micropension accounts where even ₹100 can be deposited at any time (like topping up a prepaid phone). These could invest in a balanced fund and convert to annuity later. Ease of access and flexibility will attract informal workers who have irregular incomes. Likewise, insurers should develop annuity options that have inflation-indexed payouts or escalating payouts. Also, products like deferred annuities that one can buy at, say, age 40 which start paying at 60 could be popular if designed well. The regulator IRDAI can ease norms to allow more experimentation here. A robust annuity market will be crucial as more people retire with lump sums from NPS/EPF and need to convert to lifelong income. Government can also consider issuing longevity bonds or supporting insurers for offering annuities to reduce their risk. Integration of Health and Retirement Planning may also be thought as a possible solution.

(3). Gender Gap and Inclusion: Our results showed that women in the sample are slightly lagging in retirement allocation. This reflects a broader concern: women often have interrupted careers and longer life expectancy, meaning they actually need to be more prepared, yet they tend to be less prepared. As India pushes for Viksit Bharat, women's financial inclusion is paramount. Policymakers might consider targeted measures for women's retirement security—for example, special incentives for female contributors to NPS or APY (perhaps a higher government co-contribution for women in APY to encourage enrolment). Financial literacy programs should especially reach out to women, who historically might have left retirement planning to husbands. Making retirement planning gender-inclusive remains a goal. Microfinance self-help groups, which mostly involve women, could be leveraged to impart retirement planning as part of their training.

(4). Role of Formal Schemes—EPF, NPS, APY: One striking insight of our empirical findings is that inclusion in a formal scheme correlates with better retirement saving behaviour. Far from inducing complacency, having a formal pension seems to anchor one's retirement strategy. This supports the government's multi-pronged approach of expanding coverage: bring more people under EPF (through extending it to smaller firms, the ongoing formalization of the economy) and aggressively enrolling people in APY/NPS. But ensuring continuation of contributions and eventual adequacy is key. Perhaps APY can evolve to offer higher pension tiers (beyond Rs.5000/month) as the economy grows. Employers who don't currently offer any pension could consider facilitating NPS subscriptions for their employees (even if not mandated) as part of CSR or employee welfare—effectively bringing more people into the fold. For the informal sector, the challenge is harder, but the APY model of auto-debit from bank accounts is a good start. Perhaps linking APY with other government benefits (like if you have an active APY, you get a slight preference or bonus in other schemes) could nudge participation. The government should explicitly incorporate retirement planning metrics into the financial inclusion index with stipulated targets. For instance, alongside bank account ownership, track the percentage of adults contributing to a pension or retirement scheme. This would place retirement inclusion on the radar of policymakers at all levels and would drive efforts.

(5). The Delay of Gratification Challenge: A recurring theme is the difficulty many have in prioritising a distant goal over present needs or wants. This is a classic behavioural issue. Our data showed many start late or invest little because of this. Tackling it may require innovative approaches, for instance, tying retirement savings to aspirational goals. One idea could be to promote retirement saving as "financial freedom" for pursuing second careers or passions post-60.

(6). Adequacy and Portfolio Considerations: While our study focused on participation and effort in retirement saving, an important next step is adequacy—are these individuals on track to have enough? Many in our sample allocating 10–20 per cent of their income may still not accumulate a sufficiently large corpus depending on longevity and inflation. There is a need for tools that help individuals gauge adequacy (the planning calculation was one—those who did it realised perhaps they need to allocate more, as evidenced by our data). Policymakers might consider mandating or encouraging pension providers to give projected pension or corpus estimates annually, so people can adjust contributions. Also, the risk tolerance effect reminds us that portfolio mix matters: too conservative an approach can lead to shortfall due to lower returns. Financial inclusion should include providing access to instruments that yield real returns (like equities) in a prudent manner. Thus, default lifecycle funds (as in NPS where younger investors have more equity automatically) are a good feature to maintain.

(7). Social Security and "Viksit Bharat 2047": A developed India by 2047 would presumably have a robust social security system. Our findings feed into what that system might entail. Currently, India's approach is largely self-funded retirement savings (with some employer backing for formal workers). Social pensions for the very poor (a few hundred rupees a month from government) exist but are minimal. As the population of elderly swells to 300 + million, can we rely purely on individual saving? Likely a combination is needed: encourage/maximise self-provision for those who can, and provide a stronger safety net for those who cannot. The government's vision could include a universal or means-tested pension by 2047 that ensures no senior is destitute. That zero pillar would complement personal savings. Towards this end, the following suggestions are worth considering:

- For those earning below a threshold who contribute regularly for 5 years, give a one-time bonus contribution. This reward could improve persistence. It also makes the habit of contribution more rewarding.
- The new tax regime, which is gaining importance, should incentivise retirement savings. On the same line, for people belonging to low-income strata, fresh account holders, more especially under 30 years of their age, may be offered higher interest rates on PPF, SCSS, etc. to encourage early-age participation in retirement planning. Similarly, cash-back or lottery incentives for sustained contributions in schemes like APY (e.g., every year of continuous contribution enters a draw for a reward) may also be explored. While these might seem unusual, they can capture the interest of the uninvolved and get them on board.
- EPF like benefits should also be expanded to Gig/contract workers, like cab drivers, delivery boys, etc.

- Even with all efforts, there will be a segment that either never earned enough to save or outlived their savings. Viksit Bharat must have a heart for its senior citizens who are vulnerable. Towards this end, increasing the old-age pension under National Social Assistance Programme (NSAP) and indexing the same to inflation as well as providing community support and services (e.g., expanding senior citizen discounts or public transport, utilities, and healthcare) are some crucial steps.

(8). The Need for Ongoing Research and Monitoring: This study, while informative, covers a specific segment. To truly secure "golden years" nationwide, more data is needed on varied groups—farmers, small shop owners, gig economy workers—to tailor inclusion strategies. The government should strengthen data collection on pension scheme usage and adequacy. PFRDA's annual reports, EPFO's data, surveys like ours, and perhaps a dedicated panel study on household finances (like an Indian Retirement Survey) can feed into policy tweaks. The government could in fact, implement a periodic Retirement Readiness Survey across India to monitor how prepared different cohorts are. This would be analogous to how some countries track consumer confidence, etc., but focused on retirement readiness. Over time, that can show if policies are moving in the desired direction. Perhaps technology (fintech) can help—app-based micro-investing platforms could bring pension saving to the smartphone user who may not be reached by traditional agents.

In conclusion, the discussion reiterates that retirement planning is both an individual behaviour issue and a systemic issue. Financial inclusion efforts must address both: educate and motivate individuals (so they want to participate) and build and reform systems (so that they can participate easily and effectively). Our study has shown that when individuals are knowledgeable, willing to take informed risks, and plan proactively, they do make better provision for old age. The challenge is to make this the norm rather than the exception, which requires policy support, industry innovation, and cultural change.

References

Agarwalla, S. K., Barua, S. K., Jacob, J., & Varma, J. R. (2015). Financial literacy among working young in urban India. *World Development, 67*, 101–109. https://doi.org/10.1016/j.worlddev.2014.10.004

Ajzen, I. (1991). The theory of planned behaviour. *Organizational Behavior and Human Decision Processes, 50*(2), 179–211. https://doi.org/10.1016/0749-5978(91)90020-T

Albert, A., & Modigliani, F. (1963). The 'life cycle' hypothesis of saving: Aggregate implications and tests. *American Economic Review, 53*, 55–84.

Atchley, R. C. (1989). A continuity theory of normal aging. *The Gerontologist, 29*(2), 183–190.

Atkinson, A., McKay, S., Kempson, E., & Collard, S. (2006). *Levels of financial capability in the UK: Results of a baseline survey*. Financial Services Authority. Accessed on April 22, 2025 at https://www.bristol.ac.uk/media-library/sites/geography/migrated/documents/pfrc0602.pdf

Basu, S. (2023). Rethinking India's pension system: Inclusion, returns and regulation. *Economic & Political Weekly, 58*(24), 40–45.

Bhushan, P., & Medury, Y. (2013). Financial literacy and its determinants: An empirical study of Indian investors. *International Journal of Economic and Financial Issues, 3*(2), 395–402.

Bucher-Koenen, T., Lusardi, A., Alessie, R., & van Rooij, M. (2017). How financially literate are women? An overview and new insights. *Journal of Consumer Affairs, 51*(2), 255–283. https://doi.org/10.1111/joca.12121

Chaurasia, A., & Sahu, S. (2020). Retirement planning in India: An analysis using IHDS data. *Indian Journal of Human Development, 14*(2), 219–236.

Duflo, E., & Saez, E. (2003). The role of information and social interactions in retirement plan decisions: Evidence from a randomized experiment. *Quarterly Journal of Economics, 118*(3), 815–842.

Feldman, D. C., & Beehr, T. A. (2011). A three-phase model of retirement decision making. *American Psychologist, 66*(3), 193–203.

Feldstein, M. (1974). Social security, induced retirement, and aggregate capital accumulation. *Journal of Political Economy, 82*(5), 905–926.

Feldstein, M. (1976). Social security and saving: The extended life cycle theory. *American Economic Review, 66*(2), 77–86.

Friedman, M. (1957). *A theory of the consumption function*. Princeton University Press.

Gallego-Losada, R., Montero-Navarro, A., Rodríguez-Sánchez, J.-L., & González-Torres, T. (2022). Retirement planning and financial literacy, at the crossroads: A bibliometric analysis. *Finance Research Letters, 44*, Article 102109. https://doi.org/10.1016/j.frl.2021.102109

Guo, J., Nazri, M., & Fernandez, K. (2024). Psychological factors and retirement planning behaviour among Chinese university faculty members: The mediating effects of retirement planning intention. *Educational Gerontology*, 1–16. https://doi.org/10.1080/03601277.2024.2417459

Hassan, K. H., Rahim, R. A., Ahmad, F., Zainuddin, T. N. A. T., Merican, R. R., & Bahari, S. K. (2016). Retirement planning behaviour of working individuals and legal proposition for new pension system in Malaysia. *Journal of Politics and Law, 9*(4), 43–52. https://doi.org/10.5539/jpl.v9n4p43

Hershey, D. A., Jacobs-Lawson, J. M., & Austin, J. T. (2013). Effective financial planning for retirement. In A. M. Ferraro, F. M. Scogin, & J. M. Brady (Eds.), *Retirement planning and financial literacy* (pp. 29–50). Nova Science Publishers.

Hershey, D. A., & Mowen, J. C. (2000). Psychological determinants of financial preparedness for retirement. *The Gerontologist, 40*(6), 687–697.

Hershey, D. A., Henkens, K., & van Dalen, H. P. (2007). Mapping the minds of retirement planners: A cross-cultural perspective. *Journal of Cross-Cultural Psychology, 38*(3), 361–382. https://doi.org/10.1177/0022022107300274

IRDAI. (2023). *Annual report 2022–23*. Insurance Regulatory and Development Authority of India. Accessed on March 1, 2024 at https://irdai.gov.in/document-detail?documentId=4273788

Kahneman, D., & Tversky, A. (1979). Prospect theory: An analysis of decision under risk. *Econometrica, 47*(2), 263–291.

Kaur, M., Arora, A., & Rastogi, A. (2021). Retirement planning behaviour among Indian millennials: An empirical analysis. *Asian Journal of Economics and Banking, 5*(1), 1–20.

Kaur, M., & Arora, A. (2020). Exploring the role of employer and financial advisor in influencing retirement saving decisions: Evidence from India. *Indian Journal of Economics and Development, 16*(4), 727–732.

Khan, A., Laskar, N. A., & Das, B. (2022). Financial literacy and retirement saving behaviour among public sector employees in India. *International Journal of Social Economics, 49*(8), 1112–1126.

Locke, E. A., & Latham, G. P. (2002). Building a practically useful theory of goal setting and task motivation. *American Psychologist, 57*(9), 705–717.

Lusardi, A., & Mitchell, O. S. (2017). How ordinary consumers make complex economic decisions: Financial literacy and retirement readiness. *Quarterly Journal of Finance, 7*(3), 1750008. https://doi.org/10.1142/S2010139217500082

Lusardi, A., & Mitchell, O. S. (2011). Financial literacy and planning: Implications for retirement wellbeing. In O. S. Mitchell & A. Lusardi (Eds.), *Financial literacy: Implications for retirement security and the financial marketplace* (pp. 17–39). Oxford University Press.

Lusardi, A., & Mitchell, O. S. (2007). Financial literacy and retirement preparedness: Evidence and implications for financial education. *Business Economics, 42*(1), 35–44.

Madrian, B. C., & Shea, D. F. (2001). The power of suggestion: Inertia in 401(k) participation and savings behavior. *The Quarterly Journal of Economics, 116*(4), 1149–1187. https://doi.org/10.1162/003355301753265543
Mayer, T. (1972). *Permanent income, wealth and consumption.* University of California Press.
Modigliani, F. (1970). The life cycle hypothesis of saving and intercountry differences in the saving ratio. In W. A. Eltis, M. F. G. Scott, & J. N. Wolfe (Eds.), *Induction, growth, and trade: Essays in honour of Sir Roy Harrod.* Clarendon Press.
Modigliani, F., & Brumberg, R. H. (1954). Utility analysis and the consumption function: An interpretation of cross-section data. In K. K. Kurihara (Ed.), *Post-Keynesian economics* (pp. 388–436). Rutgers University Press.
Modigliani, F., & Brumberg, R. H. (1980). Utility analysis and aggregate consumption functions: An attempt at integration. In A. B. Abel (Ed.), *The collected papers of Franco Modigliani: Volume 2, The life cycle hypothesis of saving* (pp. 128–197). The MIT Press.
Mulligan, C. B. & Martin, X. S-I. (1999a). *Social security in theory and practice (I): Facts and political theories* (NBER Working Paper 7118). Accessed on December 5, 2023 at https://www.nber.org/system/files/working_papers/w7118/w7118.pdf
Mulligan, C. B. & Martin, X. S-I. (1999b). *Social security in theory and practice (II): Efficiency theories, narrative theories and implications for reform* (NBER Working Paper 7119). Accessed on December 5, 2023 at https://www.nber.org/system/files/working_papers/w7119/w7119.pdf
NITI Aayog. (2024). *Senior care reforms in India—Reimagining the senior care paradigm: A position paper.* Accessed on March 27, 2025 at https://www.niti.gov.in/sites/default/files/2024-02/Senior%20Care%20Reforms%20in%20India%20FINAL%20FOR%20WEBSITE_compressed.pdf
OECD. (2021). *Pensions at a glance 2021: OECD and G20 indicators.* OECD Publishing https://doi.org/10.1787/ca401ebd-en
OECD. (2022). *OECD/INFE Toolkit for measuring financial literacy and financial inclusion 2022.* Accessed on June 6, 2024 at https://www.oecd.org/content/dam/oecd/en/publications/reports/2022/03/oecd-infe-toolkit-for-measuring-financial-literacy-and-financial-inclusion-2022_54dba970/cbc4114f-en.pdf
Rooij, M. V., Lusardi, A., & Alessie, R. (2011). Financial literacy and retirement planning in the Netherlands. *Journal of Economic Psychology, 32*(4), 593–608.
Sane, R. & Shah, A. (2011). *Civil service and military pensions in India* (NIPFP Working Paper 91). National Institute of Public Finance and Policy, New Delhi. Accessed on July 23, 2018 at https://www.nipfp.org.in/media/medialibrary/2013/04/wp_2011_91.pdf

Shefrin, H. M., & Thaler, R. H. (1988). The behavioural life-cycle hypothesis. *Economic Inquiry, 26*(4), 609–643.

Simon, H. A. (1955). A behavioural model of rational choice. *The Quarterly Journal of Economics, 69*(1), 99–118.

Sivaramakrishnan, S., Srivastava, M., & Rastogi, A. (2017). Attitudinal factors, financial literacy, and financial behaviour: Evidence from India. *Vision, 21*(4), 365–373.

Tabellini, G. (2000). A positive theory of social security. *The Scandinavian Journal of Economics, 102*(3), 523–545.

Tan, E. C. D., Lee, C., & Lee, N. (2017). Household risk tolerance and retirement planning: Evidence from Malaysia. *Economic Modelling, 60*, 71–83.

Thaler, R. H. (1999). Mental accounting matters. *Journal of Behavioral Decision Making, 12*(3), 183–206.

United Nations. (2017). *World population aging 2017*. The Department of Economic and Social Affairs (DESA), UN Secretariat. Accessed on September 20, 2024 at https://www.un.org/en/development/desa/population/publications/pdf/ageing/WPA2017_Report.pdf

Wiener, R. L., & Doescher, T. A. (2008). A framework for promoting retirement savings. *Journal of Financial Planning, 21*(4), 48–55.

CHAPTER 6

Disability and Financial Inclusion in India: Rights, Access, and Realities

Shilpi Mayank Awasthi, Tanwi Shams, Rilina Basu Banerjee, Vikas Dixit, and Joan Maria E. I.

1 Introduction

1.1 Background and Context

The Constitution of India enshrines the principles of equality, freedom, justice, and dignity for all citizens, including persons with disabilities (PwDs), thereby laying a foundational mandate for an inclusive

S. M. Awasthi (✉)
Yuvaan Research Foundation, Noida, India
e-mail: shilpi@specialsaathi.com; shilpi@yrf.org.in

T. Shams
Centre for Disability Law and Advocacy, National Law University (Odisha), Cuttack, India
e-mail: tanwi@nluo.ac.in

R. Basu Banerjee · V. Dixit
Department of Economics, Jadavpur University, Kolkata, India
e-mail: rilina.basu@jadavpuruniversity.in

© The Author(s), under exclusive license to Springer Nature Singapore Pte Ltd. 2026

V. Dixit et al. (eds.), *Financial Inclusion for Viksit Bharat*,
https://doi.org/10.1007/978-981-92-0807-4_6

and equitable society. Reflecting this constitutional vision, India's policy framework has evolved to proactively address the challenges faced by disadvantaged populations, with disability emerging as a critical area requiring sustained policy attention, targeted implementation, and robust monitoring. Globally, the call for disability inclusion has gained momentum. The United Nations Secretary-General, in his message on the International Day of Persons with Disabilities, reiterated the global community's resolve to collaborate with persons with disabilities in building a just, inclusive, and sustainable future—one in which every individual, regardless of gender, age, or ability, can realize their full potential.[1] This global commitment aligns with the overarching principle of the Sustainable Development Goals (SDGs): "Leave no one behind." The 2020 theme for the International Day of Persons with Disabilities—"Building Back Better: Toward a Disability-Inclusive, Accessible and Sustainable Post COVID-19 World"—highlighted the persistent barriers and systemic discrimination that PwDs face daily, impeding their full and equal participation in society.[2] Addressing these challenges and promoting meaningful inclusion demands a paradigm shift rooted in evidence-based planning, inclusive governance, and strong institutional accountability. In this context, integrating disability into the discourse on financial inclusion is not only a matter of rights and justice but also an essential step toward realizing inclusive development for all.

Financial inclusion of persons with disabilities may be understood as the ability of individuals with disabilities to access, use, and independently manage affordable financial services—including savings, payments, credit, insurance, and digital financial services—without facing physical, informational, technological, or institutional barriers. This definition emphasises that financial inclusion for persons with disabilities goes beyond mere

V. Dixit
e-mail: vikas.dixit@jadavpuruniversity.in

J. M. E. I.
Department of English, Sree Sankaracharya University of Sanskrit, Kalady, India
e-mail: reg@ssus.ac.in

[1] https://www.un.org/en/observances/day-of-persons-with-disabilities/message.

[2] https://social.desa.un.org/issues/disability/events/international-day-of-persons-with-disabilities-idpd-3-december-2020.

account ownership and requires accessibility, usability, and independence in financial decisionmaking. However, the issue of financial inclusion has rarely been examined from a disability perspective. Most national and international studies on financial inclusion focus either on macroeconomic expansion of banking systems or on specific groups such as women, rural populations, or the elderly. The particular barriers faced by persons with disabilities remain largely underexamined. Given this gap, the present study begins by establishing the broader context within which disability and financial exclusion intersect. It delves into the institutional, legal, infrastructural, and behavioural dimensions of financial inclusion, and offers evidence-informed reflections and actionable recommendations aimed at strengthening financial access, literacy, and trust among PwDs as India charts its course toward Viksit Bharat @2047.

1.2 Research Objectives and Guiding Hypotheses

The specific objectives of this study are as under:

I. To examine the conceptual and policy foundations of disability inclusion within national and international legal frameworks.
II. To analyse the socioeconomic context of persons with disabilities in India and its implications for financial inclusion.
III. To review regulatory guidelines and institutional initiatives aimed at improving accessibility of financial services.
IV. To understand the lived experiences of persons with disabilities in accessing banking and financial services.

In order to support these objectives, the following testable hypotheses are developed and tested during the course of this study:

H1: Despite the presence of progressive legal and policy frameworks, persons with disabilities continue to face significant barriers in accessing financial services.

H2: The gap between regulatory guidelines and their implementation contributes significantly to financial exclusion of persons with disabilities.

H3: Financial inclusion for persons with disabilities requires not only physical accessibility but also institutional and technological accessibility.

1.3 Methodological Approach

This chapter adopts an exploratory mixed method approach to examine the intersection between disability and financial inclusion in India. Given the limited availability of systematic empirical research on financial inclusion of persons with disabilities as well as the lack of any large scale survey in this area, the study combines multiple sources of evidence to develop a comprehensive understanding of the issue. First, the chapter undertakes a policy and institutional analysis of international conventions, national legislations, and regulatory guidelines relating to disability rights and accessibility in financial services. Key frameworks examined include the United Nations Convention on the Rights of Persons with Disabilities (UNCRPD), the Rights of Persons with Disabilities (RPwD) Act, 2016, and relevant guidelines issued by financial regulators in India. Second, the study utilises secondary statistical sources, including population census data and nationally representative surveys such as the National Family Health Survey (NFHS), to highlight the socio-economic conditions of persons with disabilities and their implications for financial inclusion. Third, the chapter incorporates instances from specific court cases (pertaining to the matters of discrimination of PwDs in banking and insurance services), relevant findings of two audit reports, released by Comptroller and Auditor General of India (CAG), qualitative insights from semi-structured interviews conducted with persons with disabilities, their parents/caregivers, NGO representatives, disability rights activists, and stakeholders associated with financial institutions. These interviews provide valuable perspectives on the practical barriers faced by persons with disabilities in accessing financial services. Thus, by combining policy analysis, statistical evidence, and stakeholder perspectives, the study seeks to provide a multidimensional understanding of the structural and institutional factors influencing financial inclusion of persons with disabilities in India.

1.4 Outline of the Chapter

The rest of this chapter is divided as follows:

The next section (Sect. 2) discusses the evolving concept of disability from its narrow focus on medical conditions to a broader, rights-based framework that views it in relation to structural, attitudinal, and environmental barriers. It then reviews international and national definitions, including those in UNCRPD and RPwD Act, 2016. The section concludes by highlighting the need for a rights-based and inclusive understanding of disability. Section 3 briefly analyses data from Census 2011 and NSS 76th Round to understand the prevalence of disability as well as its socio-economic and demographic background in terms of the distribution of persons with disabilities by gender, location, and age, along with their educational and employment status. Keeping in view the ultimate purpose of this chapter, the discussion of all the trends has been kept brief, both at national and subnational levels, to the extent that is necessary to emphasise the role of inclusive policies and programmes. Section 4 on Legal and Policy Foundations of Disability Rights and Financial Inclusion starts by reviewing international frameworks (UNCRPD, SDGs, and Incheon Strategy). It then summarises relevant provisions of the Indian constitution, early legislative frameworks and key national policies and schemes for PwDs. The key provisions and implications of the RPwD Act, 2016 and RPwD Rules, 2017 are then discussed at some length. This is followed by an outline of the regulatory framework of financial inclusion for PwDs in India which has evolved over past two decades in terms of the guidelines by the Reserve Bank of India (RBI), Insurance Regulatory and Development Authority of India (IRDAI), Securities and Exchange Board of India (SEBI), Department of Financial Services (DFS), and judicial interventions from time to time. Section 5 highlights persistent barriers in accessing financial services by PwDs in light of findings from accessibility audits and stakeholder interviews. In particular, based on secondary literature as well as stakeholder interviews with eight individuals (serving in various capacities), this section highlights exclusion of PwDs in banking, insurance, and pension systems due to infrastructural, digital, attitudinal, and procedural challenges. Section 6 on Inclusive Financial Education and Employment Practices shares insights from interviews conducted in Kerala. This section emphasises early financial literacy and inclusive workplace practices as two important channels of financial inclusion and empowerment, especially in case of PwDs. It highlights lived experiences of nine individuals with disabilities and their recommendations for systemic reform. Finally, Sect. 7 concludes the chapter.

2 Understanding Disability—Definitions and Perspectives

Disability is a complex and evolving concept that extends beyond the presence of physical or mental impairments. It encompasses a dynamic interaction between individuals with impairments and the structural, attitudinal, and environmental barriers that hinder their full participation in society. Contemporary definitions of disability have moved away from viewing it solely through a medical lens and now increasingly reflect a rights-based and inclusive framework.

The United Nations Convention on the Rights of Persons with Disabilities (UNCRPD), adopted in 2006, marked a global shift in how disability is understood and addressed.[3] Article 1 of this Convention defines persons with disabilities as:

> Persons with disabilities include those who have long-term physical, mental, intellectual, or sensory impairments which, in interaction with various barriers, may hinder their full and effective participation in society on an equal basis with others.

This definition underscores the social model of disability (Oliver, 1983, 2013), which argues that it is not the impairment itself but rather the societal barriers—such as inaccessible infrastructure, discriminatory norms, or lack of institutional support—that create disability. It contrasts with the medical model (Crow, 1996; Silvers, 1998), which treats disability primarily as a problem inherent in the individual—something to be cured, treated, or rehabilitated.[4] These two models of disabilities are depicted in Figs. 1 and 2. In the medical model of disability, the problem is the disabled person: is house-bound, confined to a wheelchair, can't walk,

[3] The UNCRPD can be accessed at https://www.un.org/disabilities/documents/convention/convoptprot-e.pdf.

[4] For a review of various models of disabilities, please see Zaks (2023); also see Olkin (2002) for a summary.

can't get up steps, can't see/hear/speak, is sick, looking for a cure, has fits, needs help and caregivers (Fig. 1).

The social model of disability states that the oppression and exclusion people with impairments face is caused by the way the society is organised and operates. The problem is the disabling world: badly designed buildings, stairs not ramps, no lifts, no special schools, few sign-language interpreters, discrimination, inaccessible transport, no parking places, isolated families, poor job prospects (Fig. 2).

However, as acknowledged by the World Health Organization (WHO) and the World Bank's World Report on Disability (2011), a balanced

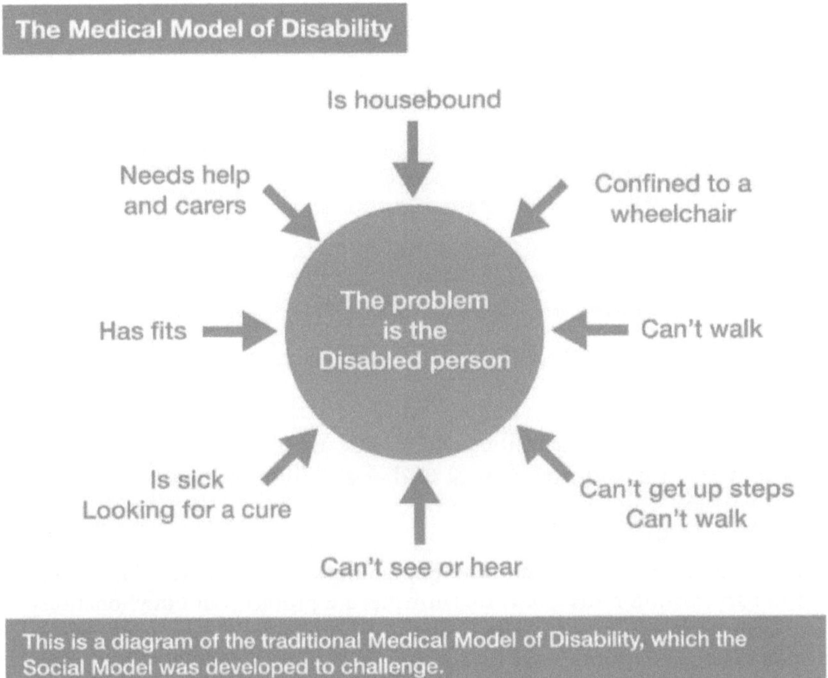

Fig. 1 Medical model of disability (*Source* https://www.inclusionlondon.org.uk/about-us/disability-in-london/social-model/the-social-model-of-disability-and-the-cultural-model-of-deafness/)

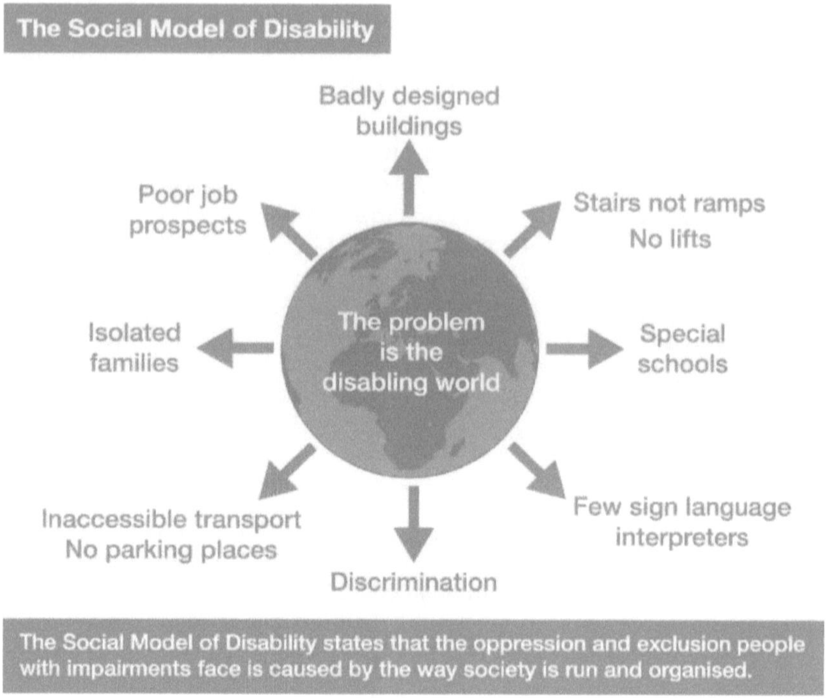

Fig. 2 Social model of disability (*Source* Same as for Fig. 1)

approach is needed. Disabilities often arise from complex health conditions and can carry both medical and social implications. According to WHO:

> Disability is an umbrella term, covering impairments, activity limitations and participation restrictions. Impairments are problems in body functions or structures while activity limitations are difficulties encountered by an individual in executing tasks or actions. Problems experienced by an individual in life situations are called participation restrictions. In other words, disability is not just one health problem. It is a complex phenomenon, reflecting the interaction between features of a person's body and features of the society in which he or she lives.[5]

[5] https://www.afro.who.int/health-topics/disabilities.

In this way, disability reflects an interplay between an individual's health condition and the environment in which they live.

India signed UNCRPD, 2006 on 30th March, 2007 and ratified it on 1st October, 2007. The Convention came into force in the country with effect from 3rd May 2008. It places the following three important obligations on each State Party:

i. To respect the rights and freedoms of persons with disabilities.
ii. To protect individuals with disabilities from rights violations by others.
iii. To fulfil these rights by taking appropriate legislative, administrative, and policy measures. India's Rights of Persons with Disabilities (RPwD) Act, 2016 (Government of India, 2016), which is aligned with UNCRPD, 2006, defines person with disability in its Section 2(s) as:

> "person with disability" means a person with long term physical, mental, intellectual or sensory impairment which, in interaction with barriers, hinders his full and effective participation in society equally with others.

The Schedule to the RPWD Act, 2016, under Clause ZC of Section 2 specifies 21 types of disabilities, including cerebral palsy, autism spectrum disorder, intellectual disability, thalassemia, and multiple disabilities. This Act adopts a rights-based framework and emphasises accessibility, non-discrimination, and the empowerment of persons with disabilities as equal citizens.

According to the World Health Organisation, An estimated 1.3 billion people—or 16% of the global population—experience a significant disability today.[6] Various rough estimates suggest that around one-sixth of world's disabled people live in India alone. Many of them experience layered vulnerabilities—including poverty, inadequate access to health-care, education, and employment—and often encounter deep-rooted social stigma. These intersecting disadvantages not only limit personal development but also systematically exclude persons with disabilities from economic participation. A nuanced understanding of disability is crucial in any policy discourse—particularly in the realm of financial inclusion,

[6] https://www.who.int/news-room/fact-sheets/detail/disability-and-health.

where structural and behavioural barriers may remain invisible yet deeply exclusionary. Recognising disability as both a social and human rights issue is foundational to designing inclusive systems that empower persons with disabilities to live with dignity and independence.

Once in an interview with the New York Times by Claudia Dreifus, Physicist Stephen Hawking, responding to the question: "Given all you've experienced, what words would you offer someone who has been diagnosed with a serious illness, perhaps A.L.S.?" said: "My advice to other disabled people would be, concentrate on things your disability doesn't prevent you doing well, and don't regret the things it interferes with. Don't be disabled in spirit, as well as physically." (The New York Times, 2011).

This chapter builds on such perspectives, seeking to shift the narrative from disability as a limitation to disability as a dimension of diversity that must be accommodated within inclusive financial systems. The conceptual evolution of disability from a purely medical condition to a socially mediated phenomenon has important implications for access to economic opportunities and public services. When physical environments, institutional procedures, or digital systems are not designed to accommodate diverse abilities, persons with disabilities encounter structural barriers in participating fully in economic life. Financial systems are no exception. Access to banking infrastructure, digital payment platforms, credit facilities, and financial information can be significantly constrained by such barriers. Understanding disability through this broader social lens therefore becomes essential for analysing the specific challenges that persons with disabilities face in accessing and using financial services.

3 Socio-Economic and Demographic Status of Persons with Disabilities in India

Understanding the socio-economic and demographic profile of persons with disabilities (PwDs) is vital for framing targeted financial inclusion strategies. In India, the two primary sources of disability statistics—Census 2011 and NSS 76th Round (conducted during July-December, 2018) (Government of India, 2019)—offer valuable but divergent perspectives on the extent and nature of disability, each shaped by distinct methodologies.[7]

3.1 *Prevalence of Disability and Gender Disparity*

As per the Census 2011, the disabled population in India stood at 2.68 crore, representing 2.21% of the total population of 121.08 crore (Table 1). There existed a noticeable gender disparity: 1.50 crore males and 1.18 crore females reported having a disability. The proportion of persons with disabilities was 2.41% among males and 2.01% among females, indicating underreporting or social barriers affecting female disclosure of disability status. Out of total disabled persons, 69% reside in rural areas, and 31% in urban areas.

While Census 2011 reports a disability rate of 2.21%, NSS 76th Round (Government of India, 2019) places it at 2.2%, highlighting an overall consistency in magnitude but differences in definitions and diagnostic criteria. As per NSS 76th round also, the prevalence of disability is higher among males at 2.4% as compared to females at 1.9%. In rural areas 2.3% of total rural population are living with disabilities, while this prevalence is 2% in urban areas. Importantly, NSS 76th round on Persons with Disabilities provides more nuanced data on types of disability and their impact

Table 1 Total and disabled population (Census 2011)

Category	*Persons*	*Males*	*Females*
Total Population of India	121.08 crore	62.32 crore	58.76 crore
Of Which Disabled Population	2.68 crore (2.21%)	1.5 crore (2.41%)	1.18 crore (2.01%)
Sex Ratio of Total Population (M:F)	51:49		
Sex Ratio of Disabled Population (M:F)	56:44		
Rural–Urban Ratio of Disabled Population	69:31		

Figures inparentheses indicate percentage to total
Source Census 2011, as cited in Government of India (2021)

[7] For a review of these two approaches of collecting data on persons with disabilities in India as well as definitions of disabilities covered by each of them over the years, please see Chapter 2 of "Persons with Disabilities (Divyangjan) in India—A Statistical Profile: 2021 (Government of India, 2021).

Table 2 Disabled population share by social groups (Census 2011)

Social Group	*Persons (%)*	*Males (%)*	*Females (%)*
Total	2.21	2.41	2.01
Scheduled Castes	2.45	2.68	2.2
Scheduled Tribes	2.05	2.18	1.92
Other than SC/ST	2.18	2.37	1.98

Source Same as for Table 1

on education, employment, and living conditions—vital for constructing holistic financial inclusion strategies.

3.2 Social Group Differentiation

Disability prevalence differs across social groups. Census 2011 data shows that Scheduled Castes (SCs) and Scheduled Tribes (STs) reported disability rates of 2.45% and 2.05%, respectively (Table 2). These figures are slightly above and below the national average (2.21%), suggesting an intersection of disability with socio-economic marginalisation.

3.3 Distribution of Disabled Population by Age

Shown in Fig. 3 is the percentage distribution of disabled population by age group. Figure 3 reveals that out of total disabled population in India, elderly (60+ years) constituted 21%. 18% of total disabled males, and 23% of total disabled females are elderly (60+ years). The top two age groups accounting for the highest disabled population (both males as well as females) are 10–19 and 20–29.

3.4 State-Level Variation

While the national disability rate stands at 2.21%, the significant inter-state variation highlights the need for differentiated strategies in disability planning and service delivery. There are as many as fourteen States and two Union Territories (UTs) which have a disability prevalence above the national average of 2.21% (Fig. 4). Andhra Pradesh with 4.57% followed by Sikkim (2.98%), Odisha (2.96%), Jammu and Kashmir (2.88%), and Maharashtra (2.64%) are the top five States having disability

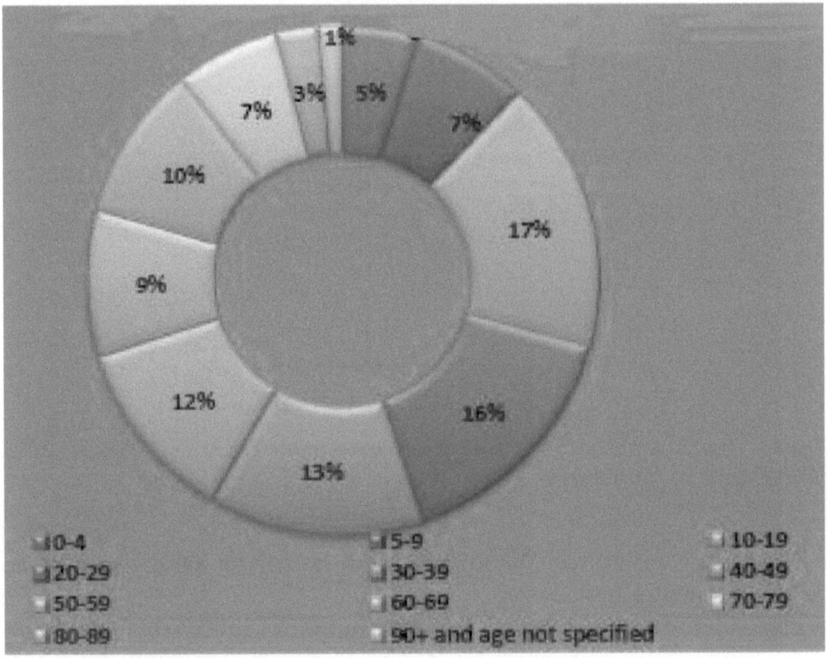

Fig. 3 Percentage distribution of disabled population by age in India–Census 2011 (*Source* Same as for Table 1)

prevalence significantly above the national average. Several States/UTs, like Kerala, Rajasthan, Goa, Himachal Pradesh, Bihar, and West Bengal cluster around the national average. While Sikkim has the second highest prevalence of disability, except Manipur, all other North Eastern States have a disability rate below 2%. Commenting on the regional variation, it may be seen from Fig. 4 that Southern India shows a wide range—from Andhra Pradesh (4.57%) to Tamil Nadu (1.64%), indicating heterogeneity even within a region typically seen as advanced in social development. On the other hand, North-East India consistently reports lower disability prevalence (mostly below 2%), which raises questions about under-identification in tribal and remote areas. Central-Eastern belt (Odisha, Chhattisgarh, Jharkhand, Bihar) exhibits moderate to high prevalence—possibly reflecting poor health indicators and higher exposure to developmental risks. Finally, Union Territories show mixed

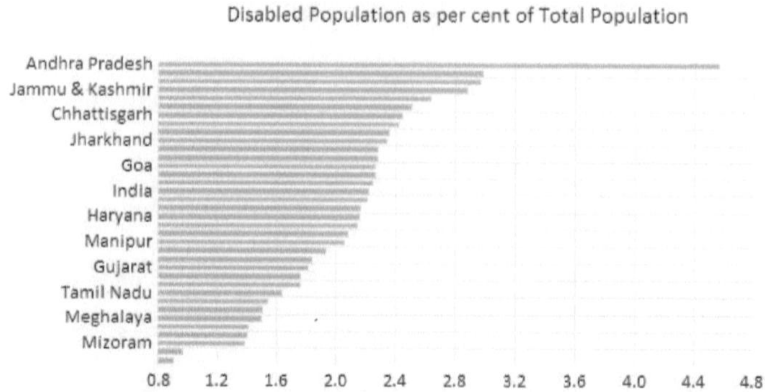

Fig. 4 Disability prevalence across States and Union Territories—Census 2011 (*Source* Same as for Table 1)

patterns—low in Delhi, Chandigarh, and Daman & Diu, but high in Puducherry and Lakshadweep.

Figure 5 portrays the percentage distribution of India's disabled population across states and union territories. It can be seen from this figure that seven States, namely, Uttar Pradesh, Maharashtra, Bihar, Andhra Pradesh, West Bengal, Rajasthan, and Madhya Pradesh alone account for over 62% of India's disabled population. On the other extreme are the seventeen States and UTs that account for less than 1% of India's disabled population. Among these seventeen States/UTs, the North-East region as a whole (Except Assam) contributes less than 1% spread across seven states. All Union Territories, including Chandigarh, Puducherry, Daman & Diu, Dadra & Nagar Haveli, Andaman & Nicobar Islands, and Lakshadweep, together account for less than 0.25%.

3.5 *Educational Status of Persons with Disabilities in India*

Education serves as a foundational pillar for empowerment and inclusion. For persons with disabilities (PwDs), however, access to formal education continues to be limited due to infrastructural, attitudinal, and systemic barriers. As per Census 2011, around 61% of disabled children aged 5–19 years were attending educational institutions, but participation was significantly lower among children with multiple disabilities (only 46%)

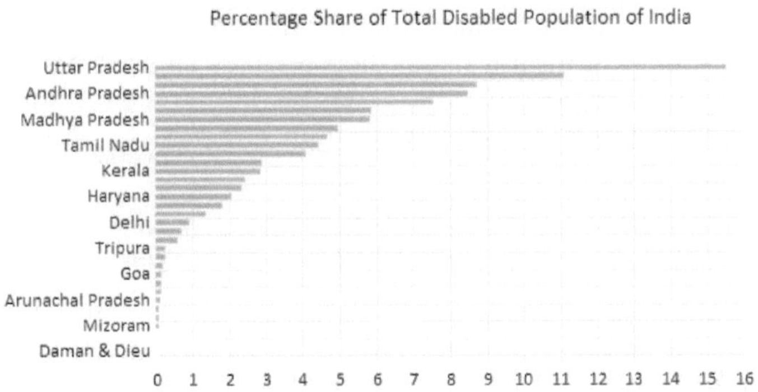

Fig. 5 State-wise percentage distribution of India's disabled population—Census 2011 (*Source* Same as for Table 1)

and those with mental illnesses (only 50%). Overall, 54.5% of India's disabled population was literate, with considerable gender disparity—62% among males and only 45% among females. Educational attainment levels were also low: 45% of all disabled individuals were illiterate, 13% had completed secondary education, and only 5% were graduates or above. Among literate disabled persons, merely 8.5% had attained graduate-level qualifications. Notably, female disabled persons showed much lower educational outcomes compared to males across all levels.

State-level data reveal sharp disparities. Kerala and Goa had the highest literacy rates among PwDs, exceeding 70%, while Arunachal Pradesh and Rajasthan recorded the lowest, below 41%. Similarly, the proportion of graduates among disabled persons was highest in Chandigarh and Delhi and lowest in smaller states and Union Territories such as Lakshadweep and Meghalaya.

The NSS 76th Round (Government of India, 2019) reinforces these trends. It found that only 52.2% of PwDs aged 7 years and above were literate, and 19.3% of those aged 15 and above had completed secondary education or higher. Among those aged 3 to 35 years, just 10.1% had attended preschool intervention programmes. While 62.9% had been enrolled in ordinary schools at some point, only 4.1% had attended special schools when mainstream education was inaccessible.

These figures underscore the educational exclusion faced by PwDs in India, particularly disabled girls and those from under-resourced regions. Ensuring inclusive education requires targeted policy interventions, early childhood support, accessible infrastructure, trained educators, and greater social awareness to dismantle persistent barriers.

3.6 Economic Activity and Employment Status of Persons with Disabilities in India

Participation in economic activity is central to the empowerment and inclusion of persons with disabilities (PwDs). However, persistent structural, attitudinal, and environmental barriers continue to restrict their integration into the labour market. As per Census 2011, only about 36% of the total disabled population in India was engaged in work. The gender gap in employment is stark—47% of disabled men reported being workers, compared to just 23% of disabled women. Rural disabled women (25%) were somewhat more likely to be engaged in work than their urban counterparts (16%), indicating layered disadvantages of gender, disability, and urban exclusion.

At the state level, significant disparities persist. Nagaland (51.9%), Sikkim (49%), and Arunachal Pradesh (44.7%) reported the highest workforce participation among PwDs, whereas Lakshadweep (19.9%), Kerala (23.6%), and Delhi (27.9%) recorded the lowest. In absolute terms, Uttar Pradesh and Maharashtra accounted for the largest number of disabled workers, consistent with their population size.

The NSS 76th Round (Government of India, 2019) provides further insight. Among persons with disabilities aged 15 years and above, the Labour Force Participation Rate (LFPR) in usual status (considering both principal and subsidiary activities) stood at 23.8%, while the Worker Population Ratio (WPR) was 22.8%. The unemployment rate was 4.2%, which, while modest on paper, reflects deeper issues of underemployment, job quality, and exclusion from formal sector opportunities.

These statistics highlight the urgent need for inclusive skilling programmes, employment support services, workplace accommodations, and policy incentives to boost labour force engagement among PwDs. Realizing the goals of inclusive economic development under Viksit Bharat @2047 requires that the disabled population be not only included in employment metrics but also enabled to participate meaningfully in productive work. The socio-economic profile discussed above highlights that persons with disabilities in India continue to experience disadvantages in education, employment, and income opportunities. These inequalities directly influence their participation in formal financial systems. Limited employment opportunities may restrict the ability to maintain regular banking relationships, while lower income levels and informational barriers may reduce the usage of financial products such as savings instruments, insurance, and credit facilities. Consequently, financial inclusion for persons with disabilities must be understood not only as a banking issue but also as a broader question of socio-economic participation.

4 Legal and Policy Foundations of Disability Rights and Financial Inclusion in India

Legal and policy frameworks play a crucial role in shaping the accessibility of economic and institutional systems. In the context of financial inclusion, legislation and regulatory guidelines influence the extent to which banking infrastructure, digital financial services, and institutional practices accommodate the needs of persons with disabilities. International conventions and national legal frameworks therefore provide an important foundation for promoting accessibility and equal participation in financial systems.

4.1 International Commitments Shaping Financial Inclusion for Persons with Disabilities

The right to accessibility is not a new or separate human right, but rather an integral part of existing human rights frameworks. Accessibility is embedded within several international human rights treaties, reinforcing its foundational role in ensuring equality and dignity for all individuals, including those with disabilities. For example, access to the physical environment and public transportation is essential for the realisation of freedom of movement, which is guaranteed under Article 13 of the Universal Declaration of Human Rights (UDHR)[8] and Article 12 of

[8] Accessed at https://www.un.org/en/about-us/universal-declaration-of-human-rights.

the International Covenant on Civil and Political Rights (ICCPR).[9] Similarly, access to information and communication is crucial for exercising the right to freedom of opinion and expression, as articulated in Article 19 of the UDHR and Article 19(2) of ICCPR. Furthermore, Article 21(2) of UDHR and Article 25(c) of ICCPR guaranty the right of equal access to public service. These rights are foundational for enabling PWDs to live independently, participate in society, and enjoy their rights on an equal basis with others. Their principles have significantly influenced Indian constitutional law and jurisprudence, often cited by the Supreme Court to interpret and expand the scope of fundamental rights.

The global discourse on disability rights and inclusive development underwent a radical transformation with the introduction of the United Nations Convention on the Rights of Persons with Disabilities (UNCRPD) (2006). This Convention lays the normative and operational groundwork for advancing financial inclusion of persons with disabilities (PWDs). The UNCRPD affirms the right of PWDs to participate fully and equally in society—including in economic and financial domains. Accessibility is woven throughout the Convention as a cross- cutting right, reinforcing its critical role in achieving social inclusion. It is highlighted in paragraph (e) of the Preamble, which calls for an environment that supports full personal development and societal participation. Article 3 of the UNCRPD sets out accessibility as a general principle, which highlights the necessity of removing both tangible and intangible barriers to ensure that PWDs can fully exercise their rights. These barriers can be physical, such as inaccessible buildings and transportation systems, or intangible, such as discriminatory attitudes or inaccessible digital content. Article 9(1) mandates that States take proactive steps to ensure persons with disabilities have equal access to public spaces, transportation, information, communication systems, and services. This directive encompasses the development, implementation, and monitoring of standards and guidelines that promote access. Article 9(2)(a) elaborates on these obligations by detailing the areas that require targeted action, such as ensuring that the design and construction of buildings and public facilities adhere to universal design principles. This commitment extends to digital spaces and information technologies.

[9] Accessed at https://www.ohchr.org/en/instruments-mechanisms/instruments/international-covenant-civil-and-political-rights.

Some other articles relevant to the context, such as Article 5 (Equality and non- discrimination), Article 8 (Awareness raising), Article 19 (Living independently and being included in the community), Article 21 (Freedom of expression and opinion, and access to information), Article 25 (Health) (especially, clause (e): "Prohibit discrimination against persons with disabilities in the provision of health insurance, and life insurance where such insurance is permitted by national law, which shall be provided in a fair and reasonable manner"), Article 27 (Work and employment), Article 28 (Adequate standard of living and social protection), Article 31 (Statistics and data collection) explicitly uphold the rights of persons with disabilities to access banking, credit, insurance, pensions, and financial infrastructure along with financial literacy on an equal basis with others. The Convention also mandates states to ensure legal capacity, remove physical and digital barriers, and promote inclusive economic opportunities.

Parallelly, the UN Sustainable Development Goals (SDGs)[10]—particularly SDGs 1 (End poverty in all its forms everywhere), 2 (End hunger, achieve food security and improved nutrition and promote sustainable agriculture), 4 (Ensure inclusive and equitable quality education and promote lifelong learning opportunities for all), 8 (Promote sustained, inclusive and sustainable economic growth, full and productive employment and decent work for all), 9 (Build resilient infrastructure, promote inclusive and sustainable industrialization and foster innovation), 10 (Reduce inequality within and among countries), 11 (Make cities and human settlements inclusive, safe, resilient and sustainable), 16 (Promote peaceful and inclusive societies for sustainable development, provide access to justice for all and build effective, accountable and inclusive institutions at all levels), and 17 (Strengthen the means of implementation and revitalize the Global Partnership for Sustainable Development)—underscores the imperative to leave no one behind, including PWDs. These goals promote inclusive finance through universal access to social protection, employment-linked finance, digital banking infrastructure, financial literacy, and disaggregated data systems.

[10] Please visit https://sdgs.un.org/goals for details.

Apart from these two prominent global frameworks, India also adopted the Incheon Strategy[11] in 2012. It offers the first set of regionally agreed inclusive development goals aimed at making the rights of persons with disabilities a reality in the Asia—Pacific region. Notably, ICT (Information and Communication Technology) accessibility is specifically referenced in Goal 3 of the strategy. This goal emphasizes the need to enhance access to the physical environment, public transportation, knowledge, information, and communication systems for persons with disabilities.

Taken together, all these three frameworks provides a rights-based foundation and an implementation roadmap for ensuring that persons with disabilities are fully included in the financial systems of every country. India, as a signatory to both the UNCRPD and the SDG agenda as well as Incheon Strategy, has reiterated its commitment through the enactment of the Rights of Persons with Disabilities Act, 2016, and various inclusive schemes under Digital India, PM Jan Dhan Yojana, Accessible India Campaign, and more. These efforts reflect the nation's growing resolve to foster an accessible, equitable, and enabling financial ecosystem for persons with disabilities, moving towards the vision of Viksit Bharat that is inclusive in both letter and spirit. The subsequent subsections of this current section will delve upon various legal and policy frameworks that reflect India's commitment for inclusive financial and other services for differently abled people.

4.2 Constitutional and Legislative Foundations of Disability Rights in India

The Constitution of India lays a robust normative foundation for promoting justice, equality, and dignity for all citizens, including persons with disabilities (PwDs). While Part III of the Constitution, which guarantees fundamental rights, does not specifically mention disability, the rights enshrined therein—such as the right to equality (Article 14), protection from discrimination (Article 15), and the right to life and personal liberty (Article 21)—apply equally to PwDs. The Preamble affirms the values of justice, liberty, and equality, providing the philosophical basis for inclusive and non-discriminatory laws and policies.

[11] The strategy can be viewed at https://www.unescap.org/sites/default/files/Incheon%20%20Strategy%20pocket%20version.pdf.

Importantly, Article 41 of the Directive Principles of State Policy calls upon the State to secure the right to work, education, and public assistance in cases of disablement, subject to its economic capacity. Similarly, Article 46 mandates the State to promote the educational and economic interests of weaker sections of society and protect them from social injustice and exploitation—provisions that encompass PwDs. Although disability was originally listed under the State List (Entry 9, List II), provisions under Article 249 empower Parliament to legislate on matters in any list if doing so serves India's international obligations, such as those under the UNCRPD. Further constitutional backing can be found in the Eleventh and Twelfth Schedules of the Constitution (Articles 243G and 243W), which recognize the welfare of the "handicapped and mentally retarded" as essential functions of panchayats and municipalities respectively.

4.3 *Evolution of Disability-Related Legislations in India*

India's legal regime for PwDs has evolved progressively over the past few decades. A brief overview of the key legislations is provided below:

a. The Mental Health Act, 1987 & The Mental Healthcare Act, 2017 (referred to as Mental Health Act, 1987 and Mental Health Act, 2017 respectively hereafter):

Originally enacted to regulate care for persons with mental illness, the Mental Health Act, 1987[12] was later superseded by the Mental Healthcare Act, 2017[13]. The latter adopts a rights-based approach and aims to ensure access to mental health services while safeguarding the rights and dignity of persons with mental illness.

b. The Rehabilitation Council of India (RCI) Act, 1992[14]:

[12] Accessed on June 20, 2025 at https://ncwapps.nic.in/acts/THEMENTALHEALTHACT1987.pdf.

[13] Accessed on June 20, 2025 at https://www.indiacode.nic.in/bitstream/123456789/2249/1/A2017-10.pdf.

[14] Accessed on June 20, 2025 at https://www.indiacode.nic.in/bitstream/123456789/19048/1/rehabilitation_council_of_india_act_1992.pdf.

This Act established the RCI as the statutory authority responsible for regulating training and maintaining standards among rehabilitation professionals. It mandates registration and accreditation to ensure quality service delivery for PwDs.

c. The Persons with Disabilities (Equal Opportunities, Protection of Rights and Full Participation) Act, 1995 (referred to as PWD Act, 1995 hereafter)[15]:

A landmark legislation, the PWD Act, 1995 was India's first comprehensive legal instrument to recognize disability rights. It covered seven types of disabilities and addressed employment, education, affirmative action, barrier-free access, and institutional support.

d. THE NATIONAL TRUST FOR WELFARE OF PERSONS WITH AUTISM, CEREBRAL PALSY, MENTAL RETARDATION AND MULTIPLE DISABILITIES ACT, 1999 (referred to as the National Trust Act, 1999 hereafter)[16]:

This Act was introduced to ensure care and protection of persons with developmental disabilities, including Autism, Cerebral Palsy, Mental Retardation, and Multiple Disabilities. It enables legal guardianship and independent living arrangements for PwDs who require lifelong support.

4.4 *National Policy for Persons with Disabilities, 2006*[17]

The National Policy for Persons with Disabilities (PwDs), 2006, was formulated in light of constitutional guarantees of equality, justice, and dignity. It responded to the growing realisation that PwDs could lead fulfilling lives if granted equal opportunities and access to services. The policy aimed at shifting focus from medical to social rehabilitation and

[15] Accessed on June 20, 2025 at https://www.indiacode.nic.in/bitstream/123456789/12890/1/the_persons_with_disabilities_act%2C_1995_no._1_of_1996_date_01.01.1996.pdf.

[16] Accessed on June 21, 2025 at https://www.indiacode.nic.in/bitstream/123456789/1951/1/A1999_44.pdf.

[17] Accessed on July 2, 2025 at https://cdnbbsr.s3waas.gov.in/s3e58aea67b01fa747687f038dfde066f6/uploads/2023/10/20231013248779923.pdf.

mainstreaming based on capability rather than charity. In particular, the policy aimed at promoting equal opportunities and non-discrimination; protection of rights and dignity; full participation in society; empowerment through education, employment, and access to facilities. The policy builds upon three core legislations, namely, the PWD Act, 1995, the National Trust Act, 1999, and the Rehabilitation Council of India Act, 1992. Seven National Institutes and over 120 District Disability Rehabilitation Centres (DDRCs) form the backbone of the infrastructure. These are supported by multiple state institutions and over 250 private training institutions.

The National Policy lays out a broad, multi-dimensional strategy to tackle the needs and rights of persons with disabilities (PwDs). The rehabilitation framework outlined in the policy is three-pronged:

- Physical rehabilitation entails timely medical interventions, provision of assistive aids, and the development of trained personnel for delivery of these services.
- Educational rehabilitation envisions a fully inclusive schooling system from early childhood to higher education, supported by special schools, open learning options, and suitable learning aids.
- Economic rehabilitation is advanced through proactive efforts to provide dignified employment—via wage employment (with a mandated 3% reservation in government and PSU sectors) and via self-employment schemes enabled by concessional finance through National Handicap Finance and Development Corporation (NHFDC), and training via skill-building centres.

The policy pays particular attention to women and children with disabilities, acknowledging their distinct vulnerabilities. For women with disabilities, provisions include special hostels, vocational training, and mechanisms to prevent exploitation. Notably, programmes must include at least 25% representation of women. Recognizing their caregiving challenges, the policy supports temporary financial aid to mothers with disabilities for hiring child care support. For children with disabilities, the policy underscores the need for an enabling environment that ensures their development with dignity. This includes not only inclusive and barrier-free education but also specialised services for children with severe or multiple disabilities.

A major thrust of the policy is the creation of a barrier-free physical and digital environment that enables independent functioning and mobility for PwDs. The policy mandates that all public infrastructure—government buildings, transport facilities, educational institutions, and recreational spaces—must be redesigned using universal design principles. This includes the implementation of disability-friendly building codes and space standards, adoption of ramps, accessible toilets, tactile flooring, and auditory signals in transportation systems. Moreover, information and communication technologies (ICTs) are to be rendered accessible. This means that websites—particularly of government departments—must conform to accessibility standards that allow screen-reading tools and text-to-speech software. Sign language, augmentative and alternative communication methods, and large print formats are also to be widely promoted. Recognising the gap in professional expertise, the policy encourages the training of architects, engineers, and urban planners in accessibility norms, and the development of a cadre of access auditors to monitor compliance. This shift marks a significant departure from mere tokenistic approaches to genuine infrastructural inclusion.

Social protection for PwDs is recognized as essential to reduce the economic burden associated with disability. The policy promotes a simplified, decentralised, and citizen-friendly disability certification process, ensuring legal recognition of disability status, which is essential for availing benefits. A strong focus is laid on financial security, particularly for persons with severe disabilities and their families. Provisions include tax exemptions for PwDs and their guardians, disability pensions and unemployment allowances to be rationalised and expanded by states and UTs, and long-term care support through the National Trust, including legal guardianship and the Supported Guardianship Scheme for destitute or abandoned individuals with high support needs. This comprehensive view of social security treats PwDs not as dependents, but as rights-holders entitled to structural and institutional support across their lifespan.

Robust and up-to-date data is the bedrock of informed policy. The policy mandates regular collection and analysis of disability-related socio-economic data through both the Census and the National Sample Survey Organisation (NSSO), with a frequency of at least every five years. Efforts are to be made to standardize definitions and data classifications across agencies to ensure comparability and accuracy. A second transformative provision is the push toward technological innovation. The policy envisions a dedicated Rehabilitation Technology Centre under the Ministry of Science & Technology to spearhead research on adaptive aids and digital tools. Priority is given to developing low-cost, durable, and user-friendly assistive devices, drawing on partnerships with premier institutions and global expertise. This orientation toward technology not only promotes independence but also lays the foundation for universal access to the digital economy.

A well-structured governance mechanism is proposed to ensure policy execution. The Ministry of Social Justice and Empowerment serves as the nodal ministry, with support from an Inter-Ministerial Coordinating Body that includes NGOs, DPOs, and family groups. Each line ministry is expected to prepare five-year perspective plans and annual reports detailing disability inclusion outcomes. Importantly, Panchayati Raj Institutions and urban local bodies are entrusted with local-level planning and monitoring. Chief Commissioners and State Commissioners for Disabilities are given a central role in statutory compliance and grievance redressal. The provision of a comprehensive policy review every five years ensures accountability, adaptability, and progress tracking at both central and state levels. The policy recognises that NGOs are indispensable allies in the disability movement. It proposes a systematised approach to register, map, and strengthen disability-focused NGOs, especially in underserved areas. NGOs are encouraged to develop ethical codes of conduct, diversify their funding sources to reduce dependency on state aid, and participate more actively in training, monitoring, and innovation. This pluralistic approach reinforces that disability inclusion is a shared social responsibility, not just a state obligation.

To conclude, the National Policy for Persons with Disabilities, 2006, marks a transformative shift in India's approach to disability—from charity-based to rights-based. By combining legislative backing with institutional support and a multi-sectoral strategy, the policy lays a foundational framework for building an inclusive society. It emphasises empowerment, mainstreaming, dignity, and independent living for all persons with disabilities, particularly focusing on rural outreach, education, employment, and accessibility. Together, these interlinked policy measures reflect a comprehensive vision that goes beyond welfare to assert the rights, autonomy, and dignity of persons with disabilities. By emphasizing barrier-free design, legal identity, data-driven governance, and technology-based empowerment, the policy sets the foundation for a more inclusive and equitable India.

4.5 *National Policy on Universal Electronic Accessibility*[18]

Recognising that access to technologies and the Internet is fundamental for ensuring democratic, effective, efficient and equitable participation in an information society, the Government of India released the National Policy on Universal Electronic Accessibility in 2013 to eliminate discrimination on the basis of disabilities as well as to facilitate equal access to electronics and Information and Communication Technologies (ICTs). It proposes universal access to electronic and ICT products and services and sets out implementation guidelines for the policy. The accessibility standards and guidelines under this policy have been formulated or adapted from the prevailing standards including W3C accessibility standards[19], and guidelines including ATAG (Authoring Tools Accessibility Guidelines); WCAG 2.0 (Web Content Accessibility Guidelines); and UAAG (User Agent Accessibility Guidelines).[20] The policy mandated the creation of all electronic contents in an accessible format including local language support. The policy would be reviewed from time to time by the Department of Electronics and Information Technology.

4.5.1 India's Follow-Up of Web Accessibility Content

India has recognized the importance of web accessibility and has taken legal and policy measures to ensure compliance with the Web Content Accessibility Guidelines (WCAG). The Indian government has adopted WCAG principles to promote digital inclusion, especially for persons with disabilities, in line with both national and international commitments. The Guidelines for Indian Government Websites and Apps (GIGW),

[18] The policy document can be accessed at https://www.meity.gov.in/static/uploads/2024/02/18rpr.pdf.

[19] The Web Content Accessibility Guidelines (WCAG) are a set of internationally recognized standards developed by the World Wide Web Consortium (W3C) to ensure that web content is accessible to all users, including persons with disabilities. These guidelines provide technical and design recommendations to make websites, applications, and digital content more inclusive.

[20] For an overview along with further details and latest updates of these various accessibility standards and guidelines, please visit https://www.w3.org/WAI/standards-guidelines/.

issued by the Ministry of Electronics and Information Technology, aligns with WCAG 2.0 Level AA standards.[21]

National Informatics Centre (NIC) has released three versions of Guidelines of Indian Websites—the first version was released in 2009, the second version in 2019, and the latest third version was released in March 2023. These guidelines serve as a single point of reference for all three aspects of digital systems of the internet i.e., quality, accessibility and security:

- GIGW 1.0—The 2009 version, based on the Web Content Accessibility Guidelines (WCAG) 1.0, provided detailed information on various accessibility features such as text alternatives for images, resizable text, and colour contrast. The guidelines also mandated that all government websites should be compatible with assistive technologies such as screen readers and provided guidelines for testing the accessibility of government websites.
- GIGW 2.0—A significant improvement over the previous version, the 2019 version was based on WCAG 2.0 and covered a wider range of disabilities including visual, auditory, physical, and cognitive impairments. The guidelines included detailed information on various accessibility features such as keyboard accessibility, colour contrast, and text resizing. It mandated that all new government websites should comply with the WCAG 2.0 Level AA accessibility standards.
- GIGW 3.0—Released in March 2023, this is the most advanced version of GIGW formulated jointly with Standardisation Testing and Quality Certification (STQC), Directorate of the Ministry of Electronics and Information Technology and Indian Computer Emergency Response Team (CERT- In). It is aimed at improving the user interface and user experience of government websites. These guidelines are especially designed to incorporate features like intuitive page loading (using AI and analytics) based on user profile. It takes special cognizance of mobile revolution and seeks to enhance accessibility and usability of mobile apps developed by government agencies. The guidelines have been designed keeping in mind the

[21] For details of these guidelines, please see the document at https://cdnbbsr.s3waas.gov.in/s3c92a10324374fac681719d63979d00fe/uploads/2025/02/2025021775.pdf.

public digital infrastructure initiatives that will enhance government's delivery of services, benefits and information. It also includes critical aspects such as API level integration with social media, India Portal, DigiLocker, Aadhaar- based identity, single sign- on and data sharing on open formats.

4.6 Accessible India Campaign (Sugamya Bharat Abhiyan): Toward Universal Accessibility

Launched on December 3, 2015, the Accessible India Campaign (AIC) is a nationwide flagship initiative of the Department of Empowerment of Persons with Disabilities (DEPwD) aimed at creating a barrier-free and inclusive environment for Persons with Disabilities (PwDs) across India.[22] Aligned with Article 9 of the UN Convention on the Rights of Persons with Disabilities (UNCRPD) and Sects. 40–46 of the Rights of Persons with Disabilities (RPwD) Act, 2016, the campaign targets three critical verticals:

(1) the built environment,
(2) the transportation system, and
(3) the information and communication ecosystem.

1. Built Environment Accessibility

AIC promotes the transformation of public infrastructure—government buildings, schools, hospitals, and workplaces—into universally accessible spaces. This includes provisions for ramps, accessible toilets, tactile pathways, Braille signage, alarm systems, and accessible parking. The campaign mandates accessibility audits and adherence to standards such as the Harmonized Guidelines and Space Standards for Barrier-Free Environment, ensuring that retrofitting is consistent with both international norms (e.g., ISO) and local realities. Accessibility is emphasized not just in urban but also in peri-urban and rural areas, ensuring that equity extends to all geographic regions.

[22] Please visit https://depwd.gov.in/accessible-india-campaign/ for more details.

2. Transportation System Accessibility

Recognizing mobility as a precondition for inclusion, the campaign focuses on accessible travel infrastructure—airports, railway stations, and bus terminals—as well as on transport carriers themselves (low-floor buses, accessible coaches, aerobridges). It encompasses associated services such as ticket booking, travel information systems, and digital platforms, advocating universal design and requiring conformity with standards like the Code of Practice for Bus Body Design.

3. Information and Communication Accessibility

The campaign addresses digital and informational barriers by enhancing the accessibility of government websites, public documents, audiovisual media, and communication formats. It promotes adoption of the WCAG 2.0 standards (ISO/IEC 40,500:2012), use of sign language interpreters, and captioning of public news broadcasts. Accessibility audits of websites are undertaken in collaboration with the National Informatics Centre (NIC).

AIC has functioned through a structured system of proposals, grants, audits, and monitoring, with dedicated Programme Management Units (PMUs) and a Management Information System (MIS) for real-time tracking. As per the revised guidelines, the campaign is set to be merged into the Barrier Free Environment component under SIPDA (Scheme for Implementation of the Rights of Persons with Disabilities Act, 2016) (from April 2024)[23], thus continuing its objectives through an integrated framework. In order to ensure a barrier free environment more effectively, in 2021, the Sugamya Bharat App was launched to enable citizens to report inaccessibility issues in public infrastructure. This app strengthens the campaign's Jan-Bhagidari (people's participation) approach and feeds into policymaking through real-time data and feedback.

Thus, the Accessible India Campaign has laid a transformative foundation for mainstreaming accessibility into India's developmental agenda. By systematically addressing environmental, transportation, and digital barriers, and by setting enforceable standards, AIC operationalizes India's

23 Please refer to the document at https://cdnbbsr.s3waas.gov.in/s3e58aea67b01fa747687f038dfde066f6/uploads/2023/10/202408141618446982.pdf.

legal obligations under the RPwD Act and its international commitments under the UNCRPD. As it transitions into the SIPDA framework, the campaign continues to play a pivotal role in making financial services, public infrastructure, and civic spaces equally accessible for persons with disabilities, thus reinforcing the vision of an inclusive and empowered India.

4.7 *The Rights of Persons with Disabilities Act*[24]*, 2016 and Rights of Persons with Disabilities Rules, 2017*[25]

The Government of India had enacted the Rights of Persons with Disabilities (RPWD) Act, 2016, to give domestic effect to India's obligations under the United Nations Convention on the Rights of Persons with Disabilities (UNCRPD) and for matters connected therewith or incidental thereto.[26] The enactment of RPWD Act, 2016 marks a significant legislative shift in conceptualising disability from the earlier medical and technical model of disability under the PWD Act, 1995, which carried a significant burden of stigma, to a rights-based and social model. The RPWD Act, 2016 recognises disability as a condition arising not only from impairments but also from communicational, cultural, economic, environmental, institutional, political, social, attitudinal or structural factors which hampers the full and effective participation of persons with disabilities in society. These barriers, as mentioned in Section 2(c) of the RPWD Act, 2016, lie at the heart of the exclusion experienced by persons with disabilities, preventing them from realizing their full potential and participating as full and equal members and citizens—a vision enshrined by the framers of the Indian Constitution.

As a significant development, the RPWD Act, 2016 incorporates the principle of 'reasonable accommodation', which is defined in Section 2(y) of this act as:

[24] Accessed on July 2, 2025 at https://www.indiacode.nic.in/bitstream/123456789/15939/1/the_rights_of_persons_with_disabilities_act%2C_2016.pdf.

[25] Accessed on July 2, 2025 at https://upload.indiacode.nic.in/showfile?actid=AC_CEN_25_54_00002_201649_1517807328299&type=rule&filename=Rules_notified_15.06.pdf.

[26] The RPWD Act came into force on April 19, 2017.

> "Reasonable accommodation" means necessary and appropriate modification and adjustments, without imposing a disproportionate or undue burden in a particular case, to ensure to persons with disabilities the enjoyment or exercise of rights equally with others.

Section 3 of the RPWD Act, 2016 deals with 'Equality and Non-discrimination', and reads as follows:

1. "The appropriate Government shall ensure that the persons with disabilities enjoy the right to equality, life with dignity and respect for his or her integrity equally with others.
2. The appropriate Government shall take steps to utilise the capacity of persons with disabilities by providing appropriate environment.
3. No person with disability shall be discriminated on the ground of disability, unless it is shown that the impugned act or omission is a proportionate means of achieving a legitimate aim.
4. No person shall be deprived of his or her personal liberty only on the ground of disability.
5. The appropriate Government shall take necessary steps to ensure reasonable accommodation for persons with disabilities."

In connection with Section 3 of the RPWD Act, 2016, it should be noted that Rule 3(4) of the Rights of Persons with Disabilities (RPWD) Rules, 2017 mandates that no establishment shall compel a person with disability to partly or fully pay the costs incurred for reasonable accommodation.

Section 13(1) of the RPWD Act, 2016 mandates the 'appropriate government' to ensure that the persons with disabilities have right, equally with others, to own or inherit property, movable or immovable, control their financial affairs and have access to bank loans, mortgages, and other forms of financial credit. Section 19(2)(d) mandates the provision of loans at concessional rates including that of microcredit to facilitate and support employment of persons with disabilities. That apart, Section 21(1) states that every establishment shall notify equal opportunity policy detailing measures proposed to be taken by it in pursuance of the provisions of this Chapter in the manner as may be prescribed by the Central Government. Rule 8 of the RPWD Rules, 2017 deals with 'Manner of publication of equal opportunity policy'. Under this rule, all establishments are mandated to publish equal opportunity policy for persons with disabilities, and display the same preferably on their websites, failing which, at conspicuous places in their premises. The equal opportunity policy of a private establishment having 20 or more employees and the Government establishments is also required to contain, among other things, provisions for assistive devices, barrier-free accessibility and other provisions for persons with disabilities.

Section 19 (1) read in conjunction with (2d) provides for loans at concessional rates including that of microcredit to facilitate and support employment of persons with disabilities especially for their vocational training and self- employment. Section 24 concerns with social security schemes and programmes to safeguard and promote the right of persons with disabilities for adequate standard of living to enable them to live independently or in the community. In particular, subsection 3 of Section 24 provides for, among other facilities, (g) disability pension to persons with disabilities subject to such income ceiling as may be notified; (h) unemployment allowance to persons with disabilities registered with Special Employment Exchange for more than two years and who could not be placed in any gainful occupation; (i) care- giver allowance to persons with disabilities with high support needs; and (j) comprehensive insurance scheme for persons with disability, not covered under the Employees State Insurance Schemes, or any other statutory or Government- sponsored insurance schemes. Section 26 further requires the appropriate Government to make (by notification) insurance schemes for their employees with disabilities.

Section 40 of the RPWD Act, 2016 deals with 'Accessibility' and the same reads as under:

"The Central Government shall, in consultation with the Chief Commissioner, formulate rules for persons with disabilities laying down the standards of accessibility for the physical environment, transportation, information and communications, including appropriate technologies and systems, and other facilities and services provided to the public in urban and rural areas."[27] Consequently, Rule 15 of the RPWD Rules, 2017, lays down 'Rules for Accessibility' and reads as under[28]:

1. "Every establishment shall comply with the following standards relating to physical environment, transport and information and communication technology, namely:-
   a. standard for public buildings as specified in the Harmonised Guidelines and Space Standards for Barrier Free Built Environment for Persons With Disabilities and Elderly Persons as issued by the Government of India, Ministry of Urban Development in March, 2016;
   b. standard for Bus Body Code for transportation system as specified in the notification of the Government of India in the Ministry of Road Transport and Highways, vide number G.S.R. 895(E), dated the 20th September, 2016;
   c. Information and Communication Technology- (i) website standard as specified in the guidelines for Indian Government websites, as adopted by Department of Administrative Reforms and Public Grievances, Government of India; (ii) documents to be placed on websites shall be in Electronic Publication (ePUB) or Optical Character Reader (OCR) based pdf format: Provided that the standard of accessibility in respect of other services and facilities shall be specified by the Central Government within a period of six months from the date of notification of these rules.
2. The respective Ministries and Departments shall ensure compliance of the standards of accessibility specified under this rule through the concerned domain regulators or otherwise."

[27] According to Section 2(x) of this Act, "public facilities and services" includes all forms of delivery of services to the public at large, including housing, educational and vocational trainings, employment and career advancement, shopping or marketing, religious, cultural, leisure or recreational, medical, health and rehabilitation, banking, finance and insurance, communication, postal and information, access to justice, public utilities, transportation.

[28] Please note that Rule 15 has undergone substantial amendments via notifications from 2023 to 2024, broadening its scope across multiple sectors including education, finance, transport, healthcare, and rural development.

Rule 16 further requires the Central Government to review from time to time the accessibility standards notified based on the latest scientific knowledge and technology.

Section 42 of the RPWD Act, 2016 deals with 'Access to information and communication technology'. This section requires the appropriate Government to take measures to ensure that,—(i) all contents available in audio, print and electronic media are in accessible format; (ii) persons with disabilities have access to electronic media by providing audio description, sign language interpretation and close captioning; (iii) electronic goods and equipment which are meant for every day use are available in universal design. Section 43, dealing with 'Consumer goods', requires the appropriate Government to take measures to promote development, production and distribution of universally designed consumer products and accessories for general use for persons with disabilities. Section 44 imposes strict compliance with accessibility norms during building construction and occupation. According to this section, No establishment can receive permission to construct any structure unless the proposed plan follows the accessibility rules prescribed by the Central Government under Section 40. Furthermore, buildings cannot be certified as complete or occupied unless they fully adhere to these accessibility requirements. The provision ensures that universal design is embedded from the outset of the construction process, rather than as a later retrofit.

Section 45 of the RPWD Act, 2016 sets a five-year deadline (from the date of relevant rule notification) for making all existing public buildings accessible in accordance with Central Government rules. States may be granted extensions on a case-by-case basis depending on their level of preparedness. Additionally, the appropriate Government and local authorities are mandated to prepare and publish an action plan prioritising accessibility improvements in essential service spaces, such as primary health centres, civil hospitals, schools, railway stations, and bus stops. This section recognizes both the urgency and logistical challenges in retrofitting older infrastructure. Section 46 requires that all service providers, whether government or private, must make their services accessible in line with the Central Government's rules under Section 40 within two years of notification. In special cases, the Central Government, in consultation with the Chief Commissioner for Persons with Disabilities, may extend the deadline for specific categories of services.

The section reinforces that accessibility is not limited to physical infrastructure—it extends to all forms of service delivery, including transport, communication, finance, and digital services.

To sum up, the RPWD Act, 2016 is not only a civil rights statute but a social justice framework designed to integrate persons with disabilities into the mainstream of Indian society—economically, politically, and culturally. The emphasis on accessibility, legal capacity, and equality in financial and employment sectors directly underpins the broader agenda of financial inclusion. While implementation challenges persist, the Act lays a solid legal foundation for realising a rights-based, inclusive model of development for persons with disabilities in India.

While the legal and policy frameworks discussed so far in this section establish broad principles of equality and accessibility, their practical implications become particularly visible in sectors where individuals interact directly with public and private institutions. The banking and financial services sector represents one such critical domain. Financial regulators and banking institutions have issued various guidelines aimed at improving accessibility of financial services for persons with disabilities. Examining these guidelines provides an opportunity to understand how broader legal commitments are translated into institutional practices affecting financial inclusion.

4.8 Bridging Law and Practice: Implementation Gaps and Institutional Responses in Disability-Inclusive Finance

Despite decades of progressive legislation in India—including the Mental Health Act (1987), the Rehabilitation Council of India Act (1992), the National Trust Act (1999), the Persons with Disabilities Act (1995), and most recently, the Rights of Persons with Disabilities (RPwD) Act (2016)—persons with disabilities (PwDs) continue to face persistent structural and institutional barriers in accessing basic financial services. The laws may have evolved, but their implementation has often lagged, especially in the absence of enforceable norms or clear operational guidelines for financial institutions.

It is against this backdrop of normative advancement and practical exclusion that India has witnessed a long and uneven trajectory of regulatory and judicial interventions—from early litigations by visually impaired individuals to more recent cases dealing with digital inaccessibility and denial of insurance. This subsection narratively maps the two-decade-long evolution of institutional responses to financial inclusion for PwDs—anchored in a chronological record of judicial decisions and circulars of the Reserve Bank of India (RBI) between 2005 and 2025, recent circulars of Insurance Regulatory and Development Authority of India (IRDAI) and Securities and Exchange Board of India (SEBI), and some recent guidelines of the Department of Financial Services (DFS).

4.8.1 Judicial Trigger and Early Regulatory Responses (2005–2009)

The journey began with the landmark case of V. P. Singhania v. Ministry of Finance & Others (CCPD Order, 2005)[29], in which the petitioner, representing the National Federation of the Blind, challenged the denial of cheque books, lockers, and loans to visually impaired persons who were unable to sign. The Chief Commissioner for Persons with Disabilities (CCPD) ruled in favour of the petitioner, affirming that visually impaired persons must be treated at par with others in banking services. The CCPD directed that thumb impressions or signatures be accepted without additional undertakings and mandated the provision of ATM, locker, and cheque book services on equal terms. This landmark ruling prompted a wave of regulatory responses by the Reserve Bank of India (RBI) in terms of a series of circulars reinforcing the legal and operational competence of visually impaired persons to access banking services. For instance, in its notification dated November 19, 2007, RBI recognised guardianship certificates under the National Trust Act, 1999, and Mental Health Act, 1987, allowing guardians to open and operate bank accounts on behalf of persons with developmental or mental disabilities (Reserve Bank of India, 2007). Going forward, RBI issued a series of notifications during June-July, 2008, thereby directing scheduled commercial banks (SCBs), State and Central Co-operative Banks, and Regional Rural Banks (RRBs) to offer full access to banking services, such as cheque books (including third-party cheques), lockers, ATM, net banking, retail loans, credit cards, etc. to visually challenged customers without discrimination (Reserve Bank of India, 2008a, 2008b, 2008c). A significant infrastructural push came through RBI notifications issued in April, 2009, which mandated accessible ATM infrastructure—ramps, adjusted heights, and Talking ATMs with Braille keypads—for all SCBs, RRBs,

[29] The copy of the court case is accessed from https://rbidocs.rbi.org.in/rdocs/content/pdfs/85806.pdf.

and Urban Cooperative Banks (UCBs) (Reserve Bank of India, 2009a, 2009b, 2009c).

4.8.2 *Renewed Judicial Vigilance and Expansion of Regulatory Scope (2012–2015)*

The litigation by Ramji Tripathi v. State Bank of India, BHU Branch (CCPD Order, 2012) (Indian Banks Association, 2017) reinforced the ongoing marginalisation of PwDs despite the 2005 judicial and 2008–2009 regulatory directions. Mr. Tripathi, a visually impaired government employee, was denied an ATM card and cheque book due to perceived risk. CCPD overruled SBI's discriminatory practices and reaffirmed RBI and IBA guidelines, and censured the additional requirements imposed on disabled persons.

Reacting to continuing non-compliance, RBI issued fresh circulars for SCBs (Reserve Bank of India, 2012a) as well as for RRBs (Reserve Bank of India, 2012b) reaffirming previous mandates. It instructed all these banks to comply with the 2008 and 2009 circulars and ensure that all banking facilities, like ATM, internet banking, etc. are accessible without any hurdle and discrimination to visually challenged/persons with disabilities. Furthermore, in order to facilitate hassle-free opening/operating of bank accounts by the guardian/manager on behalf of persons with autism, cerebral palsy, mental retardation and multiple disabilities, RBI issued fresh guidelines (Reserve Bank of India, 2014a) which superseded its 2007 directive (Reserve Bank of India, 2007) and clarified the legal validity of guardianship under both the Mental Health Act, 1987 and the National Trust Act, 1999 for account operations. It emphasised that banks must honour guardianship certificates issued under the Mental Health Act and the National Trust Act and should ensure that their branches give proper guidance to their customers so that the guardians/managers of the disabled persons do not face any difficulties in this regard.

With infrastructural accessibility still lagging, and after receiving suggestions from the Government of India and other public representatives, RBI reinforced its earlier directions (Reserve Bank of India, 2009a, 2009b, 2009c), making Talking ATMs equipped with Braille keypads mandatory from July 1, 2014, and requiring branches to provide magnifying glasses and ramps (Reserve Bank of India, 2014a, 2014b). It reiterated that banks must put in place an inclusive architectural design in their branches, and ensure accessibility of ATMs by persons with disabilities for undertaking day-to-day banking transactions. Banks were also advised to report the progress made in this regard periodically to their respective Board of Directors/Customer Service Committee of the Board and ensure compliance. Additionally, RBI (2014c) extended these responsibilities to non-banking financial companies (NBFCs) and called for anti-discriminatory practices against physically/visually challenged persons in making available various business facilities, including loan offerings, staff sensitisation and disability training modules, and grievance redressal. Perhaps most transformative was RBI's inclusion of PwDs under the Weaker Sections category of Priority Sector Lending (PSL), thereby incentivising banks to lend to PwDs on preferential/concessional terms (Reserve Bank of India, 2015a).

4.8.3 *Consolidation through Master Circulars and Pension-Related Protections (2015–2017)*

In a bid to consolidate and clarify various previous directions, RBI issued Master Circulars on Customer Service in Banks to SCBs and UCBs to systematize inclusive customer service (Reserve Bank of India, 2015b, 2015c). These master circulars laid out comprehensive norms on bank infrastructure and branch accessibility, staff training along with the use of technology such as Talking ATMs with Braille keypads and magnifying glasses. They also introduced mandatory display of guardianship rules and obligations. To clarify misinterpretations, RBI (2016) reiterated that guardianship should only be demanded when the individual demonstrably lacks capacity. Judicial scrutiny further strengthened this area in Naresh Bansilal Soni v. Municipal Commissioner (2016, Gujarat HC) (Government of India, 2024a), where pension was arbitrarily stopped for a person with intellectual disability. The court reaffirmed the right of dependent PwDs to receive family pensions under Rule 93 of the Gujarat Civil Services Pension Rules, and ordered the payment with interest (Government of India, 2024a).

4.8.4 *Digital Transition and the Rise of Inclusive Technology Mandates (2017–2020)*

With a growing push for digital services and recognising the vulnerability of aged and disabled pensioners, RBI (2017a) mandated agency banks to adopt witness-certified withdrawal mechanisms and staff sensitization. In a significant move, RBI (2017b) introduced new directives for branch-level services: dedicated counters, proactive issuance of cheque books, doorstep banking, digital form support, and automatic account conversion for senior citizens and visually impaired customers. These measures were to be implemented by December 31, 2017. Yet, compliance remained uneven. Thus, RBI (2020a) made doorstep banking services mandatory for senior citizens and differently abled persons across all SCBs (including RRBs), Payment Banks, Small Finance Banks, and Local Area Banks. Quarterly progress reporting and public disclosure of implementation were mandated. Meanwhile, the case of Gopalan P. V. v. Union of India & Ors. (2020, Kerala HC) (Government of India, 2024a) addressed procedural delays in the appointment of legal guardians. The court emphasized the concept of "limited guardianship" under Section 14 of the RPwD Act, 2016 and directed the competent authority to process the application without delay.

The enactment of the Rights of Persons with Disabilities (RPWD) Act, 2016, and the subsequent framing of the RPWD Rules, 2017, catalysed a regulatory shift within the insurance sector. In response, the Insurance Regulatory and Development Authority of India (IRDAI) issued a series of circulars aimed at ensuring that persons with disabilities are not discriminated against in insurance coverage and are provided equitable access to insurance products and services. These circulars of IRDAI are directly downloadable from the IRDAI website under "Circulars" section by reference number and date. They are also cited in Government of India (2024b). These different circulars of IRDAI are briefly discussed here.

The IRDAI issued a circular on March 27, 2018, addressing the exemption of reinsurance schemes from paying Goods and Services Tax, for some specified insurance schemes, which included Niramaya Health Insurance Scheme implemented by the National Trust for the Welfare of Persons with Autism, Cerebral Palsy, Mental Retardation and Multiple Disabilities Act, 1999. This was to ensure reduced premium cost for persons with disabilities (PWDs) under this insurance scheme. The circular emphasised that the benefit of premium Goods and Service Tax Exemption reduction due to non- payment of the Goods and Services Tax should be passed on to PWDs. Through another circular, dated August 16, 2018, the IRDAI directed all insurance companies to comply with the provisions of the Mental Healthcare Act, 2017. As per Section 21(4) of the Mental Healthcare Act, 2017, every insurer is required to make provision for medical insurance for treatment of mental illness on the same basis as is available for treatment of physical illness.[30]

In alignment with the Accessible India Campaign and the RPWD Act, the Mobile Aided Note Identifier (MANI) app was launched by RBI on January 1, 2020 (Reserve Bank of India, 2020b, 2018). This smartphone-based tool helped visually impaired users identify denominations of currency notes, offering audio and vibration feedback in Hindi and English (later expanded to 13 Indian languages (Reserve Bank of India, 2022)).

4.8.5 *Expanding the Accessibility Regime: Further Mandates, Misses, and Momentum (2020–2025)*

In February 2020, the IRDAI has mandated that insurance companies include persons with disabilities, those affected by HIV/AIDS, and people with mental illnesses in their Inclusive Health Insurance Policies (as cited in Government of India, 2024b). Insurers are required to develop underwriting policies that address not only standard applicants but also those with additional health challenges. These policies must be in line with the IRDAI (Health Insurance) Regulations, 2016 and comply with laws such as the HIV and AIDS Prevention and Control Act, 2017 and the Mental Healthcare Act, 2017, ensuring that these individuals are not unfairly excluded. Further, insurers are required to publicly disclose their approach to offering coverage to these groups and publish their underwriting philosophy on their websites, providing clear information about how they assess and offer insurance to PWDs, people with HIV/AIDS, and those with mental illnesses. This step ensures transparency and promotes inclusivity in health insurance practices.

In its another circular, dated June 9, 2020, the IRDAI permitted issuing a stand- alone 'Compulsory Personal Accident' cover for owners/drivers under Motor Insurance Policies, in cases of death and permanent disability (total and partial) (as cited in Government of India, 2024b). With regards to the Individual Life Term Insurance Products, the IRDAI clarified that riders can be included in Standard Individual Term Life Insurance Product for total/partial payment of insured sum, in case of

[30] Please refer to the relevant section of the original Act at https://www.indiacode.nic.in/bitstream/123456789/2249/1/A2017-10.pdf.

Permanent Disability.[31] The IRDAI issued detailed guidelines on Standard Personal Accident Insurance Products.[32] These guidelines include the following provisions for persons with disabilities:

- The insurer is required to pay 100% of the sum insured if the insured person suffers permanent total disablement directly due to an accident during the policy period.
- The insurer is required to pay up to 50% of the sum insured if the insured person suffers permanent partial disablement directly due to an accident during the policy period.
- Compensation is payable if the insured person suffers from temporary total disablement and is incapacitated from engaging in employment due to an accident, at the rate of 0.2% of the base sum insured per week, for up to 100 weeks, provided the disablement period exceeds 4 weeks; and
- Following an admissible claim under the policy for Death or Permanent Total Disability of the insured person, a one- time educational grant of 10% of the base sum insured per child is payable.

Regarding Standard Domestic Travel Insurance Products, the IRDAI's detailed guidelines, issued on May 5, 2021, include the following provisions for persons with disabilities (as cited in Government of India, 2024b):

- The insurer is required to pay 100% of the insured sum if the insured person suffered permanent total disablement (as specified in Section 3 of the Guidelines) due to an accident during the period of insurance, while travelling on a passenger on a common carrier; and
- The insurer is required to pay 50% of the insured sum if the insured person suffered permanent partial disablement (as specified in Section 4 of the Guidelines) due to an accident during the period of insurance, while travelling on a passenger on a common carrier.

[31] The circular, as cited in Government of India (2024a) can be accessed at https://irdai.gov.in/document-detail?documentId=395579.

[32] The circular, as cited in Government of India (2024a) can be accessed at https://irdai.gov.in/documents/37343/0/Final+guidelines+on+standard+PA+product-25.02.2021+(2).pdf/ba6be748-a838-530a-ea7d-c5be5dd7b8c3?t=1633499581090.

Despite regulatory guidelines from IRDAI, the instances of violation were reported. For example, the judicial stance matured in Saurabh Shukla v. Max Bupa Health Insurance Co. Ltd. & Ors. (2022, Delhi HC) (Government of India, 2024a), where the petitioner with tetraplegia was denied insurance. The court held that denial of health coverage on the basis of disability violates both the RPwD Act, 2016 and the UNCRPD, and directed IRDAI to abolish the discriminatory classification of "substandard lives." Consequently, the IRDAI, through its circular issued on May 27, 2022, modified the definitions of 'Multiple Sclerosis with Persisting Symptoms' and 'Loss of Speech' contained in the Master Circular on Standardization of Health Insurance Products issued on July 22, 2020, which prescribes the nomenclature and procedure for 22 'Critical Illnesses' that may form part of health insurance policies (as cited in Government of India, 2024b). Further, in its Master Circular on Health Insurance Business[33], issued on May 29, 2024, the IRDAI directed all health insurers to ensure that specific health insurance products are designed and offered to persons with disabilities, individuals affected by HIV/AIDS, and persons with mental illness. Health insurance products are designed in line with the scope and parameters of such policies, as outlined in a previous IRDAI circular issued on February 27, 2023. This circular specifies that insurers may broaden the scope of these health insurance products for persons with disabilities, but they cannot narrow the coverage beyond the minimum standards set by the model product. Likewise, in another Master Circular on Life Insurance Business, issued on June 12, 2024 (Government of India, 2024b), the IRDAI directs all life insurers to ensure equitable access to life insurance products for persons with disabilities. It specifies the following:

- Inclusivity Requirement: Life insurers are required to design products and riders that cater to all customer segments, including persons with disabilities.
- Wide Choice: Insurers are required to provide a variety of products that suit the specific needs of persons with disabilities.

[33] The relevant circular, as also cited in Government of India (2024b) can be accessed at https://irdai.gov.in/documents/37343/365525/%25e0%25a4%25b8%25e0%25a5%258d%25e0%25a4%25b5%25e0%25a4%25be%25e0%25a4%25b8%25e0%25a5%258d%25e0%25a4%25a5%25e0%25a5%258d%25e0%25a4%25af+%25e0%25a4%25ac%25e0%25a5%2580%25e0%25a4%25ae%25e0%25a4%25be+%25e0%25a4%25b5%25.

- Flexibility and Affordability: Products should be flexible and affordable to ensure accessibility for persons with disabilities.
- Clear Information: Insurers must present customer information (benefits, exclusions, etc.) in a simple, easy- to- understand format to help persons with disabilities make informed decisions, including information of the size of benefit payable on disability due to accident before the end of the policy term.
- Partial Withdrawal: Persons with disabilities should be allowed to partially withdraw amounts for their life insurance products to meet medical and incidental expenses arising from disability or incapacitation.

In a transformative policy shift aligned with the Rights of Persons with Disabilities Act, 2016 and the Accessible India Campaign, the Department of Financial Services in 2024 issued comprehensive accessibility standards and guidelines for the banking, insurance, and broader financial sector (Government of India, 2024c, 2024d, 2024e). These guidelines mandate a universal design approach—ensuring that all physical premises, self-service technologies, digital platforms, and customer-facing services are inclusive, dignified, and responsive to the diverse needs of persons with disabilities (PwDs) across all financial entities—banks, insurance companies, and financial institutions. The standards emphasise:

- Barrier-free infrastructure with ramps, tactile paths, accessible counters, signage, lifts, and toilets designed to meet the needs of wheelchair users, the visually impaired, and others with functional limitations.
- Inclusive self-service systems, including Talking ATMs, kiosks, POS devices, and card readers with Braille and tactile features, audio instructions, and height-adjustable components.
- Digitally accessible platforms—websites, apps, and documents—compliant with WCAG 2.1, IS 17802, and GIGW, featuring customizable settings, keyboard navigation, screen-reader compatibility, and alternative text support.
- Customer-centric service provisions like doorstep delivery/collection of documents, trained staff assistance in form-filling, magnifiers for low-vision users, and priority counters.

- Institutional accountability through mandatory nodal officers at all branches, regular training on disability etiquette and rights, monitoring mechanisms, and inclusion of PwD service indicators in internal reporting and customer service governance.

Collectively, these standards represent a paradigm shift: from reactive adjustments to proactive design, embedding accessibility not as charity or compliance but as a core operational ethic across India's financial ecosystem.

Recognising the gaps in access to basic financial services, the Reserve Bank of India in its Master Circular on Deendayal Antyodaya Yojana—National Rural Livelihoods Mission (DAY-NRLM) (Reserve Bank of India, 2024a) included following specific provisions related to persons with disabilities:

- The circular specifies that self- help groups for persons with disabilities may include both men and women. This provision is an exception to the usual gender- specific self- help groups promoted by DAY- NRLM, which are predominantly women- centric.
- In the case of self- help groups for persons with disabilities, the group size can be reduced to a minimum of 5 members, unlike the usual self- help groups, which typically consist of 10–20 members.
- Banks are required to open savings accounts for all self- help groups, including those with members with disabilities. Self- help groups that promote savings among their members are eligible to open such accounts.

These provisions aim to ensure that individuals with disabilities are integrated into the financial inclusion initiatives under DAY- NRLM, making the scheme more inclusive.

Furthermore, in an attempt to promote inclusive digital payments, RBI (2024b) directed all Payment System Participants to make their infrastructure accessible and submit time-bound action plans, in compliance with February 2024 DFS guidelines (Government of India, 2024c). Moreover, RBI (2025) updated pension disbursement protocols, reinforcing the right to agency and dignity for pensioners who are disabled or incapacitated.

In a significant ruling on the rights of persons with disabilities and survivors of acid attacks, the Supreme Court of India in Pragya Prasun & Ors. v. Union of India & Ors. (W.P. C.No. 289 of 2024) and Amar Jain v. Union of India & Ors. (W.P. C.No. 49 of 2025), delivered on April 30, 2025, held that digital exclusion caused by inaccessible e-KYC procedures violates fundamental constitutional rights.[34] The petitioners—acid attack survivors in the former case, and a 100% visually challenged individual in the other—challenged the design of biometric-based authentication systems (such as facial recognition and iris scans) used for banking and mobile services. The Court ruled that these procedures violate Articles 14 (equality), 15 (non-discrimination), and 21 (life and dignity) of the Constitution. Citing the Rights of Persons with Disabilities Act, 2016 and the UN Convention on the Rights of Persons with Disabilities (UNCRPD), the Court emphasised the state's obligation to provide reasonable accommodation and ensure that digital platforms are universally accessible. The Court directed regulators including the RBI, SEBI, and the Department of Telecommunications to:

- Immediately introduce alternative KYC procedures such as thumbprint authentication, paper-based verification, and screen-reader-compatible forms.
- Issue detailed accessibility standards for all digital financial services.
- Ensure compliance with IS 17802, WCAG, and other digital accessibility norms.

The judgment marks a watershed moment, affirming that digital financial inclusion is a constitutional entitlement, not a technical choice—and exclusion by design is tantamount to discrimination.

In response to the Supreme Court's April 2025 judgment affirming digital access as a constitutional right under Article 21, SEBI has very recently issued a circular directing all regulated entities—including stock exchanges, brokers, mutual funds, depositories, portfolio managers, and KYC agencies—to ensure their digital platforms are fully accessible to persons with disabilities, thereby ensuring their compliance with the provisions of RPwD Act, 2016 and RPwD Rules, 2017 (Securities and

[34] The judgement can be accessed at https://api.sci.gov.in/supremecourt/2024/17879/17879_2024_13_1501_61229_Judgement_30-Apr-2025.pdf.

Exchange Board of India, 2025). All regulated entities are now required to carry out a phased set of actions: prepare and submit an inventory of their digital platforms within one month; appoint an IAAP-certified accessibility auditor within 45 days; complete a comprehensive accessibility audit within three months; and implement necessary remediations to ensure full compliance within six months. Accessibility audit reports must also be submitted annually within 30 days after the financial year ends. Each entity is required to designate a senior-level Nodal Officer to oversee accessibility efforts and serve as the liaison with SEBI. Additionally, they must establish a dedicated grievance redressal mechanism for accessibility-related issues, train their staff and developers in inclusive digital design, and ensure that investor-facing platforms conform to standards such as WCAG 2.1, GIGW, and IS 17802. Special emphasis has been placed on making KYC and e-KYC processes inclusive by incorporating features like assistive technology compatibility, voice-guided support, ISL video guidance, and manual review of rejections involving disability. No automated denial of service should occur without human oversight.

4.8.6 Concluding Observations

This evolving chronology from 2005 to 2025 reflects a sustained yet staggered institutional response to the demands of disability-inclusive banking. The consistent issuance of RBI circulars, DFS guidelines, judicial orders, and a recent SEBI circular reveals a policy ecosystem gradually aligning with the letter and spirit of the RPWD Act, 2016. Yet, the repetition of court cases even two decades after the first intervention underlines the persistence of implementation gaps—shifting from physical to digital domains in more recent years. As we proceed to the next two sections, we aim to assess how these regulatory efforts translate into actual outcomes and what the broader landscape of financial inclusion for persons with disabilities in India currently looks like.

5 Persistent Barriers in Accessing Basic Financial Services by Persons with Disabilities (PwDs)

Despite progressive legislative and regulatory frameworks such as RPwD Act, 2016 and the issuance of accessibility standards and guidelines for the banking, insurance and other financial institutions, significant implementation gaps persist that hinder the inclusion of PwDs in the formal financial system. While there exists no systematic data on the access to basic financial services by PwDs, multiple studies and audits reveal consistent barriers in access to basic financial services such as banking, insurance, and digital financial platforms.

5.1 *Gaps in Accessibility of Banking Infrastructure and Services*

Motivated by a report of the Centre for Internet and Society (CIS) on Accessibility of Government Websites in India, published in 2012[35], an accessibility evaluation of 48 public sector and private sector banking websites in India by Kaur and Dani (2014) found that none of the website was fully accessible. Only 9 websites were highly accessible, 3 websites came under low accessibility category and 36 websites were inaccessible. This showed that Indian banks were not able to provide accessible and barrier free environment in online services and websites were difficult to be accessed by users with disabilities. The result also showed that there was no difference between public and private sector bank website with respect to WCAG 1.0, WCAG 2.0 and accessibility score but there was a difference between them in complexity score suggesting that complex object design make the website less popular.

Three years later, a similar attempt was made by Mathew Martin and Rabindranath (2017), who tested the accessibility of 103 websites of banking and financial institutions (BFIs) in India for their compliance of WCAG2.0, focusing on several parameters, like interactivity, accessibility, and information inputs. Among the 103 websites of BFIs in India, only 11 websites had full compliance as per the norms of W3C. 14.5% of Indian BFIs websites passed the accessibility test, thus proving that most of the websites of BFIs were inaccessible to PWDs. Moreover, vernacular

[35] The report can be accessed at https://cis-india.org/accessibility/accessibility-of-government-websites-in-india.

language facility was offered by only 28% of the BFIs, thus losing out on rural banking customers, who might understand only the vernacular language. The disability-specific graphics or alternative text to images in the website was offered only by 9.7% of the BFIs in India, thus limiting the use of the website by visually challenged customers. A surprising finding of the study was that majority of the content in the website of these organizations was about information regarding the financial instruments aspects, instead of services for customers of BFIs. Majority of them (63.1%) do not even have feedback or complaint form details.

The 2022 study by the Xavier's Resource Centre for the Visually Challenged (XRCVC) (referred to as XRCVC Report, 2022 hereafter)[36] also conducted a preliminary examination to check accessibility of Indian bank websites and their mobile applications, covering 22 banks, including 11 public sector banks, 6 private sector banks, and 5 foreign banks. In addition to these 22 bank websites and Apps, the study also tested the accessibility features of 6 third-party wallets and UPI Apps. All basic accessibility features, such as keyboard/gesture operability, form elements, CAPTCHA, descriptive link, zooming, colour contrast, etc. were tested. The accessibility test results reveal that only 6 out of 11 public sector banks, 3 out of 6 private sector banks, and 2 out of 5 foreign bank websites passed keyboard operability test. This indicates that nearly half or more of these websites failed to meet basic operability standards for users navigating via keyboards or assistive technologies. Accessibility of form fields was poor across all categories, with only 2 public, no private, and 3 foreign bank websites passing this test. Thus, out of 22 bank websites tested, only 11 passed the basic accessibility benchmark for keyboard operability and form accessibility, revealing a 50% accessibility success rate, with private banks performing the worst. All 11 public sector banking apps and 4 out of 6 private sector banking apps were found to be operable via keyboard/gesture-based navigation. Foreign bank apps showed slightly lower compliance, with only 4 out of 5 passing. However, only 2 public sector apps, none from private banks, and just 1 from foreign banks had accessible form fields. This highlights a serious usability issue for visually impaired users trying to fill information. Thus, 19 out of 22 banking Apps passed the operability test, but only 3 passed the form element test, suggesting that while basic navigation is mostly functional, interaction

[36] The report can be accessed at https://xrcvc.org/docs/Banking%20on%20Accessibility%20by%20XRCVC%20June%202022.pdf.

with the content remains largely inaccessible. All 6 third-party wallet/UPI Apps passed operability test, indicating good navigation support. Only 1 app had accessible forms, and the remaining 5 failed, echoing the trend seen with banking apps. None of the apps provided accessible CAPTCHA mechanisms. All 6 were marked "Not Found/NA", posing a significant barrier for screen reader users and people with cognitive disabilities. Thus, while navigation scored high, interaction and security layers (e.g., CAPTCHA) were exclusionary. Only one app out of six passed more than one test, showing limited overall accessibility.

These accessibility testing results were further confirmed by the XRCVC report, 2022 itself when it tried to examine the user feedback through Access India Mailing List and Project Eyeway where users have filed repeated complaints on a range of issues that need to be resolved. Apart from the digital accessibility issues of bank websites, Apps, and other third-party wallets and UPI Apps, some other issues, like banks' continued attitude to treat PwDs as illiterate; untrained bank staff; signature mismatch; procedural hurdles in money transfer; non-compliance with accessible bank branch infrastructure; poor compliance with accessible ATM regulations; poor customer care; lack of awareness on redressal mechanism; communication challenge for hearing impaired customers; and issues in handling currency notes and coins were also reported by users. Yet another study by Singanamalla et al. (2019) conducted a survey of 107 ATM machines across four cities in India, and found that less than 18% of surveyed machines were accessible. Many other instances reported through blogs/interviews also highlight institutional apathy and lack of awareness among front-line bank staff.[37] Visually impaired respondents recounted being asked to return with sighted companions for even simple transactions such as balance inquiries or account openings. Others were denied access to lockers or loans without valid reasons, despite producing government-issued disability certificates.

Some of the authors of the present chapter also conducted a personal in-depth interview during April-June 2025 of eight stakeholders, involving PwDs, parents/caregivers of PwDs, disability right activists,

[37] See for example, a recent blog published on American India Foundation website: https://aif.org/banking-barriers-the-struggle-for-accessibility-in-indias-financial-institutions/.

NGO representatives, and financial service providers so as to understand their perspectives on financial inclusion for PwDs.[38] To facilitate systematic presentation of the qualitative insights obtained from interviews, the key observations from persons with disabilities and financial sector stakeholders are summarised in Tables 3 and 4. While some bankers described financial inclusion narrowly as providing basic services "at par with so-called abled persons," NGO representatives and the disability-rights activist offered broader definitions. They view it as enabling PwDs to access all services—banking, insurance, education, employment, health care, legal provisions—independently and without discrimination. For them, financial inclusion begins with accessible identity documents, extends to inclusive education and employment, and ultimately supports independent living. They stress that inclusive banking must include access to health insurance and social security, areas where PwDs currently face outright denials. On the broader question of accessibility gaps and barriers in accessing financial services by PwDs (or by their parents/caregivers on their behalf), PwD respondents consistently describe banking services as hard to use, mainly due to complicated bank procedures and documentation burdens (instance: denial of valid UDID card while requiring legal documents along with a trust deed in case of person with intellectual disability), attitudinal barriers and lack of staff sensitisation and training (staff makes things difficult instead of easing out; insists on unnecessary documents; calls many times for a single-day task), lack of awareness of relevant policies/guidelines and implementation gaps (bank representatives are found almost ignorant about relevant and specific banking accessibility guidelines; NGO representatives reported serious gaps in implementation of accessible infrastructure and other guidelines despite a clearcut mandate under RPwD Act, 2016). NGOs highlight that guardianship applications and UDID forms are cumbersome, suggesting that reliance on complex documentation undermines independence. Bank/insurance representatives acknowledge that accessible infrastructure is partial: branches may have ramps, lifts and talking ATMs, but features such as braille statements or fully accessible apps are rare. One representative admitted that people with disabilities are often denied ATM and chequebook facilities, car loan facility, especially in small towns. The mathura-based bank representative confirmed that customers

[38] Six out of eight respondents were located in Delhi/Noida, one in Jammu, and one in Mathura. They comprised of three females and five males, ranging from 21 to 65 years.

still need witnesses for basic services such as opening accounts, and that banks impose stringent signature verification or refuse chequebook requests for PwDs. Two bank representatives said no specific training had been organised, and another recalled only one training session back in 2018. These lived experiences reveal that social and attitudinal barriers persist alongside physical ones. Even where infrastructure exists, lack of staff training and absence of grievance redressal mechanisms nullify the impact of legal mandates. Across stakeholders, several reforms recur:

- Accessible infrastructure and technology: expand ramps, lifts and fully accessible ATMs; make mobile banking apps and websites compatible with assistive technologies; provide braille or audio statements.
- Simplify processes and recognise UDID: accept a single disability proof (UDID), eliminate unnecessary legal documentation, and streamline guardianship or trust formation.
- Mandatory staff training and attitudinal change: regular sensitisation programmes for bank staff and awareness campaigns for the public; NGOs call for training on autism communication, sensory management and behavioural strategies.
- Policy enforcement and data collection: enforce the RPD Act's accessibility provisions, develop clear guidelines for inclusive banking, and conduct a comprehensive census of PwDs to inform planning.
- Collaborative initiatives: scale up good practices by working with organisations like Enable India; initiate discussions between government, banks and NGOs to co-create a shared vision of financial inclusion.

5.2 *Low Penetration and Discriminatory Practices in Insurance and Pension*

A persistent challenge in the domain of financial services is the low penetration and discriminatory exclusion from insurance products faced by PwDs. Despite clear guidelines, insurance companies in India exclude those with intellectual and developmental disabilities from coverage.[39]

[39] https://behanbox.com/2023/01/13/indian-insurers-are-denying-health-cover-for-intellectual-developmental-disabilities/.

Table 3 Basic profile of interviewees

Stakeholder category	*Location*	*Age in years*	*Gender*	*Education level*	*Occupation*	*Monthly Household Income Level (INR)*	*What type of disability do you suffer from (or deal with)*	*In your view, what does "financial inclusion" mean for persons with disabilities?*
Caregiver/ Family Member of a Person with Disability	Noida	44	Female	Graduation or above	Self-employed	100,000–150,000	ASD	More inclusive and accessible services for all
Bank/Insurance Representative	Delhi	38	Male	Graduation or above	Employed in private sector	50,000–100,000	Visual	Not sure
Person with Disability	Noida	21	Male	Higher Secondary	Parttime engagement/ Student	50,000–100,000	Hearing	When all the services are accessible to PWDs. Without any discrimination eg. Medical Insurance
NGO Representative	Jammu	65	Male	Graduation or above	Employed in private sector	Below 50,000	Intellectual	Financial inclusion will play a vital role to provide security for their future
Disability Rights Activist	New Delhi	52	Female	Graduation or above	Employed in private sector	50,000–100,000	Intellectual; Multiple; Autism Spectrum	Financial inclusion is to have access to useful and affordable financial products and services in all areas like banking, insurance etc

Stakeholder category	*Location*	*Age in years*	*Gender*	*Education level*	*Occupation*	*Monthly Household Income Level (INR)*	*What type of disability do you suffer from (or deal with)*	*In your view, what does "financial inclusion" mean for persons with disabilities?*
NGO Representative	New Delhi	45	Female	Graduation or above	Employed in private sector	50,000–100,000	ASD	It means access to everything that is available to a non-disabled person, in accordance with specific needs, so that a person can access it independently. It starts with having access to their identity first, so they can claim what is rightfully theirs, and moves into access to education, employment, home, medical services, therapeutic and mental health services, community and civic services, legal provisions and so on It is driven by laws and policies and implemented by people and within systems
Bank/Insurance Representative	New Delhi	32	Male	Graduation or above	Employed in public sector	100,000–150,000	Visual;Locomotor	Persons with disabilities should have access to various financial services/facilities at par with so-called abled persons

(continued)

Table 3 (continued)

Stakeholder category	*Location*	*Age in years*	*Gender*	*Education level*	*Occupation*	*Monthly Household Income Level (INR)*	*What type of disability do you suffer from (or deal with)*	*In your view, what does "financial inclusion" mean for persons with disabilities?*
Bank/Insurance Representative	Mathura	43	Male	Graduation or above	Employed in public sector	100,000–150,000	Visual;Locomotor	For me, financial inclusion for PWD means independent access to financial services by PWD himself/herself, whether it is using ATM, depositing cash or withdrawing money, etc. There used to be a time when for opening a bank account of PWD as well as for other banking operations, the PWD customer was required to bring some witness. The counter staff used to be louder while asking how much to withdraw? Or this is the required amount (loudly speaking the denomination), thereby threating the privacy of the customer. Things have improved a bit, but not at the desired pace

Source Authors' compilation from interview responses

Table 4 Views of interviewees on challenges and possible improvements of financial services for PwDs

Stakeholder category	*What challenges or barriers have you faced yourself or on behalf of your PwD client/ relative while accessing financial services?*	*What would make financial services more trustworthy or accessible to you?*	*Do you think financial inclusion of PwDs is more of a policy issue, infrastructure issue, or awareness issue?*	*What policy or operational reforms do you suggest to improve access for PwDs?*	*If you could recommend one priority reform, what would it be to make India's financial system more inclusive for PwDs?*	*Can you share any real-life story (positive or negative) related to access, trust, or financial literacy?*	*Are there any local innovations or good practices that should be scaled up to promote financial inclusion of PwDs?*
Caregiver/ Family Member of a Person with Disability	Very complicated services with discriminatory approach and attitude of bank staff/ management for PwDs and/ or their parents/ caregivers	Better accessibility, simplified banking procedures, and friendly attitude/ behaviour of bank staff towards PwD customers	The issue of financial inclusion is due to all, policy flaws, poor infrastructure, and low awareness	Better accessibility, simplified banking procedures, and friendly attitude/ behaviour of bank staff towards PwD customers	I don't know	Despite being independent in other terms I am dependent related to financial services and their use	I don't know
Bank/ Insurance Representa-tive	Unfriendly attitude of bank colleagues towards PwD colleagues and PwD customers. No specific sensitisation training for bank staff	Friendly attitude of bank staff with regular staff sensitisation trainings and workshops, covering modules on disability	Awareness issues	Staff sensitisation towards customers with special needs through regular training	Can't say	Can't remember	Don't know

(continued)

Table 4 (continued)

Stakeholder category	*What challenges or barriers have you faced yourself or on behalf of your PwD client/ relative while accessing financial services?*	*What would make financial services more trustworthy or accessible to you?*	*Do you think financial inclusion of PwDs is more of a policy issue, infrastructure issue, or awareness issue?*	*What policy or operational reforms do you suggest to improve access for PwDs?*	*If you could recommend one priority reform, what would it be to make India's financial system more inclusive for PwDs?*	*Can you share any real-life story (positive or negative) related to access, trust, or financial literacy?*	*Are there any local innovations or good practices that should be scaled up to promote financial inclusion of PwDs?*
Person with Disability	Bank staff insensitive towards PWDs and don't have much knowledge about the rights of PWDs and makes things difficult instead of easing out. They asked me to present a document from a lawyer and did not accept my UDID card	Sensitization of the staff and simplified steps. Acceptance of UDID and not complicate the formalities	More of a policy issue and awareness issues	Policy simplification with staff sensitisation	One identification should be sufficient eg.UDID as a proof of disability and trust formation for the family members should be an easy process	I had to get my Bank account made but I was asked to get documents from Lawyer and had to make a trust as well. I made multiple visits but I was hassled by the bank account people and eventually I got an account from a private bank without disclosing my disability	Not aware
NGO Representative	No	No reason as such	Don't know	Separate counter for all Disabled people	We must have a complete Data of disabled community which is not a place at present.no census after 2011.	A paren who having two sons with international disability have no money in their account due and left them without shelter. We arrange their pension, provide them shelter	No

Stakeholder category	*What challenges or barriers have you faced yourself or on behalf of your PwD client/ relative while accessing financial services?*	*What would make financial services more trustworthy or accessible to you?*	*Do you think financial inclusion of PwDs is more of a policy issue, infrastructure issue, or awareness issue?*	*What policy or operational reforms do you suggest to improve access for PwDs?*	*If you could recommend one priority reform, what would it be to make India's financial system more inclusive for PwDs?*	*Can you share any real-life story (positive or negative) related to access, trust, or financial literacy?*	*Are there any local innovations or good practices that should be scaled up to promote financial inclusion of PwDs?*
Disability Rights Activist	Single account opening, availing ATM and chequebook facility, locker, loan, etc. are still challenging in far flung areas, especially for customers with intellectual disability	Banks must follow guidelines of RBI and implement them in their true letter and spirit	Policy and awareness both have problems	There should be policy framed including all 21types. To my knowledge currently the policies hanging to previous disability group	1. Section 40 of the Rights of Persons With Disabilities (RPD) Act, 2016 requires that the public facilities and services be made accessible in line with the standards notified by the Central Government.Governments must establish and enforce laws that protect the financial rights of persons with disabilities and promote inclusive financial products 2.Tailored education initiatives should be developed to enhance financial literacy among persons with disabilities, their family and proffesional working with them	Well known special educator with orthopedic disability suddenly removed from job and no support from delhi disability ministry, we battle everywhere to get leagal guidance. But all went in strain. Finally we approached an NGO, the case stretching for 7yrs.till date no financial support she has received Same with a mother who is a government school teacher in Utter-pradesh,unfortunately her first child turned as autism, and she applied for transfer to get training for her son. She is on leave without salary for three years. The state is not listening to her. What's in the law is only written in paper	I don't have any idea

(continued)

Table 4 (continued)

Stakeholder category	*What challenges or barriers have you faced yourself or on behalf of your PwD client/relative while accessing financial services?*	*What would make financial services more trustworthy or accessible to you?*	*Do you think financial inclusion of PwDs is more of a policy issue, infrastructure issue, or awareness issue?*	*What policy or operational reforms do you suggest to improve access for PwDs?*	*If you could recommend one priority reform, what would it be to make India's financial system more inclusive for PwDs?*	*Can you share any real-life story (positive or negative) related to access, trust, or financial literacy?*	*Are there any local innovations or good practices that should be scaled up to promote financial inclusion of PwDs?*
NGO Representative	Bank staff/management lacks knowledge of circulars and guidelines for banking services to PwDs; health insurance companies hesitate to subscribe to PwDs	Staff training along with proper implementation of banking guidelines, and insurance regulations are desirable	Actually, even after lots of efforts by the Government of India, the issue of financial inclusion for PWDs continues to be experienced on all fronts; there are gaps in policy implementation, lack of adequate and reasonable infrastructure persists, and awareness challenges are also observed among PWDs and/or their parents/caregivers thereby impeding their financial inclusion	Based on the findings of this study identify the gaps that currently exist and start from there. The first step for me would be creating a document on what 'financial inclusion' could look like for PwDs. There are many different yet parallel trajectories for this. What would those look like. Share that with the others including the government and NGOs, so discussions can begin	It would be to start a discussion on what is possible immediately. Join forces to make that happen. The more people there are, the more likelihood for change. More than other things, it is misinformed attitude and knowledge of people who think of PwDs as people to be 'supported' or taken care of. Concerted efforts are required to make this attitudinal change	We have supported several autistic people get jobs. The support then needed to be extended to people having a bank account to receive their salary, knowledge or connection to correct professional for filing taxes. We support people get enrol for guardianship or to access Nirmaya schemes	There are several disability groups who are already doing some great work. It is important to contextualise those... what works in one culture, one region may not necessarily work in other places

Stakeholder category	*What challenges or barriers have you faced yourself or on behalf of your PwD client/ relative while accessing financial services?*	*What would make financial services more trustworthy or accessible to you?*	*Do you think financial inclusion of PwDs is more of a policy issue, infrastructure issue, or awareness issue?*	*What policy or operational reforms do you suggest to improve access for PwDs?*	*If you could recommend one priority reform, what would it be to make India's financial system more inclusive for PwDs?*	*Can you share any real-life story (positive or negative) related to access, trust, or financial literacy?*	*Are there any local innovations or good practices that should be scaled up to promote financial inclusion of PwDs?*
Bank/ Insurance Representative	Poor physical infrastructure inside bank branches, accessibility issues of bank websites, lack of Braille statements, and Apps, and above all, attitudenal barrier are major hurdles. No sensitisation programme as such organised	Monitoring mechanisms should be strengthened, fines for non-compliance should be introduced by RBI. There should be regular access and accessibility audits of bank branches, bank websites and Apps	To me, it is more of a policy issue, because without proper policies, we cannot have adequate infrastructure as well as awareness creation	I think creating accessible infrastructure and providing reasonable accommodation is very essential to improve financial access for persons with disabilities	It is most urgent to provide all basic financial facilities and services to persons with disabilities at par with other customers. This is possible through accessible physical infrastructure as well as accessible websites and apps of the financial service providers with properly trained and sensitised staff	No, I don't remember any such story	Enable India is one such organisation that works towards enhancing the independent living and working conditions for persons with disabilities. The government at different levels should collaborate and partner with such organisations to scale up their activities for the promotion of independent living and working of PWDs

(continued)

Table 4 (continued)

Stakeholder category	*What challenges or barriers have you faced yourself or on behalf of your PwD client/relative while accessing financial services?*	*What would make financial services more trustworthy or accessible to you?*	*Do you think financial inclusion of PwDs is more of a policy issue, infrastructure issue, or awareness issue?*	*What policy or operational reforms do you suggest to improve access for PwDs?*	*If you could recommend one priority reform, what would it be to make India's financial system more inclusive for PwDs?*	*Can you share any real-life story (positive or negative) related to access, trust, or financial literacy?*	*Are there any local innovations or good practices that should be scaled up to promote financial inclusion of PwDs?*
Bank/Insurance Representative	Lack of knowledge on the part of bank staff about banking services for PwDs, lack of willingness to bring change in the ecosystem, denial of banking services to PwDs, lack of staff training at regular intervals; just one general training in 2018	Banks must conduct sensitisation workshops and trainings, covering a mandatory module on disability needs and banking facilities and services for PwDs. This should be necessary for new employees	The issue is at all stages, more especially on awareness side. Staff needs more sensitisation training for their special needs customers. In respect of policies, we regularly observe gaps in providing access to financial services to PWDs at par with other customers. For instance, even as on date, 90–95% health insurance companies simply deny their health insurance to PWDs	Health insurance must be made accessible for PWDs in all respects. Similarly, adequate and accessible infrastructure should be put in place in banks and other financial institutions to provide reasonable accommodation to PWDs	The urgent priority reform is to make basic financial services such as ATM and chequebook facility available to all customers with special needs and further simplification of rules and procedures for such basic services for PWDs. Till date, banks (including that of mine) are often found to deny ATM service to PWD; the problem is more serious in small cities/towns as compared to large cities, what to talk of rural areas. Even if PWD customer is given the ATM facility, the service cannot be used independently by the PWD customer due to lack of accessible infrastructure and fully accessible ATM machine. Furthermore, despite the guideline that third-party cheques can be issued by PWDs, PWD customers are often denied the chequebook facility, and if they insist on availing the chequebook, the chequebook is issued in their name by the bank, but only for withdrawing money from their own account. Even in that case, PWD customers are required to follow strict procedure of verification of their signatures, witness, etc	In my own bank, the authority generally escapes to serve differently abled customers. Whethher it is giving an ATM to a visually challenged customer, or any other service, they create hurdles/barriers. Once, an orthopedically customer came to apply for car loan, the loan manager simply refused saying that you are not eligible for car loan, ignoring banking guidelines of RBI and IBA for persons with disabilities	No, I am not aware of any such local initiatives

James et al. (2019) have reported accessibility issue and coverage gap in Swavlamban health insurance scheme for persons with disabilities in Karnataka. Lack of professional knowledge/information, social attitudes and stigma, lack of proper data on the demands and distribution channels of specific health insurance products, and unclear guidelines from IRDAI are cited as major barriers in providing health insurance services to mentally ill patients (Zoya et al., 2025). A nationwide survey conducted under the 'Ayushman for All' campaign by the National Centre for Promotion of Employment for Disabled People (NCPEDP) revealed alarming gaps in insurance coverage for persons with disabilities (PwDs) in India (Business Standard, 2025). Of the over 5,000 PwDs surveyed across 34 states and UTs, 82% lacked any form of insurance, and 42% were unaware of Ayushman Bharat PM-JAY, the government's flagship health scheme. Only 28% had ever applied for the scheme, despite its mandate to serve vulnerable populations. Disability rights activists at the National Disability Network (NDN) meeting highlighted systemic barriers, including lack of awareness, exclusionary eligibility norms, and persistent denials of coverage by private insurers. Arman Ali of NCPEDP criticised the absence of unconditional inclusion for PwDs under Ayushman Bharat—despite such coverage being extended to senior citizens over 70—and emphasised the need for representation, policy reform, and accessible, cashless insurance systems. The discussions called attention to high out-of-pocket medical costs, rising debt among PwDs, and the broader exclusion of PwDs from health equity frameworks, especially for disabled women and politically underrepresented groups. The discussion advocated state-wise action, better data, inclusive outreach, and political will to make universal healthcare truly accessible.

The two recent performance audit reports on the implementation of the RPwD Act, 2016, released by the Comptroller and Auditor General (CAG) of India highlight several deficiencies in the implementation of insurance and pension schemes. The audit report for the Government of Karnataka (CAG, 2024a) highlights serious implementation lapses in the Niramaya Health Insurance Scheme. Despite nominal renewal fees, there was poor policy renewal among enrolled beneficiaries (only 201 renewals out of 2,379), and no effective departmental measures to ensure continuity of coverage. This undermined the potential benefit of the scheme for persons with disabilities. Likewise, the audit observed weak implementation of the insurance scheme for parents/guardians of persons with mental retardation in the State. With only 787 enrolled beneficiaries across six districts and no registrations in five major districts, the report indicates poor awareness and outreach. The same list was reused yearly without updates, reflecting lack of efforts to identify new beneficiaries or publicise the scheme. On the issue of credit facilities provided by the National Handicap Finance and Development Corporation (NHFDC), the report (CAG, 2024a) found that post-2014, NHFDC-linked concessional credit schemes were largely non-operational in Karnataka due to failure to execute a required loan agreement with NHFDC. As a result, schemes like Swavalamban Kendras and Divyangjan Swavalamban Yojana could not be implemented, depriving PwDs in the state of vital self-employment and skill development loans.

The audit of disability welfare schemes in Rajasthan revealed limited pension coverage (only 36.89% of PwDs), delayed inclusion of newly recognised disability categories under the RPwD Act, 2016, and widespread documentation lapses (CAG, 2024b). Self-employment schemes and aid distribution efforts were poorly managed, with delays, lack of verification, and subsidy irregularities. Accessibility efforts for departmental buildings also remained inadequate.

6 Inclusive Financial Education and Employment Practices as Channels of Financial Inclusion: Some Insights from Kerala

Before concluding this chapter, it is imperative to highlight the role of early and inclusive financial education, and financial power through inclusive employment practices as two major channels of financial inclusion of PwDs. According to a report by UNESCO, in India, only around 61% of children with disability between the ages of 5 and 19 attend school regularly, mostly due to inaccessible learning environments and limited inclusive practices (UNESCO, 2019). Moreover, as per the National Financial Literacy and Inclusion Survey (NCFE-FLIS), only twenty-seven per cent of Indian adults possess basic financial knowledge (National Centre for Financial Education [NCFE], 2019). Furthermore, globally, persons with disabilities have significantly lower employment rates than those without. People with disabilities in OECD countries have a twenty seven per cent lower employment rate than those without disabilities. They are also 2.3 times more likely to be unemployed (OECD, 2022). Exclusion of persons with disabilities from employment may reduce a country's GDP by three per cent to seven per cent (World Bank & International Labour Office, 2022). The low labour force participation rate of 23.8% as per NSS 76th round of Persons with Disabilities (Government of India, 2019) indicate a poor scenario in terms of employment of PwDs in India. Although the RPwD Act, 2016 laid a strong foundation for inclusion, many states have not held the required review meetings, and full-time commissioners have yet to be appointed to ensure its implementation (Bagival, 2024).

The literature on these two channels of financial inclusion is scarce, especially for India. Kang et al. (2025) examined that people with intellectual and developmental disabilities are rarely taught essential financial skills in school, such as budgeting or understanding interest. A recent global review further stressed the challenges in low- and middle-income countries, such as poor infrastructure and limited access to digital tools (Puli et al., 2024). Thohari and Rizky (2021) observed that many disabled people face barriers such as inaccessible financial services and limited learning support. Fernández-Batanero et al. (2022) emphasised that assistive technologies like screen readers and tactile tools improve access to learning but are not widely implemented due to lack of trained teachers and resources. However, most existing studies focus primarily on general educational access or assistive tools rather than exploring how inclusive, early financial education impacts financial decision-making and financial security among persons with disabilities. Existing studies also underline the need for further research on how inclusive employment influences the financial empowerment of persons with disabilities. A CSRBOX (2023) study found that in selected districts of India, most persons with disabilities were self-employed, while only 20% held regular salaried jobs, indicating limited access to inclusive and stable employment. A case study by Deorukhkar and Shaikh (2025) found that a therapeutic income generation program based on supported employment significantly improved self-confidence, workplace acceptance and financial independence among persons with intellectual and developmental disabilities. Mendoza (2021) studied persons with disabilities in General Trias and Rosario, Philippines, and found that most were female, single, college-educated, and earned low incomes; while they showed moderate entrepreneurial capability and engagement, major challenges included limited financial resources, lack of access to credit and business information, insufficient skills and weak family support. Santoso (2023), using a systematic literature review and descriptive data, found that persons with disabilities in both developed and developing countries face key barriers to financial access, including information asymmetry, complicated banking procedures and a lack of disability-sensitive services, which points that inclusive digital banking and better financial literacy are critical to advancing their economic empowerment. These studies reveal important gaps, indicating the need for qualitative research based on lived experiences.

In light of the above background, the present study conducted an interview with 9 persons with both congenital and acquired disabilities in the State of Kerala. The choice of this State is guided by the fact that while it has over 70% literacy rate among PwDs, it is counted among the States with low work force participation rate of PwDs (please refer to Sects. 3.5 and 3.6 of this chapter). As per Census 2011, Goa and Kerala together accounted for 73% of disabled children (5–19 years) attending educational institution. Those children will now be comprising of a sizable portion of the working-age population. A semi-structured questionnaire was developed to explore the awareness of the PwDs related to financial literacy, their access to financial education and the challenges they face. Early exposure to financial concepts, the use of inclusive curricula and assistive technologies as well as challenges related to cognitive, communication or sensory barriers were the primary focus areas. The questionnaire also attempted to understand their experiences about inclusive work environment with reasonable accommodation, financial advise from employers/ colleagues, and the impact of these on their overall financial empowerment. Purposive sampling was used to ensure relevant and diverse insights. Participants' names have been omitted from the discussion to protect their anonymity. The interviews were conducted either in person or via phone, depending on each participant's preference and accessibility needs. A prior informed consent was obtained from each participant before the interview with clear explanation of the purpose of the interview. The responses were recorded and transcribed for the study. The primary data obtained from the interviews were analyzed thematically to identify the challenges, concerns and suggestions related to financial education for persons with disabilities. Table 5 presents socio-economic and demographic profile of the nine participants, while Table 6 provides their experiences with financial education and accessible contents. Finally, Table 7 summarises the challenges faced by these participants as well as support received by them in understanding financial concepts and processes.

Table 5 Socio-economic and demographic profile of participants

Participant	*Age*	*Gender*	*Marital status*	*Whether congenital or Acquired (Disability)*	*Education in special, integrated or Regular school*	*Educational qualification*	*Income level (in INR)*	*Employment status*
1	31	Female	Unmarried	Not sure and diagnosed at the age of 5	Regular school	M.A., M.Phil., B.Ed. and cleared UGC NET	55,000–65,000	Public sector
2	25	Male	Unmarried	Congenital	Both in special school and in regular school	M.A. and cleared UGC NET	Receiving UGC fellowship	Research scholar
3	36	Male	Unmarried	Congenital	Special school	M.A., B.Ed. and cleared UGC NET	55,000–65,000	Public sector
4	28	Female	Unmarried	Congenital	Regular school	M.A. and cleared UGC NET	Receiving UGC fellowship	Research scholar
5	32	Female	Unmarried	Congenital	Regular school	M.A. and cleared UGC NET with JRF	55,000–65,000	Public sector
6	48	Male	Married	Congenital	Special school	B.A. discontinued	10,000–15,000	Private sector
7	38	Male	Unmarried	Congenital	Integrated school	M.A., B.Ed. and cleared UGC NET	75,000–85,000	Public sector

(continued)

Table 5 (continued)

Participant	*Age*	*Gender*	*Marital status*	*Whether congenital or Acquired (Disability)*	*Education in special, integrated or Regular school*	*Educational qualification*	*Income level (in INR)*	*Employment status*
8	52	Male	Married	Acquired	Regular school	Diploma, B.A. and B.Ed	45,000–55,000	Public sector
9	26	Male	Unmarried	Acquired	Regular school	B.A	Below 10,000	Self employed

Source Author's compilation from interviews

Table 6 Participants' experiences with financial education and accessible contents

Participants	*Received financial literacy in school*	*When first learned financial concepts*	*Early financial education is important*	*Adapted financial educational materials provided in school*	*Used assistive technologies to learn or manage finances*	*Opinion on how accessible are financial literacy resources in your local language or accessible formats*
1	No. A saving scheme called Sanjika existed briefly but was discontinued	First learned about financial concepts when opening a zero-balance account in higher secondary school for a scholarship. Learned more during college through screen readers and technology	Strongly agree	No	Yes	Haven't explored many financial literacy resources in my local language. Mostly use English as the medium and several accessibility issues still exist on the websites and applications
2	No. Basic banking concepts were included in Economics in higher secondary, but no focus on financial management	After tenth standard opened a bank account at eighteen. Tried to gain knowledge through personal experience, not from a formal education	Strongly agree	Some tactile graphs were provided to me in my eleventh and twelfth grades. Other than that, there was nothing	Yes	Mostly use English. Experienced accessibility issues in accessing certain websites and applications

(continued)

Table 6 (continued)

Participants	*Received financial literacy in school*	*When first learned financial concepts*	*Early financial education is important*	*Adapted financial educational materials provided in school*	*Used assistive technologies to learn or manage finances*	*Opinion on how accessible are financial literacy resources in your local language or accessible formats*
3	No. Only taught to identify currency notes by size	First encountered financial concepts during higher secondary studies in humanities, but with no practical application. Opened a bank account in college to receive a grant. Gained awareness after starting a job	Strongly agree	No	Yes	In our local language, accessible resources are rare. Experienced accessibility issues
4	No	Began thinking seriously about financial matters only after postgraduation	Strongly agree	No	Yes	Though they are not provided in my local language but mostly in English, I found them accessible and also am comfortable with English

Participants	*Received financial literacy in school*	*When first learned financial concepts*	*Early financial education is important*	*Adapted financial educational materials provided in school*	*Used assistive technologies to learn or manage finances*	*Opinion on how accessible are financial literacy resources in your local language or accessible formats*
5	No	Started learning financial concepts after postgraduation while receiving fellowship. Earlier, it was managed by parents	Strongly agree	No	Yes	I haven't made a deliberate attempt to search for financial literacy resources
6	No	Tried to learn about financial matters mostly through self-exploration in early twenties	Strongly agree	No	Yes	Have not come across many financial literacy resources in my local language. Accessibility issues exist

(continued)

Table 6 (continued)

Participants	*Received financial literacy in school*	*When first learned financial concepts*	*Early financial education is important*	*Adapted financial educational materials provided in school*	*Used assistive technologies to learn or manage finances*	*Opinion on how accessible are financial literacy resources in your local language or accessible formats*
7	No. Teachers helped open a bank account, but financial decisions were handled by others	Started to think seriously and took charge of finances after getting a job in 2012	Strongly agree	No	Yes	Comfortable with English, so I don't feel the need to use my local language to understand financial resources. Accessibility issues exist

Participants	*Received financial literacy in school*	*When first learned financial concepts*	*Early financial education is important*	*Adapted financial educational materials provided in school*	*Used assistive technologies to learn or manage finances*	*Opinion on how accessible are financial literacy resources in your local language or accessible formats*
8	Studied in a regular school that had a saving scheme and involved students in managing school programs, which gave some financial experience, though not formal education	Opened a bank account after tenth standard but learned structured financial concepts during graduation at the seminary	Strongly agree	During my school days, I had no visual difficulties. I lost my vision at the age of 26	Yes	Not widely available. Still accessibility issues exist
9	No	Opened a bank account at sixteen and gradually learned financial concepts, with the help of technology	Strongly agree	No	Yes	Only limited resources are available in my local language and accessible format. Mostly use English

Source Same as for Table 5

Table 7 Participants' challenges and support in understanding financial concepts and processes

Participant	*Faced challenges in understanding financial concepts due to sensory, cognitive, or communication barriers*	*Support or modifications from educators to overcome these barriers*	*Support or modifications from family to overcome these barriers*	*Support or modifications from technology to overcome these barriers*	*Are there any specific financial terms or processes you still find difficult to understand or navigate*
1	Yes	No	Yes	Yes	Yes, I find it difficult to understand how interest is calculated, especially compound interest. I also struggle with understanding how loan interest works, how rates are fixed for fixed deposits, and how to use credit cards safely. Navigating financial processes is also challenging- for example, using the YONO app of SBI. ATMs are inaccessible for people like me who are visually challenged
2	Yes	No	Sometimes	Yes	Yes, I am not fully aware of how to use credit cards, so I prefer not to use them. ATMs are inaccessible, and I face challenges in withdrawing money. Personally, I haven't faced negative attitudes from bank staff. Canara Bank provided me with an ATM card without objections. But many visually challenged friends were denied services due to their disability
3	Yes	No	Yes	Yes	Yes, I find it difficult to understand technical financial terms. I also face challenges with financial processes. I cannot withdraw cash from ATMs as they are not accessible. Banking apps like YONO are also not accessible. Though I received an ATM card, the bank staff showed scepticism because of my disability

Participant	*Faced challenges in understanding financial concepts due to sensory, cognitive, or communication barriers*	*Support or modifications from educators to overcome these barriers*	*Support or modifications from family to overcome these barriers*	*Support or modifications from technology to overcome these barriers*	*Are there any specific financial terms or processes you still find difficult to understand or navigate*
4	No	No	Yes	Yes	I can search and understand financial terms to a great extent. But withdrawing money from ATMs remains a dream for people like me with locomotor disabilities. Independent movement in bank branches is not possible due to the lack of proper ramps. Most ramps are poorly built and unsafe. I avoid visiting banks because of this. I have not used an ATM ever in my life. Even if ramps were provided, the limited space inside the ATM counter is another challenge
5	Yes	No	Yes	Yes	Yes, I still find it difficult to understand terms like mutual funds, stock markets, exchange rates, and EMIs. Without basic practical knowledge, it's uncomfortable to deal with such matters. I have never used an ATM. I use Google Pay, and for physical cash, my family helps me
6	Yes	No	No	Yes	Yes, some banking and financial terms are still difficult for me, though I can't recall specific ones. ATMs are inaccessible to me as a visually challenged person, and I rely on others for cash. I also face difficulty identifying currency. Apps like Cash Reader sometimes give inaccurate results. I didn't face issues getting an ATM card from Federal Bank, but I am not satisfied with SBI services

(continued)

Table 7 (continued)

Participant	*Faced challenges in understanding financial concepts due to sensory, cognitive, or communication barriers*	*Support or modifications from educators to overcome these barriers*	*Support or modifications from family to overcome these barriers*	*Support or modifications from technology to overcome these barriers*	*Are there any specific financial terms or processes you still find difficult to understand or navigate*
7	Sometimes	No	Yes	Yes	Yes, I use YouTube and AI tools to understand financial topics. But accessibility issues exist (e.g., Indian Overseas Bank's website). My bank denied me a cheque book and discouraged me from using an ATM card. I had to insist to get one. Net banking was initially inaccessible, and a friend helped me deposit money. I use apps like Groww, but the pen signature requirement was inaccessible. I contacted support and, after follow-up, they resolved the issue. I also face issues identifying currency in public, so I sort notes with family support. ATMs are inaccessible, so I rely on Google Pay or friends to withdraw cash. In another instance, a company cut the call when I asked to use a thumb impression instead of a signature due to my disability

Participant	*Faced challenges in understanding financial concepts due to sensory, cognitive, or communication barriers*	*Support or modifications from educators to overcome these barriers*	*Support or modifications from family to overcome these barriers*	*Support or modifications from technology to overcome these barriers*	*Are there any specific financial terms or processes you still find difficult to understand or navigate*
8	No	Yes	No	Yes	I can understand most financial terms, but ATMs are still inaccessible. I started using internet banking in 2012 through SBT without issues. But in 2017, at SBI, the staff doubted my ability due to my disability. I had to prove myself by using their system. I also had to raise my voice to get an ATM card. There was no issue with my first credit card, but Axis Bank denied my second one because of my disability. I had to hide my disability and complete the KYC process using video. Many friends were denied such services
9	Sometimes	No	No	Yes	I use software on Android phones and computers to read printed material. Technology helps me overcome barriers. At present, I don't face major difficulties with financial terms or processes in my everyday life. I use internet searches to clarify doubts

Source Same as for Table 5

6.1 Early Exposure to Financial Education

Participants consistently reported a lack of structured financial education during their schooling, whether in regular or special schools. Most recalled only basic exposure such as identifying currency notes or participating in informal schemes like 'Sanjika,' where students pooled money weekly and received it with interest later.

While Participant 8 experienced some financial engagement through school event budgeting and later received structured financial training during higher studies, the rest largely began understanding money matters in adulthood—through self-exploration, grants, and screen-reader-enabled banking apps.

Several began managing finances only after receiving fellowships, scholarships, or employment. Participant 5 relied on her parents to operate her bank account until postgraduate studies, while Participant 7 began handling finances after receiving awards in school and later through employment. The consensus: financial education came late and informally, leaving them unprepared for independent financial management in early adulthood.

All participants strongly advocated for introducing financial literacy early, particularly for children with disabilities. They highlighted how early financial knowledge builds self-confidence, reduces dependency, and counters societal stereotypes of persons with disabilities as burdens. Participant 2 noted the heightened financial needs faced due to reliance on private transport and assistive services, further necessitating early planning skills.

6.2 Inclusive Curriculum and Assistive Technologies for Financial Education

None of the participants received accessible financial learning materials in school. Participant 2 recalled limited use of tactile graphs in economics classes; most others had no access to screen-reader-compatible content, tactile tools, or inclusive formats. Participant 9 confirmed no materials were adapted for visually impaired learners.

In adulthood, participants relied heavily on assistive technologies to bridge this gap. Screen readers, UPI apps, and tools like MANI and Cash Reader enabled them to manage accounts, identify currency, and access services. Participant 1 used toll-free numbers and apps for transactions.

Participant 9 mentioned talking ATMs and the general helpfulness of trained bank staff.

Despite digital tools, physical accessibility remains limited. Participant 4, a wheelchair user, could not access ATMs due to inadequate infrastructure. Others noted inaccessible websites, English-only financial materials, and unlabelled digital interfaces. These physical and digital exclusions highlighted the need for both infrastructural and content-based inclusivity.

6.3 Cognitive and Communication Barriers in Understanding Financial Concepts

Visually challenged participants struggled with abstract as well as technical financial concepts such as budgeting, interest calculation, inflation, mutual fund, and loan EMIs, especially due to inaccessible diagrams and lack of real-life application during schooling. Participants were often unsure whether these difficulties stemmed from cognitive barriers, language gaps, or lack of adapted instruction.

Most learned financial concepts independently using technology and online resources. Participant 7 actively explored mutual funds through YouTube and apps like Groww. Participant 9 credited assistive software and talking ATMs with enhancing his financial independence.

Educator support was minimal. Apart from Participant 2's economics teacher, few recalled any teaching guidance on financial matters. Participants faced challenges navigating inaccessible banking apps, using ATMs, and handling physical currency. Participant 5 relied on family for transactions, and Participant 4 avoided physical bank visits due to unsafe infrastructure.

Institutional ableism was another concern. Participants reported being denied ATM cards or credit facilities due to disability status. Participant 7 faced difficulties in completing KYC processes due to rigid identification requirements that do not consider the needs of visually challenged customers. Participant 8 had to hide his blindness to obtain a credit card. Many were forced to prove their competence to sceptical bank staff, underscoring persistent attitudinal barriers.

6.4 Recommendations for Inclusive Financial Literacy

Participants offered actionable suggestions grounded in lived experience. All emphasized the importance of early, practical, and inclusive financial education.

Key recommendations included:

- Embedding financial literacy into school curricula for all students.
- Ensuring accessibility in currency design, banking apps, and ATMs.
- Offering inclusive savings schemes and tailored awareness programs at workplaces.
- Training educators and employers to recognise persons with disabilities as financially capable individuals.

Participants stressed that financial literacy must go beyond theory—demonstrating, for example, how to manage accounts, use assistive tech, avoid scams, and assert financial rights. Participant 7 emphasized automatic account conversion at age 18 and streamlined ATM access. Participant 8 advocated for staff training and the use of inclusive documentation.

These suggestions reinforce the view that financial inclusion must begin early and continue through adult life, supported by systems designed to accommodate, not exclude.

6.5 Inclusive Workplaces and Accommodations

Participants reported varying degrees of workplace inclusion. While some worked in institutions for the visually challenged that offered a degree of support, most described environments where inclusion was informal, partial, or self-managed.

Participant 1 had to adapt herself without receiving accommodations. Participant 2 and Participant 3 found their workplaces "mostly inclusive," though social attitudes remained problematic. Participant 4 worked remotely but noted the lack of consultation about her needs, while Participant 5 was only accommodated in her first job, not in subsequent roles. Others cited physical barriers (Participant 6), lack of assistive software (Participant 7), and the need to rely on informal support (Participant 9). Only Participant 8 described a consistently supportive environment.

The findings highlight that while some employers comply with the RPwD Act nominally, meaningful consultation and systemic support for reasonable accommodation are often absent.

6.6 *Employment and Financial Independence*

All participants described employment as the turning point in gaining financial independence and confidence. Even modest earnings allowed them to make personal decisions, contribute to family expenses, and invest in tools that enhanced productivity and autonomy.

Participants associated employment with dignity, empowerment, and reduced dependency. For example, Participant 1 noted that scholarships and fellowships empowered her to pursue education independently. Participant 4 joined a savings scheme and supported her family, while Participant 5 used earnings to buy smartphones and productivity tools. Participant 7 provided several examples of financial decisions made independently, such as managing property or hiring help.

The narratives consistently emphasized that stable income enables persons with disabilities to assert their choices in both personal and social spheres.

6.7 *Gaps in Workplace-Based Financial Empowerment*

Participants largely agreed that their workplaces did not provide structured financial guidance. Discussions around pensions, savings, or insurance were rare and informal.

Participant 1 received investment advice from a colleague but not through any formal program. Participants 2, 3, 5, and 6 confirmed that no systematic awareness efforts existed. Participant 9 reported a complete absence of financial guidance at work. Even in inclusive environments, employers did not prioritize financial literacy or planning as part of workplace inclusion.

6.8 *Role of Employers and Government*

Participants urged both employers and the government to ensure accessibility in digital financial tools, enhance awareness of rights and schemes, and integrate financial literacy into early education and onboarding processes.

Participant 1 called for universal design in apps and portals. Participant 2 emphasized inclusive design from the outset. Participant 3 recommended early financial education and structured awareness programs. Participant 4 described persistent physical and procedural banking barriers, even after employment. Participant 5 proposed including financial education in induction and faculty development.

Suggestions included simplifying account opening, training staff to treat disabled clients equally, assigning higher deposit interest rates (Participant 7), and securing savings through protected salary-linked accounts. Participant 8 pointed out discriminatory practices in health insurance, calling for government-backed data to counter such bias. Participant 9 stressed increasing employment opportunities as a foundational step.

These responses reflect a call for systemic reform, from inclusive infrastructure and accessible information to proactive employer engagement.

6.9 Experiences of Financial Empowerment

Participants shared varied personal journeys toward financial empowerment. Some began managing money after employment, others through fellowships or training roles. Across cases, the transition to earning income brought confidence, self-worth, and control.

Participant 1 framed empowerment as internal motivation. Participant 3 cited technology as pivotal in his financial learning. Participant 4 described the liberating experience of earning and making independent decisions. Participant 5 preferred short-term savings like chitties over long-term investments. Participant 6 learned through self-exploration, highlighting budgeting and expense management. Participant 7 emphasized social responsibility alongside financial control. Participant 8, who shifted careers after vision loss, credited financial independence with restoring dignity. Participant 9 stressed the importance of saving habits and permanent employment.

Collectively, their accounts underscore that financial empowerment is not just about income—it is about control, respect, inclusion, and opportunity.

6.10 *Suggestions by Participants*

Although laws like the RPwD Act provide a framework for inclusion, implementation gaps persist in employment and financial systems. Most participants encountered informal or incomplete accommodations, inaccessible infrastructure, and attitudinal barriers.

Employment was seen as central to achieving financial and personal autonomy, yet workplace-based financial education and planning remained largely absent. Recommendations included early curriculum reform, digital accessibility, policy enforcement, and proactive employer engagement.

Ultimately, financial empowerment for persons with disabilities requires more than income. It demands systemic change—universal design, early intervention, rights-based policies, and institutional accountability—to ensure persons with disabilities are treated as full and equal participants in economic life.

7 Conclusion

While financial inclusion has emerged as a central policy objective in India's development strategy, the discussion in this chapter highlights that the experiences of persons with disabilities have received relatively limited attention within mainstream financial inclusion discourse. Evidence from demographic and socio-economic indicators suggests that persons with disabilities in India continue to face multiple forms of disadvantage, including lower educational attainment, reduced labour force participation, and limited economic opportunities. These factors, in turn, influence their ability to participate effectively in formal financial systems. The review of international conventions and national legislative frameworks demonstrates that the normative foundations for disability inclusion are well established. Instruments such as UNCRPD and RPwD Act, 2016 articulate important principles relating to accessibility, equality, and non-discrimination. In the financial sector, regulatory authorities have also issued guidelines aimed at improving accessibility of banking infrastructure, digital financial services, and institutional practices. However, the existence of regulatory provisions does not automatically translate into effective implementation. Evidence from judicial interventions, policy reports, and stakeholder interactions indicates that persons with disabilities continue to encounter various barriers in accessing financial services, including physical inaccessibility of banking infrastructure, limited availability of accessible digital platforms, and inadequate awareness among service providers. The insights obtained from interactions with persons with disabilities and financial sector stakeholders further underline the importance of viewing financial inclusion not merely as account ownership but as meaningful and independent access to financial services. Accessibility, usability, and autonomy in financial decision-making remain critical elements in achieving genuine inclusion.

Overall, the findings of this chapter highlight the need for sustained efforts to bridge the gap between policy commitments and practical implementation. Strengthening accessibility standards, improving institutional awareness, and incorporating disability-sensitive design in financial systems will be essential for ensuring that the broader goals of inclusive growth and equitable development extend to persons with disabilities. As India advances towards the vision of Viksit Bharat, ensuring meaningful financial inclusion for persons with disabilities will remain an important component of building an inclusive and equitable economic system.

Acknowledgements The authors gratefully acknowledge Dr. Malabika Roy (Professor of Economics at Jadavpur University), whose original idea of including a chapter on disability and inclusion in this volume inspired the development of the present work. We also thank our Palgrave Editor (Ms. Aparajita Singh) for her encouragement to pursue this theme further and explore authorship possibilities. Their support at the conceptual stage was instrumental in bringing this chapter to fruition.

References

Bagival, P. K. (2024, December 3). Citizens with disabilities, making their rights real. *The Hindu*. https://www.thehindu.com/opinion/lead/citizens-with-disabilities-making-their-rights-real/article68939410.ece

Comptroller and Auditor General of India. (2024a). Performance audit on implementation of the rights of persons with disabilities act, 2016 (RPWD), Government of Karnataka. Report No. 02 of the year 2024.

Comptroller and Auditor General of India. (2024b). Performance audit on implementation of rights of persons with disabilities act, 2016, Government of Rajasthan. Report No. 1 of the year 2023.

Crow, C. (1996). Including all of our lives. In Morris (Ed.), *Encounters with strangers*. The Women's Press Ltd.

CSRBOX. (2023). *Economic empowerment & social inclusion of persons with disabilities in selected districts of India*. https://csrbox.org/Impact/description/Article_full_Economic-Empowerment-%26-Social-Inclusion-of-Persons-with-Disabilities-in-Selected-Districts-of-India_163

Deorukhkar, M. Y., & Shaikh, E. A. (2025). Re-integration and empowerment of persons with disabilities through therapeutic income generation program: A case study approach. *International Journal of Intellectual Disability, 6*(1), 01–04.

Fernández-Batanero, J. M., Montenegro-Rueda, M., Fernández-Cerero, J., & García-Martínez, I. (2022). Assistive technology for students with disabilities: A systematic review. *Education and Information Technologies, 70*(1), 1–20.

Government of India. (2016). The Rights of Persons with Disabilities Act, 2016. https://www.indiacode.nic.in/bitstream/123456789/15939/1/the_rights_of_persons_with_disabilities_act%2C_2016.pdf

Government of India. (2017). The Rights of Persons with Disabilities Rules, 2017. https://upload.indiacode.nic.in/showfile?actid=AC_CEN_25_54_00002_201649_1517807328299&type=actfile&filename=a2016-49.pdf

Government of India. (2019). Persons with Disabilities in India. NSS Report No. 583, National Statistical Office, Ministry of Statistics and Programme Implementation. https://www.mospi.gov.in/sites/default/files/publication_reports/Report_583_Final_0.pdf

Government of India. (2021). Persons with Disabilities (Divyangjan) in India—A Statistical Profile: 2021. Ministry of Statistics and Programme Implementation, National Statistical Office, Social Statistics Division. https://ndfdc.nic.in/upload/nhfdc/Persons_Disabilities_31mar21.pdf

Government of India. (2024a). Pathways to Access: Courts on Disability Rights. Compilation of summaries of important judgements of Supreme Court of India and High Courts across India. https://divyangjan.depwd.gov.in/upload/pathways_to_access/Tagged_Recognised.pdf

Government of India. (2024b). Pathways to access (Part III)—rights of persons with disabilities related to financial services, Compilation of summaries of important orders/circulars/notifications of the Government of India pertaining to financial services for persons with disabilities. Accessed on July 12, 2025 at https://cdnbbsr.s3waas.gov.in/s3e58aea67b01fa747687f038dfde066f6/uploads/2024/12/2024120211865O6453.pdf

Government of India. (2024c). Accessibility Standards and Guidelines for Banking Sector. Department of Financial Services. https://financialservices.gov.in/beta/sites/default/files/2024-08/Guidelines-for-Banking-Sector.pdf

Government of India. (2024d). Accessibility Standards and Guidelines for infrastructure and services in Insurance Sector. Department of Financial Services. https://financialservices.gov.in/beta/sites/default/files/2024-08/guidelines-E.pdf

Government of India. (2024e). Annexure to Notification no. 17/24/2024-IF-I dated 02.09.2024, Accessibility Standard Guidelines for infrastructure and services in Financial Institutions across India. Department of Financial Services. https://financialservices.gov.in/beta/sites/default/files/2024-09/Guidelines-FI.pdf

Indian Banks Association. (2017). Bankers' guide for customers with special needs and persons with disabilities. Downloaded from the website of the Punjab National Bank (PNB): https://www.pnbindia.in/downloadprocess.aspx?fid=IlHD3R3RXcrUkwUZyv+pgA==

James, J. W., Basavarajappa, C., Sivakumar, T., Banerjee, R., & Thirthalli, J. (2019). Swavlamban health insurance scheme for persons with disabilities: An experiential account. *Indian Journal of Psychiatry, 61*(4), 369–375. https://doi.org/10.4103/psychiatry.IndianJPsychiatry_77_19

Kang, S., Kastberg, S., & Mason, B. (2025). Financial literacy for individuals with intellectual and developmental disabilities: Border crossing required. *School Science and Mathematics, 125*(1), 18–32.

Kaur, A., & Dani, D. (2014). Banking websites in India: An accessibility evaluation. *CSIT, 2*(1), 23–34. https://doi.org/10.1007/s40012-014-0040-x

Mendoza, X. L. D. (2021). Entrepreneurial capability and engagement of persons with disabilities toward a framework for inclusive entrepreneurship. *Asian Intellect Research and Education Journal, 20*(1), 179–186.

Mathew Martin, P. J., & Rabindranath, M. (2017). Digital inclusion for access to information: A study on banking and financial institutions in India. *SAGE Open, 7*(3), 1–8. https://doi.org/10.1177/2158244017720479

National Centre for Financial Education. (2019). National Financial Literacy and Inclusion Survey (NCFE-FLIS) 2019. https://ncfe.org.in/wp-content/uploads/2023/12/NCFE-2019_Final_Report.pdf

OECD. (2022). Disability, work and inclusion: Mainstreaming in all policies and practices. *OECD Publishing*. https://doi.org/10.1787/1eaa5e9c-en

Olkin, R. (2002). Could you hold the door for me? Including disability in diversity. *Cultural Diversity and Ethnic Minority Psychology, 8*, 130–137.

Oliver, M. (1983). *Social work with disabled people*. Red Globe Press.

Oliver, M. (1996). *Understanding disability: From theory to practice*. St. Martin's Press.

Oliver, M. (2013). The social model of disability: Thirty years on. *Disability & Society, 28*(7), 1024–1026. https://doi.org/10.1080/09687599.2013.818773

Puli, L., Layton, N., Bell, D. & Shahriar, A. Z. (2024). Financial inclusion for people with disability: A scoping review. *Global Health Action, 17*(1). https://doi.org/10.1080/16549716.2024.2342634

Reserve Bank of India. (2025). Master circular—Disbursement of government pension by agency banks. https://rbidocs.rbi.org.in/rdocs/notification/PDFs/05MC010420252ED8A74EE428468287D815016A33587F.PDF

Reserve Bank of India. (2024a). Master circular—Deendayal Antyodaya Yojana—National Rural Livelihoods Mission (DAY-NRLM). https://rbidocs.rbi.org.in/rdocs/notification/PDFs/20MCNRLM1604202436A6E96BA7C44362A93B85BA99A3A906.PDF

Reserve Bank of India. (2024b). Facilitating accessibility to digital payment systems for Persons with Disabilities—Guidelines. https://rbidocs.rbi.org.in/rdocs/notification/PDFs/NOT838196C0F37571427181419D7ADF9FFCC0.PDF

Reserve Bank of India. (2022). MANI (Mobile Aided Note Identifier)—Introduction of multi-lingual audio notification (press release). https://rbidocs.rbi.org.in/rdocs/PressRelease/PDFs/PR899EF7232BBA8624431BAD98CE9E8FC84F4.PDF

Reserve Bank of India. (2020a). Doorstep banking services for senior citizens and differently abled persons (circular). https://rbidocs.rbi.org.in/rdocs/notification/PDFs/203CDBC69575209AF64C93AB73B3E65A86ADF1.PDF

Reserve Bank of India. (2020b). Launch of Mobile Aided Note Identifier (MANI) by RBI (press release). https://rbidocs.rbi.org.in/rdocs/PressRelease/PDFs/PR1570BF3200BEC962474ABF72CF5A0B118EFE.PDF

Reserve Bank of India. (2018). Statement on developmental and regulatory policies (press release). https://rbidocs.rbi.org.in/rdocs/PressRelease/PDFs/PR3191F15F5759EFA74292BBB6D21A0EC2EC5A.PDF

Reserve Bank of India. (2017a). Master circular—Disbursement of government pension by agency banks. https://rbidocs.rbi.org.in/rdocs/notification/PDFs/01MC010720179FA825279A0F4515AC45A306EE04C43A.PDF

Reserve Bank of India. (2017b). Statement on developmental and regulatory policies—October 4, 2017-Banking facility for senior citizens and differently abled persons (circular). https://rbidocs.rbi.org.in/rdocs/notification/PDFs/NOTI89F9DD47A9F3FA440E94C254135F95E728.PDF

Reserve Bank of India. (2016). Legal guardianship certificates issued under the Mental Health Act, 1987 (circular). https://rbidocs.rbi.org.in/rdocs/notification/PDFs/321CN1102166DE8AE4289E045B1BF596576D65FB238.PDF

Reserve Bank of India. (2015a). Priority sector lending—Persons with disabilities (PwD)—Inclusion under Weaker Sections (circular). https://rbidocs.rbi.org.in/rdocs/notification/PDFs/499IPDPSL0315.pdf

Reserve Bank of India. (2015b). Master circular on customer service in banks. https://www.rbi.org.in/commonman/Upload/English/Notification/PDFs/59FM04072F58B1DD44DFADD486B9B0A59E9D.pdf

Reserve Bank of India. (2015c). Master Circular on Customer Service—UCBs. https://www.rbi.org.in/commonman/Upload/English/Notification/PDFs/61CS99D0093EF958451186E35A661DC233B6.pdf

Reserve Bank of India. (2014a). Legal Guardianship Certificates Issued under the Mental Health Act, 1987and National Trust for the Welfare of Persons with Autism, Cerebral Palsy, Mental Retardation and Multiple Disabilities Act, 1999 (circular). https://rbidocs.rbi.org.in/rdocs/notification/PDFs/CIRBC13012014.PDF

Reserve Bank of India. (2014b). Need for Bank Branches/ATMs to be made accessible to persons with disabilities. (circular for all scheduled commercial banks). https://rbidocs.rbi.org.in/rdocs/notification/PDFs/DB13NT0514FS.PDF

Reserve Bank of India. (2014c). Need for bank branches/ATMs to be made Accessible to persons with disabilities (circular for UCBs). https://rbidocs.rbi.org.in/rdocs/notification/PDFs/CA110614FSM.pdf

Reserve Bank of India. (2014d). Master circulars—Miscellaneous instructions to all non-banking financial companies. https://rbidocs.rbi.org.in/rdocs/notification/PDFs/52MBFC010714F.pdf

Reserve Bank of India. (2012a). Banking facilities to visually challenged/persons with disabilities (circular for all SCBs). https://rbidocs.rbi.org.in/rdocs/notification/PDFs/C191BF050912.PDF

Reserve Bank of India. (2012b). Banking facilities to visually challenged/persons with disabilities (circular for RRBs). https://rbidocs.rbi.org.in/rdocs/notification/PDFs/CE249BF121012.PDF

Reserve Bank of India. (2009a). Need for Bank Branches/ATMs to be made accessible to persons with disabilities (circular for all SCBs). https://rbidocs.rbi.org.in/rdocs/notification/PDFs/CIRCULARBC123.PDF

Reserve Bank of India. (2009b). Need for Bank Branches/ATMs to be made accessible to persons with disabilities (circular for all RRBs). https://rbidocs.rbi.org.in/rdocs/notification/PDFs/CNo441210409.pdf

Reserve Bank of India. (2009c). Need for Bank Branches/ATMs to be made accessible to persons with disabilities (circular for all UCBs). https://rbidocs.rbi.org.in/rdocs/notification/PDFs/ATM290409.pdf

Reserve Bank of India. (2008a). Banking facilities to the visually challenged (circular for all SCBs). https://www.rbi.org.in/commonman/Upload/English/Notification/PDFs/84791.pdf

Reserve Bank of India. (2008b). Banking facilities to the visually challenged (circular for all Central/State Cooperative Banks). https://www.rbi.org.in/commonman/Upload/English/Notification/PDFs/85684.pdf

Reserve Bank of India. (2008c). Banking facilities to the visually challenged (circular for all RRBs). https://rbidocs.rbi.org.in/rdocs/notification/PDFs/85805.pdf

Reserve Bank of India. (2007). Legal Guardianship Certificate issued under the National Trust Act, 1999 empowering the disabled persons with autism, cerebral palsy, mental retardation and multiple disabilities (circular for all SCBs). https://rbidocs.rbi.org.in/rdocs/notification/PDFs/81351.PDF

Santoso, B. (2023). Inclusive digital financial services for persons with disabilities: Impact on economic empowerment and financial inclusion. *Indonesian Journal of Disability Studies, 10*(1), 105–124.

Securities and Exchange Board of India. (2025). Rights of Persons with Disabilities Act, 2016 and rules made thereunder- mandatory compliance by all Regulated Entities. (July 31) (Circular). https://www.sebi.gov.in/legal/circulars/jul-2025/rights-of-persons-with-disabilities-act-2016-and-rules-made-thereunder-mandatory-compliance-by-all-regulated-entities_95745.html

Silvers, A. (1998). A fatal attraction to normalizing. In Parens (Ed.), *Enhancing human traits* (pp. 95–123). Georgetown University Press.

Singanamalla, S., Potluri, V., Scott, C., & Medhi-Thies, I. (2019). Pocket ATM: Understanding and improving ATM accessibility in India. *ICTD 19: Proceedings of the Tenth International Conference on Information and Communication Technologies and Development*, Article No. 14. https://doi.org/10.1145/3287098.3287106

Thohari, S. A., & Rizky, U. F. (2021). Persons with disabilities' financial literacy and access to financial services. *Jurnal Ekonomi dan Bisnis, 24*(1), 47–64. https://doi.org/10.24914/jeb.v24i1.3675

The New York Times. (2011, May 9). *Life and the Cosmos, Word by Painstaking Word*. Restricted https://www.nytimes.com/2011/05/10/science/10hawking.html?register=email&auth=register-email

UNESCO. (2019). *State of the education report for India 2019: Children with disabilities*. UNESCO. https://unesdoc.unesco.org/ark:/48223/pf0000368780

United Nations Convention on the Rights of Persons with Disabilities. (2006). https://www.un.org/disabilities/documents/convention/convention_accessible_pdf.pdf

World Health Organisation and World Bank. (2011). *World report on disability*. https://www.who.int/teams/noncommunicable-diseases/sensory-functions-disability-and-rehabilitation/world-report-on-disability

World Bank, & International Labour Office. (2022). *Technical note on accessibility: The narrative (Part 1)*. https://thedocs.worldbank.org/en/doc/2c15b0291da3107e5a324e8d261c674b-0320012022/original/WBG-TECHNICAL-NOTE-PART-1.pdf

Zaks, Z. (2023). Changing the medical model of disability to the normalization model of disability: Clarifying the past to create a new future direction. *Disability & Society, 39*(12), 3233–3260. https://doi.org/10.1080/09687599.2023.2255926

Zoya, S., Jagannathan, A., Sivakumar, T., & Padmavati, R. (2025). Status of inclusion of mental illness under health insurance coverage in India—An exploratory study. *Indian Journal of Psychiatry, 67*(3), 323–332. https://doi.org/10.4103/indianjpsychiatry.indianjpsychiatry_590_24

CHAPTER 7

The Pandemic Divide: Gender Inequality in Terms of Financial Inclusion in India

Chandralekha Ghosh and Rimita Hom Chaudhury

1 Introduction

The COVID-19 pandemic brought unprecedented challenges to economies worldwide. In India, its impact has been multifaceted, with the financial sector witnessing a significant acceleration in digitalization. Digital financial services became essential during lockdowns, facilitating transactions, savings, and access to government relief measures. During the pandemic, governments leveraged digital channels to efficiently distribute emergency funds directly into bank accounts, ensuring timely support to vulnerable populations. This shift underlined the critical role of technology in expanding financial services, especially amidst restrictions that limited physical interactions. Globally, there was a significant increase in digital payments during the pandemic, and India was no

C. Ghosh
Department of Economics, West Bengal State University, Kolkata, India

R. H. Chaudhury (✉)
Department of Economics, Nalanda University, Rajgir, India
e-mail: rimitahomchaudhury@gmail.com

© The Author(s), under exclusive license to Springer Nature Singapore Pte Ltd. 2026

V. Dixit et al. (eds.), *Financial Inclusion for Viksit Bharat*,
https://doi.org/10.1007/978-981-92-0807-4_7

exception. In 2021, 15.52% of adults used a mobile phone or the internet to check their account balance, which was only 6.72% in 2017 (Demirgüç-Kunt et al.,. Regarding digital payments, it has been observed that in 2021, 24.69% of adults reported making digital payments, compared to 19.97% in 2017 (Demirgüç-Kunt et al.,. Similarly, 19.40% reported receiving digital payments in 2021, up from 16.46% in 2017 (Demirgüç-Kunt et al.,. There has been a remarkable surge in mobile money account ownership, increasing from 1.99% to 10.44% (Demirgüç-Kunt et al.,. The onset of the COVID-19 pandemic has cast a spotlight on the indispensable role of digital finance. However, despite this surge, the percentage of Indian adults engaging in digital payments remains relatively lower compared to global averages. A notable challenge highlighted during this period is the gender gap in digital finance usage. There exists a significant double-digit disparity between men and women in accessing and utilizing digital financial services (Demirgüç-Kunt et al., 2022a). In this regard, this research delves into the impact of the COVID-19 pandemic on gender inequality in financial inclusion in India, focusing on the digital financial landscape.

Women have endured discrimination in almost every aspect of their lives for ages. They have fewer economic opportunities than men and, therefore, less economic participation. Moreover, women are frequently found working in informal organizations or low-paying jobs. Another concern is the disproportionate burden of unpaid care and domestic work, which severely limits women's participation in the labor force (Ferrant et al., 2014). Women's health is also ignored in many societies. Furthermore, women, irrespective of their age, class, caste, or educational background, have long been victims of exploitation in case of their social and economic lives. Such exploitation and exclusion hurt not just their own life but also the growth and development of a country (Cavalcanti & Tavares, 2016; Esteve-Volart, 2009; Fatima, 2013; Klasen & Lamanna, 2009; Raghavendra et al., 2017; World Bank, 2012). Because of these, the elimination of gender disparity has recently become a fundamental aspect of the Sustainable Development Goals 2030 (SDG 5). Women were disproportionately affected by the COVID-19 pandemic, facing increased unpaid care work (Alon et al., 2020; Bahn et al., 2020; Kabeer et al., 2021; UN Women, 2020), rising gender-based violence, and greater job and income losses, especially in the informal sector. The crisis also deepened educational disruptions for girls, threatening progress in gender equality (Malala Fund, 2020). Financial resources certainly have the potential to bring about positive changes in women's lives. Effective access to the full range of formal financial services allow them to achieve social, economic, and political empowerment (Al-Mamun et al., 2014; Ashraf et al., 2010; Bhatia & Singh, 2019; Hashemi et al., 1996; Hendriks, 2019; Kim, 2022). Furthermore, women use financial resources in such a way that, in addition to enhancing their living standards, it also improves the well-being of the family, especially children (Kabeer, 2001; Nader, 2008; Swamy, 2014). Because of this, financial inclusion, especially in the form of digital finance remains an important strategy to strengthen women even during the crisis. Therefore addressing gender disparities in financial inclusion has become more urgent than ever.

Gender inequality in case of financial inclusion has long been a concern in India, rooted in socioeconomic (Ghosh & Hom Chaudhury, 2019), cultural, and systemic barriers (Ghosh & Vinod, 2017; Sabherwal et al., 2019). The pandemic worsened women's financial challenges, with job losses, reduced earnings, and limited safety nets increasing their reliance on informal borrowing and cash, further distancing them from digital financial services (Demirgüç-Kunt et al., 2022a). In this regard the study examines the impact of the COVID-19 pandemic on gender inequality in case of financial inclusion in India, with a specific focus on digital financial services. While financial inclusion has been a policy priority, initiatives have often failed to address the distinct barriers faced by women, leading to persistent disparities. By conducting a comparative analysis between 2017 and 2021, the study seeks to understand how the crisis has reshaped the gender gap in accessing both traditional and digital financial services, an area that remains under-researched. A critical dimension of this analysis lies in identifying the factors predominantly influencing the gender gap in financial inclusion. This analysis will further identify whether there are any shifts in the factors contributing to this gender disparity. By focusing on the intersection of gender, digital finance, and pandemic response, this study fills a critical gap in existing literature. It offers novel empirical insights into how external shocks reshape financial inclusion dynamics and provides actionable recommendations for developing more gender-responsive financial inclusion policies in post-pandemic recovery efforts.

The paper is organized as follows. Section 2 critically examines the past studies on gender gap in financial inclusion. Section 3 deals with data, variable details and methodology. Section 4 presents the results and analysis. And finally, Sect. 5 presents the conclusion and prescribes policies.

2 Gender Gap in Financial Inclusion

Gender inequality is widely acknowledged as a formidable impediment to global progress and development (Cavalcanti & Tavares, 2016; Esteve-Volart, 2009; Fatima, 2013; Klasen & Lamanna, 2009; World Bank, 2012). Its persistent inclusion in international development frameworks such as the Universal Declaration of Human Rights, the Millennium Development Goals (MDGs), and the Sustainable Development Goals (SDGs) reflects its enduring relevance as a paramount global development objective. A pivotal strategy in advancing gender equality is enhancing women's access to financial services, as articulated by Ohiomu and Ogbeide-Osaretin (2019). Research consistently demonstrates that integrating financial services into women's lives yields substantial benefits, including bolstering economic autonomy, amplifying decision-making authority within households, and facilitating broader participation in social and economic realms. Financial inclusion is crucial as it aims to ensure universal access to formal financial services for all individuals, irrespective of their income, gender, ethnicity, or geographical location. By extending access to savings, credit, insurance, and other financial services to every person, financial inclusion promotes not only economic empowerment but also enhances social inclusion and resilience within communities. Over the past few years, the concept of financial inclusion has emerged as a critical focus in India's policy landscape. Despite advancements in financial inclusion efforts, a significant gender gap persists within India's financial landscape. Women face numerous barriers that hinder their access to essential financial services such as savings, credit, and insurance, creating a substantial disparity compared to men's access levels. Ghosh and Vinod (2016) found that female-headed households are 10% less likely to access formal financial services compared to male-headed households, with similar trends in service usage. Their follow-up study in 2017 highlighted barriers that provide hindrances to financial inclusion for families headed by females. They established the fact education and wages are important factors in explaining access to finance, while political and social factors are more relevant in determining how these services are used. Ghosh and Hom Chaudhury (2019) suggested that women are significantly less likely to be financially included as compared to their male counterparts. They also revealed that gender differences in socio-economic variables largely explain the gender gap in financial inclusion. More precisely, lower employment status among females was observed to be a crucial reason for not having formal accounts, formal savings, and formal credit requirements. However, lower education among females predominantly prohibits them from using digital financial services. Sabherwal et al. (2019) underlined the barriers women face in accessing their entitlements from DBT programmes. Kaur et al. (2020) recognized the factors (education, monthly household consumption expenditure, land size holding, irrigated area, and penetration of scheduled commercial banks) that positively influence FHHs' (Female-headed Households) access to IF (Institutional Finance). While digital financial services offer new pathways for inclusion, they can also reinforce existing divides. Many studies have expanded their research emphasizing digital finance for India and explored the positive gender gap in the adoption of digital financial services (Ghosh, 2022; Ghosh & Hom Chaudhury, 2022). These prior studies prompt us to understand how the crisis reshaped the gender gap in accessing traditional and digital financial services as no comparative analysis has been conducted in this regard between 2017 (pre-covid) and 2021 (middle era of the pandemic).

3 Research Design

3.1 Data Source

For our analysis, we utilized microdata from the World Bank's Global Findex database for 2017 and 2021 (Demirgüç-Kunt et al., 2018, specific to India. The dataset comprises responses from approximately 3,000 individuals in each survey year, drawn from a nationally representative sample of adults aged 15 and above. This comprehensive dataset includes over 100 indicators related to financial inclusion and digital finance, such as account ownership, savings, payments, credit, online transactions, cards, and financial resilience for India. These indicators are based on survey data collected by Gallup, Inc. in collaboration with its annual Gallup World Poll. The gender distribution in both years is nearly balanced, with male and female respondents each constituting about 50% of the sample. It is important to note that the data do not follow the same individuals across years; rather, different individuals were surveyed in 2017 and 2021, meaning changes in indicators reflect population-level trends rather than individual-level transitions.

3.2 Explanatory variables

The explanatory variables used in our analysis are age, gender, income, education, and employment. Four dummy variables for income have been constructed i.e. Income level 1 (poorest 20%), Income level 2 (second 20%), Income level 3 (third 20%), and Income level 4 (fourth 20%). The fifth richest quintile has been used as the base dummy. Income level 1 is a dummy variable equal to one if income is in the first income quintile, zero elsewhere, and so on for the other dummies. There are two dummies for education level namely Secondary education and Tertiary education. The base category is primary education dummy or less. Age as well as age square has been undertaken. A female dummy variable has been taken which takes a value equal to 1 if the individual is female, and for male, it takes zero value. Employment dummy variable takes one if the individual is in the workforce, and zero otherwise.

3.3 Dependent Variables

Indicators of traditional and digital financial services, such as formal account, formal saving, deposit, formal borrowing, mobile account, debit card ownership, credit card ownership, debit card usage, digital transaction, and digitally check account balance have been considered as dependent variables. All these are binary variables, constructed as taking the value '1' for yes, and '0' for others. Formal account takes the value 1 if the respondent has an account at a financial institution, and 0 otherwise. Formal saving takes the value 1 if the respondent 'saved using an account at a financial institution', and 0 otherwise. Deposit takes the value 1 if the respondent 'made any deposit into the account', and 0 otherwise. While both formal saving and deposit relate to financial behavior at formal institutions, the former reflects an individual's intent to save, whereas the latter includes any deposit made into the account, regardless of purpose or depositor. Formal borrowing takes the value of 1 if the respondent 'borrowed from a financial institution', and 0 otherwise. Mobile account takes the value 1 if the respondent 'has a mobile money account', and 0 otherwise. Debit card ownership takes the value 1 if the respondent 'has a debit card', and 0 otherwise. Credit card ownership takes the value 1 if the respondent 'has a credit card', and 0 otherwise. Debit card usage takes the value 1 if the respondent 'used a debit card', and 0 otherwise. Digital transaction takes the value 1 if the respondent 'used a mobile phone or internet to access account', 0 otherwise. Digitally check account balance takes the value 1 if the respondent 'used a mobile phone or internet to check account balance', 0 otherwise.

3.4 *The Fairlie Nonlinear Decomposition Technique*

This research employs the Fairlie nonlinear decomposition technique (Fairlie, 1999, 2006) to examine the gender gap across various indicators of traditional and digital finance in India for the years 2017 and 2021. The Fairlie decomposition is an extension of the Blinder-Oaxaca decomposition, specifically designed for cases where the outcome is binary, using coefficients from a Logit or Probit model. This method allows for a detailed understanding of how different factors contribute to the observed gender disparities in financial inclusion.

Fairlie decomposition model can be specified as:

$$\overline{Y}^{M} - \overline{Y}^{F} = \left[\sum_{i=1}^{N^{M}} \frac{F(X_i^{M}\hat{\beta}^{M})}{N^{M}} - \sum_{i=1}^{N^{F}} \frac{F(X_i^{F}\hat{\beta}^{M})}{N^{F}}\right] + \left[\sum_{i=1}^{N^{F}} \frac{F(X_i^{F}\hat{\beta}^{M})}{N^{F}} - \sum_{i=1}^{N^{F}} \frac{F(X_i^{F}\hat{\beta}^{F})}{N^{F}}\right] \ldots\ldots\ldots \quad (1)$$

where, N^{j} represents the sample size for gender j (M = male, F = Female). $\overline{Y}^{j}$ is the mean probability of the outcome variable for gender j, X_i^{j} is the vector of independent variables for case i in gender j, $\hat{\beta}^{j}$ is the vector of coefficient estimates, which includes a constant term. F refers to the cumulative distribution function from the logistic distribution. The equation is structured such that the first term in brackets captures the portion of the gender gap attributable to group differences in the distribution of the independent variables X (i.e., the characteristics between men and women). The second term represents the portion of the gap due to differences in how these characteristics influence the outcome variable Y, essentially capturing the differences in coefficients between the groups. This term also accounts for the portion of the gender gap that may be explained by unmeasurable or unobserved factors (endowments). In this equation, the male coefficient estimates $\hat{\beta}^M$ are used as weights in the first term, while the female distribution of independent variables X^F is used as weights in the second term, allowing for a comparison of how each group's characteristics and processes contribute to the gender gap in financial inclusion.

An equally valid expression for the decomposition is:

$$\overline{Y}^M - \overline{Y}^F = \left[\sum_{i=1}^{N^M} \frac{F(X_i^M \hat{\beta}^F)}{N^M} - \sum_{i=1}^{N^F} \frac{F(X_i^F \hat{\beta}^F)}{N^F}\right] + \left[\sum_{i=1}^{N^M} \frac{F(X_i^M \hat{\beta}^M)}{N^M} - \sum_{i=1}^{N^M} \frac{F(X_i^M \hat{\beta}^F)}{N^M}\right] \ldots\ldots\ldots \quad (2)$$

In this approach, the female coefficient estimates, $\hat{\beta}^F$ are applied as weights for the first term in the decomposition, while the male distribution of independent variables X^M are used for the second term. This method may yield different results due to the "index problem" often seen in the Blinder-Oaxaca decomposition technique. An alternative is to weight the first term using coefficient estimates from a pooled sample of both groups. In our study, we have adopted this pooled approach, using logit regression coefficient estimates from a sample that includes all gender groups. This method allows for a more comprehensive comparison, capturing characteristics and influences across both male and female groups.

To isolate the contribution of gender differences in specific variables, such as X_1, to the overall gap, an additional calculation is required. Suppose the set of independent variables X includes two variables, X_1 and X_2. The independent contribution of X_1 to the gender gap can be expressed as:

$$\frac{1}{N^F} \sum_{i=1}^{N^F} F\left(\hat{\alpha}^* + X_{1i}^M \widehat{\beta}_1^* + X_{2i}^M \widehat{\beta}_2^*\right) - F\left(\hat{\alpha}^* + X_{1i}^F \widehat{\beta_1}^* + X_{2i}^M \widehat{\beta_2}^*\right) \ldots\ldots \quad (3)$$

Similarly, the contribution of X_2 can be expressed as:

$$\frac{1}{N^F}\sum_{i=1}^{N^F} F\left(\hat{\alpha}^* + X_{1i}^F\widehat{\beta_1}^* + X_{2i}^M\widehat{\beta_2}^*\right) - F\left(\hat{\alpha}^* + X_{1i}^F\widehat{\beta_1}^* + X_{2i}^F\widehat{\beta_2}^*\right) \ldots\ldots \quad (4)$$

One key advantage of this method is that the total contribution of individual variables equals the combined contribution of all variables when evaluated on the full sample. This allows us to estimate how much gender differences in independent variables contribute to the gender gap in the dependent variable. It also enables the assessment of each variable's specific contribution to the overall gap. The contribution is calculated by observing changes in average predicted probabilities when the female distribution is replaced by the male distribution for each variable while keeping others constant. The decomposition process involves matching male and female cases based on predicted probabilities. Since sample sizes differ, a random female sub-sample is generated to match the male sample size. To address the sensitivity of decomposition estimates to the choice of sub-sample, we draw 1,000 distinct sub-samples. Our findings are then derived from the average values obtained through decompositions performed across these sub-samples. To ensure accuracy, the order of variables is randomized across simulations. This method enables us to calculate the estimates and their standard errors. Using this method, we compute estimates to quantify the total gap, the explained gender gap from socioeconomic variables, and the unexplained portion separately for the years 2017 and 2021 for all the finance variables mentioned in Sect. 3.3. The 'bootstrap' method is applied to ensure robust inference and significance levels for all gaps.

4 Gender Diversity in Financial Inclusion: A Comparative Analysis Between 2017 and 2021

This section provides a comprehensive analysis of the relationship between gender and financial inclusion, employing the "Fairlie non-linear decomposition" technique to delve into the contributions of various socioeconomic variables to gender disparities. The results of this analysis are presented in Table 1, Table 2, and Table 3, offering a structured breakdown of the factors driving disparities in financial inclusion between men and women. This approach not only quantifies the extent of gender disparities but also identifies the specific socioeconomic dimensions that play a pivotal role in shaping these differences. By combining statistical testing with decomposition analysis, this study enhances our understanding of gender dynamics in financial behaviors and provides a basis for targeted interventions aimed at promoting gender equality in financial inclusion initiatives.

As indicated in Table 1, a significant gender gap in account ownership was evident only in 2017, with a rate of 0.0598. This gap was mainly attributed to differences in several socioeconomic variables (62.71%), mainly in education, and employment status. Employment status contributed the most, explaining 34.62% of the gender gap. However, by 2021, no significant gender gap is observed in formal account ownership. This holds also for formal borrowing. In contrast, data from 2017 indicated a modest 3.41% difference in formal borrowing between males and females. Socioeconomic factors explain 38.71% of this gap, highlighting their significance but incomplete role in shaping gender disparities in formal credit usage. Specifically, employment status alone accounted for 29.03% of the observed gender gap. Despite this, a substantial portion of the gap remained unexplained, suggesting the presence of additional, unidentified factors influencing differences in formal borrowing behavior across genders beyond socioeconomic considerations. The decomposition estimates for formal savings align with the observation that a significant gender gap exists in savings at financial institutions. However, this gap has narrowed in 2021 compared to 2017. Currently, males are 2.62% more likely to save formally than females, a decrease from 4.93% in 2017. This positive gap indicates a persistent disparity favouring males in formal savings behavior. Our analysis shows that observable characteristics explain the entire gender gap, highlighting the role of socioeconomic factors. In 2021, education has emerged as the primary explanatory factor, whereas employment status held this role in 2017. Specifically, differences in secondary education contribute 27.10% to the gender gap, an increase from 19.68% in 2017. Meanwhile, disparities in tertiary education account for 53.44% of the gap, a significant rise compared to 21.10% in 2017. This shift likely reflects the increasing importance of financial literacy especially among women, which are strongly correlated with educational attainment. Income's role

Table 1 Gender gap in traditional finance

Variable	*Formal Account*		*Formal Saving*		*Formal Borrowing*		*Deposit*	
	2017	*2021*	*2017*	*2021*	*2017*	*2021*	*2017*	*2021*
Age	−0.0062	0.0074***	0.0003	−0.0005	0.0006	0.0037	−0.0002	0.0020
Age square	0.0006	−0.0058**	−0.0007	0.0001	−0.0006	−0.0051**	−0.0004	−0.0021
Secondary education	0.0146* (24.41%)	0.0124*	0.0097* (19.68%)	0.0071* (27.10%)	0.0026	0.0049*	0.0122* (13.22%)	0.0079* (5.43%)
Tertiary education	0.0076* (12.71%)	0.0107*	0.0104* (21.10%)	0.0140* (53.44%)	0.0005	0.0006	0.0066* (7.15%)	0.0092** (6.33%)
Income level 4	−0.0008	−0.0011	−0.0009	−0.0011	0.0001	0.0004	−0.0024	−0.0022
Income level 3	−0.0001	0.0005	0.0001	0.0044* (16.79%)	−0.0001	−0.0003	0.0009	0.0042
Income level 2	0.0004	−0.0038	0.0025** (5.07%)	0.0084* (32.06%)	0.0002	−0.0020	0.0033	0.0169* (11.62%)
Income level 1	0.0008	−0.0018	0.0036*** (7.30%)	0.0077* (29.39%)	0.0000	0.0004	0.0089* (9.64%)	0.0150* (10.32%)
Employment	0.0207* (34.62%)	0.0221*	0.0258* (52.33%)	0.0048*** (18.32%)	0.0099** (29.03%)	0.0140*	0.0272* (29.47%)	0.0049
Observation	3000	3000	3000	3000	3000	3000	2379	2365
Group (male)	0.8238	0.7892	0.2154	0.1514	0.0833	0.0989	0.4637	0.3641
Group (female)	0.7641	0.7873	0.1661	0.1252	0.0491	0.0941	0.3714	0.2188
Difference/gap	0.0598*	0.0020	0.0493*	0.0262**	0.0341*	0.0048	0.0923*	0.1454*

(continued)

Table 1 (continued)

Variable	*Formal Account*		*Formal Saving*		*Formal Borrowing*		*Deposit*	
	2017	*2021*	*2017*	*2021*	*2017*	*2021*	*2017*	*2021*
Unexplained gap	0.0222	−0.0386	−0.0017	−0.0188*** (~0.00%)	0.0210*** (61.58%)	−0.0117	0.0362*** (39.22%)	0.0895* (61.55%)
Explained gap	0.0375* (62.71%)	0.0406*	0.0509* (~100%)@	0.0450* (~100%)@	0.0132* (38.71%)	0.0166*	0.0561* (60.78%)	0.0559* (38.45%)

Source Author's calculation

Note Parenthesis denotes percentage in respect of total gap

@The percentage comes to more than 100% this means the total gap can be completely explained by the explanatory variables incorporated in our model

*Significant at 1% level, **significant at 5% level, ***significant at 10% level

Table 2 Gender gap in access to digital finance

Variable	*Mobile Account*		*Debit Card Ownership*		*Credit Card Ownership*	
	2017	*2021*	*2017*	*2021*	*2017*	*2021*
Age	0.0019	0.0033	−0.0005	0.0169** (8.23%)	0.0001	0.0027
Age square	−0.0043	−0.0044	0.0058	−0.0116	−0.0001	−0.0031
Secondary education	0.0014*** (7.78%)	0.0121* (10.06%)	0.0334* (20.98%)	0.0208* (10.13%)	0.0018	0.0055* (8.89%)
Tertiary education	0.0111* (61.67%)	0.0304* (25.27%)	0.0163* (10.24%)	0.0215* (10.47%)	0.0048* (26.82%)	0.0088* (14.22%)
Income level 4	−0.0009	−0.0009	−0.0007	−0.0023	−0.0010**	−0.0005
Income level 3	0.0002	0.0056* (4.66%)	0.0004	0.0052	0.0000	0.0017*** (2.75%)
Income level 2	0.0005	0.0107* (8.89%)	0.0042*** (2.64%)	0.0211* (10.27%)	0.0003	0.0048* (7.75%)
Income level 1	0.0005	0.0090* (7.48%)	0.0064*** (4.02%)	0.0189* (9.20%)	0.0006	0.0043* (6.95%)
Employment	−0.0014	0.0152* (12.64%)	0.0199* (12.50%)	0.0175* (8.52%)	0.0041	0.0090* (14.54%)
Observation	3000	3000	3000	2365	3000	2365
Group (male)	0.0310	0.1768	0.3964	0.4683	0.0385	0.0932
Group (female)	0.0129	0.0564	0.2372	0.2629	0.0207	0.0313
Difference/ gap	0.0180*	0.1203*	0.1592*	0.2054*	0.0179*	0.0619*
Unexplained gap	0.0092*** (51.11%)	0.0394* (32.75%)	0.0741* (46.55%)	0.0975* (47.47%)	0.0073	0.0287* (46.37%)
Explained gap	0.0089* (49.44%)	0.0810* (67.33%)	0.0851* (53.45%)	0.1080* (52.58%)	0.0106* (59.22%)	0.0332* (53.63%)

Source Author's calculation
Note Parenthesis denotes percentage in respect of total gap
*Significant at 1% level, **significant at 5% level, ***significant at 10% level

in explaining the gender gap in formal savings has become more significant in 2021. The contribution of employment status to the gender gap has decreased significantly to 18.32% in 2021, down from 52.33% in 2017. In contrast to formal saving practices, the disparity in deposit behavior between genders has intensified in 2021 compared to 2017. The data reveals a notable increase in the overall difference between males and females in terms of deposit, rising from 9.23% in 2017 to 14.54% in 2021.

Table 3 Gender gap in the usage of digital finance

Variable	*Debit Card Usage*		*Digital Transaction*		*Digitally Check Account Balance*	
	2017	*2021*	*2017*	*2021*	*2017*	*2021*
Age	0.0001	−0.0007	0.0019	0.0051	0.0015	0.0075
Age square	0.0012	0.0026	−0.0043	−0.0058	−0.0035	−0.0080
Secondary education	0.0126* (19.57%)	0.0124* (5.63%)	0.0067* (27.35%)	0.0222* (11.78%)	0.0106* (17.58%)	0.0221* (11.95%)
Tertiary education	0.0128* (19.88%)	0.0114* (5.17%)	0.0129* (52.65%)	0.0322* (17.09%)	0.0159* (26.37%)	0.0298* (16.11%)
Income level 4	−0.00001	0.0022*** (.998%)	−0.0006	−0.0008	−0.0005	−0.0012
Income level 3	0.0009	0.0131* (5.94%)	0.0005*** (2.04%)	0.0069* (3.66%)	0.0006	0.0066** (3.57%)
Income level 2	−0.0030**	0.0164* (7.44%)	0.0000	0.0166* (8.81%)	−0.0004	0.0180* (9.73%)
Income level 1	0.0027	0.0133* (6.03%)	0.0015** (6.12%)	0.0151* (8.01%)	0.0024* (3.98%)	0.0161* (8.70%)
Employment	0.0022	0.0205* (9.30%)	0.0004	0.0168* (8.92%)	−0.0033	0.0160* (8.65%)
Observation	943	884	2379	2365	2379	2365
Group (male)	0.3750	0.5351	0.0727	0.2702	0.1111	0.3054
Group (female)	0.3106	0.3147	0.0482	0.0818	0.0508	0.1204
Difference/ gap	0.0644**	0.2204*	0.0245*	0.1884*	0.0603*	0.1850*
Unexplained gap	0.0349	0.1291* (58.58%)	0.0057	0.0801* (42.52%)	0.0371* (61.53%)	0.0780* (42.16%)
Explained gap	0.0295*** (45.81%)	0.0913* (41.42%)	0.0188* (76.73%)	0.1083* (57.48%)	0.0233* (38.64%)	0.1070* (57.84%)

Source Author's calculation
Note Parenthesis denotes percentage in respect of total gap
*Significant at 1% level, **significant at 5% level, ***significant at 10% level

Interestingly, while socioeconomic variables historically played a significant role in narrowing this gap, their influence has noticeably decreased in 2021. Specifically, socioeconomic factors now account for 38.45% of the total gender gap in deposit, whereas they explained 60.78% of the gap in 2017. Despite efforts to understand and address these gaps through socioeconomic lenses, a substantial portion of the disparity remains unexplained in 2021. This suggests the existence of additional, unidentified factors influencing differences in deposit behaviors across genders. The evolving dynamics of gender gaps in deposit behaviors highlight shifts in the factors influencing these disparities over time. In 2021, income levels have emerged as the primary contributor to the gender gap in depositing, replacing employment, which held this role in 2017. Employment status played a notable role (29.47%) in contributing to these disparities in 2017, but its influence has become insignificant in the current context. The effect of education also has diminished in the year 2021.

Tables 2 and 3 showcase the results from the "Fairlie non-linear decomposition" technique, applied to different indicators of digital financial services, highlighting significant trends in gender disparities. The results indicate that gender differences across all indicators of digital finance have widened notably in the year 2021 compared to 2017.

The analysis of mobile account ownership trends reveals a significant disparity between genders. In 2021, males are shown to be 12.03% more likely than females to possess mobile accounts, marking a substantial increase from the 1.80% gap observed in 2017. This widening gap shows a growing imbalance in mobile account ownership over the years, with males increasingly outpacing females in adopting mobile financial services. The shift is indicative of broader societal and economic factors influencing access and uptake of mobile finance. Moreover, the study highlights the evolving role of socioeconomic characteristics in explaining this gender gap. In 2017, these factors—such as age, income levels, educational attainment, and employment status accounted for 49.44% of the differences in mobile account ownership between males and females. By 2021, the explanatory power of these factors rose to 67.33%, suggesting that observable factors like education, employment, and income have become more significant in explaining why men are more likely to have mobile accounts than women. However, differences in tertiary education which previously contributed 61.67% to the gender gap now contribute only 25.27% of the gap. The importance of higher education has declined, while the significance of income and employment has grown more pronounced. The second most substantial contribution to the gender gap, now standing at 12.64%, originates from employment status—an area that previously had an insignificant impact in 2017. The examination of debit card ownership data highlights a pronounced divergence between genders. However, this discrepancy has grown wider in 2021 compared to the situation observed in 2017 (from 15.92% to 20.54%).

Gender-based discrimination in socioeconomic factors plays a substantial role in accounting for over 50% of the disparity observed in debit card ownership between men and women. Education continues to be the leading factor in explaining this disparity, yet its impact has lessened since 2017, particularly in secondary education where its contribution has dropped from 20.98% to 10.13%. In contrast, income has gained prominence as an important determinant of the gender gap in debit card ownership by 2021. Meanwhile, the influence of employment status on this gap has notably decreased to 8.52% in 2021, down from 12.50% in 2017. The landscape of credit card ownership reveals a widening gap between genders, expanding from 1.79% in 2017 to 6.19% in 2021. This shift reflects evolving ownership dynamics over time, underpinned by socio-economic factors whose collective explanatory power has diminished from 59.22% to 53.63%. In the current narrative of 2021, the spotlight on gender disparities in credit card ownership has pivoted decisively. Employment status has emerged as the principal force driving this gap, now commanding 14.54% of its totality—a mantle previously carried by education back in 2017. This transformation represents a significant departure in the factors influencing credit card ownership discrepancies. Notably, the role of employment status was insignificant in 2017, marking a notable transformation in its impact on gender differences in credit card ownership. Alongside these shifts, variations in educational attainment and income levels persist as critical contributors to this enduring divide. The difference in the gender gap between debit card and credit card ownership can be explained by how these cards are given to people. Debit cards are usually given automatically when someone opens a bank account, so it's easier for both men and women to get them. But credit cards are harder to get. To have a credit card, a person must meet extra conditions, like having a steady income, being employed, and sometimes having a good credit history. These conditions can be difficult for many women to meet, especially those working in informal or unpaid jobs. Moreover, employment status became the most important reason for the gender gap in credit card ownership, even though it didn't matter much in 2017. This shows that having a job has become more important to get a credit card, possibly because the economic shock disproportionately affected women's employment, especially in informal and service sectors. As a result, employment status became more immediate determinants of access to credit card than education levels. For debit cards, education is still the main factor, although its importance has gone down. In short, because credit cards have stricter rules and are harder to get, women, especially those without regular jobs face more barriers.

Simply having access to digital financial services does not guarantee their utilization; what truly matters is whether individuals actively engage with these services rather than merely having access to them. However, according to Table 3, there has been a more pronounced increase in the gender gap in digital finance usage compared to the rate of increase in access to digital financial services. Over the span from 2017 to 2021, the use of debit cards has shown a notable divergence between genders, with the gap expanding from 6.44% to a more pronounced 22.04%. This shift reflects evolving patterns in ownership dynamics influenced by socioeconomic factors. Initially, these factors collectively accounted for 45.81% of the gap in 2017, yet their explanatory power has slightly reduced to 41.42% by 2021. A significant transformation has been the rise of employment status as a primary driver, now explaining 9.30% of the gap—markedly surpassing its negligible role in 2017. This change represents a departure from the previous dominance of educational differences in 2017. Alongside these shifts, disparities in educational attainment and income levels continue to play crucial roles in perpetuating the gender divide in debit card usage. Despite efforts to comprehend and address these disparities through socioeconomic lenses, a substantial portion of the gap remains unexplained as of 2021. Between 2017 and 2021, there has been a significant widening of the gender gap in digital transactions, increasing from 2.45% to 18.84%. This trend indicates a pronounced disparity, with men increasingly leading in digital financial activities compared to women. Historically, socioeconomic factors played a pivotal role in narrowing this gap, but their impact has diminished. As of 2021, these factors account for 57.48% of the gender gap, down from 76.73% in 2017. Education remains a significant contributor to this disparity, although its influence has decreased since 2017. Differences in tertiary education now contribute 17.09% to the gender gap (down from 52.65% in 2017), while disparities in secondary education contribute 11.78% (down from 27.35% in 2017). Moreover, factors such as employment status and income level, previously peripheral, have gained prominence in 2021. Similar evidence also has been manifested in the case of checking account balances digitally. Analysis of trends reveals a significant disparity between genders. As of 2021, males are notably more inclined—18.50% more so than females—to engage in checking account balance digitally, a marked increase from the 6.03% gap observed in 2017. This study also emphasizes the evolving role of socioeconomic factors factors in explaining this gender gap. In 2017, factors such as age, income, education, and employment status collectively accounted for 38.64% of the gender differences in digital account usage between males and females. By 2021, this explanatory power has significantly risen to 57.84%, underscoring the increasing influence of these factors in understanding why males exhibit higher digital engagement compared to females. Education remains a key contributor to this disparity, although its impact has diminished since 2017. Discrepancies in tertiary education now contribute 16.11% to the gender gap (down from 26.37% in 2017), while disparities in secondary education contribute 11.95% (down from 17.58% in 2017). In contrast, factors such as employment status and income level, previously considered peripheral, have gained prominence in 2021 as pivotal determinants of digitally account balance-checking behavior.

In the discourse on financial inclusion, particularly in digital finance, gender disparities have become a focal point of analysis. Our findings reveal a complex picture in the case of traditional finance: the initial insights suggest progress in reducing the gender gap in formal savings but highlight persistent challenges, particularly concerning deposits. Socioeconomic factors play a crucial role in explaining these disparities, yet their impact varies across different aspects of financial inclusion. Moreover, the unexplained gap in deposits became more pronounced in 2021. On the other hand, the digital realm has both promised greater inclusivity and amplified existing gender differences. Throughout 2021, disparities across all indicators of digital finance widened significantly. This trend depicts a complex interplay where digital financial tools, while offering opportunities, also exacerbate gender inequalities. Moreover, socioeconomic factors, while influential, do not uniformly alleviate these gaps. The increasing percentage of unexplained disparities in debit and credit card ownership, debit card usage, and digital transactions signals a growing complexity that extends beyond socioeconomic explanations.

5 Conclusion and Policy Implications

The COVID-19 pandemic significantly impacted India's economy, accelerating digitalization in the financial sector. With restrictions limiting physical interactions, digital financial services became essential for transactions, savings, and government relief distribution. While digital payments surged globally, including in India, the percentage of Indian adults using such services remains lower than global averages. A critical issue highlighted during this period is the pronounced gender gap in digital payment adoption, with women significantly lagging behind men in accessing and using digital financial services (Demirgüç-Kunt et al., 2022a). In this regard, this research examines the pandemic's effect on gender inequality in financial inclusion in India, emphasizing digital financial services.

Based on the findings presented, it's evident that gender dynamics in financial inclusion are multifaceted. For traditional finance, the gender gap is reduced for formal savings but highlights persistent challenges, particularly concerning deposits. These disparities are influenced significantly by socioeconomic factors, although their impact varies across different aspects of financial inclusion. For deposits, the contribution of socioeconomic factors to the gap decreased in 2021. This study shows that the pandemic has disproportionately affected women in terms of adopting digital finance. While past measures like demonetization in India had previously narrowed gender gaps in digital financial inclusion (Ghosh & Hom Chaudhury, 2022), the pandemic had a contrasting effect, exacerbating existing disparities. Throughout 2021, disparities in various digital finance indicators widened notably, indicating a complex interaction where digital tools both offer opportunities and exacerbate inequalities. Despite the influence of socioeconomic factors, they do not uniformly mitigate these gaps. Specifically, disparities in debit and credit card ownership, usage, and digital transactions are increasingly unexplained by socioeconomic variables. Moreover, the role of education in diminishing this gap also be reduced in 2021, while employment and income levels are seeking attention. A possible reason for this shift is that without continuous income generation, sustainable financial inclusion, whether through branch banking system or digital platforms, remains unattainable. Education alone is insufficient to overcome structural barriers such as digital illiteracy, restricted mobility, and limited access to technology. The economic shock caused by the pandemic disproportionately impacted women's employment, particularly in the informal sectors, further exacerbating their financial vulnerability. This trend underlines a growing complexity that extends beyond traditional explanations, suggesting a need for more refined approaches to address gender inequalities in digital financial inclusion comprehensively. These observations are needed for policy-making purposes.

Our analysis underlines the ongoing need to bolster women's access to financial services by enhancing their participation in employment and education. While these efforts are crucial, they alone are insufficient to bridge the gender disparities evident in both traditional and digital finance, as highlighted by an exacerbated unexplained gap observed in 2021. The COVID-19 pandemic has remarkably spurred the adoption of digital finance, yet this growth has disproportionately favored men. Many women in rural and low-income urban areas have continued to face difficulties in leveraging digital platforms. The pandemic also intensified caregiving responsibilities for women, reducing their time and ability to engage with financial tools. Moreover, safety and privacy concerns, particularly in shared device environments, further discouraged usage. However, experiences following demonetization have shown a reduction in the gender gap within digital financial services (Ghosh & Hom Chaudhury, 2022). Looking ahead, it is essential to implement targeted policies that prioritize women's financial inclusion, especially in times of crisis, ensuring equitable access and opportunities in financial sectors.

Appendix

See Tables 4, 5, 6, 7 and 8.

Table A.1. Summary statistics

	2017		*2021*	
Variable	*Observation*	*Mean*	*Observation*	*Mean*
Explanatory Variables				
Female	3000	0.5157	3000	0.4607
Age	3000	37.4307	3000	36.0780
Secondary education	3000	0.2790	3000	0.3543
Tertiary education	3000	0.0620	3000	0.1023
Income level 4	3000	0.1997	3000	0.2120
Income level 3	3000	0.2007	3000	0.1990
Income level 2	3000	0.1977	3000	0.1853
Income level 1	3000	0.1820	3000	0.1847
Employment	3000	0.5623	3000	0.5563
Dependent Variables				
Formal Account	3000	0.7930	3000	0.7883
Formal Saving	3000	0.1900	3000	0.1393
Formal Borrowing	3000	0.0657	3000	0.0967
Deposit	2379	0.4178	2365	0.2973
Mobile Account	3000	0.0217	3000	0.1213
Debit Card Ownership	3000	0.3143	2365	0.3738
Credit Card Ownership	3000	0.0293	2365	0.0647
Debit Card Usage	943	0.3499	884	0.4638
Digital Transaction	2379	0.0605	2365	0.1835
Digitally Check Account Balance	2379	0.0811	2365	0.2203

Source Author's calculation

Note Except for age, all other variables are categorical, and for these, the mean represents the proportion of observations possessing the respective characteristic

Table A.2. Spearman's rank correlation between income level and education

	2017						*2021*					
	Secondary education	*Tertiary education*	*Income level 4*	*Income level 3*	*Income level 2*	*Income level 1*	*Secondary education*	*Tertiary education*	*Income level 4*	*Income level 3*	*Income level 2*	*Income level 1*
Secondary education	1						1					
Tertiary education	−0.1599*	1					−0.2501*	1				
Income level 4	0.0667*	0.0099	1				0.0471*	0.0025	1			
Income level 3	−0.0222	−0.0391**	−0.2503*	1			−0.0236	−0.0691*	−0.2585*	1		
Income level 2	−0.1053*	−0.0686*	−0.2479*	−0.2487*	1		−0.0789*	−0.0846*	−0.2474*	−0.2377*	1	
Income level 1	−0.122*	−0.0568*	−0.2356*	−0.2363*	−0.2341*	1	−0.0993*	−0.087*	−0.2468*	−0.2372*	−0.227*	1

Source Author's calculation

*Significant at 1% level, **significant at 5% level

Table A.3. Logistic results of traditional finance

Variable	*Formal Account*		*Formal Saving*		*Formal Borrowing*		*Deposit*	
	2017	*2021*	*2017*	*2021*	*2017*	*2021*	*2017*	*2021*
Female	−0.1342	0.2266**	0.0128	0.1951	−0.3804**	0.1482	−0.1607***	−0.4853*
Age	0.1030*	0.0816*	0.0435*	0.0224	0.0313	0.0864*	0.0259***	0.0080
Age square	−0.0010*	−0.0007*	−0.0003	−0.0001	−0.0002	−0.0010*	−0.0003	−0.0001
Secondary education	0.7835*	0.6075*	0.5122*	0.6746*	0.2616	0.3818*	0.3731*	0.3006*
Tertiary education	2.3139*	1.1436*	1.2429*	1.1848*	0.1561	0.1020	0.6580*	0.5326*
Income level 4	−0.2941**	−0.1105	−0.3185**	−0.4035*	0.0758	0.0947	−0.4790*	−0.3720*
Income level 3	−0.0420	−0.1161	−0.4595*	−0.8747*	−0.2566	0.1831	−0.7007*	−0.9154*
Income level 2	−0.0828	0.2871	−0.6964*	−0.8839*	−0.1037	0.2413	−0.7167*	−0.8397*
Income level 1	−0.1884	0.1323	−1.2182*	−1.5550*	−0.0177	−0.0609	−1.0570*	−1.0148*
Employment	0.3922*	0.4789*	0.5376*	0.1598	0.4233**	0.5936*	0.3551*	0.0860
Constant	−1.2015*	−1.2025*	−2.7886*	−2.5149*	−3.7064*	−4.5957*	−0.6485***	−0.4619
Observation	3000	3000	3000	3000	3000	3000	2379	2365
Pseudo R square	0.061	0.044	0.070	0.075	0.024	0.024	0.047	0.061
Log pseudo-likelihood	−1436.024	−1480.192	−1356.871	−1120.310	−709.263	−930.647	−1540.328	−1351.646
Wald chi2(10)	153.110	121.980	176.710	150.920	33.710	37.150	144.370	164.490
Prob > chi2	0.000	0.000	0.000	0.000	0.0002	0.0001	0.000	0.000

Source Author's calculation

*Significant at 1% level, **significant at 5% level, ***significant at 10% level

Table A.4. Logistic results of access to digital finance

Variable	*Mobile Account*		*Debit Card Ownership*		*Credit Card Ownership*	
	2017	*2021*	*2017*	*2021*	*2017*	*2021*
Female	−0.5920***	−0.6758*	−0.4588*	−0.5212*	−0.3154	−0.6996*
Age	0.1311**	0.0915*	0.1182*	0.0684*	0.0266	0.0375
Age square	−0.0016**	−0.0013*	−0.0014*	−0.0008*	−0.0001	−0.0004
Secondary education	0.8576**	1.6150*	1.3540*	0.7178*	0.5736**	0.8985*
Tertiary education	2.7618*	2.5722*	2.4205*	1.4723*	1.5790*	1.1388*
Income level 4	−1.3433*	−0.7490*	−0.5176*	−0.3044**	−0.9754*	−0.3828***
Income level 3	−1.2461*	−0.9757*	−0.7564*	−0.8996*	−0.6794**	−0.8064*
Income level 2	−1.6059*	−1.4915*	−1.2226*	−1.1235*	−0.8143**	−0.7884*
Income level 1	−1.5228*	−1.6112*	−1.5528*	−1.2756*	−0.7393**	−0.8154*
Employment	−0.1131	0.5868*	0.3550*	0.3307*	0.3863	0.5044**
Constant	−5.8846*	−4.0709*	−2.8810*	−1.5208*	−4.2681*	−3.6549*
Observation	3000	3000	3000	2365	3000	2365
Pseudo R square	0.224	0.252	0.191	0.141	0.071	0.093
Log pseudolikelihood	−243.155	−829.726	−1511.423	−1342.208	−369.113	−514.190
Wald chi2(10)	137.290	359.740	526.900	358.280	74.930	107.890
Prob > chi2	0.000	0.000	0.000	0.000	0.000	0.000

Source Author's calculation

*Significant at 1% level, **significant at 5% level, ***significant at 10% level

Table A.5. Logistic results of usage of digital finance

Variable	*Debit Card Usage*		*Digital Transaction*		*Digitally Check Account Balance*	
	2017	*2021*	*2017*	*2021*	*2017*	*2021*
Female	−0.1681	−0.6456*	−0.1246	−0.9408*	−0.6370*	−0.7058*
Age	−0.0112	0.0041	0.0722**	0.0358	0.0852**	0.0435***
Age square	0.0002	−0.0002	−0.0009**	−0.0006***	−0.0011*	−0.0007**
Secondary education	0.5139*	0.4128**	1.1704*	1.4600*	1.0960*	1.1786*
Tertiary education	1.2006*	0.9704*	2.1164*	2.2993*	2.1709*	1.9941*
Income level 4	−0.4537**	−0.5035*	−0.4274***	−0.8368*	−0.5089**	−0.6825*
Income level 3	−0.3610***	−1.3572*	−0.3387	−0.9796*	−0.3574	−0.9955*
Income level 2	−0.4747***	−1.6376*	−0.6790**	−1.5727*	−0.9995*	−1.4181*
Income level 1	−0.8837*	−1.2373*	−1.0312*	−1.6928*	−0.8199*	−1.4587*
Employment	0.0311	0.4109**	0.0180	0.4933*	−0.1114	0.4179*
Constant	−0.6054	0.1462	−4.3005*	−2.1949*	−3.7938*	−1.9093*
Observation	943	884	2379	2365	2379	2365
Pseudo R square	0.049	0.140	0.111	0.261	0.142	0.215
Log pseudolikelihood	−580.527	−525.157	−483.089	−833.307	−574.894	−978.822
Wald chi2(10)	53.440	132.060	111.790	402.020	181.860	384.250
Prob > chi2	0.000	0.000	0.000	0.000	0.000	0.000

Source Author's calculation

*Significant at 1% level, **significant at 5% level, ***significant at 10% level

References

Al-Mamun, A., Wahab, S. A., Mazumder, M. N. H., & Su, Z. (2014). Empirical investigation on the impact of microcredit on women empowerment in urban Peninsular Malaysia. *The Journal of Developing Areas, 48*(2), 287–306.

Alon, T., Doepke, M., Olmstead-Rumsey, J., & Tertilt, M. (2020). *The impact of COVID-19 on gender equality* (NBER Working Paper No. 26947).

Ashraf, N., Karlan, D., & Yin, W. (2010). Female empowerment: Impact of a commitment savings product in the Philippines. *World Development, 38*(3), 333–344.

Bahn, K., Cohen, J., & Rodgers, Y. (2020). A feminist perspective on COVID-19 and the value of care work globally. *Gender, Work & Organization, 27*(5), 695–699.

Bhatia, S., & Singh, S. (2019). Empowering women through financial inclusion: A study of urban slum. *Vikalpa, 44*(4), 182–197.

Cavalcanti, T., & Tavares, J. (2016). The output cost of gender discrimination: A model-based macroeconomics estimate. *The Economic Journal, 126*(590), 109–134.

Demirgüç-Kunt, A., Klapper, L., Singer, D., & Ansar, S. (2022a). The Global Findex Database 2021: Financial inclusion, digital payments, and resilience in the age of COVID-19. *World Bank.* https://doi.org/10.1596/978-1-4648-1897-4

Demirgüç-Kunt, A., Klapper, L., Singer, D., & Ansar, S. (2022b). *The Global Findex Database 2021: Financial inclusion, digital payments, and resilience in the age of COVID-19.* World Bank. Retrieved country-level data on January 11, 2023, from http://www.worldbank.org/globalfindex

Demirgüç-Kunt, A., Klapper, L., Singer, D., & Ansar, S. (2022c). *The Global Findex Database 2021: Financial inclusion, digital payments, and resilience in the age of COVID-19.* World Bank. Ref: IND_2021_FINDEX_v02_M. Accessed at https://microdata.worldbank.org/index.php/catalog/4653/get-microdata on June 19, 2023. https://doi.org/10.48529/8xhf-w759

Demirgüç-Kunt, A., Klapper, L., Singer, D., Ansar, S., & Hess, J. (2018). *The Global Findex Database 2017: Measuring financial inclusion and the fintech revolution.* World Bank. Ref: IND_2017_FINDEX_v02_M. Accessed at https://microdata.worldbank.org/index.php/catalog/3362/get-microdata on November 21, 2018. https://doi.org/10.48529/6ysd-xg80

Esteve-Volart, B. (2009). *Gender discrimination and growth: Theory and evidence from India.* York University.

Fairlie, R. W. (1999). The absence of the African-American owned business: An analysis of the dynamics of self-employment. *Journal of Labor Economics, 17*(1), 80–108.

Fairlie, R. W. (2006). *An extension of the Blinder-Oaxaca decomposition technique to logit and probit models* (IZA Discussion Papers 1917). Institute for the Study of Labor (IZA).

Fatima, G. (2013). Gender inequality in human capital accumulation and economic growth: A comparative analysis of Pakistan and Sri Lanka. *Asia Pacific Journal of Social Work and Development*, *23*(4), 242–252.

Ferrant, G., Pesando, L. M., & Nowacka, K. (2014). *Unpaid care work: The missing link in the analysis of gender gaps in labour outcomes*. OECD Development Centre. Retrieved from https://www.oecd.org/dev/development-gender/Unpaid_care_work.pdf, on April 2022.

Ghosh, C., & Hom Chaudhury, R. (2019). Gender gap in case of financial inclusion: An empirical analysis in Indian context. *Economics Bulletin, 39*(4), 2615–2630.

Ghosh, C., & Hom Chaudhury, R. (2022). Determinants of digital finance in India. *Innovation and Development, 12*(3), 343–362. https://doi.org/10.1080/2157930X.2020.1850012

Ghosh, S. (2022). Gender and financial inclusion: Does technology make a difference? *Gender, Technology and Development, 26*(2), 195–213. https://doi.org/10.1080/09718524.2022.2073323

Ghosh, S., & Vinod, D. (2016). Furthering the financial inclusion agenda in India: How important is gender? *Economic & Political Weekly, 51*(12), 126–132.

Ghosh, S., & Vinod, D. (2017). What constrains financial inclusion for women? Evidence from Indian micro data. *World Development, 92*, 60–81. https://doi.org/10.1016/j.worlddev.2016.11.011

Hashemi, S. M., Schuler, S. R., & Riley, A. P. (1996). Rural credit programs and women's empowerment in Bangladesh. *World Development, 24*(4), 635–653.

Hendriks, S. (2019). The role of financial inclusion in driving women's economic empowerment. *Development in Practice, 29*(8), 1029–1038.

Kabeer, N. (2001). Conflicts over credit: Re-evaluating the empowerment potential of loans to women in rural Bangladesh. *World Development, 29*(1), 63–84.

Kabeer, N., Razavi, S., & Rodgers, Y. (2021). Feminist economic perspectives on the COVID-19 pandemic. *Feminist Economics, 27*(1–2), 1–29.

Kaur, S., & Kapuria, C. (2020). Determinants of financial inclusion in rural India: Does gender matter? *International Journal of Social Economics, 47*(6), 747–767.

Kim, K. (2022). Assessing the impact of mobile money on improving the financial inclusion of Nairobi women. *Journal of Gender Studies, 31*(3), 306–322.

Klasen, S., & Lamanna, F. (2009). The impact of gender inequality in education and employment on economic growth: New evidence for a panel of countries. *Feminist Economics, 15*(3), 91–132.

Malala Fund. (2020). *Girls' education and COVID-19: What past shocks can teach us about mitigating the impact of pandemics*. Malala Fund.

Nader, Y. F. (2008). Microcredit and the socio-economic wellbeing of women and their families in Cairo. *The Journal of Socio-Economics, 37*, 644–665.

Ohiomu,S., & Ogbeide-Osaretin, E. N. (2019). Financial inclusion and gender inequality reduction: Evidence from Sub-Saharan Africa. *The Indian Economic Journal, 67*(3–4), 367–372.

Raghavendra, S., Duvvury, N., & Ashe, S. (2017). The macroeconomic loss due to violence against women: The case of Vietnam. *Feminist Economics, 23*(4), 62–89.

Sabherwal, R., Sharma, D., & Trivedi, N. (2019). Using direct benefit transfers to transfer benefits to women: A perspective from India. *Development in Practice, 29*(8), 1001–1013. https://doi.org/10.1080/09614524.2019.1653264

Swamy, V. (2014). Financial inclusion, gender dimension, and economic impact on poor households. *World Development, 56*(C), 1–15.

UN Women. (2020). *The impact of COVID-19 on women*. https://www.unwomen.org/en/digital-library/publications/2020/04/policy-brief-the-impact-of-covid-19-on-women

World Bank. (2012). *World Development Report 2012: Gender equality and development*. World Bank. https://openknowledge.worldbank.org/handle/10986/4391

PART III

Sectoral and Regional Pathways to Deepen Inclusion

CHAPTER 8

Financial Technology and Informal Credit: A Structuralist Macro Model

Moumita Basu and Ranjanendra Narayan Nag

1 Introduction

The nexus between financial inclusion and macroeconomic behaviour of an economy has been one of the central topics of macroeconomic discussions. In recent times the wellbeing of a nation is very much related to the process of financial inclusion as financial products and services are easily accessible and affordable to both household sector and business sector regardless of their personal net worth or size of the company. Moreover, financial literacy, which is an important dimension of financial inclusion, generates a positive impact on the marginalised people. In this context the use of financial technology (FinTech) by the informal sector, small and marginal farmers etc. is mentioned worthy. Financial inclusion

M. Basu (✉)
Department of Economics, Aliah University, New Town, Kolkata, West Bengal, India
e-mail: moumita.basu@aliah.ac.in

R. N. Nag
Department of Economics, St. Xavier's College (Autonomous), Kolkata, West Bengal, India

© The Author(s), under exclusive license to Springer Nature Singapore Pte Ltd. 2026

V. Dixit et al. (eds.), *Financial Inclusion for Viksit Bharat*,
https://doi.org/10.1007/978-981-92-0807-4_8

may produce greater overall innovation, economic growth, and consumer knowledge. As accountholders, people are more likely to use other financial services, such as credit and insurance, to start and expand businesses, invest in education or health, manage risk, and weather financial shocks, which can improve the overall quality of their lives.

The COVID-19 pandemic has underscored the critical importance of advancing digital financial inclusion, particularly for financially excluded and underserved populations. Digital financial inclusion refers to the deployment of cost-effective digital technologies to deliver a broad range of formal financial services that are accessible, affordable, and appropriate to the needs of low-income individuals, while remaining sustainable for service providers. In response to pandemic-related restrictions and economic disruptions, digital financial services — especially those enabled by mobile technologies—have rapidly expanded. As of early 2021, such services had been introduced in over 98 countries, with many achieving considerable scale. Notably, the number of registered mobile money accounts surpassed 1.35 billion globally. This expansion has enabled millions of individuals who previously relied solely on cash-based transactions to transition toward the use of formal financial services, accessed through mobile phones and other digital platforms. Consequently, digital financial inclusion has emerged as a vital instrument for promoting economic resilience and social equity in the post-pandemic recovery.

Countries such as China, Kenya, India, and Thailand have demonstrated notable progress in advancing digital financial inclusion through the private sector innovation and the promotion of low-cost accounts, including those enabled by mobile and digital payment systems. The COVID-19 pandemic further accelerated the adoption of digital payments across developing countries, highlighting the urgency of expanding financial access. Despite these advancements, the latest *Global Findex* data reveals that approximately one-third of the global adult population—equivalent to 1.4 billion individuals—remained unbanked in 2021. Encouragingly, the gender gap in account ownership in developing countries narrowed from nine percentage points in 2017 to six percentage points in 2021. Nonetheless, gender disparities persist, limiting women's ability to fully manage and benefit from financial services. Early evidence suggests that mobile money accounts may contribute to reducing this gap in several contexts.

Since 2010, over 55 countries have made formal commitments to financial inclusion, and more than 60 have launched or are developing national financial inclusion strategies (NFIS). Countries that have made significant strides in this domain typically share several characteristics: implementation of policies at scale—such as India's use of universal digital identification systems (Aadhaar) and the Jan Dhan Yojana (JDY) accounts, which collectively cover over 1.2 billion residents; integration of government-to-person (G2P) payments to drive account ownership—for instance, 35% of adults in low-income countries who received a government payment reported opening their first account to access these funds; and the enabling of mobile financial services—evident in Sub-Saharan Africa, where mobile money account ownership rose from 12% in 2014 to 33% in 2021. Additionally, innovative business models that leverage digital platforms, such as e-commerce data, have supported financial inclusion, alongside comprehensive NFIS frameworks that coordinate efforts across stakeholders, including financial regulators, telecommunications bodies, competition authorities, and education ministries. Finally, a strong emphasis on consumer protection and financial capability has proven critical in ensuring that financial services are not only inclusive but also responsible and sustainable.[1]

India has emerged as a global leader in the FinTech revolution. According to a recent global survey, the country ranks second worldwide in FinTech adoption, boasting an adoption rate of 52%.[2] With over 1,200 FinTech firms currently operating, the sector has not only created a significant number of jobs but also attracted robust investor interest. A key driver of this transformation has been the proactive stance of the Reserve Bank of India (RBI), which has consistently promoted the use of electronic payments to foster a "less-cash" society. The RBI's vision has centered on building a payment ecosystem that emphasizes safety, security, convenience, and accessibility. In addition to these core principles, affordability, interoperability, and customer awareness and protection have been crucial areas of focus. While banks have traditionally served as the primary gateway for payment services, rapid technological advancements have diversified the landscape. Today, non-bank entities are playing an increasingly important role—both by collaborating with banks as technology providers and by offering retail electronic payment services directly

[1] Source: https://www.worldbank.org/en/topic/financialinclusion/overview.

[2] EY FinTech Adoption Index 2017, available at https://www.ey.com/Publication/vwLUAssets/ey-fintech-adoption-index-2017/$FILE/ey-fintech-adoption-index-2017.pdf.

to consumers. The regulatory environment has been instrumental in supporting and encouraging this broader participation in the payments space. In recent years, India has made concerted efforts to establish cutting-edge national payments infrastructure. Innovations such as the Immediate Payments Service (IMPS), Unified Payments Interface (UPI), Bharat Interface for Money (BHIM), Bharat Bill Pay System (BBPS), and Aadhaar-enabled Payment System (AePS) have redefined the country's retail payments ecosystem. As a result, the volume of retail electronic payments has seen a staggering nine-fold increase over the past five years. These developments highlight the strength and resilience of India's digital economy, driven by technological innovation, supportive regulation, and a rapidly expanding FinTech sector.

Financial technology (FinTech) holds the potential to revolutionize access to financial services. However, its rapid expansion often reinforces existing social, economic, and regional divides. While FinTech can empower underserved populations by offering low-cost, accessible financial tools, it may also exacerbate inequality due to disparities in infrastructure, digital literacy, and regulatory capacity.

Urban regions typically enjoy better internet infrastructure, higher smartphone penetration, and greater financial literacy, facilitating smoother adoption of digital financial tools. In contrast, rural and underdeveloped areas often lack these prerequisites, resulting in limited access to FinTech services and deepening regional disparities. A 2021–2022 IMF study reveals that digital literacy in urban India stands at 61%, compared to just 25% in rural areas. The contrast is further highlighted by internet penetration rates: states such as Delhi, Kerala, and Himachal Pradesh report access above 50%, while others like Odisha fall below 10%. These gaps in digital infrastructure and literacy significantly hinder FinTech adoption in rural regions. FinTech adoption is also influenced by income levels. Higher-income individuals are more likely to own smartphones, have bank accounts, and navigate digital platforms confidently. Conversely, low-income groups often face multiple barriers, including lack of access, limited trust in digital platforms, and vulnerability to financial misinformation or scams. Moreover, automation in financial services—such as AI-driven customer support and robo-advisors—can displace lower-skilled jobs, disproportionately affecting economically weaker sections. The proliferation of high-risk, easily accessible investment platforms, such as cryptocurrency exchanges, also poses dangers. Financially inexperienced users, often from marginalized backgrounds, may suffer significant losses due to inadequate knowledge or lack of regulation.

One of the most pronounced FinTech access gaps is gender-based, especially in rural India. According to a June 2025 *Mint* report, while 76% of rural women use mobile phones, only 48% actually own them—compared to 80% ownership among rural men. IMF data highlights that just 8.5% of rural women have ever used the internet, versus 30% of urban women and 43.5% of urban men. Moreover, 29.5% of rural women are unable to read SMS messages, further limiting their ability to engage with digital platforms. These barriers—ranging from digital illiteracy and low confidence to concerns over cybersecurity and societal restrictions—constrain women's financial autonomy. Many women rely on male family members for access to mobile devices, making their engagement with FinTech tools sporadic and dependent.

Government of India initiatives like *Digital India* and the widespread adoption of the Unified Payments Interface (UPI) have expanded digital payment usage, particularly among lower- and middle-income groups. FinTech startups offering microloans have also begun reaching underserved regions. However, significant challenges still persist. The digital divide between urban centers like Bengaluru or Mumbai and economically weaker states such as Bihar or Jharkhand persists. State-level variations in both infrastructure and digital education continue to widen the gap, undermining FinTech's potential as a tool for inclusive development.

A voluminous literature deals with the role of FinTech in determining macroeconomic behaviour of the economy. Bazarbash and Beaton (2020) analyze data from 109 countries between 2015 and 2017 to examine the relationship between FinTech credit—both to businesses and consumers—and various aspects of financial development. Their findings reveal that while low-income countries have effectively leveraged FinTech credit in the consumer segment, they continue to face significant obstacles in expanding credit access to businesses. Omar and Inaba (2020) investigate the determinants and effects of financial inclusion on poverty and income inequality across 116 developing countries, using unbalanced panel data from 2004 to 2016. Their study identifies key factors influencing financial inclusion—including per capita income, internet penetration, age dependency ratio, inflation, and existing income inequality—and presents robust evidence that enhanced financial inclusion significantly reduces both poverty rates and income inequality.

Focusing on China, Xu and Sun (2022) utilize data from the 2013, 2015, and 2017 China General Social Surveys (CGSS), alongside the China Digital Inclusive Finance Development Index, to assess the impact of inclusive finance on residents' investment behavior. Their findings suggest that inclusive finance significantly increases investment participation but paradoxically reduces individuals' subjective well-being, indicating a trade-off that policymakers may need to address. Azimi (2022) adopts a global perspective to evaluate the long-term relationship between financial inclusion and economic growth using panel data from 2002 to 2020, stratified by income and regional classifications. The results confirm a stable long-run relationship between financial inclusion and economic growth across diverse country contexts.

Li et al. (2023) investigate the effects of digitized inclusive finance on consumer consumption and high-quality economic growth in China, using panel data from 30 provinces and cities from 2011 to 2020 and applying a spatial econometric model. Their findings indicate that integrating digital finance with consumer behavior promotes sustainable and high-quality economic development. Cavoli and Gopalan (2023) empirically assess the role of financial inclusion in consumption smoothing and risk sharing for 85 emerging markets and developing economies (EMDEs) over the period 1995–2017. They conclude that financial inclusion reduces consumption volatility and helps align national consumption trends with global patterns, while also enhancing domestic credit market-based risk sharing, though it does not fully eliminate unsmoothed consumption.

Mishra et al. (2024) offer a comprehensive review of the various dimensions of financial inclusion, examining its socioeconomic implications for sustainable development and outlining directions for future research. Their study underscores the importance of extending formal financial services to marginalized populations through government-led initiatives and banking system reforms. Yudaruddin et al. (2024) investigate the impact of FinTech, particularly in peer-to-peer lending and payment systems, on credit risk in conjunction with liquidity. The analysis is conducted using panel data from 142 commercial banks in Indonesia over a 15- year period from 2004 to 2018. The results reveal that higher liquidity leads to a reduction in credit risk, whereas FinTech development is found to increase credit risk, particularly in small banks (BUKU 3 and BUKU 4) and private national banks.

However, a notable gap in the existing literature is the absence of a comprehensive theoretical model that analyzes the impact of financial inclusion, particularly through FinTech, within a dualistic economic structure characterized by both formal and informal credit markets. To address this caveat, we develop a structuralist macroeconomic model grounded in the Keynesian-Kaleckian framework. The model conceptualizes a dual economy comprising two distinct sectors: an industrial sector and an agricultural sector.

In this framework, output in the industrial sector is demand-determined, with fixed prices, while the agricultural sector deals with the price flexibility. The industrial sector uses imported oil as an intermediate input along with labour and capital in the production process. Credit availability plays a pivotal role in determining the output level in the agricultural sector, which accesses financing from two sources: formal and informal credit markets. The formal interest rate is administratively set by the central bank, leading to excess demand for credit and consequent rationing in the formal credit market. This unmet demand gives rise to an informal credit market, wherein the interest rate is determined endogenously based on the market conditions. Using this framework the paper explores the role of FinTech in determining interaction between the food price, food production, industrial output and exchange rate and informal interest rate. Moreover, the paper examines the effects of credit risk in the form of higher formal interest rate and an increase in exogenous capital inflow as the consequences of FinTech. In addition, the feedback effects of improved financial inclusion on policy tools are examined in terms of an increase in interest rate subsidy for agricultural farmers.

The rest of the paper is organised as follows. In Sect. 2, we construct a two sector model focussing on inter-linkage between an industrial sector and an agricultural sector. In Sect. 3, we analyse some related issues of FinTech. Section 4 concludes the paper.

2 The Model

The model formulation is based on stylized facts about the behaviour of a dual economy.[3] The economy consists of two sectors, namely an industrial sector and an agricultural sector. Output is demand determined in the

[3] The basic framework of sectoral interlinkage follows the tradition of structural macroeconomics (see Bose(1989), Rakshit (1983) and Taylor (1977).

industrial sector. On the other hand, all commodity and factor prices are flexible in the informal agricultural sector. Industrial price is fixed. The industrial sector uses imported oil as an intermediate input along with the labour and capital in the production process. Credit plays a significant role in determining output level in the agriculture sector. There are two sources of credit, namely formal and informal credit. Though the outreach and the amount of formal credit had increased in the last decade, several weaknesses in the institutional credit system have significantly affected the viability and sustainability of these institutions, thus providing a space for the continuation of the role of informal credit in the agriculture sector. Moreover, the formal interest rate is fixed by the Central bank which causes excess demand and consequent credit rationing. This in turn leads to emergence of informal credit market in which the informal interest rate is endogenously determined. This completes the description of the economy. Thus a proper assessment of financial inclusion requires a careful understanding of different dimensions of dualism in an emerging market economy like India.

The following symbols will be used in the formal representation of the model.

Y: Industrial output
P_Y: Industrial *Price*
F: Food production
P_F: Food price
L: Formal credit
K: Informal credit
α : FinTech parameter
r: Informal interest rate
i: Formal interest rate
k: Capital inflow
ε: Profit mark-up
H: Farmers' demand for formal credit
m: Village money lenders' demand for formal credit

2.1 The agricultural sector

Agricultural farmers borrow from both formal and informal credit markets to carry out the food production process. Farmers are subject to several constraints in the formal credit market. Credit rationing takes place in the formal credit market which in turn imposes a credit ceiling on the amount of fund $(\overline{H})$ advanced to the farmers. This amount of loan is sufficient to finance farmers' demand for working capital if food production does not cross some threshold level, say F_0. However, if food production rises above F_0, farmers are compelled to take loans from village money lenders to finance their demand for working capital. Now this threshold level, that is, F_0 can be expressed as a positive function of some parameter which captures the process of financial inclusion in terms of FinTech. FinTech (α) helps the farmers to access the formal credit more quickly such that threshold level of food production can increase.

Hence, Profit of farmers is given by[4]

$$\pi_F = P_F(F - F_0(\alpha)) + P_F F_0(\alpha) - \overline{i}\overline{H} - r\left[H(F - F_0(\alpha)) - \overline{H}\right] \quad (1)$$

$$\left[\text{where, } F_{01} = \frac{\partial F_0}{\partial \alpha} > 0,\ H_1 = \frac{\partial H}{\partial \mathrm{F}} > 0,\ H_{11} = \frac{\partial^2 H}{\partial \mathrm{F}^2} > 0,\ H_2 = \frac{\partial H}{\partial \alpha} < 0\right]$$

Here, P_F is the food price; $\overline{i}$ is the fixed interest rate in the formal credit market; H is the demand for credit; and r is the interest rate in the informal credit market; $\left[H(F - F_0(\alpha)) - \overline{H}\right]$ is the demand for informal credit.

From the first order condition of profit maximization we get

$$P_F = rH_1(\mathrm{F}, \alpha)$$

Now the profit maximizing behaviour of farmers gives us food supply function as

$$F^s = F^s(P_F, \alpha, r)\left[\text{where, } \mathrm{F}_1^s = \frac{\partial F^s}{\partial P_F} > 0,\ \mathrm{F}_2^s = \frac{\partial F^s}{\partial \alpha} > 0, \text{ and } \mathrm{F}_3^s = \frac{\partial F^s}{\partial r} < 0\right] \quad (2)$$

[4] *For*, $F = F_0$, $H = \overline{H}$ and for $F > F_0$, $\left[H(F - F_0) - \overline{H}\right] > 0$

The market demand for food (F_D) is

$$F^D = F_c(Y, w, \alpha) + X\left(\frac{eP_F^*}{P_F}, \alpha\right) + I_F\left(\frac{P_F^e}{P_F}, \alpha\right) \tag{3}$$

The demand for food consists of industrial workers' consumption, exports and Inventories. Workers spend their entire wage bill $(wa_l Y)$ to purchase food.[5] Here, w is the wage rate which is considered to be fixed in the short run, a_l is fixed labour coefficient in the industrial sector (Y) and hence, $a_l Y$ measures the industrial employment level. Now the food consumption of industrial workers depends on industrial output (Y), wage rate (w) and use of FinTech which is captured by the parameter α. Exports are positively related to the world price (measured in units of domestic currency) relative to the domestic price of food $(\frac{eP_F^W}{P_F})$ and the use of FinTech (α)[6] which enhances the smooting of transactions and thereby lowers the trading cost. The increase in domestic food price reduces expected relative price of food grains which in turn causes a decrease in inventories. On the other hand, an increase in industrial output raises level of employment in the industrial sector which entails an increase in food consumption of industrial workers. The use of FinTech positively influences workers' consumption, exports and Inventories. FinTech leads to increase in the velocity of circulation of money such that demand for food as a whole increases in response to this rapid use of FinTech.

Equilibrium in the food market requires that

$$F^s = F^d$$

$$F^s(P_F, \alpha, r) = F_c(Y, w, \alpha) + X\left(\frac{eP_F^W}{P_F}, \alpha\right) + I_F\left(\frac{P_F^e}{P_F}, \alpha\right) \tag{4}$$

[5] In this paper we assume that the workers consume only food. If we assume that workers spend on both food and industrial output the qualitative results of this paper remain unaltered, only the algebra will be complicated.

[6] Kumari (2025) investigates how FinTech innovations reduce trade costs and, in turn, enhance the gains from trade. By estimating a theory-consistent gravity model based on bilateral trade flows from 106 countries over the period 2014–2019, the study finds that FinTech innovations disproportionately stimulate international trade compared to domestic trade.

From Eq. (4) we can obtain the equilibrium food price (P_F^*)

$$P_F^* = p\left(Y, e, w, r, \alpha, P_F^e\right) \tag{5a}$$

Let us explain partial effect of each variable on equilibrium food price. An increase in industrial output (Y) raises food demand leading to increase in the food price and hence, $p_1 = \frac{\partial p}{\partial Y} > 0$. An increase in exchange rate raises food export which in turn causes higher food demand leading to increase in food price such that $p_2 = \frac{\partial p}{\partial e} > 0$. An increase in wage rate raises workers' demand for food and hence, $p_3 = \frac{\partial p}{\partial w} > 0$. An increase in informal interest rate raises cost of borrowing in the agricultural sector leading to decrease in the supply of food and hence, food price rises to restore equilibrium in the food market. Therefore, we get $p_4 = \frac{\partial p}{\partial r} > 0$. An increase in use of FinTech raises both supply of and demand for food which generates an ambiguous effect on food price and consequently, we get $p_5 = \frac{\partial p}{\partial \alpha} \gtrless 0$. An increase in expected food price raises inventories leading to increase in demand for food and hence, higher food price. Therefore, we get $p_6 = \frac{\partial p}{\partial P_F^e} > 0$.

Now based on the equilibrium food price we can obtain the equilibrium level of food production which is given by

$$F^* = f\left(Y, e, w, r, \alpha, P_F^e\right) \tag{5b}$$

$$\left[\text{where, } f_1 = \frac{\partial f}{\partial Y} > 0,\ f_2 = \frac{\partial f}{\partial e} > 0,\ f_3 = \frac{\partial f}{\partial w} > 0,\right.$$
$$\left. f_4 = \frac{\partial f}{\partial r} < 0,\ f_5 = \frac{\partial f}{\partial \alpha} > 0, \text{ and } f_6 = \frac{\partial f}{\partial P_F^e} > 0\right]$$

Let us explain partial effect of each variable on equilibrium food production. An increase in industrial output (Y) raises food demand leading to increase in the food production and hence, $f_1 = \frac{\partial f}{\partial Y} > 0$. An increase in exchange rate raises food export which in turn causes higher food demand leading to increase in food production such that $f_2 = \frac{\partial f}{\partial e} > 0$. An increase in wage rate raises workers' demand for food and hence, $f_3 = \frac{\partial f}{\partial w} > 0$. An increase in informal interest rate raises cost of borrowing in the agricultural sector leading to decrease in the supply of food and hence, equilibrium food production falls. Therefore, we get $f_4 = \frac{\partial f}{\partial r} < 0$.

An increase in use of FinTech raises both supply of and demand for food which entails an increase in equilibrium food production and consequently, we get $f_5 = \frac{\partial f}{\partial \alpha} > 0$. An increase in expected food price raises inventories leading to increase in demand for food and hence, higher equilibrium food production. Therefore, we get $f_6 = \frac{\partial f}{\partial P_F^e} > 0$.

2.2 The Industrial Sector

The industrial sector uses two variable factors of production namely labour (L) and imported intermediate input, that is, oil (O) in the production process. We assume that labour coefficients (a_l) and intermediate input coefficients (a_o) are fixed. Capital is a fixed factor of production used in the production of industrial output.

The price equation for the industrial goods follows the Kaleckian mark up pricing as represented by the Eq. (6)

$$P_Y = \varepsilon[wa_l + eP_o a_o][\text{where}, \varepsilon > 1] \tag{6}$$

where, ε is the constant profit mark-up; e is the nominal exchange rate; P_o is the international price of oil which is given in the world market. Hence, domestic price of oil is eP_o. An increase in food price reduces exports leading to exchange rate depreciation which in turn raises domestic price of imported intermediate inputs.

Now percentage change in the industrial price can be expressed as a weighted average of percentage change in the wage rate and percentage change in the exchange rate as shown in Eq. (6').

$$\widehat{P_Y} = \theta_L \hat{w} + \theta_o \hat{e} \tag{6'}$$

where, $\theta_L = \frac{wa_l}{\varepsilon[wa_l + eP_o a_o]} = \frac{wa_l}{P_Y}$, $\theta_o = \frac{eP_o a_o}{\varepsilon[wa_l + eP_o a_o]} = \frac{eP_o a_o}{P_Y}$ and $\theta_L + \theta_o = 1$

Here, θ_L is the cost share of labour and θ_o is the cost share of imported intermediate inputs used in the industrial sector.

The industrial profit less taxes is given by

$$\pi_Y = Y\left(1 - \frac{wa_l}{P_Y} - \frac{eP_o a_o}{P_Y}\right) - \frac{T}{P_Y} \tag{7}$$

Here, T denotes business taxes levied on industrial producers.

The aggregate demand for industrial output (in real term) is given by

$$AD_Y = C(\pi_Y, \alpha) + I(\bar{i}) + \frac{G}{P_Y} \quad (8)$$

According to Eq. (8), the aggregate demand for industrial output consists of consumption expenditure of industrial producers, investment expenditure, government expenditure and net exports. Consumption expenditure can be expressed as a positive function of both profit of the industrial producers and the use of FinTech which stimulates transaction smoothing without cash. The industrial producers borrow from the formal credit market to finance their investment expenditures. Therefore, there exists a negative relationship between investment and domestic formal interest rate which is nothing but the cost of borrowing $[I_1 = \frac{\partial I}{\partial i} < 0]$. In nominal terms, the government expenditure is exogenously given. However, we consider the real government expenditure, measured in units of industrial output, as a component of aggregate demand for industrial output. Since the industrial output is demand determined, equilibrium condition in the industrial sector is given by

$$Y = AD_Y \quad (9)$$

From Eq. (9) we can obtain the equilibrium value of industrial output as

$$Y^* = y[e, P_Y, \alpha, w, \bar{i}, G, T, P_o] \quad (10)$$

Let us interpret the partial effect of each variable on the industrial output. An increase in exchange rate raises cost for imported intermediate input which in turn reduces profit of industrial producers leading to decrease in demand for industrial output and hence, $y_1 = \frac{\partial y}{\partial e} < 0$. An increase in industrial price lowers real government expenditure. On the other hand, the increase in industrial price reduces real costs incurred by industrial producers leading to increase in industrial profit which in turn generates a positive effect on the consumption expenditure. However, the restoration of a stable equilibrium requires that an increase in industrial price should reduce demand for industrial output, and hence, $y_2 = \frac{\partial y}{\partial P_Y} < 0$. An increase in the use of FinTech raises consumption expenditure leading to increase in the demand for industrial goods and hence, $y_3 = \frac{\partial y}{\partial \alpha} > 0$. An increase in the wage rate reduces profit of industrial firm owners leading to decrease in producers' consumption expenditure. Hence, the demand for industrial output falls due to increase in the wage rate, that is, $y_4 = \frac{\partial y}{\partial w} < 0$. An increase in domestic formal interest rate reduces investment demand. Hence, the demand for industrial output falls, that is, $y_5 = \frac{\partial y}{\partial \bar{i}} < 0$. An increase in G leads to increase in the demand for industrial output, that is, $y_6 = \frac{\partial y}{\partial G} > 0$. However, an increase in tax reduces profit of the producers leading to decrease in the demand for industrial output, that is, $y_7 = \frac{\partial y}{\partial T} < 0$. An increase in oil price in the world market leads to increase in the input cost and fall in the demand for industrial output. Therefore, $y_8 = \frac{\partial y}{\partial P_o} < 0$.

2.3 Balance of Payment Equilibrium

The balance of payment (BOP) equilibrium is

$$P_F^W X\left(\frac{eP_F^W}{P_F}, \alpha\right) + \bar{k} + k\left[\bar{i} - \left(i^* + \frac{e^e}{e} - 1\right)\right] = P_o a_o Y \qquad (11)$$

The left-hand side of the Eq. (11) consists of the agricultural exports and capital inflow. The capital inflow (k) has both exogenous ($\bar{k}$) and endogenous components. The endogenous capital flow is a positive function of the uncovered interest differential.[7] The right-hand side of the Eq. (11) shows the demand for foreign exchange which includes imports of oil.

From Eq. (11) we can determine the equilibrium exchange rate as

$$e^* = e\left(P_F, Y, \bar{k}, \bar{i}, i^*, P_o, P_F^W, \alpha\right) \qquad (12)$$

Let us consider the partial effect of each variable on the exchange rate. An increase in food price reduces exports leading to excess demand in the foreign exchange market. Hence, exchange rate depreciates, that is, $e_1 = \frac{\partial e}{\partial P_F} > 0$. An increase in the industrial output raises demand for imported

[7] The uncovered interest differential is $\left[\bar{i} - i^* - \left(\frac{e^e}{e} - 1\right)\right]$, where, $\bar{i}$ and i^* are domestic and foreign interest rates respectively. Here, risk premium is represented by the expected change in exchange rate. In this model, the expected exchange rate is assumed to be fixed. Clearly, our model departs from the Mundell-Fleming framework in the sense that we allow for imperfect capital mobility and hence, we drop the assumption of interest rate parity.

oil which in turn causes an increase in the demand for foreign exchange leading to exchange rate depreciation and hence, we get $e_2 = \frac{\partial e}{\partial Y} > 0$. An exogenous increase in capital inflow leads to excess supply in the foreign exchange market leading to exchange rate appreciation and hence, $e_3 = \frac{\partial e}{\partial \overline{k}} < 0$. An increase in the domestic interest rate raises capital inflow leading to increase in the supply of foreign exchange. Hence, exchange rate appreciates, that is, $e_4 = \frac{\partial e}{\partial \overline{i}} < 0$. An increase in the world interest rate leads to capital outflow and hence, $e_5 = \frac{\partial e}{\partial i^*} > 0$. An increase in oil price in the world market raises import spending and hence, $e_6 = \frac{\partial e}{\partial P_o} > 0$. An increase in the food price in the world market raises exports and consequently, we get $e_7 = \frac{\partial e}{\partial P_F^W} < 0$. An increase in the use of FinTech raises exports and hence, we get $e_8 = \frac{\partial e}{\partial \alpha} < 0$.

2.4 *The Credit Market*

The credit market of this economy consists of both formal and informal financial sectors, which characterises the financial structure of a developing country. In this context, we assume that the industrial sector takes loans from the formal credit market to finance investment expenditure on the fixed capital. In addition, the village money lenders can also borrow from the formal credit market. The agricultural farmers borrow from both formal and informal credit markets to finance their working capital.

2.4.1 *The Informal Credit Market*

Farmers' demand for informal credit is

$$K^d = H[F - F_0(\alpha)] - \overline{H}$$

$$\Rightarrow K^d = K^d(P_F, r, \overline{H}, \alpha)\left[\text{where, } K_1^d = \frac{\partial K^d}{\partial P_F} > 0,\ K_2^d = \frac{\partial K^d}{\partial r} < 0,\right.$$
$$\left. K_3^d = \frac{\partial K^d}{\partial \overline{H}} < 0, \text{ and } K_4^d = \frac{\partial K^d}{\partial \alpha} < 0\right] \quad (13)$$

The village money lenders take loans from the formal credit market and use this fund to provide loans to the agricultural farmers in the informal credit market. These money lenders behave like monopolists and hence, they have the power to set the informal interest rate.

The demand for loan is negatively related to the interest rate (r) of informal credit market, and the inverse demand function for loanable fund becomes

$$r = r(K, a)[\text{where, } r_K = \frac{\partial r}{\partial K} < 0 \text{ and } r_a = \frac{\partial r}{\partial a} > 0] \tag{14}$$

Here, 'a' is the shift parameter which represents an exogenous component of the loan demand function.[8] The decrease in 'a' reduces interest rate of the informal credit market.

The village money lenders are also subject to default risk, that is, a fraction of the loan may not be repaid. We take default risk (γ) as a positive function of the loan size (K). One possible justification for positive relation between the default risk and amount of loan is this. The amount of loan depends on the scale of operation. With an increase in scale of operation any harvest failure produces a stronger effect on farmers' income which in turn increases the default. Accordingly, the default risk rises with an increase in production. Hence,

$$\gamma = \rho\gamma(K)[\text{where, } \rho > 0, a \text{ constant; and } \rho\gamma_K = \frac{\partial \gamma}{\partial K} > 0] \tag{15}$$

Therefore, the revenue (R) earned by the village money lender is

$$R = \left[1 - \gamma\right] K r(K, a) \tag{16}$$

The cost incurred by the village money lender is

$$C = \bar{i}m(K) + \delta(\alpha)N(K)\left[\text{where, } m_K = \frac{\partial m}{\partial K} > 0 \right.$$
$$\left. \text{and } N_K = \frac{\partial N}{\partial K} > 0, \text{ and } \delta_\alpha = \frac{\partial \delta}{\partial \alpha} < 0\right] \tag{17}$$

Here, m is the money lender's demand for formal credit; and N represents number of trips to the bank which is positively related to the size

[8] An increase in threshold level of food production (F_0), or a decrease in food price (P_F), or an increase in credit ceiling ($\overline{H}$) in the formal credit market causes an exogenous decrease in loan demand as represented by lower 'a'.

of informal credit and δ represents cost per trip to the bank which is negatively related to the use of FinTech (α).

Now the profit of the money lender is

$$\pi^m = \left[1 - \rho\gamma(K)\right]Kr(K, a) - \bar{i}m(K) - \delta(\alpha)N(K) \tag{18}$$

The profit maximising behaviour of the money lender gives the following equilibrium condition

$$\left[1 - \rho\gamma(K)\right]\left[r(K, a) + Kr_K\right] - \rho\gamma_K Kr(K, a) = \bar{i}m_K + \delta(\alpha)N_K \tag{20}$$

From Eq. (20) we get equilibrium value of loanable fund in the informal credit market and it can be expressed as

$$K^* = K\left(a, \rho, \alpha, \bar{i}\right)\left[\text{where, } K_1 = \frac{\partial K}{\partial a} > 0, K_2 = \frac{\partial K}{\partial \rho} < 0, \right. \\ \left. K_3 = \frac{\partial K}{\partial \alpha} > 0 \text{ and } K_4 = \frac{\partial K}{\partial i} < 0\right] \tag{21}$$

Now the equilibrium value of informal interest rate (r^*) can be obtained by using Eq. (14) and Eq. (21). Hence, the equilibrium informal interest rate is

$$r^* = r\left(K^*, a\right)$$

$$\Rightarrow r^* = r\left(a, \rho, \alpha, \bar{i}\right) \tag{22}$$

$$\left[\text{where, } r_1 = \frac{\partial r^*}{\partial a} > 0, r_2 = \frac{\partial r^*}{\partial \rho} > 0, r_3 = \frac{\partial r^*}{\partial \alpha} < 0, \text{ and } r_4 = \frac{\partial r^*}{\partial i} > 0\right]$$

Equation (22) shows that equilibrium informal interest rate depends on exogenous component of loan demand (a), rate of default risk(ρ), use of FinTech (α) and formal interest rate(i). Let us interpret partial effect of each parameter on informal interest rate. An exogenous increase in loan demand leads to increase in informal interest rate and hence,

$r_1 = \frac{\partial r^*}{\partial a} = r_K K_1 + r_a > 0$. An increase in rate of default risk raises informal interest rate such that $r_2 = \frac{\partial r^*}{\partial \rho} = r_K K_2 > 0$. An increase in use of FinTech(α)[9] reduces cost of lending which in turn causes lower informal interest rate such that $r_3 = \frac{\partial r^*}{\partial \alpha} = r_K K_3 < 0$. An increase in formal interest rate also leads to increase in cost of lending and hence, $r_4 = \frac{\partial r^*}{\partial i} = r_K K_4 > 0$.

2.4.2 *The Formal Credit Market*

Interest rate in the formal credit market is assumed to be fixed.

$$i = \bar{i} \tag{23}$$

The supply of formal credit is also fixed at a given point of time, that is,

$$L^s = \overline{L} \tag{24}$$

Now the demand for formal credit comes from activities of farmers, village money lenders and industrial producers.

Farmers are subject to credit ceiling in the formal credit market and it is given by

$$H = \overline{H} \tag{25}$$

Village money lenders' demand for formal credit can be represented as

$$m^* = m\left(K^*\right) \tag{26}$$

The industrial sector also takes loans from the formal credit market to finance investment expenditure. Hence, loan demand function of the industrial sector is

$$I = I\left(\bar{i}\right) \tag{27}$$

[9] Village moneylenders and rural populations can now access credit facilities through mobile banking applications and digital wallets. These platforms allow users to open savings accounts, make digital payments, transfer money, pay bills, and access credit—all without needing to visit physical bank branches. Fintech has also introduced innovative banking models, such as agent banking and banking correspondents (BCs), to further extend services to remote communities. BCs act as intermediaries between banks and customers, offering services like account opening, cash deposits and withdrawals, and loan applications. This approach significantly enhances financial inclusion, expands banking outreach, and strengthens last-mile connectivity in underserved areas.

Therefore, total demand for formal credit is

$$L^d = \overline{H} + I(\overline{i}) + m(K^*) \tag{28}$$

Since, the formal interest rate is fixed below the equilibrium interest rate there is disequilibrium in formal credit market in the form of excess demand and hence, we get

$$L^s < L^d$$

$$\Rightarrow \overline{L} < \overline{H} + I(\overline{i}) + m(K^*) \tag{29}$$

2.5 *Macroeconomic Equilibrium*

The model can be solved for five endogenous variables namely food price, food production, the industrial output and the exchange rate and the informal interest rate from the Eqs. (5a), (5b), (10), (12) and (22) respectively.

The diagrammatic representation can be used to depict the relationship between the food price and the industrial output with simultaneous determination of other endogenous variables. For this purpose we substitute Eq. (12) and Eq. (22) into Eqs. (5a) and (5b). Equation (12) is also substituted into Eq. (10) such that we get the following three equations:

$$P_F^* = p\left[Y, e\left(P_F, Y, \overline{k}, \overline{i}, i^*, P_o, P_F^W, \alpha\right), w, r\left(a, \rho, \alpha, \overline{i}\right), \alpha, P_F^e\right] \tag{5a'}$$

$$\left[\text{where, } p_1 = \frac{\partial p}{\partial Y} > 0,\ p_2 = \frac{\partial p}{\partial e} > 0,\ p_3 = \frac{\partial p}{\partial w} > 0,\right.$$

$$\left. p_4 = \frac{\partial p}{\partial r} > 0,\ p_5 = \frac{\partial p}{\partial \alpha} \gtrless 0, \text{ and } p_6 = \frac{\partial p}{\partial P_F^e} > 0\right]$$

$$F^* = f\left(Y, e\left(P_F, Y, \overline{k}, \overline{i}, i^*, P_o, P_F^W, \alpha\right), w, r\left(a, \rho, \alpha, \overline{i}\right), \alpha, P_F^e\right) \tag{5b'}$$

$$\left[\text{where, } f_1 = \frac{\partial f}{\partial Y} > 0,\ f_2 = \frac{\partial f}{\partial e} > 0,\ f_3 = \frac{\partial f}{\partial w} > 0,\right.$$

$$\left. f_4 = \frac{\partial f}{\partial r} < 0,\ f_5 = \frac{\partial f}{\partial \alpha} > 0, \text{ and } f_6 = \frac{\partial f}{\partial P_F^e} > 0\right]$$

$$Y^* = y\left[e\left(P_F, Y, \overline{k}, \overline{i}, i^*, P_o, P_F^W, \alpha\right), P_Y, \alpha, w, \overline{i}, G, T, P_o\right] \tag{10}$$

$$\left[\text{where, } y_1 = \frac{\partial y}{\partial e} < 0, y_2 = \frac{\partial y}{\partial P_Y} < 0, y_3 = \frac{\partial y}{\partial \alpha} > 0, y_4 = \frac{\partial y}{\partial w} < 0, \right.$$

$$\left. y_5 = \frac{\partial y}{\partial \overline{i}} < 0, y_6 = \frac{\partial y}{\partial G} > 0, y_7 = \frac{\partial y}{\partial T} < 0 \text{ and } y_8 = \frac{\partial y}{\partial P_o} < 0 \right]$$

$$e^* = e\left(P_F, Y, \overline{k}, \overline{i}, i^*, P_o, P_F^W, \alpha\right) \tag{12}$$

$$\left[\text{where, } e_1 = \frac{\partial e}{\partial P_F} > 0, e_2 = \frac{\partial e}{\partial Y} > 0, e_3 = \frac{\partial e}{\partial \overline{k}} < 0, e_4 = \frac{\partial e}{\partial \overline{i}} < 0, \right.$$

$$\left. e_5 = \frac{\partial e}{\partial i^*} > 0, e_6 = \frac{\partial e}{\partial P_o} > 0, e_7 = \frac{\partial e}{\partial P_F^W} < 0, \text{ and } e_8 = \frac{\partial e}{\partial \alpha} < 0 \right]$$

$$r^* = r\left(a, \rho, \alpha, \overline{i}\right) \tag{22}$$

$$\left[\text{where, } r_1 = \frac{\partial r^*}{\partial a} > 0, r_2 = \frac{\partial r^*}{\partial \rho} > 0, r_3 = \frac{\partial r^*}{\partial \alpha} < 0, \text{ and } r_4 = \frac{\partial r^*}{\partial \overline{i}} > 0\right]$$

The Eq. (5a') represents a locus of combinations of food price and industrial output such that food market is in equilibrium as given by the FF schedule in Fig. 1. For instance, an expansion of the industrial sector requires more labour and imported intermediate inputs. This increase in level of employment raises workers' demand for food. Moreover, the increase in industrial output raises demand for imported intermediate inputs which in turn causes exchange rate depreciation and hence, an increase in agricultural exports. The resulting excess demand for food is eliminated by an increase in food price and hence, FF curve is upward sloping, as shown in Fig. 1.

Similarly, the Eq. (10'), represents a relationship between food price and industrial output so as to maintain equilibrium in the industrial sector as reflected by the YY schedule in Fig. 1. Let us intuitively explain this. An increase in food price reduces exports which entail exchange rate depreciation and hence, imported intermediate inputs become more expensive. This reduces profit of the industrial producers leading to decrease in consumption expenditure. Moreover, the increase in exchange rate raises industrial price, as represented by the Eq. (6), which in turn

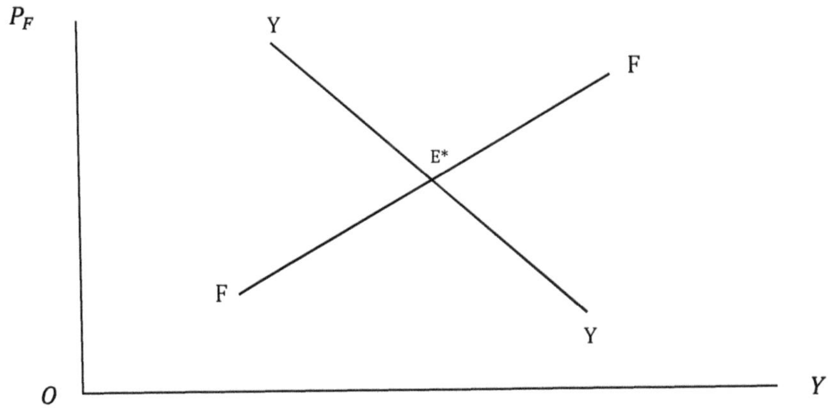

Fig. 1 Macroeconomic equilibrium with food price and industrial output

causes a fall in real government expenditure $\left(\frac{G}{P_y}\right)$. After considering all the effects, it is clear that any increase in food price reduces aggregate demand for industrial output leading to contraction of the industrial sector. Consequently, the YY schedule is negatively sloped, as shown in Fig. 1.

In Fig. 1, macroeconomic equilibrium is shown by the point E*at which the FF curve intersects the YY curve. At the point E* both the markets for food and industrial output are at equilibrium.

2.6 *FinTech and Macroeconomic Equilibrium*

An increase in use of FinTech raises threshold level of food production such that farmers' demand for informal credit declines leading to decrease in '*a*' as represented by the Eq. (22). Moreover, FinTech reduces cost per trip(δ)[10] to the bank from the perspective of village money lenders. Therefore, informal interest rate decreases.

[10] We can interpret δ as the value of the time spent on traveling to and from the bank and waiting in line for getting the cash credit.

The increase in threshold level of food production financed by borrowing from the formal credit market and a decrease in the informal interest rate together lead to increase in food production. Moreover, the increase in use of FinTech raises workers' consumption, agricultural exports and Inventories. Hence, demand for food increases. So, food price changes ambiguously such that the FF curve may shift upward as represented by the Fig. 2a or downward as shown by the Fig. 2b.

The increase in agricultural exports leads to exchange rate appreciation which in turn reduces oil price (measured in domestic currency) and hence, industrial price as represented by the Eq. (6). As a result, profit of the industrial producers rises leading to increase in consumption expenditure on industrial goods. Moreover, the decrease in industrial price causes an increase in real government expenditure $\left(\frac{G}{P_y}\right)$. So, the increased use of FinTech positively influences both the consumption and government expenditures as represented by the Eq. (8). As a result, aggregate demand for industrial output increases such that expansion of the industrial sector takes place. Consequently, the YY curve shifts rightward as represented by the Fig. 2a or b.

According to Fig. 2a, Both food price and industrial output will increase in response to increased use of FinTech. In this case we are considering that shift of the YY curve dominates shift of the FF curve. So the new equilibrium point E_2 lies to the north-east of the initial equilibrium point E_1. According to Fig. 2b, food price declines along with expansion of the industrial sector due to increased use of FinTech. In this case we are considering that shift of the FF curve dominates shift of the YY curve. Hence, the new equilibrium point E_2 lies to the south-east of the initial equilibrium point E_1. Expansion of the industrial sector raises import demand for oil which, in turn, generates a positive effect on the exchange rate.

2.7 FinTech, Credit Risk and Macroeconomic Equilibrium

One significant disadvantage of expanding FinTech lies in the increase in credit risk,[11] which can elevate the formal interest rate within the banking

[11] Anestiawati et al. (2025) find that digital lending (DL) is positively associated with an increase in non-performing loans (NPLs). They observe that innovation-driven emerging economies tend to experience both higher NPLs and faster FinTech growth, driven by

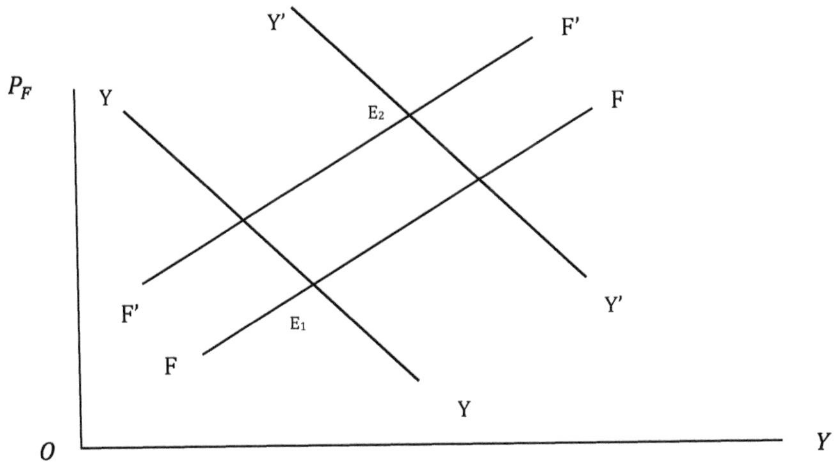

(2a): Use of FinTech, Higher Industrial Output, Higher Food Price

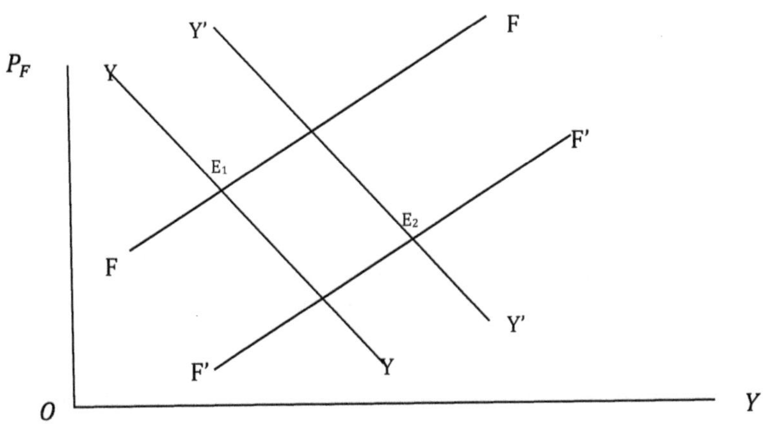

(2b): Use of FinTech, Higher Industrial Output, Lower Food Price

Fig. 2 **a** Use of FinTech, higher industrial output, higher food price. **b** Use of FinTech, higher industrial output, lower food price

sector. As a consequence, both farmers and village moneylenders face a higher cost of borrowing from formal financial institutions.

This escalation in formal borrowing costs spills over into the informal credit market, causing an increase in informal interest rates as well. As a result, the cost of borrowing from both formal and informal sources rises, leading to a decline in the profit of farmers. Hence, food production falls. Moreover, the increase in domestic interest rate raises return on domestic bonds such that foreign capital inflow increases. This causes exchange rate appreciation, which in turn reduces food exports. Therefore, food demand decreases. The decrease in both food supply and food demand generates an ambiguous effect on the food prices. If food price rises we get an upward shift of the FF schedule, as illustrated in Fig. 3a. In contrast, the fall in food price causes downward shift of the FF schedule as shown in Fig. 3b.

Simultaneously, the increase in formal interest rates reduces the investment demand in the industrial sector. However, the imported intermediate inputs become more cheeper due to exchange rate appreciation. This raises profit of the industrial producers leading to increase in consumption expenditure. Moreover, the decrease in exchange rate reduces industrial price, as represented by Eq. (6), which in turn causes an increase in real government expenditure$\left(\frac{G}{P_y}\right)$. As a whole the effect on aggregate demand for industrial goods is ambiguous. Therefore, the industrial output may decrease, causing a leftward shift of the YY schedule, as shown in Fig. 3a or may increase leading to rightward shift of the YY schedule as represented by the Fig. 3b.

The new macroeconomic equilibrium, represented by the point E_2 in Fig. 3a is characterized by higher food price, lower industrial output and reduced food production. This combination reflects a classic case of stagflation—rising prices coupled with declining output and employment. Thus, point E_2 illustrates a stagflationary outcome that can arise from unregulated or excessive financial inclusion via FinTech platforms, which elevate credit risk without adequate oversight. In Fig. 3a, we are considering that shift of the FF curve dominates shift of the YY curve.

rapid adoption that often outpaces regulatory frameworks. The authors argue that to ensure financial inclusion and sustainable economic development, developing countries must strengthen regulations in response to the accelerating FinTech landscape. Moreover, Phan et al. (2020) show that FinTech has a negative impact on banking performance in Indonesia.

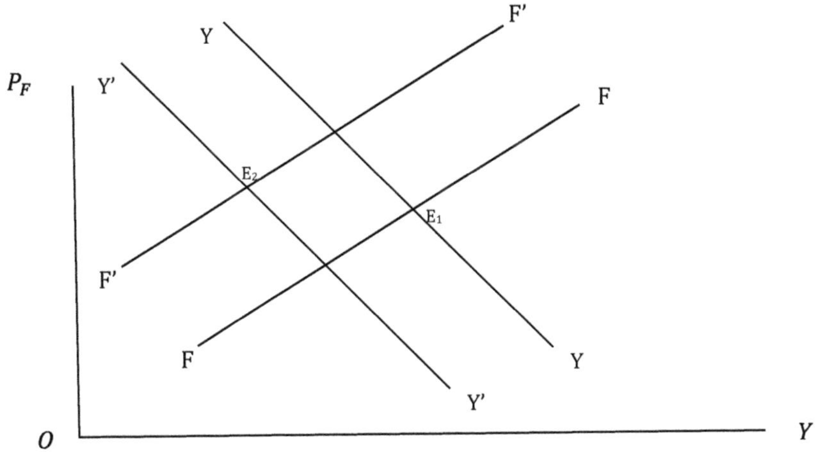

(3a): Credit Risk, Lower Industrial Output, Higher Food Price

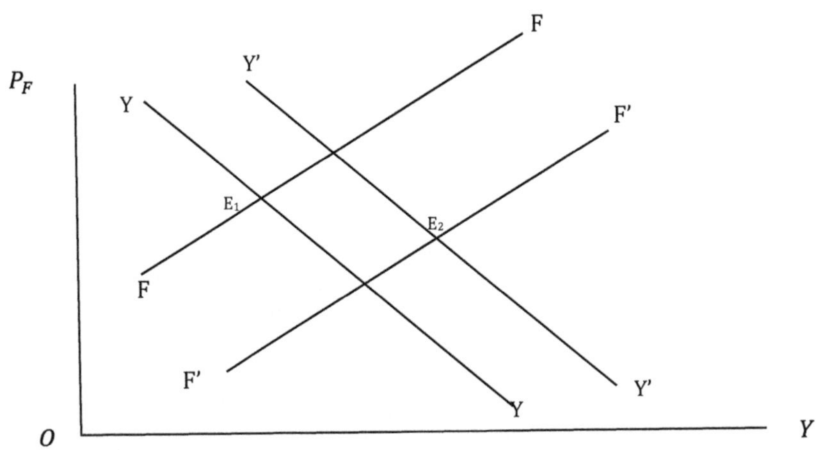

(3b): Credit Risk, Higher Industrial Output, Lower Food Price

Fig. 3 **a** Credit risk, lower industrial output, higher food price. **b** Credit risk, higher industrial output, lower food price

Hence, the new equilibrium point E_2 lies to the north-west of the initial equilibrium point E_1.

According to Fig. 3b, the new macroecoeconomic equilibrium point E_2 shows higher industrial output, lower value of food price and lower food production as well. In this case level of employment will increase corresponding to the new equilibrium. In Fig. 3b we are considering that shift of the FF curve dominates shift of the YY curve. Hence, the new equilibrium point E_2 lies to the south-east of the initial equilibrium point E_1.

2.8 *FinTech, Capital flow and Macroeconomic Equilibrium*

The rise of financial technology (FinTech) has significantly reshaped the global financial landscape, altering the dynamics of capital movement across borders. FinTech innovations—including digital payment systems, blockchain technology, peer-to-peer lending platforms, robo-advisors, and decentralized finance (DeFi)—have increased the speed, efficiency, and accessibility of financial transactions. These developments have the potential to enhance capital inflows[12] by reducing transaction costs, broadening investor participation, and improving financial inclusion, particularly in emerging and developing economies.

However, the impact of FinTech on capital flows is not unequivocally positive. While FinTech can facilitate higher inflows, it also introduces new forms of risk and complexity. The very features that enable rapid investment—such as digital mobility, algorithm-driven decision-making, and decentralized platforms—can also accelerate capital flight in response to changes in market sentiment or geopolitical uncertainty. This increased volatility raises concerns about financial stability, particularly for economies with less developed regulatory frameworks or shallow financial markets.

This paper explores the positive impact of FinTech on capital inflows: its capacity to attract more investment by improving financial infrastructure and inclusion. This is represented by an increase in exogenous capital flow$(\overline{k})$, which in turn leads to exchange rate appreciation. This decrease in exchange rate reduces exports such that food demand declines leading to generate excess supply in the food market. Hence, food price falls to

[12] Liu et. al (2025) emphasize that Fintech can break through the geographical location constraints of the traditional financial industry and expand the flow of corporate capital.

restore equilibrium in the food market. As a result the FF schedule shifts downward as represented by the Fig. 4.

The exchange rate appreciation reduces domestic currency price of the imported intermediate inputs, used as a factor of production in the industrial sector. Hence, profit of the industrial producers increases which in turn raises consumption expenditure on industrial goods. Moreover, the exchange rate appreciation lowers the industial price, as shown in Eq. (6), leading to increase in real government expenditure $\left(\frac{G}{P_y}\right)$. Consequently, aggregate demand for industrial goods increases such that the industrial sector expands. Hence, the YY schedule shifts rightward as represented by the Fig. 4.

In Fig. 4 we are considering that shift of the FF curve dominates shift of the YY curve. Hence, the new equilibrium point E_2 lies to the south-east of the initial equilibrium point E_1. Here, the new macroeconomic equilibrium point E_2 indicates higher industrial output, lower food price and lower food production as well. The decrease in food production[13]

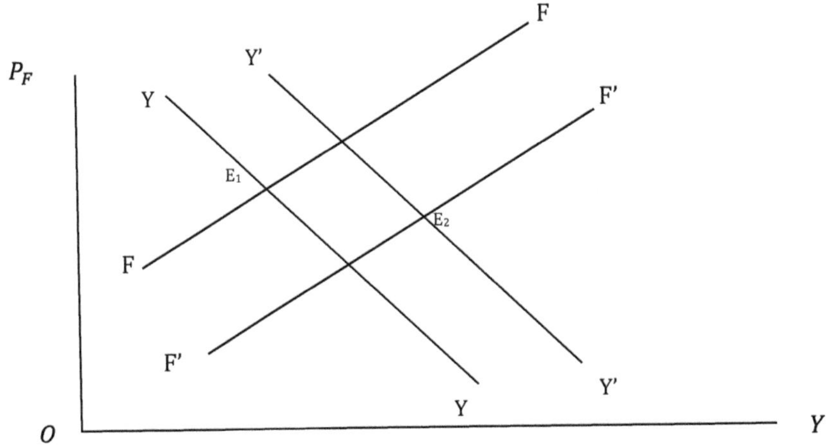

Fig. 4 Capital Inflow, Higher Industrial Output, Lower Food Price

[13] Assuming that food production crosses its threshold level.

reduces demand for loan in the informal credit market such that informal interest rate goes down.

3 Financial Inclusion and Interest Rate Subsidy

Interest rate subsidies in the agriculture sector are a key policy tool used by governments to support farmers. By reducing the effective interest rate on agricultural loans, these subsidies make it more affordable for farmers to access credit needed for a variety of farming activities — such as purchasing inputs, investing in equipment, improving irrigation, or expanding production. The primary aim of such subsidies is to promote investment in agriculture, increase productivity, and enhance the financial viability of farming operations, particularly for small and marginal farmers. By lowering borrowing costs, these initiatives also help reduce dependence on informal credit sources, thereby encouraging greater financial inclusion and long-term sustainability in the agricultural sector.

Let us now analyse the role of interest rate subsidy in determining macroeconomic behaviour of the economy. In this model we consider that threshold level of food production is inversely related to the effective formal interest rate, which is represented by the fixed formal interest rate less subsidy. So the increase in subsidy rate reduces the effective formal interest rate and hence, raises the threshold level of food production.

Profit of farmers is given by

$$\pi_F = P_F(F - F_0(\alpha, i_s)) + P_F F_0(\alpha, i_s) - i_s\overline{H} - r\left[H(F - F_0(\alpha, i_s)) - \overline{H}\right] \tag{30}$$

$$\left[\text{where, } F_{01} = \frac{\partial F_0}{\partial \alpha} > 0,\ F_{02} = \frac{\partial F_0}{\partial i_s} < 0,\ H_1 = \frac{\partial H}{\partial \mathrm{F}} > 0,\right.$$

$$\left. H_{11} = \frac{\partial^2 H}{\partial \mathrm{F}^2} > 0,\ H_2 = \frac{\partial H}{\partial \alpha} < 0,\ H_3 = \frac{\partial H}{\partial i_s} > 0\right]$$

where, effective formal interest rate is $i_s = \bar{i} - s$. Here, ′s′ is the subsidy rate.

$\left[H(F - F_0(\alpha, i_s)) - \overline{H}\right]$ is the demand for informal credit.

From the first order condition of profit maximization we get

$$P_F = r H_1(\mathrm{F}, \alpha, i_s)$$

Now the profit maximizing behaviour of farmers gives us food supply function as

$$F^s = F^s(P_F, \alpha, r, i_s) \tag{31}$$

The food market equilibrium is given by

$$F^s(P_F, \alpha, r, i_s) = F_c(Y, w, \alpha) + X\left(\frac{eP_F^W}{P_F}, \alpha\right) + I_F\left(\frac{P_F^e}{P_F}, \alpha\right) \tag{32}$$

From Eq. (4) we can obtain the equilibrium food price (P_F^*)

$$P_F^* = p\left(Y, e, w, r, \alpha, P_F^e, i_s\right) \tag{33a}$$

$$\left[\text{where, } p_1 = \frac{\partial P}{\partial Y} > 0,\ p_2 = \frac{\partial P}{\partial e} > 0,\ p_3 = \frac{\partial P}{\partial w} > 0,\ p_4 = \frac{\partial P}{\partial r} > 0,\right.$$
$$\left. p_5 = \frac{\partial P}{\partial \alpha} \gtrless 0,\ p_6 = \frac{\partial P}{\partial P_F^e} > 0 \text{ and } p_7 = \frac{\partial p}{\partial i_s} > 0\right]$$

Now based on the equilibrium food price we can obtain the equilibrium level of food production which is given by

$$F^* = f\left(Y, e, w, r, \alpha, P_F^e, i_s\right) \tag{33b'}$$

$$\left[\text{where, } f_1 = \frac{\partial f}{\partial Y} > 0,\ f_2 = \frac{\partial f}{\partial e} > 0,\ f_3 = \frac{\partial f}{\partial w} > 0,\ f_4 = \frac{\partial f}{\partial r} < 0,\right.$$
$$\left. f_5 = \frac{\partial f}{\partial \alpha} > 0,\ f_6 = \frac{\partial f}{\partial P_F^e} > 0 \text{ and } f_7 = \frac{\partial f}{\partial i_s} < 0\right]$$

Let us consider the effects of increase in interest rate subsidy for agricultural farmers on the macroeconomic equilibrium.

The increase in subsidy rate reduces the effective interest rate which in turn raises equilibrium food production and reduces the food price. Hence, the FF curve shifts downward as represented by the Fig. 5. The

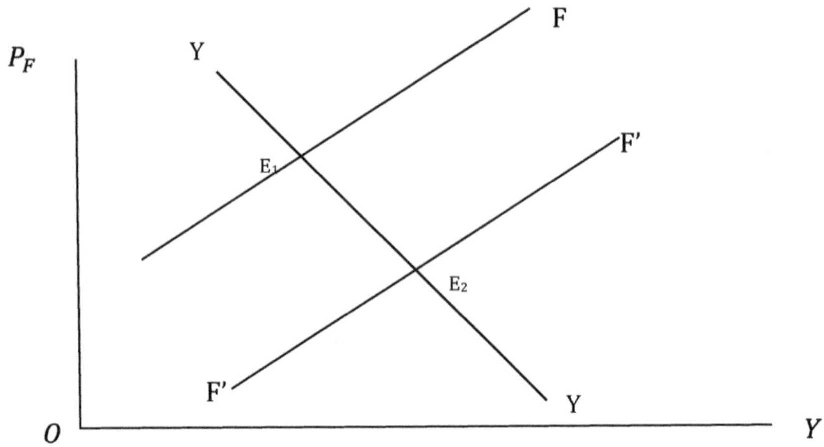

Fig. 5 Interest rate subsidy, Higher Industrial Output, Lower Food Price

macroeconomic equilibrium moves from the point E_1 to the point E_2 which corresponds to higher industrial output and lower food price. The lower effective formal interest rate reduces the demand for informal credit as threshold food production increases. Hence, informal interest rate declines in response to higher interest rate subsidy for agricultural farmers. The decrease in food price leads to increase in exports which in turn causes exchange rate appreciation such that imported intermediate becomes cheeper and industrial price declines.

4 Conclusion

In this section we summarise main results of this article and provide future direction of research. This paper explores the macroeconomic impacts of FinTech, particularly its role in influencing interactions among food price, food production, industrial output, informal interest rate, and exchange rate. The findings suggest that FinTech has a multifaceted and sometimes ambiguous effect on these variables.

The increase in the use of FinTech leads to an increase in threshold level of food production financed by borrowing from the formal credit market and a decrease in the informal interest rate. Therefore, food production rises. Moreover, the increase in use of FinTech raises workers' consumption, agricultural exports and Inventories. Hence, demand for food increases. So, food price changes ambiguously. The increase in agricultural exports leads to exchange rate appreciation which in turn reduces domestic currency price of the imported oil. Hence, profit of the industrial producers rises leading to increase in consumption expenditure. Moreover, the decrease in industrial price causes an increase in real government expenditure. Hence, aggregate demand for industrial output increases such that expansion of the industrial sector takes place. Hence, the level of employment also increases.

The increase in use of FinTech aggravates the problem of credit risk which results in higher formal interest rate in the banking sector. The higher formal interest rate produces higher informal interest rate which, in turn, curbs the food production. Moreover, the higher formal interest rate raises the capital inflow leading to exchange rate appreciation such that food exports decline. Hence, food demand falls. Consequently, food price changes ambiguously. The higher formal interest rate also reduces investment demand generating a negative effect on the aggregate demand for industrial output. However, the exchange rate appreciation reduces cost for imported oil which in turn raises profit of the industrial producers leading to increase in consumption expenditure. In addition, real government expenditure rises in response to decrease in the industrial price. These positively affect the aggregate demand for industrial output. Therefore, the industrial output also changes ambiguously in response to higher domestic formal interest rate. An important outcome of the credit risk problem may take the form of stagflationary situation, that is, lower industrial output and employment, lower food production and higher food price.

The FinTech leads to an increase in exogenous capital inflow which in turn causes exchange rate appreciation and increase in industrial output and employment. However, exchange rate appreciation reduces agricultural exports leading to decrease in food production, food price and informal interest rate as well.

The feedback effects of improved financial inclusion on policy tools can be captured in terms of an increase in interest rate subsidy for agricultural farmers. The higher subsidy rate reduces effective formal interest rate which in turn raises equilibrium food production, reduces food price and increases industrial output and level of employment. Moreover, the informal interest rate falls, exchange rate appreciates and industrial price declines in response to this increase in interest rate subsidy.

The present study can be extended by allowing for migration or labour flows between sectors and by considering wage adjustment in the informal sector.

Acknowledgements We are grateful to an anonymous reviewer for his/her constructive comments. However, the usual disclaimer applies.

Appendix

The Key Equations

$$P_F^* = p\left[Y, e\left(P_F, Y, \overline{k}, \overline{i}, i^*, P_o, P_F^W, \alpha\right), w, r\left(a, \rho, \alpha, \overline{i}\right), \alpha, P_F^e\right] \quad \text{(A1)}$$

$$\left[\text{where, } p_1 = \frac{\partial P}{\partial Y} > 0,\ p_2 = \frac{\partial P}{\partial e} > 0,\ p_3 = \frac{\partial P}{\partial w} > 0,\right.$$

$$\left. p_4 = \frac{\partial P}{\partial r} > 0,\ p_5 = \frac{\partial P}{\partial \alpha} \gtrless 0, \text{ and } p_6 = \frac{\partial P}{\partial P_F^e} > 0\right]$$

$$F^* = f\left(Y, e\left(P_F, Y, \overline{k}, \overline{i}, i^*, P_o, P_F^W, \alpha\right), w, r\left(a, \rho, \alpha, \overline{i}\right), \alpha, P_F^e\right) \quad \text{(A2)}$$

$$\left[\text{where, } f_1 = \frac{\partial f}{\partial Y} > 0,\ f_2 = \frac{\partial f}{\partial e} > 0,\ f_3 = \frac{\partial f}{\partial w} > 0,\right.$$

$$\left. f_4 = \frac{\partial f}{\partial r} < 0,\ f_5 = \frac{\partial f}{\partial \alpha} > 0, \text{ and } f_6 = \frac{\partial f}{\partial P_F^e} > 0\right]$$

$$Y^* = y\left[e\left(P_F, Y, \overline{k}, \overline{i}, i^*, P_o, P_F^W, \alpha\right), P_Y, \alpha, w, \overline{i}, G, T, P_o\right] \quad \text{(A3)}$$

$$\left[\text{where, } y_1 = \frac{\partial y}{\partial e} < 0,\ y_2 = \frac{\partial y}{\partial P_Y} < 0,\ y_3 = \frac{\partial y}{\partial \alpha} > 0,\ y_4 = \frac{\partial y}{\partial w} < 0,\right.$$

$$\left. y_5 = \frac{\partial y}{\partial \overline{i}} < 0,\ y_6 = \frac{\partial y}{\partial G} > 0,\ y_7 = \frac{\partial y}{\partial T} < 0 \text{ and } y_8 = \frac{\partial y}{\partial P_o} < 0\right]$$

$$e^* = e\left(P_F, Y, \overline{k}, \overline{i}, i^*, P_o, P_F^W, \alpha\right) \quad \text{(A4)}$$

$$\left[\text{where, } e_1 = \frac{\partial e}{\partial P_F} > 0, e_2 = \frac{\partial e}{\partial Y} > 0, e_3 = \frac{\partial e}{\partial \bar{k}} < 0, e_4 = \frac{\partial e}{\partial \bar{i}} < 0,\right.$$

$$\left. e_5 = \frac{\partial e}{\partial i^*} > 0, e_6 = \frac{\partial e}{\partial P_o} > 0, e_7 = \frac{\partial e}{\partial P_F^W} < 0, \text{ and } e_8 = \frac{\partial e}{\partial \alpha} < 0\right]$$

$$r^* = r\left(a, \rho, \alpha, \bar{i}\right) \tag{A5}$$

$$\left[\text{where, } r_1 = \frac{\partial r^*}{\partial a} > 0, r_2 = \frac{\partial r^*}{\partial \rho} > 0, r_3 = \frac{\partial r^*}{\partial \alpha} < 0, \text{ and } r_4 = \frac{\partial r^*}{\partial i} > 0\right]$$

$$P_Y = \varepsilon[wa_l + eP_o a_o][\text{where, } \varepsilon > 1] \tag{A6}$$

Now slope of the FF schedule is given by

$$\left.\frac{dP_F}{dY}\right|_{FF} = \frac{p_1 + p_2 e_2}{1 - p_2 e_1} > 0\left[\text{since, } (p_1 + p_2 e_2) > 0 \text{ and } (1 - p_2 e_1) > 0\right] \tag{A7}$$

The stability in the food market equilibrium requires that $(1 - p_2 e_1) > 0$.

Now slope of the YY schedule is given by

$$\left.\frac{dP_F}{dY}\right|_{YY} = \frac{1 - y_1 e_2}{y_1 e_1} < 0\left[\text{since, } y_1 e_2 < 0 \text{ and } y_1 e_1 < 0\right] \tag{A8}$$

The Jacobian matrix is given as

$$J = \begin{bmatrix} 1 - p_2 e_1 & -(p_1 + p_2 e_2) \\ -y_1 e_1 & 1 - y_1 e_2 \end{bmatrix}$$

The sign of the determinant J is positive and it is given by

$$\det J = (1 - p_2 e_1)(1 - y_1 e_2) - (p_1 + p_2 e_2) y_1 e_1 > 0 \tag{A9}$$

Comparative Static Execises

FinTech and Macroeconomic Equilibrium

$$\frac{dP_F}{d\alpha} = \frac{(p_5 + p_2e_8 + p_4r_3)(1 - y_1e_2) + (y_1e_8 + y_3)(p_1 + p_2e_2)}{\det J} \gtrless 0$$

If $p_5 > 0$ and if $p_5 > |p_2e_8 + p_4r_3|$, we get $\frac{dP_F}{d\alpha} > 0$ since, $(y_1e_8 + y_3) > 0$ as shown in Fig. 2a.

If $p_5 < 0$ and if $|(p_5 + p_2e_8 + p_4r_3)(1 - y_1e_2)| > (y_1e_8 + y_3)(p_1 + p_2e_2)$, we get $\frac{dP_F}{d\alpha} < 0$ as represented by the Fig. 2b.

$$\frac{dY}{d\alpha} = \frac{(y_1e_8 + y_3)(1 - p_2e_1) + (p_5 + p_2e_8 + p_4r_3)y_1e_1}{\det J} > 0$$

If $p_5 > 0$ and if $p_5 > |p_2e_8 + p_4r_3|$, we get $\frac{dY}{d\alpha} > 0$ providing $(y_1e_8 + y_3)(1 - p_2e_1) > |(p_5 + p_2e_8 + p_4r_3)y_1e_1|$ as represented by the Fig. 2a.

If $p_5 < 0$, clearly we get $\frac{dY}{d\alpha} > 0$ as shown in the Fig. 2b.

$$\frac{dF}{d\alpha} = f_5 + (f_1 + f_2e_2)Y_\alpha + f_2e_1P_{F\alpha} + f_2e_8 + f_4r_3 > 0 \text{ [since, } f_5, (f_1 + f_2e_2)Y_$$

$$f_4r_3 > 0 \text{ and } [f_5 + (f_1 + f_2e_2)Y_\alpha + f_4r_3] > |f_2e_1P_{F\alpha} + f_4r_3|]$$

Here, $Y_\alpha = \frac{dY}{d\alpha}$ and $P_{F\alpha} = \frac{dP_F}{d\alpha}$.

FinTech, Credit Risk and Macroeconomic Equilibrium

$$\frac{dP_F}{d\bar{i}} = \frac{(p_2e_4 + p_4r_4)(1 - y_1e_2) + (y_5 + y_1e_4)(p_1 + p_2e_2)}{\det J} \gtrless 0$$

If $|p_2e_4| < p_4r_4$ and $(p_2e_4 + p_4r_4)(1 - y_1e_2) > |(y_5 + y_1e_4)(p_1 + p_2e_2)|$, we get $\frac{dP_F}{d\bar{i}} > 0$ as shown in the Fig. 3a.

If $|p_2e_4| > p_4r_4$ and $|(p_2e_4 + p_4r_4)(1 - y_1e_2)| > (y_1e_4 + y_5)(p_1 + p_2e_2)$, we get $\frac{dP_F}{d\bar{i}} < 0$ as shown in the Fig. 3b.

$$\frac{dY}{d\bar{i}} = \frac{(y_5 + y_1e_4)(1 - p_2e_1) + (p_2e_4 + p_4r_4)y_1e_1}{\det J} \gtrless 0$$

If $|y_5| > y_1e_4$ and $|p_2e_4| < p_4r_4$, clearly we get $\frac{dY}{d\bar{i}} < 0$ as represented by the Fig. 3a.

If $|y_5| < y_1e_4$ and $|p_2e_4| > p_4r_4$, clearly we get $\frac{dY}{d\bar{i}} > 0$ as represented by the Fig. 3b.

$$\frac{dF}{d\bar{i}} = f_2e_4 + f_4r_4 + (f_1 + f_2e_2)Y_{\bar{i}} + f_2e_1P_{F\bar{i}} < 0 \text{ [since, } f_2e_4 \text{ and } f_4r_4 < 0$$
$$\text{and } |f_2e_4 + f_4r_4| > \left[(f_1 + f_2e_2)Y_{\bar{i}} + f_2e_1P_{F\bar{i}}\right] \text{ when } Y_{\bar{i}} \text{ and } P_{F\bar{i}} > 0]$$

Here, $Y_{\bar{i}} = \frac{dY}{d\bar{i}}$ and $P_{F\bar{i}} = \frac{dP_F}{d\bar{i}}$.

FinTech, Capital flow and Macroeconomic Equilibrium

$$\frac{dP_F}{d\bar{k}} = \frac{p_2e_3(1 - y_1e_2) + y_1e_3(p_1 + p_2e_2)}{\det J} < 0 \text{[Here, } p_2e_3 < 0 \text{ and } y_1e_3 > 0]$$

If $|p_2e_3(1 - y_1e_2)| > y_1e_3(p_1 + p_2e_2)$, we get $\frac{dP_F}{d\bar{k}} < 0$ as shown in the Fig. 4.

$$\frac{dY}{d\bar{k}} = \frac{y_1e_3(1 - p_2e_1) + p_2e_3y_1e_1}{\det J} > 0$$

[since, y_1e_3 and $(1 - p_2e_1) > 0$ and p_2e_3 and $y_1e_1 < 0$] as shown in the Fig. 4.

$$\frac{dF}{d\bar{k}} = f_2e_3 + (f_1 + f_2e_2)Y_{\bar{k}} + f_2e_1P_{F\bar{k}} < 0$$
$$\left[\text{since, } f_2e_3 \text{ and } f_2e_1P_{F\bar{k}} < 0 \text{ and } \left|f_2e_3 + f_2e_1P_{F\bar{k}}\right| > (f_1 + f_2e_2)Y_{\bar{k}}\right]$$

Here, $Y_{\bar{k}} = \frac{dY}{d\bar{k}}$ and $P_{F\bar{k}} = \frac{dP_F}{d\bar{k}}$.

Financial Inclusion and Interest Rate Subsidy

$$P_F^* = p\Big(Y, e\Big(P_F, Y, \overline{k}, \overline{i}, i^*, P_o, P_F^W, \alpha\Big), w, r\big(a, \rho, \alpha, \overline{i}\big), \alpha, P_F^e, i_s\Big) \tag{A10}$$

$$\Big[\text{where, } p_1 = \frac{\partial P}{\partial Y} > 0,\ p_2 = \frac{\partial P}{\partial e} > 0,\ p_3 = \frac{\partial P}{\partial w} > 0,\ p_4 = \frac{\partial P}{\partial r} > 0,$$

$$p_5 = \frac{\partial P}{\partial \alpha} \gtrless 0,\ p_6 = \frac{\partial P}{\partial P_F^e} > 0 \text{ and } p_7 = \frac{\partial p}{\partial i_s} > 0\Big]$$

$$F^* = f\Big(Y, e\Big(P_F, Y, \overline{k}, \overline{i}, i^*, P_o, P_F^W, \alpha\Big), w, r\big(a, \rho, \alpha, \overline{i}\big), P_F^e, i_s\Big) \tag{A11}$$

$$\Big[\text{where, } f_1 = \frac{\partial f}{\partial Y} > 0,\ f_2 = \frac{\partial f}{\partial e} > 0,\ f_3 = \frac{\partial f}{\partial w} > 0,\ f_4 = \frac{\partial f}{\partial r} < 0,$$

$$f_5 = \frac{\partial f}{\partial \alpha} > 0,\ f_6 = \frac{\partial f}{\partial P_F^e} > 0 \text{ and } f_7 = \frac{\partial f}{\partial i_s} < 0\Big]$$

$$\frac{dP_F}{di_s} = \frac{p_7(1 - y_1e_2)}{\det J} > 0 [\text{since, } p_7, (1 - y_1e_2) \text{ and } \det J > 0]$$

$$\frac{dP_F}{ds} = \frac{dP_F}{di_s} * \frac{di_s}{ds}$$

$$\Rightarrow P_{Fs} = \frac{dP_F}{ds} = -\frac{p_7(1 - y_1e_2)}{\det J} < 0$$

Here, $i_s = \overline{i} - s$.

$$\frac{dY}{di_s} = \frac{p_7y_1e_1}{\det J} < 0 [\text{since, } p_7 \text{ and } \det J > 0 \text{ and } y_1e_1 < 0]$$

$$\frac{dY}{ds} = \frac{dY}{di_s} * \frac{di_s}{ds}$$

$$\Rightarrow Y_s = \frac{dY}{ds} = -\frac{p_7y_1e_1}{\det J} > 0$$

$$\frac{dF}{ds} = -f_7 + (f_1 + f_2e_2)Y_s + f_2e_1P_{Fs} > 0$$

$$[\text{since, } f_7 < 0 \text{ and } (f_1 + f_2e_2)Y_s > 0$$

$$\text{and } [-f_7 + (f_1 + f_2e_2)Y_s] > |f_2e_1P_{Fs}|]$$

References:

Alonso, C., et.al (2023). Stacking up the benefits: Lessons from India's digital journey. *International Monetary Fund, 2023*(078). https://doi.org/10.5089/9798400240416.001

Anestiawati, C. A., Amanda, C., Khantinyano, H., & Agatha, A. (2025). Bank FinTech and credit risk: Comparison of selected emerging and developed countries. *Studies in Economics and Finance*. https://doi.org/10.1108/SEF-12-2023-0714

Azimi, M. N. (2022). New insights into the impact of financial inclusion on economic growth: A global perspective. *PLoS ONE, 17*(11), Article e0277730. https://doi.org/10.1371/journal.pone.0277730

Basu, M., & Nag, R. N. (2017). Open economy macroeconomics of balance sheets, sectoral inter-linkage and the stabilization policies: Short period equilibrium in a developing country. *Trade and Development Review, 9*(1–2), 31–56.

Bazarbash, M., & Beaton, K. (2020). *Digital credit and financial inclusion* (IMF working paper WP/20/150).

Bencivenga, V. R., & Smith, B. D. (1993). Financial intermediation and endogenous growth. *Review of Economics Studies, 58*, 195–209.

Bernanke, B.S. (1993, Spring). Credit in the macroeconomy. *FRBNY Quarterly Review*, 50–70.

Bose, A. (1989). Short period equilibrium in a less developed economy. In M. Rakshit (Ed.), *Studies in the macroeconomics of developing countries*. Oxford University Press.

Cavoli, T., & Gopalan, S. (2023). Does financial inclusion promote consumption smoothing? Evidence from emerging and developing economies. *International Review of Economics & Finance., 88*, 1529–1546.

Chari, V. V., Christiano, L. J., & Eichenbaum, M. (1995). Inside money, outside money, and short term interest rates. *Journal of Money, Credit and Banking, 27*, 1354–1386.

Khera, P. (2023). Digital financial services and inclusion. In *India's financial system building the foundation for strong and sustainable growth* (Chapter 7). International Monetary Fund. https://doi.org/10.5089/9798400223525.071

Kumari, M. (2025). Has FinTech reshaped global trade? New empirical evidence from structural gravity model. *Transnational Corporations Review, 17*(2025), Article 200105. https://doi.org/10.1016/j.tncr.2024.200105

Li, W., et al. (2023). Digital inclusive finance, consumer consumption and high-quality economic development. *PLoS One, 18*(8). https://doi.org/10.1371/journal.pone.0285695.

Liu, X., Ma, C.-Q., & Ren, Y.-S. (2025, April). ESG reactions to fintech: The role of cross-border capital flows. *Research in International Business and Finance, 76*, 102834. https://doi.org/10.1016/j.ribaf.2025.102834

Mishra, D., et al. (2024). Financial inclusion and its ripple effects on socio-economic development: A comprehensive review. *Journal of Risk and Financial Management., 17*, 105. https://doi.org/10.3390/jrfm17030105

Omar, M. A., & Inaba, K. (2020). Does financial inclusion reduce poverty and income inequality in developing countries? A panel data analysis. *Journal of Economic Structures., 9*, 37. https://doi.org/10.1186/s40008-020-00214-4

"Opportunities and Challenges of FinTech", Keynote Address by Shri Shaktikanta Das, Governor, Reserve Bank of India, Delivered at the NITI Aayog's FinTech Conclave 2019 on Monday, March 25, 2019.

Rakshit, M.(1976). *Labour surplus economy*. Macmillan.

Reserve Bank of India (RBI). (2023). *Report on financial inclusion in India*. https://www.rbi.org.in

Srivastava, P., & Bhattacharya, P. (2025, June 4). *UPI fuels rural women's digital leap-but few own their phones*. Mint.

Taylor, L. (1977). *Structuralist macroeconomics*. Basic Books.

World Bank. (2022). *The Global Findex database 2021: Financial inclusion, digital payments, and resilience in the age of COVID-19*. https://www.worldbank.org

Xu, Q., & Sun, W. (2022). Does financial inclusion promote investment and affect residents' happiness?—Evidence from China XE "China." *Frontiers in Psychology*. https://doi.org/10.3389/fpsyg.2022.988312

Yudaruddin, R., Nugroho, B. A., Mardiany, Fitrian, Z., Hapsari, P., Fitrianto, Y., & Santi, E. N. (2024). Liquidity and credit risk in Indonesia: The role of FinTech development. *SAGE Open*, *14*(2). https://doi.org/10.1177/21582440241245248

https://www.worldbank.org/en/topic/financialinclusion/overview

CHAPTER 9

Industrialization, Digital Financial Inclusion and Growth: A Subnational Level Study

Amrita Chatterjee and Pratim Saha

1 Introduction

India's economic journey has undergone a radical transformation in recent decades, shifting from a traditionally agrarian and industrial focus toward an increasingly digital future. The digitalization of the Indian economy has not merely been a technological advancement; it represents a socio-economic shift that aims to include every citizen in the financial narrative. As mobile phones, internet access, and digital payment platforms became widespread, even small villages in remote corners of the country started experiencing the winds of change. This digital tide was further accelerated by public policy missions like Digital India, which sought to bridge the digital divide and promote inclusive growth (USAID, 2019). With platforms like the Unified Payments Interface

A. Chatterjee (✉)
Madras School of Economics, Chennai, India
e-mail: amrita@mse.ac.in

P. Saha
Risk Associate, PricewaterhouseCoopers, Kolkata, India

© The Author(s), under exclusive license to Springer Nature Singapore Pte Ltd. 2026

V. Dixit et al. (eds.), *Financial Inclusion for Viksit Bharat*,
https://doi.org/10.1007/978-981-92-0807-4_9

(UPI), India has created one of the world's most robust digital payment ecosystems, reaching 100 billion transactions in 2023 alone (MSTAR, 2023). These innovations reduced paperwork, enhanced transparency, and created a more accountable ecosystem (Sarma & Pais, 2011). Digital transactions boomed in post-demonetization and post-pandemic era, with platforms like BHIM, Paytm, and Google Pay becoming household names. The government's efforts to digitize core services from banking and identity verification to direct benefit transfers have triggered new forms of connectivity and financial access. Infrastructure such as the JAM Trinity (Jan Dhan-Aadhaar-Mobile) played a central role in enabling this shift. However, the spread of Digital Financial inclusion at the sub-national level has been uneven (refer to Fig. 1 for inter-state disparity in Digital Financial Inclusion). Issues of digital literacy, lack of infrastructure, patchy internet connectivity, and trust deficits continue to hinder widespread adoption. Vulnerable groups such as the elderly, the rural poor, and women face challenges navigating this new terrain (Nassiry, 2021). On the other hand, from the public-sector-led growth of the Nehruvian era to the liberalization of the 1990s, each phase has redefined India's industrial map. Industries have played a vital role in generating employment, contributing to GDP, and fostering innovation (Kaur & Hanspal, 2022). However, industrialization has also been geographically skewed. A few states dominate the industrial output, while others lag far behind (refer to Fig. 2 for inter-state difference in industrialization). This asymmetry has major implications not just economically, but also socially and digitally. The current study intends to explore the interlinkage between Digital Financial Inclusion and Industrialization and also their interactive role in fostering the growth of the economy at the sub-national level.

1.1 Theoretical Underpinning: Growth and Industrialization

Kaldor's Growth Laws (1966, 1967) confirmed the close linkage between the expansion of the industrial activity (manufacturing in particular) and overall output growth through mechanisms such as increase in productivity and employment. Thus, in Kaldorian theory, the manufacturing sector has been considered as the main source of growth of economies through channels as such technical progress, capital accumulation, economies of scale (Szirmai & Verspagen, 2015), technological spillovers and high backward and forward linkage effects (Hirschman,

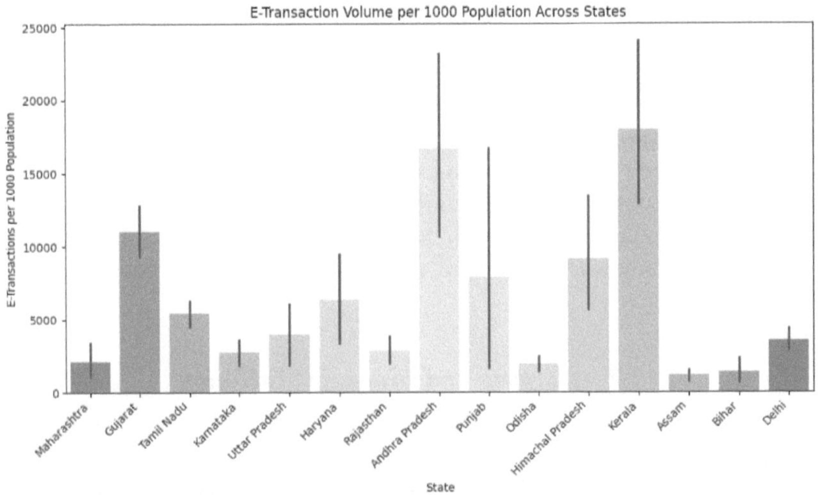

Fig. 1 E-transaction volume across states

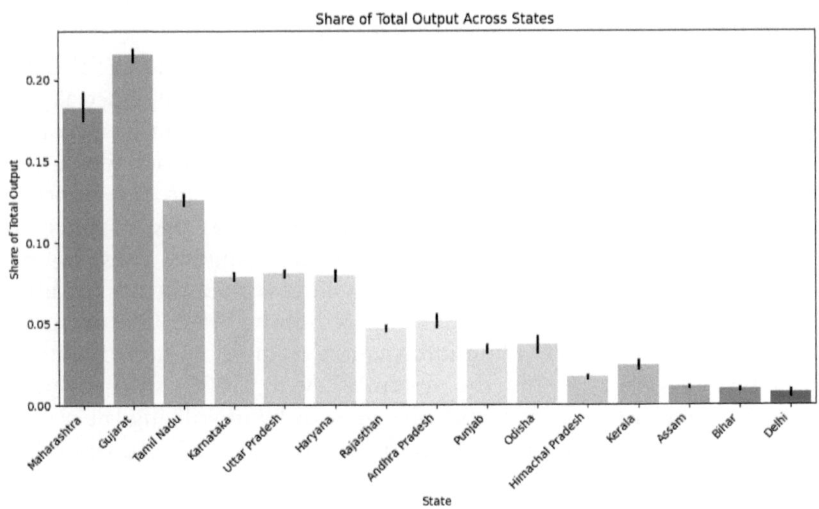

Fig. 2 Share of total output across states

1958). There have been a large body of literature that confirms the role of industrialization in growth process of developing economies (i.e., Felipe et al., 2009; Libânio & Moro, 2011; Magacho & McCombie, 2017; Marconi et al., 2016; Pacheco & Thirlwall, 2014; Szirmai, 2012a, 2012b). In Kaldorian theory, as the economy develops, labor force shifts from Agriculture to Manufacturing which leads to increase in productivity in both the sectors. Manufacturing has a spill-over effect on other sectors of the economy as well through technological progress and its role in international trade and balance of payment (Dasgupta & Singh, 2005a, 2005b).

1.2 Growth and Financial Inclusion

According to Schumpeter (1911), Gurley and Shaw (1960), McKinnon (1973) and Shaw (1973), banking development fosters economic growth because banks' activity leads to mobilization of the savings, improves the efficiency of the resource allocation, and stimulates technological innovation. Levine (2005) and Beck et al. (2007) have also agreed to the fact that a well-developed financial system has a positive impact on the growth process of the economy. As Babajide et al. (2015) have pointed out four distinct channels of economic growth through financial inclusion: (i) providing low-cost reliable means of payment to all, especially the low-income group; (ii) the role of financial intermediation in increasing the volume of transaction and allocation of resources from the surplus units to the deficit units of the economy and in the process improves resource distribution (Odeniran & Udeaja, 2010) (iii) risk management that the financial system provides by curtailing liquidity risks, thereby enabling the financing of risky but more productive investments and innovations within the economy (Bencivenga & Smith, 1991; Greenwood & Jovanovic, 1990) (iv) providing information on possible investment and availability of capital within the system (Levine, 2005). Moreover, an inclusive financial sector helps inclusive growth by mobilizing the savings and investment in the productive sector (Dabla-Norris, Ji, Townsend, & Unsal, 2015; Onaolapo, 2015).

1.3 Digital Financial Inclusion and Economy

The digital financial services, or Fintech, one of the key effective applications of information and communication technology (ICT), include a wide range of financial services like receipt of wages electronically, payment of utility bills, merchant payments and so on, which can be delivered and accessed through various digital mediums such as mobile phones, internet or electronic card that involve credit, insurance and savings (Hinson et al., 2019; Makina, 2019). It is well documented in literature that fintech has positive impact on financial inclusion (Chatterjee & Das, 2021; Demirgüç-Kunt et al., 2022; Jagtiani & Lemieux, 2018; Zetzsche et al., 2019). The share of adults making or receiving digital payments grew from 35% in 2014 to 57% in 2021 in developing countries, compared to 95% in high-income economies. Moreover, 83% of adults in developing countries who received a digital payment also made payments digitally, rising from 66% in 2014 and 70% in 2017 (Demirgüç-Kunt et al., 2022). More recently, Chatterjee (2024) shows that having formal savings and borrowing from formal financial institutions, owning mobile phone and using internet are some of the major channels through which digital receipts of income motivate individuals to make payments digitally.

1.4 Literature Gaps

The literature accepts that industrialization has its spillover effects on the other sectors of the economy though technological innovation and increase in productivity of labor. It also pulls labor from other sectors and therefore raises employment. With development of banking sector and digitalization of the financial services, it is expected to digitize the industrial sector as well. It can improve the physical as well as digital infrastructure due to industrial conglomeration. Thus, payment of wages digitally on one hand and familiarity of the labor force with digital tools on the other hand, can increase digital financial inclusion. This inter-linkage has largely been unexplored in Indian literature, especially at the subnational level. Moreover, though a large number of studies have tested Kaldor's Growth Laws in the context of Developing Economies and role of financial inclusion powered by ICT development in growth process have been explored extensively, how the entanglement of digital financial inclusion with industrial development may affect the growth process of a developing economy has not got much attention.

1.5 Research Objectives

This study explores how industrialization and digital financial inclusion interact in the diverse context of Indian states. The first objective is to examine how industrialization impacts digital financial inclusion across states. We hypothesize that industrialized states, with better infrastructure and formal employment, are more likely to have higher digital financial inclusion. The second objective is to assess whether the growth of industrialization and digital inclusion together can drive economic growth. We aim to understand whether a digitally empowered industrial sector can enhance economic performance, especially in light of India's "Digital India" and "Make in India" initiatives. The study uses a panel data from 29 Indian states between 2016 and 2023 and intend to take up a dynamic panel data analysis with system estimation approach for accomplish the objectives.

2 Data and Methodology

2.1 Data Sources and Coverage

This study uses panel data from 29 Indian states, covering eight consecutive years from 2016 to 2023 a period marked by significant changes in both industrial activity and digital adoption across the country.

To build this panel, we sourced data from several government and national databases:

- *Annual Survey of Industries (ASI):* This is our primary source for industrial information. It includes state-level panel data on factories, capital investments, wages, output, and value-added etc.
- *Ministry of Electronics and Information Technology (MeitY):* MeitY tracks digital transactions and services across the country. From this, we capture metrics like the number of digital transactions per capita and the number of e-services provided key indicators of digital financial inclusion.
- *Indiastat:* This is a comprehensive data aggregator that provides standardized statistics on demographics, education, infrastructure, and banking. We used it to fill in important contextual data like internet access, education levels (e.g., gross enrollment ratio), and the number of bank branches and accounts.

Table 1 Panel data structure

Dimension	*Value*
Total observations	232
Number of states	29
Time period	2016–2023
Total years	8
Panel type	Strongly Balanced
States covered	Andhra Pradesh, Arunachal Pradesh, Assam, Bihar, Chandigarh, Chhattisgarh, Delhi, Goa, Gujarat, Haryana, Himachal Pradesh, Jharkhand, Karnataka, Kerala, Madhya Pradesh, Maharashtra, Manipur, Meghalaya, Nagaland, Odisha, Puducherry, Punjab, Rajasthan, Tamil Nadu, Telangana, Tripura, Uttar Pradesh, Uttarakhand, West Bengal

2.2 *Summary Statistics and Variable Description*

This section provides an overview of the panel dataset employed in the study, along with detailed summary statistics for the key variables used in the empirical models. The panel dataset comprises 232 observations across 29 Indian states over an 8-year period (2016–2023), offering a balanced panel structure ideally suited for dynamic estimation techniques such as System GMM.

2.2.1 Panel Structure

The spatial and temporal distribution of the panel is outlined in Table 1.

This rich spatial–temporal coverage allows the study to capture interstate heterogeneity while also accounting for within-state dynamics over time. Please refer to Table 9 in the appendix for the summary statistics of key variables.

2.2.2 Industrialization and Digitalization: Spatial Trends

The following maps illustrate the state-wise distribution of industrialization and digital financial inclusion:

The Share of Total Output map (refer to Fig. 3) highlights states with high industrial activity, such as Maharashtra, Gujarat, and Tamil Nadu, which contribute significantly to national production. These states have better-developed infrastructure, higher employment rates, and a more extensive banking network, creating an environment where digital financial services can thrive. A strong industrial base also encourages higher incomes and financial stability, leading to greater adoption of digital transactions for both business and personal use. In contrast, states with lower industrial output, such as those in the northeast and central India, tend to have weaker financial ecosystems, potentially limiting digital financial adoption.

The E-Transaction Volume map (refer to Fig. 4) shows a strong correlation between industrialized states and high digital transaction activity.

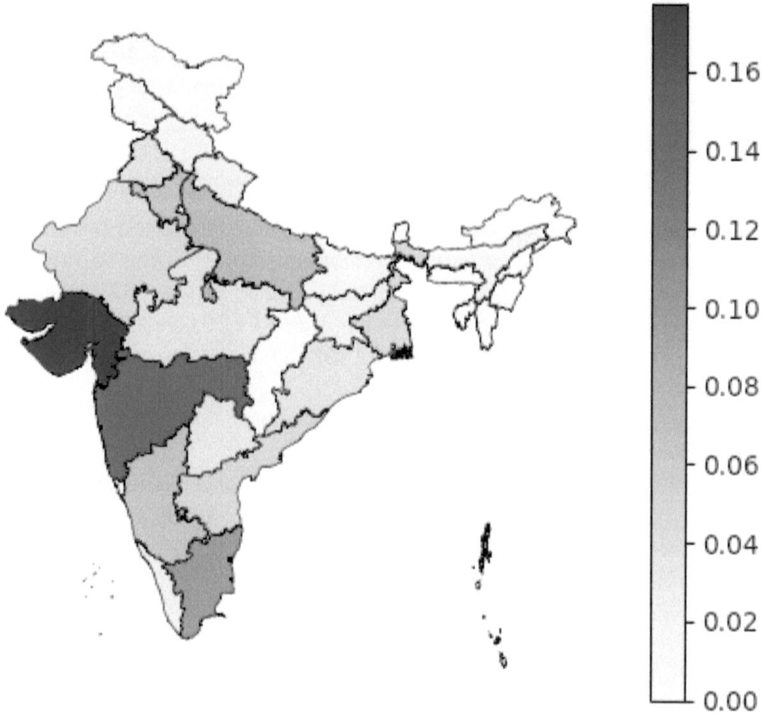

Fig. 3 Share of total output across Indian states (2023)[1]

[1] States for which data was unavailable have been assigned a value of zero in Figs. 3 and 4. This ensures completeness in visualization but may not accurately reflect the industrialization or e-transaction levels in those regions. Sources of data is already mentioned.

States like Karnataka, Maharashtra, and Delhi exhibit higher e-transaction volumes, likely driven by better financial infrastructure, widespread digital literacy, and larger economic activity. These states benefit from industrialization-driven urbanization, which increases demand for digital financial services, such as mobile banking, digital payments, and online transactions. Conversely, low-industrialization states exhibit weaker e-transaction trends, suggesting that a lack of industrial growth may hinder digital financial inclusion by limiting employment, disposable income, and access to banking services.

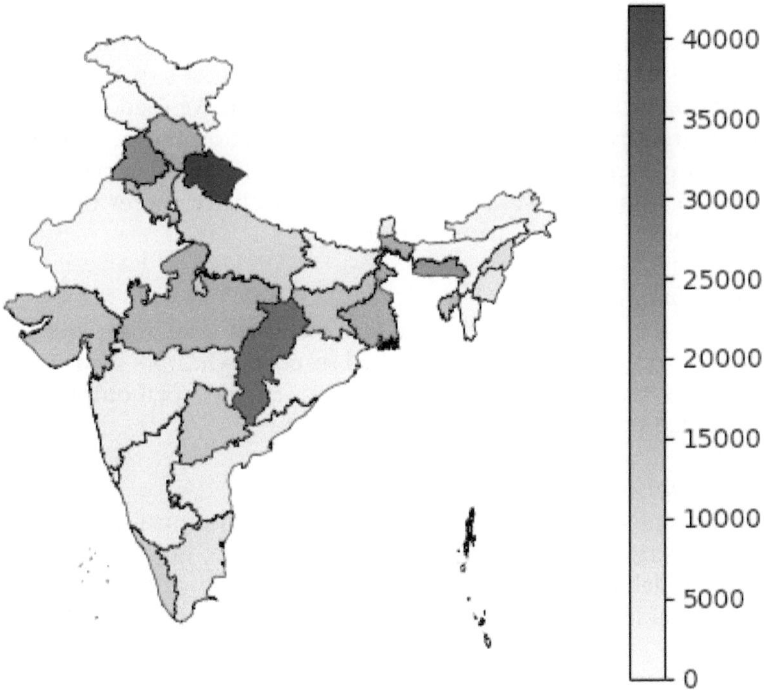

Fig. 4 Transaction volume per 1000 population across Indian states (2023)

Table 2 Variables used in the Industrialization Index

Variable	*Description*
Factories	Number of registered factories
Fixed capital	Total fixed investment in industries
Workers	Total number of industrial workers
Wages to workers	Total wages paid to industrial workers
Total output	Value of goods produced
Net value added	Output minus input costs

2.3 *Indicator Variables*

We created composite indices using Principal Component Analysis (PCA). PCA helps us distil a large set of related variables into a smaller number of components without losing essential information. We used PCA to create four key indices for our analysis: an Industrialization Index, an Infrastructure Index, a Financial Inclusion Index, and a Digital Financial Inclusion Index. Each index serves as a summary score that captures the key traits of that domain for each state over time.

2.3.1 *Industrialization Index*

To build the Industrialization Index, we used data from the Annual Survey of Industries (ASI). We selected six core indicators such as number of factories, fixed capital, total workers, wages paid, total output, and net value added (refer to Table 2).

2.3.2 *Infrastructure Index*

We constructed an Infrastructure Index using indicators like railway route length, electricity consumption, highway coverage, university count, and energy availability all normalized as shares relative to the national total (refer to Table 3).

2.3.3 *Financial Inclusion Index*

For the Financial Inclusion Index, we have included access to bank branches, the number of active bank accounts, and the Credit-to-Deposit (C-D) Ratio as an usage indicator (Table 4).

Table 3 Variables used in the Infrastructure Index

Variable	*Description*
Railway routes (share)	State share of total Indian railway network
Electricity consumption (SHARE)	Share of national electricity use
National highway length (SHARE)	Share of India's total national highways
Number of universities (share)	Educational capacity based on state university count
Energy requirement & availability (share)	Measures supply–demand balance for power

Table 4 Variables used in the Financial Inclusion Index

Variable	*Description*
Bank offices (share)	State's share of total bank branches
Bank accounts (share)	Share of national banking accounts
C-D ratio	Credit issued as a share of total deposits

2.3.4 Digital Financial Inclusion Index

Capturing the digital side of financial access required a slightly different lens. Instead of infrastructure or banking penetration, we looked at how much people actually use digital financial services. We used two practical indicators: the number of e-transactions per 1,000 people and the number of government-provided e-services available in the state. These variables serve as real-world usage proxies (refer to Table 5).

Finally, we include the Gross Enrollment Ratio (GER) in higher education, which gives us a sense of how educated and digitally ready a state's population is. A higher GER (education in Eq. 1) means more students are in college or similar programs. The national average is about 31%,

Table 5 Variables used in the Digital Financial Inclusion Index

Variable	*Description*
E-transactions per 1000	Digital financial usage intensity
Number of e-services	Digital services accessible to citizens

but some states are much lower, while others go beyond 66%. There's clear variation across states and some steady improvement over time. Since education influences how easily people can adopt and trust digital tools, GER acts as a useful control variable in our model.

3 Model Specification

We estimate two models using System GMM (Generalized Method of Moments) a dynamic panel estimation technique particularly suited for datasets like ours, where we observe the same states repeatedly over time (2016–2023) and suspect that the past might influence the present (i.e., the presence of autocorrelation), and possible reverse causality (i.e., endogeneity).

Let's now walk through the models and the logic behind each variable included.

Model 1: Understanding What Drives Digital Financial Inclusion

In our first model, the dependent variable is the Digital Financial Inclusion Index, which measures.

The model is represented as:

Model 1 (DFI vs Industrialization):

$$\begin{aligned} DFI_{it} = \alpha &+ \beta_1 DFI_{it-1} + \beta_2 Industrialization_{it} \\ &+ \beta_3 Financial\ Inclusion_{it} + \beta_4 Infrastructure_{it} \\ &+ \beta_5 GER_{it} + \beta_6 (Financial\ Inclusion \times Education)_{it} \\ &+ \beta_7 (Financial\ Inclusion \times Industrialization)_{it} \\ &+ \alpha_i + \delta_t + \varepsilon_{it} \end{aligned} \quad (1)$$

In estimating Eq. (1), Digital financial index (DFI) is taken as the dependent variable and lagged value of DFI is incorporated as an explanatory variable in the model. Another regressor treated as endogenous is industrialization index as there is a possible reverse causality from DFI to industrialization giving rise to a possible endogeneity problem. Indicators of financial inclusion, infrastructure, gross enrolment ratio are the control variables added in Eq. (1). We have also added a couple of interaction terms such as interaction between financial inclusion and education (captured by Gross enrolment ratio) and financial inclusion and industrialization.

Model 2: Evaluating the Impact on Economic Growth

In Model 2, we examine the joint effect of industrialization and digital financial inclusion on economic growth, as measured by the natural logarithm of GSDP per capita (a standard measure to monitor economic growth across regions).

Model 2 (Growth Model):

$$\begin{aligned} ln(GSDP)_{it} = \alpha &+ \gamma_1 \ln(GSDP)_{it-1} + \gamma_2 Industrialization_{it} \\ &+ \gamma_3 DFI_{it} + \gamma_4 Financial\ Inclusion_{it} \\ &+ \gamma_5 (DFI \times Industrialization)_{it} \\ &+ \gamma_6 Infrastructure_{it} + \gamma_7 GER_{it} \\ &+ \mu_i + \delta_t + \varepsilon_{it} \end{aligned} \quad (2)$$

In estimating Eq. (2), GSDP per capita growth, measured as log of GSDP per capita, is taken as the dependent variable and lagged value of log of GSDP per capita is incorporated as an explanatory variable in the model. Other regressor treated as endogenous is industrialization. Financial inclusion index, Infrastructure index, Digital Financial Index and Gross enrolment ratio are considered as purely exogenous control variables. We have also added an interaction term between Digital Financial Index and Industrialization index as we are interested in the joint effect of both on growth process of the economy.

3.1 Choice of Methodology

In estimation of panel data model, the fixed estimator can provide biased estimations if the number of time periods is small, and if the lagged value of the dependent variable, Yi,t − 1, is also correlated with the individual effects α_i. In that case, the estimation of growth regression may have some problems such as explanatory variables being endogenous and be correlated to the idiosyncratic error term because of reverse causality or measurement errors. The fixed-effects estimator fails to deal with the problems of endogeneity and hence leads to inconsistent estimations of results that are expected to have a downward bias. Moreover, omitted variables can bias the estimation. In such a situation Holtz-Eakin et al. (1988) and Arellano and Bond (1991) suggested estimating dynamic panel data models using the first differenced generalized method of moments (GMM). GMM solves the problem of endogeneity by adding the lagged value of the dependent variable as an explanatory variable. However, to deal with the potential bias and imprecision of the first-differenced GMM estimators, additional moment conditions are proposed for an equation expressed in levels (Arellano & Bover, 1995; Blundell & Bond, 1998) known as system GMM estimator. The consistency of the system GMM estimator is based on two hypotheses. First, the set of instrumental variables must not be correlated with the error terms. This hypothesis is tested using the Sargan/Hansen test of overidentifying restrictions. Second, the absence of second-order autocorrelation (AR2) in residuals must be verified, while a negative first-order autocorrelation (AR1) may be detected. This second hypothesis is tested using Arellano-Bond tests for AR1 and AR2.

Hence for the purpose of our study, given the sample size, we use the system GMM estimator (Blundell and Bond (1998)) to assess the nexus between digitalization and industrialization and subsequently their joint effect on per capita growth.

4 Results and Discussion

4.1 Industrialization and Digital Financial Inclusion

We apply the system GMM method[2] to a panel of 29 states to estimate Eq. (1) and the results are presented in Table 6. Results suggest that industrialization index has a positive and significant impact on Digital Financial Inclusion which validates our hypothesis. This means that states with higher levels of industrial development with more factories, greater capital investment, and stronger formal employment are also the ones showing faster adoption of digital financial services.

There are several plausible channels. First, industries generate formal employment, and formal workers are more likely to use formal financial services, including digital platforms for salary receipts, payments, and savings. Second, industrial clusters often catalyse infrastructure development power, roads, telecom which provides the backbone for digital

[2] We have used xtabond2 command in STATA 18.

Table 6 Nexus between industrialization and digital financial inclusion

Variables	*Dependent var: DFI*
L. Digital Financial Inclusion Index	0.832***
	(0.158)
Industrialization Index	0.239*
	(0.119)
Financial Inclusion Index	0.056
	(0.316)
Infrastructure Index	−0.065
	(0.085)
GER	0.001
	(0.001)
Financial Inclusion*GER	0.001
	(0.006)
Financial Inclusion Index*Industrialization Index	−0.365
	(0.234)
Time Dummy	Yes
Constant	−0.038
	(0.028)
Observations	203

Standard errors in parentheses
*** $p < 0.01$, ** $p < 0.05$, * $p < 0.1$

services to function efficiently. Third, supply chains in industrial zones are increasingly digitized, from GST e-filing to vendor payments via NEFT/RTGS, nudging small and medium enterprises (SMEs) toward adopting digital tools.

4.2 *Industrialization and Economic Growth: Core Findings from the Growth Model*

This section explores how industrialization and digital financial inclusion have shaped the economic performance of Indian states between 2016 and 2023. Using a dynamic panel data model (System GMM) on 29 Indian states, we examine what drives differences in per capita income represented by the log of GSDP per capita (lnGSDP) and how these factors play out over time. Estimation results of Eq. (2) are presented in Table 7 which suggests that industrialization and Digital Financial Inclusion have positive and significant impact on the growth process. Industrialization which mostly reflect the performance of the manufacturing sector is expected to have a positive impact on the growth process as per Kaldorian growth laws which get validated here. Digital financial inclusion represented by electronic transaction volume on the other hand reflect increased financial activity in the economy and that too in cashless mode. That means less chances of tax evasion and therefore less corruption. This in turn is also expected to improve the growth performance of the economy. However, the interaction term between digital financial inclusion and industrialization is turning out to be statistically significant but negative which apparently is counterintuitive. To get a deeper idea about the role of digital inclusion on growth for a threshold value of industrialization and the effect of industrialization for a meaningful value of digital inclusion we calculate the marginal effects of both (Table 8).

The respective marginal effect of industrialization and DFI on economic growth are the following (refer to Table 8):

- Evaluated at mean DFI (0.255), industrialization still has a strong, positive impact. That means for states with average level of Digital inclusion, industrialization leads to higher growth performance. Thus, if the industrialized states can achieve a threshold level of digital inclusion, they can grow at a higher level.

Table 7 Nexus between economic growth, digital financial inclusion and industrialization

Variables	*Economic growth*
Lagged ln (GSDP)	0.869***
	(0.046)
Industrialization Index	1.333***
	(0.320)
Digital Financial Inclusion Index	0.739***
	(0.194)
Financial Inclusion Index	−0.189
	(0.185)
DFI*Industrialization Index	−2.653***
	(0.712)
GER	−0.002
	(0.003)
Infrastructure Index	0.254*
	(0.140)
Constant	1.510***
	(0.514)
Observations	203

Standard errors in parentheses.
*** $p<0.01$, ** $p<0.05$, * $p<0.1$

Table 8 Marginal effects of industrialization and DFI on GSDP per capita at mean levels

Variable	*Coefficient*	*Standard error*	*t-value*	*p-value*	*95% confidence interval*
Industrialization (at mean DFI)	0.656	0.156	4.22	0.000	[0.337, 0.975]
DFI (at mean Industrialization)	0.264	0.116	2.28	0.030	[0.027, 0.502]

Note This table reports the marginal effects of interaction terms evaluated at the mean of DFI and Industrialization (0.255 and 0.179, respectively)

- Evaluated at mean Industrialization (0.179), the marginal effect of DFI is significant and positive. That suggests that DFI can also act as an engine of growth provided the states can reach a threshold of industrialization. This is obvious as the usage of digital tools will increase only when the states have enough level of formal employment that can come through mostly industrialization.

4.3 *Diagnostics and Model Validity*

One of the key assumptions in a dynamic panel model like System GMM is that while the error terms from one year may be related to those from the previous year (first-order correlation), they should not be related across two or more years (second-order correlation). If there is a pattern of errors beyond one year, our instruments could be invalid, and the model could be mis-specified.

To test this, we use the Arellano-Bond autocorrelation tests. In our Growth Model, AR(1) came out significant ($p = 0.000$) just as we expected. It means last year's outcomes influence this year's, which fits our logic. But more importantly, AR(2) was not significant ($p = 0.737$), which reassures us that there's no longer-term error spillover and our instruments are correctly specified.

Dynamic models rely on instrumental variables instruments are basically trusted reference points that help us estimate our variables more reliably. The Sargan test checks whether all the instruments as a group are uncorrelated with the error term. If they are correlated, the model is biased. The Hansen test, which is more robust especially when the number of instruments is small (as in our model), gives a similar test but adjusts for heteroskedasticity. In both the Growth Model and the Digital

Inclusion Model, these tests gave reassuring results. The Hansen test p-values were 0.413 and 0.184 respectively, which are comfortably above the 0.1 threshold. This means we cannot reject the assumption that our instruments are valid.

5 Concluding Remarks, Policy Implications and Research Limitations

It is well documented in the literature that manufacturing sector acts as the engine of growth for an economy through increase in productivity and employment through channels like technological progress and economies of scale. Given the movement of India towards a cashless economy, the current study intends to investigate the interactive effect of digital financial inclusion with that of industrialization in promoting growth. By examining data from 29 states between 2016 and 2023 and using a dynamic System GMM approach with carefully constructed PCA-based indices, we found that industrialization and digital financial inclusion are deeply intertwined. In states where factories and industrial output boomed, we see a corresponding surge in the use of digital financial services. In other words, when factories hire more people and expand production, workers earn steady wages and businesses keep formal accounts, there is a possible enhancement of mobile payments, and online transactions. Industrial jobs bring regular income and often require the formal exchange of money, which naturally leads people and firms to adopt digital payment tools. This in turn raises the total volume of electronic transaction.

The estimates of the growth model suggest that both digital inclusion and industrialization separately foster economic growth. Moreover, the marginal effects of both industrialization and digital financial inclusion on economic growth are positive. This implies that a given level of digitalization is necessary to foster the growth-industrialization nexus. On the other hand, a threshold level of industrialization facilitates digital financial tools to act as an engine of growth. These results have immense practical implications.

When customers, suppliers, and workers can pay instantly and securely through digital channels, it lowers barriers for businesses. A merchant in a small town can take UPI payments and immediately expand his supplier network; a manufacturer can pay wages by bank transfer and thus formalize operations faster. These secured and easy electronic transactions can encourage entrepreneurs to invest more in machinery and factories, knowing that financial exchanges are safe and efficient. In econometric terms, the positive coefficients in our GMM results suggest that not only does industrialization lift digital inclusion, but higher levels of digital financial activity tend to go hand-in-hand with faster economic activity and growth. In short, industrialization boosts digital uptake, and growing digital uptake supports business expansion—a bi-directional dynamic that my analysis has brought to light.

Yet this interplay is not uniform across the country. A striking finding is that regional disparities persist. The industrial heartlands—states like Maharashtra, Tamil Nadu, and Gujarat—stand out with both high industrialization indices and advanced digital payment usage. These regions have benefited from both manufacturing clusters and investments in digital infrastructure, so the two trends reinforce each other there. By contrast, some states with historically lower industrial development (for example, parts of the eastern and northeastern regions) still lag behind. In these areas, limited factory activity means fewer formal jobs and lower banking access, which translates into slower adoption of e-payments. This uneven picture tells us that where industry is weak, digital financial inclusion also suffers, leaving whole communities on the sidelines of India's modern economy. Such patterns underscore a broader truth: simply rolling out digital payment technology is not enough on its own if the underlying industrial base and financial ecosystem are not there to support it.

Reflecting on these results, a couple of broad implications emerge. First, industrial development can be a powerful catalyst for inclusive, digital financial growth. Policies that encourage factories, manufacturing zones, and small-scale industries do more than create jobs—they set the stage for financial modernization in local communities. Second, the investments in digital finance (like expanding banking infrastructure or mobile networks) can boost industrial entrepreneurship by smoothing transactions. In practical terms, an investor or policymaker should recognize that digital finance and industrial policy need to be crafted together, not in isolation. Encouraging to see, our analysis suggests that coordinated efforts have multiplicative effects: a unit of effort in one domain echoes in the other.

This convergence of industry and finance has clear lessons for development policy. It suggests that integrated strategies can yield rich rewards. For example, when a government sets up an industrial corridor or special economic zone, pairing that with digital-connectivity projects—such as high-speed internet, fintech services, and local banking correspondents—will magnify the impact. Workers in a new industrial park should be enrolled in banking programs and taught to use digital wallets, so the moment they start earning wages they join the digital finance system. Likewise, boosting financial literacy and trust in digital payments is especially crucial in regions where industry is still taking off. People in rural areas and smaller towns may not leap into online banking on their own, but if factories and agri-businesses in their region adopt digital payment systems, they are gently drawn into the formal financial fold.

The findings of the current study align with observations on the ground—that in cities like Pune or Coimbatore, manufacturers and tech firms go hand in hand with widespread use of e-payments. For policymakers and development practitioners, this study offers a kind of map: it shows where digital finance is likely to take off and how it can be encouraged through industrial policy. Rather than treating a factory grant or a subsidy for digital wallets as separate initiatives, the evidence suggests bundling them. For instance, small and medium enterprises (SMEs) could be offered special credit lines tied to digital transactions, so that as they grow their use of online payments is rewarded. Similarly, national schemes like BharatNet or rural broadband could prioritize coverage in industrializing regions, ensuring that the expansion of factories comes with the fiber optics and mobile towers needed for e-commerce and mobile banking.

Our study has its share of limitations. The empirical analysis could not incorporate indicators of digital infrastructure such as number of mobile phone users per 1000 population, especially usage of smart phones, internet users or network availability due to lack of data for all 29 states. Moreover, due to a small panel we could not do any subsample analysis for groups of states showing similar level of industrialization or digitalization. As a future extension of this study, a broader measure of digitalization can be tired as there is a large body of literature on role of digitalization in Industrialization. However, whether industrialization can stimulate digitalization of the economy has not been explored much. Due to lack of appropriate data, we are confined to only digital volume of transaction which basically reflects the digital financial inclusion.

Appendix

See Table 9.

Table 9 Summary statistics of key variables (Number of States: 29, Number of years: 8)

Variable	*Category*	*Mean*	*Std. Dev.*	*Min*	*Max*
GSDP per capita	Overall	667,205.90	673,549.20	18,509	3,645,884
	Between		653,503.00	26,822.75	2,637,941
	Within		198,856.10	−4,509.71	1,675,149
Factories	Overall	8,251.78	9,459.32	102	39,666
	Between		9,584.20	138.88	38,484.63
	Within		636.67	4,853.66	11,458.66
Fixed capital	Overall	11,900,000	15,300,000	12,754	81,000,000
	Between		15,300,000	16,293.38	69,400,000
	Within		2,327,626	−4,562,663	23,400,000
Workers	Overall	429,208.20	515,485.70	1,742	2,283,043
	Between		519,710.00	2,566.75	2,106,758
	Within		61,739.81	127,291.20	737,785.20
Wages to workers	Overall	742,063.80	926,049.90	1,331	4,380,919
	Between		909,147.50	2,478	3,220,683
	Within		236,783.10	−167,066.40	1,920,285
Total output	Overall	31,900,000	42,200,000	36,295	257,000,000
	Between		40,600,000	49,526.75	165,000,000
	Within		13,300,000	−17,700,000	124,000,000
Net value added	Overall	4,566,531	5,850,168	−22,919	31,300,000
	Between		5,744,671	8,674.38	22,700,000
	Within		1,491,058	−372,013.50	13,200,000
Railway route share	Overall	0.0345	0.0346	0.0000151	0.1515
	Between		0.0351	0.0001333	0.1344
	Within		0.00156	0.0289	0.0516
Electricity (GWh)*	Overall	59,380.68	375,033.40	370.82	5,722,318
	Between		140,832.10	444.25	769,180.80
	Within		348,449.90	−651,647.80	5,012,518
National highway share*	Overall	0.0345	0.0295	0.0001	0.1404
	Between		0.0296	0.00012	0.1297
	Within		0.0044	-0.0179	0.0451

(continued)

Table 9 (continued)

Variable	*Category*	*Mean*	*Std. Dev.*	*Min*	*Max*
No. of universities share	Overall	0.0345	0.0248	0.0024	0.0926
	Between		0.025	0.0028	0.0861
	Within		0.0026	0.0263	0.0475
GER (higher education, %)*	Overall	31.06	10.05	13.60	66.10
	Between		9.01	16.21	50.10
	Within		4.73	11.47	51.62
Annual branches share	Overall	0.0345	0.0299	0.001	0.1087
	Between		0.0303	0.0011	0.1071
	Within		0.001	0.0311	0.0384
Annual accounts share	Overall	0.0345	0.0479	0.0004	0.2834
	Between		0.0475	0.0004	0.2071
	Within		0.0102	-0.0138	0.1108
C-D ratio	Overall	59.55	27.06	23	144.7
	Between		25.09	25.36	122.71
	Within		11.04	22.7	105.8
E-transactions per 1000	Overall	6,505.14	8,062.41	57.8	42,076.75
	Between		5,018.31	1,129.07	18,656.94
	Within		6,370.41	−6,191.59	36,612.92
No. of E-services	Overall	96.69	53.19	25	273
	Between		41.81	38.13	182.63
	Within		33.68	−11.31	226.19

Note For variables marked with * in the table, missing values for certain years were estimated using the linear interpolation method. This approach ensures continuity in the dataset while maintaining the overall trend of industrial and economic indicators

References

Arellano, M., & Bond, S. (1991). Some tests of specification for panel data: Monte Carlo evidence and an application to employment equations. *The Review of Economic Studies, 58*(2), 277–297. https://pages.stern.nyu.edu/~wgreene/Econometrics/Arellano-Bond.pdf

Arellano, M., & Bover, O. (1995). Another look at the instrumental variable estimation of error-components models. *Journal of Econometrics, 68*(1), 29–51. https://doi.org/10.1016/0304-4076(94)01642-D

Arora, R., & Anand, S. (2021). Financial inclusion and regional disparities in India. *Journal of Development Studies, 57*(3), 321–340. https://bradscholars.brad.ac.uk/entities/publication/b0fddb9c-a7a1-4f01-b8cc-cb2f65857a76

Ayyar, V. (2021). The evolution of digital public infrastructure in India. *Economic and Political Weekly, 56*(29), 14–17. https://www.epw.in/journal/2021/29

Babajide, A. A., Adegboye, F. B., & Omankhanlen, A. E. (2015). Financial inclusion and economic growth in Nigeria. *International Journal of Economics and Financial Issues, 5*(3), 629–637.

Beck, T., Demirgüç-Kunt, A., & Levine, R. (2007). Finance, inequality, and the poor. *Journal of Economic Growth, 12*(1), 27–49. https://doi.org/10.1007/s10887-007-9010-6

Bencivenga, V. R., & Smith, B. D. (1991). Financial intermediation and endogenous growth. *Review of Economic Studies, 58*(2), 403–440.

Blundell, R., & Bond, S. (1998). Initial conditions and moment restrictions in dynamic panel data models. *Journal of Econometrics, 87*(1), 115–143. https://doi.org/10.1016/S0304-4076(98)00009-8

Chakrabarty, K. C. (2011, July). Financial inclusion: A road India needs to travel. *RBI Speeches*. https://www.bis.org/review/r111013f.pdf

Chakravorti, B., Bhalla, A., & Chaturvedi, R. (2020). *Digital in India: Value of inclusion*. The Fletcher School, Tufts University. https://digitalplanet.tufts.edu/publications/digital-in-india/

Chatterjee, A. (2020). Financial inclusion, information and communication technology diffusion, and economic growth: A panel data analysis. *Information Technology for Development, 26*(3), 1–29. https://doi.org/10.1080/02681102.2020.1734770

Chatterjee, A., & Das, S. (2021). Information communication technology diffusion and financial inclusion: An inter-state analysis for India. *Innovation and Development, 11*(1), 1–23. https://doi.org/10.1080/2157930X.2019.1678803

Chatterjee, A. (2024). Digital finance: a developing country perspective with special focus on gender and regional disparity. *Digital Policy, Regulation and Governance, 26*(4), 394–419. https://doi.org/10.1108/DPRG-10-2023-0149

Chatterjee, S., Saha, A., & Das, R. (2020). Digital India and the financial inclusion challenge. *Journal of Economic Policy and Research, 15*(1), 89–104. https://nibmindia.org/journal-of-economic-policy-and-research/

Chattopadhyay, A., Mitra, S., & Sen, A. (2021). Regional gaps in digital transformation in India. *Economic and Political Weekly, 56*(42), 45–53. https://www.epw.in/journal/2021/42

Dabla-Norris, E., Ji, Y., Townsend, R., & Unsal, D. (2015). *Indentifying constraints to financial inclusion and their impact on GDP and inequality: A structural framework for policy* (IMF Working papers 15/22).

Das, R., & Chatterjee, S. (2023a). Regional barriers to digital inclusion in rural India. *Indian Journal of Economics and Development, 19*(1), 23–38. https://www.ijed.in/

Das, S., & Chatterjee, A. (2023b). Impacts of ICT and digital finance on poverty and income inequality: A sub-national study from India. *Information Technology for Development, 29*(2–3), 378–405. https://doi.org/10.1080/02681102.2022.2151556

Dasgupta, S., & Singh, A. (2005a). Will services be the new engine of Indian economic growth? *Dev. Change, 36*(6), 1035–1058.

Dasgupta, S., & Singh, A. (2005b). Will services be the new engine of Indian economic growth? *Development and Change, 36*(6), 1035–1057. https://doi.org/10.1111/j.0012-155X.2005.00449.x

Demirgüç-Kunt, A., Klapper, L., Singer, D., & Van Oudheusden, P. (2022). *The Global Findex Database 2014: Measuring financial inclusion around the world.* World Bank. https://documents.worldbank.org/en/publication/documents-reports/documentdetail/187761468179367706

Felipe, J., León-Ledesma, M., Lanzafame, M., & Estrada, G. (2009). Sectoral engines of growth in developing Asia: Stylised facts and implications. *Malaysian Journal of Economic Studies, 46*(2), 107–133.

Gelb, A., Mukherjee, A., & Navis, K. (2020). *Citizens and states: How can digital ID and payments improve state capacity and effectiveness?* Center for Global Development. https://www.cgdev.org/publication/citizens-and-states-how-can-digital-id-and-payments-improve-state-capacity

Ghosh, S., & Vinod, D. (2017). What constrains financial inclusion for women? Evidence from Indian micro data. *World Development, 92*, 60–81. https://doi.org/10.1016/j.worlddev.2016.11.011

Greenwood, J., & Jovanovic, B. (1990). Financial development, growth, and the distribution of income. *Journal of Political Economy, 98*(5), 1076–1107.

Gurley, J. G., & Shaw, E. S. (1960). *Money in a theory of finance*. Brookings Institution.

Hinson, R., Lensink, R., & Mueller, A. (2019). Transforming agribusiness in developing countries: SDGs and the role of FinTech. *Current Opinion in Environmental Sustainability, 41*, 1–9. https://doi.org/10.1016/j.cosust.2019.07.002

Hirschman, A. O. (1958). *The Strategy of Economic Development*. Yale University Press.

Holtz-Eakin, D., Newey, W., & Rosen, H. (1988). Estimating vector autoregressions with panel data. *Econometrica, 56*(6), 1371–1395.

Jagtiani, J. and Lemieux, C. (2018). Do fintech lenders penetrate areas that are underserved by traditional banks? *Journal of Economics and Business, 100*(C), 43–54.

Kaldor, N. (1966). *Causes of the slow rate of economic growth of the United Kingdom*. Cambridge University Press.

Kaur, N., & Hanspal, M. (2022). Financial inclusion—A theoretical framework. *Journal of Production, Operations Management and Economics, 2*(25), 9–23. https://doi.org/10.55529/jpome.25.9.23

Levine, R. (2005). Finance and growth: Theory and evidence. In *Handbook of economic growth* (Chapter 12, 1(1), pp. 865–934). Elsevier.

Libânio, G., & Moro, S. (2011). Manufacturing industry and economic growth in Latin America. Anais do XXXVII Encontro Nacional de Economia. In *Proceedings of the 37th Brazilian Economics Meeting, ANPEC–Associação Nacional dos Centros de Pós-graduação em Economia*. Brazilian Association of Graduate Programs in Economics.

Liu, B., Wang, Y., Jiang, N., & Zhang, X. (2024). The impact of digital industrialization and industrial digitalization on regional green innovation efficiency in China: From the perspective of the innovation value chain. *Journal of Cleaner Production, 478*, Article 144015. https://doi.org/10.1016/j.jclepro.2024.144015

Magacho, G. R., & McCombie, J. S. L. (2017). Verdoorn's law and productivity dynamics: An empirical investigation into the demand and supply approaches. *Journal of Post Keynesian Economics, 40*(3), 1–22.

Makina, D. (2019). The potential of FinTech in enabling financial inclusion. *Extending Financial Inclusion in Africa, Elsevier, Amsterdam*. https://doi.org/10.1016/B978-0-12-814164-9.00014-1

Marconi, N., de Borja, F., Reis, C., & de Araújo, E. C. (2016). Manufacturing and eco- nomic development: The actuality of Kaldor's first and second laws. *Struct. Change Econ. Dyn., 37*, 75–89.

Mayer, J. (2020, September 30). *Digitalization and industrialization: Friends or foes*. WITA. https://www.wita.org/atp-research/digitalization-and-industrialization/

McKinnon, R. I. (1973). *Money and capital in economic development*. Brookings Institution.

McKinsey Global Institute. (2019). *Digital India: Technology to transform a connected nation*. McKinsey & Company. https://www.mckinsey.com/capabilities/mckinsey-digital/our-insights/digital-india-technology-to-transform-a-connected-nation

Mehrotra, S. (2020). 'Make in India': The components of a manufacturing strategy for India. *The Indian Journal of Labour Economics, 63*(1), 161–176. https://doi.org/10.1007/s41027-019-00201-9

Mehrotra, S. K. (2019). *Informal employment trends in the Indian economy: Persistent informality, but growing positive development*. International Labour Organization. https://ideas.repec.org/p/ilo/ilowps/995066393502676.html

Michael Debabrata Patra. (2023). *India's financial sector—From exuberance to resilience*. Bank for International Settlements. https://www.bis.org/review/r230922h.pdf

Nassiry, D. (2021). *The role of fintech in unlocking green finance: Policy insights for developing countries*. Lab for Innovation Finance. https://www.labinovacaofinanceira.com/wp-content/uploads/2021/06/3.4.-The-role-of-fintech-in-unlocking-green-finance.pdf

Nautiyal, T., & Ismail, S. (2022). Financial inclusion in India: A regional and district level analysis. *Asian Journal of Economics, Business and Accounting, 22*(22), 280–290. https://doi.org/10.9734/ajeba/2022/v22i2230732

Odeniran, S. O., & Udeaja, E. A. (2010). Financial sector development and economic growth: Empirical evidence from Nigeria. *Central Bank of Nigeria Economic and Financial Review, 48*(3), 91–124.

Onaolapo, A. R. (2015, September). Effects of financial inclusion on the economic growth of Nigeria (1982–2012). *International Journal of Business and Management Review, 3*(8), 11–28.

Pacheco, P., & Thirlwall, A. P. (2014). A new interpretation of Kaldor's first growth law for open developing economies. *Review of Keynesian Economics, 3*, 384–398.

Parminder Jeet Singh. (2018). *Digital industrialisation in developing countries: A review of the business and policy landscape*. IT for Change. https://itforchange.net/sites/default/files/1468/Digital-industrialisation-May-2018.pdf

Pekmezovic, A., & Walker, G. (Eds), *Sustainable development goals: Harnessing business to achieve the SDGs through finance, technology, and law reform*. Wiley. https://doi.org/10.1002/9781119541851.ch10

Rodrik, D. (2013). Unconditional convergence in manufacturing. *The Quarterly Journal of Economics, 128*(1), 165–204. https://doi.org/10.1093/qje/qjs047

Sarma, M., & Pais, J. (2011). Financial inclusion and development. *Journal of International Development, 23*(5), 613–628. https://doi.org/10.1002/jid.1698

Schumpeter, J. A. (1911). *The theory of economic development*.

Shaw, E. S. (1973). *Financial deepening in economic development*. Oxford University Press.

Škare, M., & Soriano, D. R. (2020). A dynamic panel study on digitalization and firm's agility: What drives agility in advanced economies (2009–2018)? *Technological Forecasting and Social Change, 163*, Article 120418. https://doi.org/10.1016/j.techfore.2020.120418

Szirmai, A. (2012a). *Industrialisation as an engine of growth in developing countries, 1950–2005*. Cambridge University Press.

Szirmai, A. (2012b). Industrialisation as an engine of growth in developing countries, 1950–2005. *Struct. Change Econ. Dyn., 23*(4), 406–420.

Szirmai, A., & Verspagen, B. (2015). Manufacturing and economic growth in developing countries, 1950–2005. *Structural Change and Economic Dynamics, 34*, 46–59.

USAID. (2019). *India digital financial inclusion: Journey map report* (mSTAR Project Report). https://www.fhi360.org/sites/default/files/media/documents/resource-mstar-india-digital-financial-inclusion-report.pdf

Yuan, S., Musibau, H. O., Genç, S. Y., Shaheen, R., Ameen, A., & Tan, Z. (2021). Digitalization of economy is the key factor behind fourth industrial revolution: How G7 countries are overcoming with the financing issues? *Technological Forecasting and Social Change, 165*, Article 120533. https://doi.org/10.1016/j.techfore.2020.12053

Zetzsche, D. A., Buckley, R. P., & Arner, D. W. (2019). FinTech for financial inclusion. In J. Walker (Ed.), *Sustainable development goals: Harnessing business to achieve the SDGs through finance, technology, and law reform* (pp. 1–25). Wiley.

CHAPTER 10

Access to Credit-Linked Crop Insurance in India: Does Farm Size Matter?

Saurav Priyotosh Munshi and Arindam Laha

1 Introduction

Agriculture in developing economies is characterised by a predominant presence of smallholders, with an average farm size of one to two hectares. In India, 80% of farmers belong to 'small and marginal' farmer households operating less than two hectares (Mahul et al., 2012). They are vulnerable and exposed to extreme weather events. Due to climate change in agriculture, weather shocks pose a major challenge to increasing productivity among smallholder farmers in developing countries (Ankrah et al., 2021; De Janvry et al., 2014). Investment in infrastructure (e.g., water irrigation system), technological innovations (e.g., drought-tolerant cultivars), crop management practices (e.g., changes to the timing of production activities), and access to financial instruments (e.g., credit and insurance)

S. P. Munshi (✉) · A. Laha
Department of Commerce, University of Burdwan, Burdwan, India
e-mail: spmunshi.sxc@gmail.com

A. Laha
e-mail: alaha@com.buruniv.ac.in

© The Author(s), under exclusive license to Springer Nature Singapore Pte Ltd. 2026

V. Dixit et al. (eds.), *Financial Inclusion for Viksit Bharat*,
https://doi.org/10.1007/978-981-92-0807-4_10

are considered as a novel strategy in addressing agricultural risk. However, these strategies are either not available or not feasible for many resource-constrained smallholders in developing countries (Ankrah et al., 2021). As a result, most of the resource-constrained farmers are left with no options but to suffer devastating crop loss, food insecurity, dispossession, and migration (Abdul-Razak & Kruse, 2017; Mahul & Stutley, 2010).

Small-scale farmers tend to lack savings, have limited access to credit, and rely on inefficient money transfer mechanisms and insurance markets to cushion them against shocks (Raithatha & Priebe, 2020; Moore et al., 2019). Farmers use various kinds of risk management strategies to safeguard themselves. These strategies include crop management and usage of pest, disease, and damage-resistant seeds, and financial strategies such as saving money, reducing investments, reducing consumption, seeking credit, and accessing insurance. Access to insurance is considered as a risk management (financial) strategy to improve the resilience of small-scale farmers by enhancing their capacity to absorb, adapt to, and/or recover from shocks (Jensen & Barrett, 2017). However, a lack of access to external finance constrained them in investing in productivity-enhancing technologies (Tadesse, 2014). Inability to have collateral often reflected in a lack of access to credit provided by formal financial institutions. Less than one-third of the farming community avails of institutional credit in India (Nair, 2010). As insurance is bundled with credit, insurance access is abysmally low among smallholders. In fact, India also has the largest number of uninsured farmers in the world (Mahul et al., 2012). Globally, less than 20% of small-scale farmers are included under insurance coverage. The uninsured include 97% of small-scale farmers in sub-Saharan Africa, almost 80% of those in Asia, and two-thirds of those in Latin America (Raithatha & Priebe, 2020).

Insurance in Indian agriculture is more challenging than in developed countries due to a large number of small and scattered landholdings, varying climatic and soil conditions, a lack of basic data, and a variety of agricultural practices (Nair, 2010). Insurance providers perceive small-scale farmers as risky (Hazell et al., 2021). In the presence of the imperfect nature of credit and insurance markets, there is a need to adopt a comprehensive approach (Alderman & Haque, 2007), as separate access to credit or insurance is seriously limited. Alternatively, bundling of credit and insurance markets can be an innovative solution in reducing the cost of borrowing and making credit more accessible to the smallholder farmers (Tadesse, 2014) by considering insurance as collateral against the loan.

The Indian government has undertaken several policy measures to improve the insurance penetration among smallholders through several initiatives since the Comprehensive Crop Insurance Scheme was put into place in 1985. For the first time, non-loanee farmers were included in these policies to provide smallholders with insurance access. Moreover, the Government continued to include non-food grain and non-oilseed crops in the program while giving a premium subsidy to small and marginal farmers. Furthermore, post-harvest losses were also included in the crop insurance scheme. Additionally, the unit area of the crop cutting experiment was reduced to reduce the basis risk to an acceptably low limit (Comptroller and Auditor General, 2017). A series of targeted policies are implemented by the Government of India to improve the coverage of smallholders under the Pradhan Mantri Fasal Bima Yojana. The decoupling of crop insurance from agricultural credit is considered a substantial advancement in this direction (PIB Delhi, 2020). This action is expected to contribute to the expansion of risk coverage to vulnerable farming groups that were previously excluded. Additionally, the crop insurance is delinked from subsidies, and thereby ensured that the insured farmers could access indemnity even if State Governments fail to provide subsidies in time (PIB Delhi,. DigiClaim, a digitised module that facilitates the real-time automated disbursement of insurance claims directly into the farmer's bank account through integration with the National Crop Insurance Portal (NCIP) and Public Financial Management System (PFMS), was introduced by the Ministry of Agriculture to further simplify claim settlement and enhance transparency (PIB Delhi,; 2024). The Government has also introduced several innovations for accurate crop loss estimation[1] in addition to the technological advancements. To strengthen the institutional framework, the government has signed a formal Memorandum of Understanding (MoU) with the United Nations Development Program (UNDP). With a focus on small and marginal farmers, women farmers, sharecroppers, tenants, and non-loanee farmers in particular, UNNDP offers technical support, capacity building, and

[1] These innovations include remote sensing tools like YES-TECH, CROPIC, and WINDS, which use automated weather data, satellite imagery, and drone mapping to ensure precise assessment and minimize disputes (PIB Delhi,; 2024; 2025).

IEC (information, education, and communication) support for the efficient implementation of crop insurance and agricultural credit schemes under this collaboration. This collaboration is anticipated to enhance the delivery of the scheme and its inclusiveness (PIB Delhi, 2022a;. The government has launched a pilot program called the Farmers Grievance Portal[2] which offers an online platform for real-time complaint tracking and registration (PIB Delhi,. The government has also implemented nationwide campaigns to increase awareness and encourage farmer participation. These campaigns include *Meri Policy, Mera Haath*, which markets a crop insurance scheme and delivers policy documents directly to the farmers at their homes, and *Fasal Bima Pathsala*, which is a grassroots education program[3] (PIB Delhi, 2022a;. Since the Union government realises the importance of the State government's role in the effective implementation of the crop insurance scheme, it actively engages with those States that had previously left the program.[4] The government has made these changes to transform the PMFBY into a more technologically advanced, transparent, and inclusive program.

This study bridges this gap in knowledge in two ways: Firstly, some studies in the existing literature identified the determinants of crop insurance in Indian farmers (Aditya et al., 2018; Akber et al., 2023; Biswal & Bahinipati, 2023; Cariappa et al., 2021; Cole et al., 2013; Dey & Maitra, 2017; Giné et al., 2008; Kaur et al., 2021; Rajeev & Nagendran, 2019; Ranganathan et al., 2019). This evidence motivates us to develop a theoretical framework to examine how landholding determines crop insurance access. Secondly, Access to crop insurance reduces liquidity constraint (Duchoslav & Van Asseldonk, 2018), increases productivity in agriculture (Shee & Turvey, 2012), increases access to loans (Carter et al., 2016; Farrin & Miranda, 2015; Meyer et al., 2018; Mishra et al., 2021), reduces interest rate (Carter et al., 2016; Farrin & Miranda, 2015), and increases technology adoption and entrepreneurial risk-taking in a low collateral environment (Carter et al., 2016). Credit-linked insurance contracts can facilitate the adoption of new technology, which in turn boosts their farm

[2] It is initially available in Chhattisgarh and is being expanded across the country.

[3] These events have been organised in over one lakh locations to inform farmers about the benefits of the crop insurance scheme, the enrolment process, and grievance redressal mechanisms.

[4] Andhra Pradesh and Punjab have rejoined the program, and talks to rejoin Telangana, Jharkhand, and Gujarat are still underway (PIB Delhi,.

income and demand for insurance (Carter et al., 2017; Hess et al., 2016). However, the effects of introducing formal insurance do not always have positive environmental or social impacts (Müller et al., 2017). In some contexts, empirical evidence suggests that formal insurance can crowd out traditional risk-coping mechanisms (group savings or community self-help networks). The varying impact of crop insurance across farmer categories necessitates a disaggregated impact assessment. This study gives a better understanding of this issue by considering the impact of crop insurance on farmer households in general and smallholders in particular.

The rest of the paper is systematically arranged as follows. In the next section, a theoretical model is developed. Section 3 highlights the data source and methodology. Results and discussions are given in Sect. 4. Finally, the conclusions and policy implications are provided in Sect. 5.

2 Formulation of the Theoretical Model

In this model, it is assumed that a farmer finances the cost of cultivation through a combination of savings, S, and credit, C. The farmer utilizes their savings to meet the cost of cultivation and resorts to credit to cover the deficit. Under a credit-linked insurance contract, there is a provision of crop insurance while accessing credit from the bank. They can also borrow the amount from an informal moneylender if they don't participate in the crop insurance scheme.

It is reasonable to assume that the farmer harvests a quantity q_1 during crop success, with a probability of z and a quantity q_2 during crop failure, with a probability of $1 - z$. Quantity of output q_1 and q_2 is assumed to be a function of land L and input $S + C$. The farmer is required to purchase insurance at a premium π, which is equivalent to the present value of expected indemnity payout, discounted by the interest rate charged by the bank. The indemnity payout would include the credit, premium, and interest amount $(C + \pi)(1 + r)$. Following Giné and Yang (2009), the premium is equivalent to $\pi = \frac{1-z}{z}C$.

Insured farmer: The insured farmers receive a payoff of $U(I_S) = \rho p q_1(L, (S + C)) - \left(C + \frac{1-z}{z}C\right)(1 + r)$ during crop success and a payoff of $U(I_F) = \rho p q_2(L, (S + C))$ during crop failure, where $\rho = \frac{1}{1+r}$ and p is the selling price of the product. It is assumed that the bank collects the principal amount of the loan and its interest payment from the indemnity payment in case of crop failure. So, the expected payoff of the insured farmer is as follows:

$$U(I) = z\rho pq_1(L, (S + C)) - z\left(C + \frac{1 - z}{z}C\right)(1 + r)$$
$$+ (1 - z)\rho pq_2(L, (S + C))$$
$$=> U(I) = z\rho pq_1(L, (S + C)) - C(1 + r) + (1 - z)\rho pq_2(L, (S + C))$$

Uninsured farmer: The uninsured farmer would receive a payoff of $U(N_S) = \rho pq_1(L, (S + C)) - C(1 + m)$ in crop success and a payoff of $U(N_F) = \rho pq_2(L, (S + C)) - C(1 + m)$ during crop failure, where m is the rate of interest charged by the moneylender, which is greater than r. So, the expected payoff of an uninsured farmer is as follows:

$$U(N) = z\rho pq_1(L, (S + C)) - C(1 + m) + (1 - z)\rho pq_2(L, (S + C))$$

Comparing the expected payoff of an insured farmer vis-a-vis uninsured farmer, it can be said that

$$U(I) = z\rho pq_1(L, (S + C)) - C(1 + r) + (1 - z)\rho pq_2(L, (S + C))$$
$$> U(N) = z\rho pq_1(L, (S + C)) - C(1 + m) + (1 - z)\rho pq_2(L, (S + C)).$$

Thus, variation in the interest rate ($m > r$) is considered a condition under which a farmer will go for a crop insurance contract.

Proposition 1 The payoff of insured farmers is higher than non-insured farmers.

Comparing the payoffs of insured vis-a-vis uninsured farmers under two different situations can be made as follows:

$$\text{Crop success}: U(I_S) = \rho pq_1(L, (S + C)) - \frac{C}{z}(1 + r) >=< U(N_S)$$
$$= \rho pq_1(L, (S + C)) - C(1 + m)$$

$$\text{Crop failure}: U(I_F) = \rho pq_2(L, (S + C)) > U(N_F)$$
$$= \rho pq_2(L, (S + C)) - (C)(1 + m)$$

Proposition 2 The payoff of insured farmers is higher than non-insured farmers in crop failure only.

Figure 1 presents the relationship between the expected payoff of farmers and land size. Regardless of insurance status, the vertical axis presents each farmer's expected payoff, and the horizontal axis presents their landholding. The variations in payoff are presented by the variations in the slopes between the two curves. The payoff of insured smallholders is higher than non-insured farmers. For a higher farm size, the payoff gap between insured and uninsured is greater. It is conceivable that farmers having relatively large farm sizes possess sufficient savings, which would enable them to finance the inputs without the need for formal credit, and they can self-insure without formal insurance. Except for large farmers, however, insurance access increases with farm sizes, and thereby have a favaourable impact on payoffs. Therefore, the difference in payoffs between the insured and the uninsured increases with farm sizes. Payoffs across different farm sizes are shown similarly in Appendix Fig. 4 for crop success. The result is also more or less similar to that of Fig. 1. In Appendix Fig. 5, the differences in payoffs for crop failure are prominent. Insured farmers can cover the principal and interest from indemnity amount and thereby payoff remains unaffected. However, uninsured farmers are worse affected as they are obliged to repay the informal credit. As the credit is proportional to the land size, relatively large uninsured farmers are badly affected.

3 Materials and Methods

Data Source: In this paper, the propositions derived from the theoretical model are tested in - light of empirical evidence from India. For this purpose, an exhaustive dataset from a nationally representative survey is considered. Specifically, the unit-level data is collected from the first visit of NSS 77th round of Land and Livestock Holdings of Households and Situation Assessment Survey of Agricultural Households, 2018–2019. The survey was conducted over 58,040 agricultural households in India. However, only 34,755 crop-wise observations related to 31,621 households cultivating cereals are considered for this study. Farmer households comprise 17,751 marginal farmers (below 1 hectare), 8604 small farmers (1–2 hectare), 4254 medium farmers(2–4 hectare),and 1012 large farmers (more than 4 hectare). Smallholder farmers are defined as those marginal

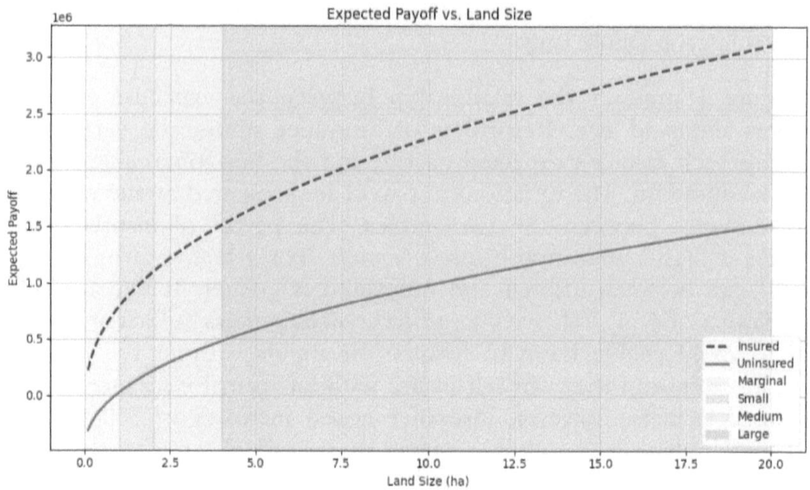

Fig. 1 Relationship between expected payoff and land size (*Note* Figure generated using Python (Matplotlib and NumPy). The results reflect a plausible scenario based on assumptions specific to the author's analytical framework)

and small farm households that own or/and cultivate less than 2.0 hectares of land.

Methods: At first, binary logistic regression analysis is employed to find the correlates of crop insurance adoption. Finally, Propensity Score Matching is utilized to assess the impact of crop insurance on farm income.

Logistic regression analysis: as the influence of independent variables on non-continuous binary dependent variables cannot be done using a multiple regression model, logistic regression is used. In this study, logistic regression analysis is used to find out the determinants of crop insurance adoption (insured vs uninsured), by considering loanee and non-loanee farmers as a singular category (insured farmer).

Let us assume $T_i = 1$ for loanee farmers, $T_i = 2$ for non-loanee farmers, and $T_i = 3$ uninsured farmers. First, to find out the determinants of crop insurance adoption, a linear relationship showing the effect of independent variables on the log-odds of insurance access will be $ln\frac{P_{T_i=1}+P_{T_i=2}}{P_{T_i=3}} = \beta_0 + \beta X + u_i$. The probability of being an insured farmer and the probability of being an uninsured farmer are $\frac{e^{z_i}}{1+e^{z_i}}$ and $\frac{1}{1+e^{z_i}}$ respectively, and $z_i = \beta_0 + \beta X + u_i$ (Gujarati, 2011).

Table 1 presents a list of independent variables and the expected sign of the coefficient of the independent variable (i.e., hypothesized sign).

Impact evaluation method: Randomized evaluations are the perfect method for evaluating causal relationships. However, when we cannot randomize, it is better to mimic randomized experiments. For this purpose, a control group is identified that is quite similar to the treatment group in observed determinants. The objective is to find a group of non-insured households that are observationally similar to insured households in characteristics but not affected by the treatment. However, it is impossible to match households manually based on multiple characteristics. A common way of matching the participants is Propensity Score Matching (PSM). PSM establishes a statistical comparable group based on a model of the probability of the household participating in the treatment to observed covariates. Assumptions of PSM (Rosenbaum, 2002) are as follows:

- Stable Unit Treatment Value Assumption (SUTVA)—the potential outcome of any unit is not impacted by the treatment provided to other units, and there are no different versions of the treatment.
- Conditional Independence Assumption—treatment status may be deemed to be assigned at random, contingent on all confounders being observed and
- Common Support Assumption (Overlap Assumption)—the probability of treatment assignment for both groups should be between zero to one.

Fulfilling these three conditions, the matching of propensity scores can be considered as equivalent to the matching of covariates. In this method, each insured household is matched to a non-insured household based on propensity score. Four matching algorithms are utilized in this study: 1:1 nearest neighbour matching (PSM), 1:5 nearest neighbor matching (NMM), radius matching (RM), and kernel matching (KM).[5]

[5] Bryson et al. (2002) noted that the inclusion of non-significant variables would increase the variances after matching. Hence, this study only considers covariates that are found significant by ordinary least square regression and logistic regression.

Table 1 List of independent variables and their hypothesised sign

Variable	*Description*	*Expected sign*	*Cited in the literature*
Age	Age of household head in years	+	Aditya et al. (2018), Mukhopadhyay et al. (2018) and Panda et al. (2020)
Age sq	Square of the age of the household head	–	Aditya et al. (2020) and Panda et al., (2020)
Male	Dummy variable (1 if head is male, 0 otherwise)	+	Aditya et al. (2018) and Carippa et al. (2021)
Till +12	Dummy variable (1 if head is educated above primary but below higher secondary, 0 otherwise)	+	Aditya et al. (2018), Cariappa et al. (2021) and Ranganathan et al. (2019)
Above +12	Dummy variable (1 if head is educated above higher secondary, 0 otherwise)	+	Aditya et al. (2018), Cariappa et al. (2021) and Ranganathan et al. (2019)
Agricultural training	Dummy variable (1 if the head has obtained training, 0 otherwise)	+	Aditya et al. (2018) and Cariappa et al. (2021)
Landholding (in hectare)	Area of land in hectares	+	Aditya et al. (2018) and Akber et al. (2023)
Land sq	Square of area of land in hectare	–	Aditya et al. (2018)
Average monthly consumption	Natural log of (monthly consumption in Rs. +1)	+	Cariappa et al. (2021)
Head engaged in farming	Dummy variable (1 if head has engaged in farming, 0 otherwise)	+	Ranganathan et al. (2019)
Household size	House size in person	–	Cariappa et al. (2021), Panda et al. (2020) and Ranganathan et al. (2019)
Scheduled tribe	Dummy variable (1 if belonging to ST caste, 0 otherwise)	–	Cariappa et al. (2021), Rajeev and Nagendran (2019) and Ranganathan et al. (2019)
Scheduled caste	Dummy variable (1 if belonging to SC caste, 0 otherwise)	–	Cariappa et al. (2021), Rajeev and Nagendran (2019) and Ranganathan et al. (2019)

(continued)

Table 1 (continued)

Variable	*Description*	*Expected sign*	*Cited in the literature*
OBC	Dummy variable (1 if belonging to OBC caste, 0 otherwise)	–	Cariappa et al. (2021) and Ranganathan et al. (2019)
Katcha	Dummy variable (1 if residing in katcha house, 0 otherwise)	–	Cariappa et al. (2021)
Semi-paka	Dummy variable (1 if residing in semi-paka house, 0 otherwise)	–	Cariappa et al. (2021)
Bank account	Dummy variable (1 if having Kisan Credit Card, 0 otherwise)	+	Lan et al. (2024)[6]
MGNREGA work	Dummy variable (1 if undertaken MGNREGA work, 0 otherwise	+	Cariappa et al. (2021)
Registered farmers organization	Dummy variable (1 if member of a registered farmers organisation work, 0 otherwise)	+	Giné et al. (2008)
Kisan Credit Card	Dummy variable (1 if having bank account, 0 otherwise)	+	Lan et al. (2024)[7] and Ranganathan et al. (2019)
ln(Yield +1)	Natural log of (yield +1)	–	Cariappa et al. (2021)[8]
Crop loss	Dummy variable (1 if crop loss, 0 otherwise)	+	Aditya et al. (2018)

Source Authors' compilation

PSM creates a statistical comparison group that is based on a model of the probability of household participation in crop insurance T conditional on observed covariates X. The propensity score can be written as: $Ps(X) = P(T = 1|X)$. PSM is based on the following two assumptions: conditional independence and common support (Rosenbaum, 2002):

[6] Huong Lan et al. (2024) considered savings in their logit model, we have used bank account as an alternative for savings.

[7] .Huong Lan et al. (2024) considered borrowings in their logit model, we have used kisan credit card as an alternative for borrowing.

[8] Cariappa et al. (2020) found total farm output significantly influences crop insurance access, we have considered yield as an alternative.

The average treatment effect on the treated can be estimated as $ATT = E_{Ps(X)|T=1}\{E[T=1, Ps(X)] - E[T=0, Ps(X)]\}$ (Khandker et al., 2009). The PSM method is employed in this study to estimate the impact of insurance access on farm income. Following NSS methodology, farm income is measured by the total income generated by the sale of crops after excluding income derived from selling byproducts.

4 Results and Discussion

4.1 *Survey Highlights at the National Level*

It is evident from the NSS survey that only 7.99% of crops were insured. Among the insured category, 5.44% of crops were insured by the loanee farmers, while 2.55% were insured by non-loanee farmers. An in-depth analysis based on farm size revealed that crop insurance coverage improves with farm size. Unbelievably, 92% of the crops were still not insured. Not knowing about insurance was the main reason for this (42.75%), followed by not knowing about the facilities that are available for such plans (14.14%). Moreover, 19.72% were not interested in purchasing a crop insurance contract, and 6.04% expressed no need for crop insurance. Segregating based on farm size, it can be seen that unawareness gradually increases from large to marginal farmers. The percentage of farmers citing not interested in crop insurance steadily increased from marginal to large farmers.

Survey evidence also suggested that 75.81% of claims were denied. The majority of the claims of marginal and small farmers are denied. Disbursement of claims was mainly realized by a higher percentage of medium and large farmers. Farmers suffered a loss as the threshold yield was lower than expected, however, non-materialization of claims left them empty-handed (Kakvi & Sharma, 2022) (Table 2).

One reason for not availing of crop insurance was reported as delayed claim payout. Only 35.56% of them received the indemnity amount in time (within 6 months). Delays were primarily caused by the inefficiency of the State Government in releasing the results of the crop cutting experiment and the subsidies in time (Rajeev & Nagendran, 2019; Vyas & Singh, 2006). It was observed that 94.04% don't know the reasons why the claims were rejected. Other reasons for rejection of claims were outside coverage and loss of documents. Private companies use these schemes to boost their profitability, and thereby, many claims

Table 2 Access to insurance and its related issues[9]

Insurance Category	*Marginal*	*Small*	*Medium*	*Large*	*Total*
Loanee Farmer	976 (2.86)	1175 (6.24)	955 (9.27)	499 (16.76)	3605 (5.44)
Non-loanee Farmer	509 (1.49)	577 (3.07)	431 (4.18)	173 (5.81)	1690 (2.55)
Uninsured Farmer	32,623 (95.65)	17,072 (90.69)	8921 (86.55)	2306 (77.43)	60,922 (92.00)
Total	34,108 (100.00)	18,824 (100.00)	10,307 (100.00)	2978 (100.00)	66,217 (100.00)
Reason for being uninsured					
Not aware	14,515 (44.49)	7248 (42.46)	3495 (39.18)	784 (34.00)	26,042 (42.75)
Not aware about the availability of facility	4644 (14.24)	2374 (13.91)	1285 (14.40)	310 (13.44)	8613 (14.14)
Not interested	5972 (18.31)	3473 (20.34)	1991 (22.32)	578 (25.07)	12,014 (19.72)
No need	2135 (6.54)	949 (5.56)	442 (4.95)	155 (6.72)	3681 (6.04)
Insurance facility not available	1715 (5.26)	901 (5.28)	428 (4.80)	134 (5.81)	3178 (5.22)
Lack of resources for premium payment	752 (2.31)	335 (1.96)	155 (1.74)	36 (1.56)	1278 (2.10)
Not satisfied with terms and conditions	503 (1.54)	381 (2.23)	316 (3.54)	118 (5.12)	1318 (2.16)
Nearest bank at a long distance	59 (0.18)	30 (0.18)	25 (0.28)	1 (0.04)	115 (0.19)
Others	1324 (4.06)	697 (4.08)	384 (4.30)	100 (4.34)	2505 (4.11)
Complex procedures	837 (2.57)	514 (3.01)	281 (3.15)	55 (2.39)	1687 (2.77)
Delay in claim Payment	167 (0.51)	170 (1.00)	119 (1.33)	35 (1.52)	491 (0.81)
Total	32,623 (100.00)	17,072 (100.00)	8921 (100.00)	2306 (100.00)	60,922 (100.00)
Status of claim					
Fully received	24 (9.38)	32 (9.73)	35 (14.29)	14 (14.00)	105 (11.29)
Partly received	37 (14.45)	39 (11.85)	32 (13.06)	12 (12.00)	120 (12.90)
Not received	195 (76.17)	258 (78.42)	178 (72.65)	74 (74.00)	705 (75.81)
Total	256 (100.00)	329 (100.00)	245 (100.00)	100 (100.00)	930 (100.00)

(continued)

[9] The frequencies mentioned in this document represent the crop-wise frequencies, based on individual crop observations.

Table 2 (continued)

Insurance Category	*Marginal*	*Small*	*Medium*	*Large*	*Total*
Time in disbursing claim					
Within 6 months	24 (39.34)	33 (46.48)	21 (31.34)	2 (7.69)	80 (35.56)
6–12 months	32 (52.46)	27 (38.03)	31 (46.27)	19 (73.08)	109 (48.44)
More than 12 months	5 (8.20)	11 (15.49)	15 (22.39)	5 (19.23)	36 (16.00)
Total	61 (100.00)	71 (100.00)	67 (100.00)	26 (100.00)	225 (100.00)
Reasons for croploss					
Inadequate rainfall	6618 (52.57)	4062 (55.36)	2370 (57.95)	887 (69.24)	13,937 (55.09)
Farm specific loss	3400 (27.01)	1858 (25.32)	946 (23.13)	192 (14.99)	6396 (25.28)
Other natural cause	1869 (14.85)	1053 (14.35)	597 (14.60)	159 (12.41)	3678 (14.54)
Other causes	703 (5.58)	364 (4.96)	177 (4.33)	43 (3.36)	1287 (5.09)
Total	12,590 (100.00)	7337 (100.00)	4090 (100.00)	1281 (100.00)	25,298 (100.00)

Note Frequencies are given along with the column percentage value in parentheses
Source Authors' compilation from Situation Assessment Survey, 2018–2019 (National Sample Survey Organization, 2021)

were rejected without providing adequate reason (Shagun, 2021). Inadequate rainfall (55.09%) was the main reason for crop loss, followed by farm-specific loss (25.28%), loss due to other natural causes (14.54%), and other losses (5.09%). The percentage of farmers reporting crop loss due to inadequate rainfall and farm-specific loss decreases steadily from marginal to large farmers.

4.2 *Inter-State Variation*

The situational assessment survey showed that states with comparatively high insurance penetration rates include Chhattisgarh (24.7%), Haryana (24.62%), Andhra Pradesh (21.15%), Maharashtra (20.36%), Rajasthan (16.62%), and Telangana (16.12%). Although they have high insurance coverage, the proportion of smallholders relative to the insured is relatively low. On the other hand, insurance coverage is very low in some states, especially in the north-eastern and hilly areas. These states include Assam (0.39%), Jammu & Kashmir (0.41%), Meghalaya (0.39%), Mizoram (0.66%), and Tripura (1.18%). Farmers in these states encounter obstacles in accessing formal insurance, despite their agro-climatic vulnerability. Smallholders are, nevertheless, the main users of crop insurance in many of these states (Table 3).

A regional variation suggests that central and western states (including Madhya Pradesh, Rajasthan, and Maharashtra) exhibit a higher uptake of crop insurance, whereas eastern and north-eastern states are lagging behind. Southern India (Andhra Pradesh, Telangana, and Tamil Nadu) exhibits moderate to high levels of coverage (Fig. 2), Overall, it can be suggested that crop insurance coverage increases with landholding size across most regions. State-wise variation in insurance coverage for smallholder farmers is presented in (Fig. 3) and the coverage of insured farmers across farm size is presented in Appendix Figs. 6, 7, 8 and 9.

Table 4 suggests that states like Chhattisgarh, Karnataka, and Tamil Nadu have a high degree of insurance penetration and smallholders' participation. The only two states with a low level of insurance coverage and a low level of smallholders' coverage are Jammu and Kashmir and Punjab. States having high insurance coverage but low smallholders' coverage are Andhra Pradesh, Gujarat, Haryana, Madhya Pradesh, Maharashtra, Rajasthan, and Telangana. The majority of the states have high smallholders' participation but low insurance participation. These states include Andaman & Nicobar, Arunachal Pradesh, Assam, Bihar, Goa, Himachal Pradesh, Jharkhand, Kerala, Manipur, Meghalaya, Mizoram, Puducherry, Sikkim, Tripura, Uttarakhand, Uttar Pradesh, and West Bengal. In Appendix Fig. 10, we plot the relationship between insurance coverage and smallholders' coverage. In this figure, the scatter dots represent the observations of various states. It has been found that a majority of the observations lie within the south-east and north-west portions of the scatter diagram. This suggests that the degree of insurance coverage is

Table 3 Inter-state variations of crop insurance coverage

State	*Loanee*	*Non-loanee*	*Uninsured*	*Total*	*Insured/total surveyed hh*	*Insured smallholders/ total insured*
Andaman & Nicobar	0	1	136	137	0.73	100.00
Andhra Pradesh	326	32	1335	1693	21.15	57.54
Arunachal Pradesh	3	14	752	769	2.21	100.00
Assam	4	7	2793	2804	0.39	90.91
Bihar	80	73	4092	4245	3.6	66.67
Chhattisgarh	187	102	881	1170	24.7	65.40
Goa	0	3	122	125	2.4	100.00
Gujarat	245	7	2124	2376	10.61	57.54
Haryana	201	61	802	1064	24.62	43.89
Himachal Pradesh	37	15	1057	1109	4.69	69.23
Jammu & Kashmir	5	1	1465	1471	0.41	33.33
Jharkhand	39	62	2090	2191	4.61	78.22
Karnataka	138	138	2687	2963	9.31	61.96
Kerala	30	85	3002	3117	3.69	72.17
Madhya Pradesh	287	75	3062	3424	10.57	56.63
Maharashtra	397	630	4018	5045	20.36	55.31
Manipur	6	9	1396	1411	1.06	100.00
Meghalaya	5	1	1533	1539	0.39	100.00
Mizoram	4	4	1202	1210	0.66	100.00
Odisha	223	67	2356	2646	10.96	67.24
Puducherry	1	3	59	63	6.35	75.00
Punjab	5	4	1334	1343	0.67	44.44
Rajasthan	623	40	3327	3990	16.62	53.09
Sikkim	4	8	907	919	1.31	83.33
Tamil Nadu	82	143	1755	1980	11.36	73.33
Telangana	211	9	1145	1365	16.12	56.82
Tripura	7	7	1175	1189	1.18	100.00
Uttarakhand	53	1	1337	1391	3.88	68.52
Uttar Pradesh	206	33	7735	7974	3.00	64.85
West Bengal	196	55	3990	4241	5.92	86.06
India	3605	1690	59,669	64,964	8.15	61.13

Source Authors' calculation based on data from Situation Assessment Survey, 2018–2019 (National Sample Survey Organization, 2021)

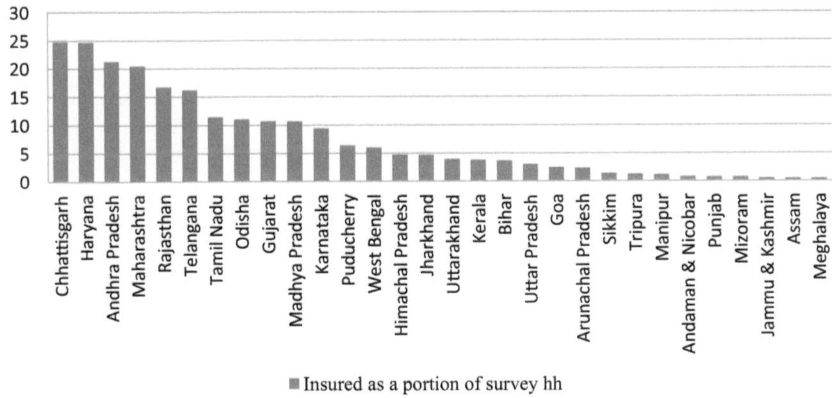

Fig. 2 Insurance coverage across Indian states (*Source* Same as Table 3)

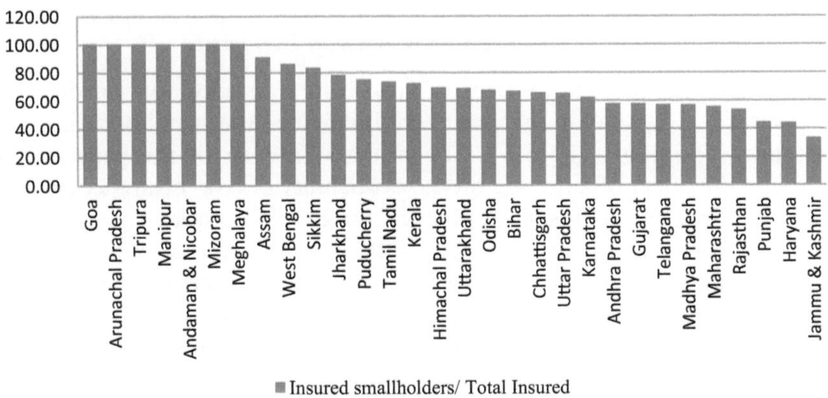

Fig. 3 State-wise variation in insurance coverage of smallholders (*Source* Same as Table 3)

a negative correlate of smallholders' coverage. The estimated correlation coefficients between insurance coverage and smallholders' coverage are estimated to be about −0.553 (Pearson Correlation), −0.473 (Kendall's tau-b), and −0.568 (Spearman's rho). All these coefficients are found to be highly statistically significant at the 0.002 or 0.001 percent level of significance (2-tailed).

Table 4 Classification of states based on values of insurance coverage and smallholders' coverage

Smallholder coverage *Insurance coverage*	*Above the national average*	*Below the national average*
Above the national average	Chhattisgarh, Karnataka, Odisha, and Tamil Nadu	Andhra Pradesh, Gujarat, Haryana, Madhya Pradesh, Maharashtra, Rajasthan, and Telangana
Below the national average	Andaman & Nicobar, Arunachal Pradesh, Assam, Bihar, Goa, Himachal Pradesh, Jharkhand, Kerala, Manipur, Meghalaya, Mizoram, Puducherry, Sikkim, Tripura, Uttarakhand, Uttar Pradesh, and West Bengal	Jammu & Kashmir and Punjab

4.3 *Determinants of Crop Insurance*

The results on the determinants of crop insurance adoption (insured vs uninsured) suggest that age positively influences the likelihood of crop insurance adoption (Table 5). The primary interest of the paper is to examine the effect of farm size on the probability of crop insurance access. Land holding has a positive influence on crop insurance access up to a point; after that, it has a negative influence on crop insurance access. Large farmers potentially have adequate collateral to access formal credit and hence are included in the insurance scheme (Aditya et al., 2018). After a certain threshold, they begin to rely less on crop insurance schemes and instead use their savings to self-insure. Male-headed households are more willing to access crop insurance than their non-male counterparts; the marginal effects show an increase in the likelihood of crop insurance access by 1.3 percentage points. Having post-elementary education and formal agricultural training facilitates farmers in accessing crop insurance. Since farmers with no basic education or formal training would not understand the benefits of insurance schemes, they are less likely to harness the benefits of crop insurance schemes (Aditya et al., 2018). The marginal effects of trained farmers show an increase in the probability of crop insurance by 3.5 percentage points to their non-trained counterparts. Household size negatively influences the likelihood of crop insurance. Households with a large family size would prefer mutual insurance over formal insurance. Farmers belonging to the SC/ST category (backward caste) are less likely to adopt crop insurance than those in the general category. However, such lower adaptation of crop insurance is not evident to the farmers belonging to the OBC category. It can be explained by a significant land ownership difference between General and SC/ST households. However, OBC holding possessed on average a landholding which is more or less the same as that of general households. Farmers residing in non-concrete houses (i.e.,katcha and semi-paka) are less likely to access crop insurance when compared to residents of concrete houses. Farmers who have accessed the benefits of the employment guarantee scheme (MGNREGA)and financial inclusion (Kisan credit card) are more likely to accept crop insurance, as shown by the marginal effect. Getting crop insurance is more likely for farmers who belong to a registered organization. This suggests that social networks play a part in getting crop insurance. Farmers with crop loss are more likely to adopt crop insurance; the probability of crop insurance purchase increases by 2.3 percentage points for farmers suffering a loss.

4.4 Impact of Crop Insurance on Farm Income

To evaluate the impact of crop insurance on farm income propensity score matching is utilised. PSM is an effective tool in a cross-sectional observational study to address the selection bias, which may arise while comparing the treated against a faulty control group. In propensity score matching, the average treatment on treated (ATT) compares the effect of treatment on outcome variables of participants receiving treatment. In this study, the effects of crop insurance on farm income are measured. The result of the ATT under different matching algorithms (i.e., 1:1 nearest neighbour matching (NNM), 1:5 NNM, radius matching, and kernel matching) is shown in Table 6. It can be seen that, in general, there is a positive effect of crop insurance on farm income. The ATT value is Rs. 7532.2 (in nearest matching algorithm), indicating that the insured farmer would have experienced a loss in farm income by Rs. 7532.2 if they would not have accessed the crop insurance scheme. The estimates of the ATT range from Rs. 7532.2 to Rs. 13,363.1 across the different matching algorithms. This result is consistent with that of Yu (2015), Agbenyo et al. (2022), Cariappa et al. (2021), Akber et al. (2023). Therefore, it can be

Table 5 Results of logistic regression along with their marginal effects

Variables	*Coef*	*dy/dx*
Age	0.047***	0.003***
Age sq	−0.000***	−0.000***
Male	0.218**	0.013**
Till +12	0.105**	0.007**
Above +12	0.061	0.004
Agricultural training	0.477***	0.035***
Landholding (in hectare)	0.427***	0.027***
Land sq	−0.020***	−0.001***
Average monthly consumption	−0.014	−0.001
Head engaged in farming	−0.076	−0.005
Household size	−0.094***	−0.006***
Scheduled tribe	−0.656***	−0.033***
Scheduled caste	−0.215**	−0.013***
OBC	0.304***	0.022***
Katcha	−0.287***	−0.018***
Semi-paka	−0.285***	−0.018***
Bank account	0.270	0.016
MGNREGA work	0.620***	0.044***
Registered farmers organization	0.742***	0.059***
Kisan Credit Card	1.334***	0.107***
ln (Yield +1)	0.059***	0.004***
Crop loss	0.352***	0.023***
Constant	−5.231***	

Note ***$p < 0.01$, ** $p < 0.05$, * $p < 0.1$ (Standard error adjusted for 31,700 clusters) dy/dx for factor levels is the discrete change from the base level
Source Authors calculation

concluded that access to crop insurance significantly impacts in achieving higher farm income.

To check whether the positive relationship between crop insurance access is consistent amongst the different farming groups (i.e., marginal, small, medium and large) we have estimated the ATT values for each farming group using the earlier matching algorithms. For marginal farmers crop insurance access increased farm income by Rs. 3197.7 (in nearest matching algorithm) than if they would not have accessed crop insurance. This increased income falls in the range from Rs. 2777.9 to Rs. 4936.8 in other algorithms. Similarly, the ATT estimates for small and medium farmers are Rs. 12,497.6 and Rs. 11,006.3 respectively. There is

Table 6 Results of PSM

Matching algorithm	*Matching: Insured vs uninsured*				
	Overall	*Marginal*	*Small*	*Medium*	*Large*
Nearest Neighbour Matching (1:1)	7532.2 (0.026) [2.22]	3197.7 (0.003) [2.99]	12,497.6 (0.000) [5.67]	11,006.3 (0.040) [2.06]	−24,304.9 (0.524) [-0.64]
Nearest Neighbour Matching (5:1)	8285.5 (0.003) [2.94]	2777.9 (0.001) [3.28]	11,521.8 (0.000) [6.06]	16,825.9 (0.000) [4.11]	−11,538.5 (0.637) [-0.47]
Radius Matching (0.1)	15,100.9 (0.000) [6.13]	4936.8 (0.000) [6.56]	13,333.4 (0.000) [7.56]	19,256.0 (0.000) [4.11]	−8054.8 (0.692) [-0.40]
Kernel Matching (0.1)	13,363.1 (0.000) [5.33]	4630.5 (0.000) [6.12]	12,947.4 (0.000) [7.30]	18,496.9 (0.000) [4.92]	−7936.6 (0.699) [−0.39]

Note ATT values are given with t-values in square brackets and *p*-values in round brackets
Source Author's calculation

no significant impact of crop insurance on farm income for large farmers. It can be seen that the magnitude of the ATT steadily declines from medium to small and then to marginal farmers in all matching algorithms except 1:1 nearest neighbour matching. Thus, this evidence supports our first theoretical proposition that insured farmers generally benefited from crop insurance in compared to uninsured farmers. However, the result is tenable across all farm sizes (except large farmers).

However, it is pertinent to ask whether a higher farm income of insured farmers is explained by the differences in productivity under different situations (crop success or failure). In the estimates of the ATT, as given in Table 7, two different situations are considered: crop success (yield is greater than or equal to the mean yield) and crop failure (yield is lower than the mean yield). In crop failure, the insured farmers were able to hedge a loss of Rs. 6807.8 by accessing crop insurance. Similarly, the ATT estimates are Rs. 1410.5, Rs. 6232.8 and Rs. 6419.4, respectively, for marginal, small and medium farmers. Similar findings are observed in situations of crop success. Estimated ATT values are Rs. 4385, Rs. 15,769, Rs. 28,364 for marginal, small, and medium farmers, respectively. It supports our second theoretical proposition that insurance is an effective risk-mitigating tool in crop failure. However, findings of the study validate the importance of insurance regardless of crop success or failure

Table 7 Results of PSM under crop success and failure

Farmer category	*Matching: Insured vs uninsured*			
	Crop success (Yield > Mean Yield)		*Crop failure (Yield ≤ Mean Yield)*	
	ATT	*t-value*	*ATT*	*t-value*
Overall	9912.4 (0.112)	1.59	6807.8 (0.001)	3.33
Marginal	4385.8 (0.010)	2.58	1410.5 (0.098)	1.66
Small	15,769.2 (0.000)	4.10	6232.8 (0.000)	3.66
Medium	28,364.6 (0.000)	3.52	6419.4 (0.074)	1.79
Large	60,309.1 (0.200)	1.29	6409.9 (0.668)	-0.43

Note ATT values are given with *p*-values in parentheses
Source Authors' calculation

for all farm sizes[10]. In particular, as firm size increases, the impact of crop insurance on farm income is observed, regardless of crop success or crop failure. This finding is in alignment with our earlier results that crop insurance access increases with land size (Table 5) and with those of the existing literature (Aditya et al., 2018; Akber et al., 2023; Mukhopadhyay et al., 2018).

5 Conclusions and Policy Implications

This paper presents a theoretical model on the relationship between farm size on insurance access. Propositions of such a model are tested in the light of evidence from a nationally representative survey in India. Initially, this investigation identifies the primary factors that influence insurance coverage of farmer households. The findings of logistic regression indicate that the factors that facilitate the access of crop insurance are age, formal agricultural training, participation in the employment guarantee scheme, possession of the Kisan Credit Card, size of land holding, and crop failure.

[10] However, there are no significant results for large farmers in the situation of crop failure or crop success.

Conversely, household size, backward caste, and poor dwelling conditions impede the acquisition of crop insurance. This study also evaluates the impact of crop insurance on farm income across farm sizes. Overall, it can be suggested that the availability of crop insurance impacts farm income: the magnitude of impact increases as firm size increases, from smallholders to medium farmers. However, the benefits of the crop insurance in addressing downward risk are evidenced. Thus, the findings of the study gather evidence in supporting the hypothesis drawn from the theoretical framework of the paper.

The evidence from the paper provides some policy suggestions as follows: Firstly, findings of the paper show that crop insurance is not widely utilised for crops harvested by marginal and small farmers, who are the most vulnerable among farming populations. Relying solely on credit-linked insurance mechanisms runs the risk of excluding farmers who cannot get formal credit. This emphasizes the necessity of separating insurance from credit and letting the farmers actively enrol, simplifying the enrolment process, and enhancing the outreach and claim settlement process. Improving access to financial services and making programs tailor-made to satisfy the needs of each region and type of farming. In addition, to make the insurance affordable for the smallholder's government should find mechanisms to facilitate co-financing of insurance between farmers and other private stakeholders like buyers and input dealers.[11] Secondly, survey evidence suggests that women and farmers classified as SC/ST are less likely to have access to crop insurance. The government should use social networks and associations to increase outreach to women farmers.[12] Similarly, initiatives must be taken to drive the outreach towards farmers belonging to the SC/ST caste. Thirdly, as evidence suggests that obtaining crop insurance is significantly influenced by formal agricultural training, a financial literacy training program on insurance awareness, showing the benefits and drawbacks of parametric

[11] In ACRE Africa, an agribusiness sponsor pays half of the premium price, and the farmer pays the remaining half.

[12] Basix provides a weather-based insurance product in drought-prone areas to the members of a women's self-help group.

insurance over traditional insurance, can motivate smallholders to participate in the crop insurance scheme. Finally, findings in this paper suggest that many of the farmers who suffered losses did not receive their claim, or they did not receive the claim on time. Data analytics can be employed to accurately predict loss. It can incentivize farmers by reducing their basis risk and the timely payment of indemnity payouts.

Appendix

See Figs. 4, 5, 6, 7, 8, 9 and 10.

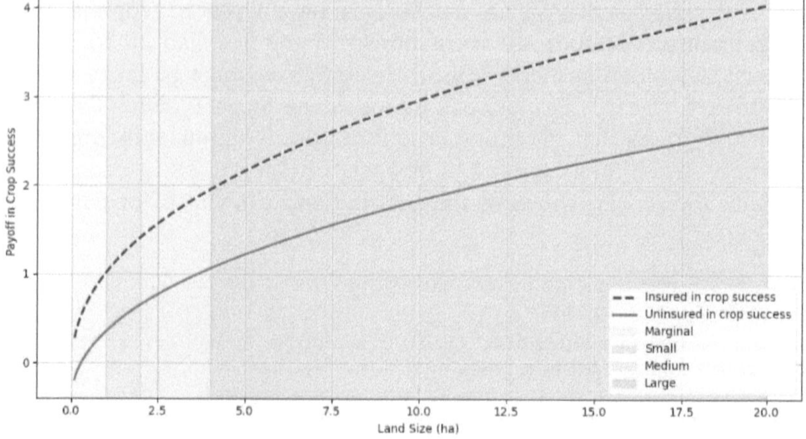

Fig. 4 Payoffs in crop success (*Note* Same as Fig. 1)

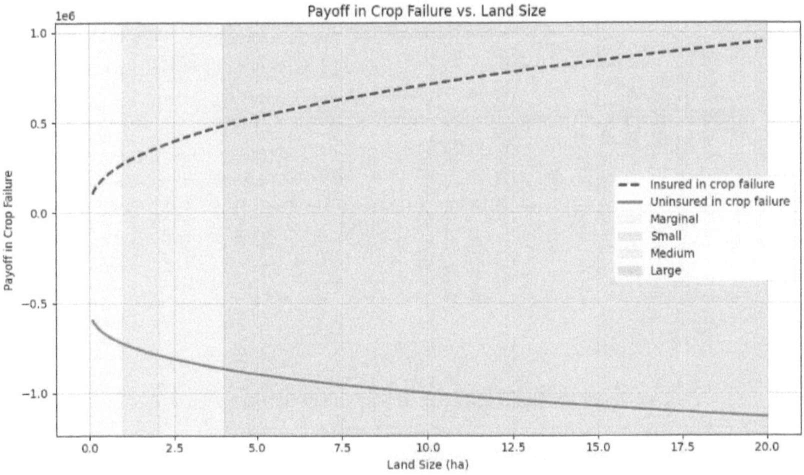

Fig. 5 Payoffs in crop failure (*Note* Same as Fig. 1)

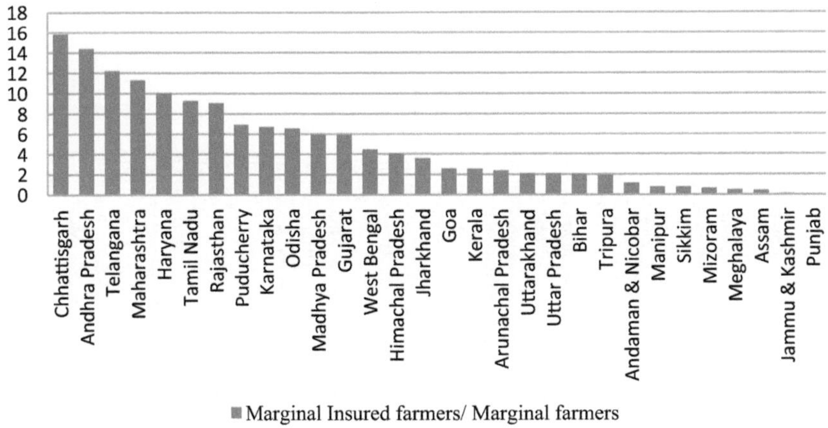

Fig. 6 Percentage of marginal farmers insured by state (*Source* Same as Table 3)

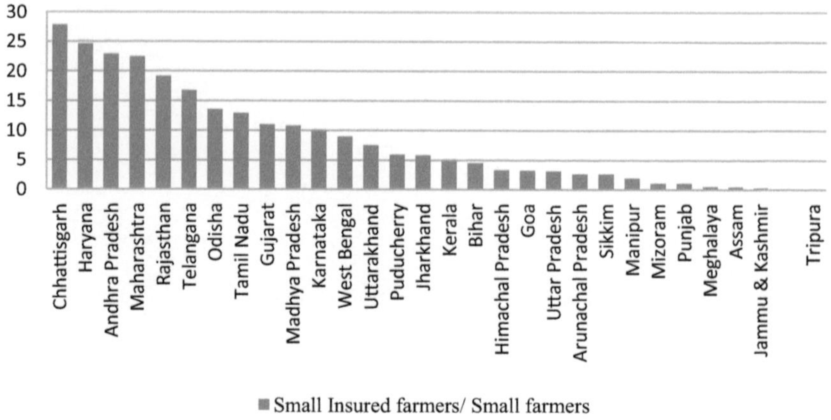

Fig. 7 Percentage of small farmers insured by the states (*Source* Same as Table 3)

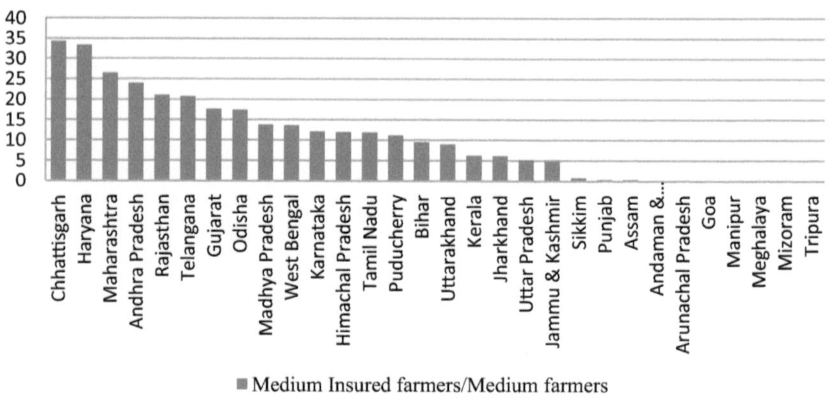

Fig. 8 Percentage of medium farmers insured by the states (*Source* Same as Table 3)

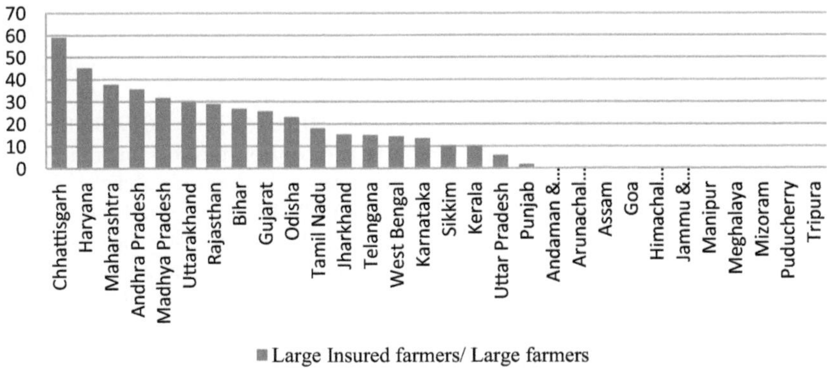

Fig. 9 Percentage of large farmers insured by the states (*Source* Same as Table 3)

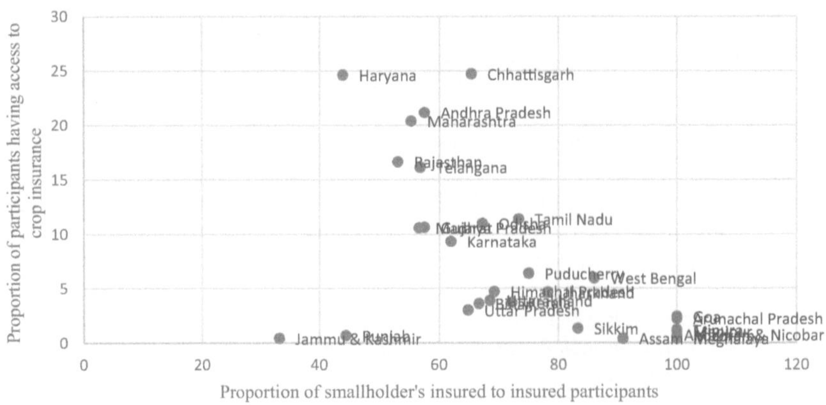

Fig. 10 Relationship between Insurance coverage and smallholders' coverage (*Source* Same as Table 3)

References

Abdul-Razak, M., and S. Kruse. 2017. The adaptive capacity of smallholder farmers to climate change in the Northern Region of Ghana. *Climate Risk Management* 17: 104–122. https://doi.org/10.1016/j.crm.2017.06.001.

Aditya, K. S., Khan, T., & Kishore, A. (2018). Adoption of crop insurance and impact: Insights from India. *Agricultural Economics Research Review*, *31*(2). https://doi.org/10.5958/0974-0279.2018.00034.4

Agbenyo, W., Jiang, Y., & Ntim-Amo, G. (2022). Impact of crop insurance on cocoa farmers' income: An empirical analysis from Ghana. *Environmental Science and Pollution Research*, *29*(41). https://doi.org/10.1007/s11356-022-20035-1

Akber, N., Paltasingh, K. R., & Mishra, A. K. (2023). Does crop insurance ensure food security for Indian farmers? Evidence from a nationally representative survey. *Agribusiness*. https://doi.org/10.1002/agr.21884

Alderman, H., & Haque, T. (2007). *Insurance against covariate shocks: The role of index-based insurance in social protection in low-income countries of Africa* (World Bank Working Paper No. 95). Africa Region Human Development Department, The World Bank, Washington, DC.

Ankrah, D. A., N. A. Kwapong, D. Eghan, F. Adarkwah, and D. Boateng-Gyambiby. 2021. Agricultural insurance access and acceptability: Examining the case of smallholder farmers in Ghana. *Agriculture & Food Security* 10 (1): 1–14.

Biswal, D., and C. S. Bahinipati. 2023. Crop-insurance adoption and impact on farm households' well-being in India: Evidence from a panel study. *Journal of the Asia Pacific Economy*. https://doi.org/10.1080/13547860.2023.2266204.

Bryson, A., Dorsett, R., & Purdon, S. (2002). *The use of propensity score matching in the evaluation of labour market policies* (Working Paper No. 4). Department for Work and Pensions.

Cariappa, A. G. A., D. P. Mahida, P. Lal, and B. S. Chandel. 2021. Correlates and impact of crop insurance in India: Evidence from a nationally representative survey. *Agricultural Finance Review* 81 (2): 204–221. https://doi.org/10.1108/AFR-03-2020-0034.

Carter, M., A. de Janvry, E. Sadoulet, and A. Sarris. 2017. Index insurance for developing country agriculture: A reassessment. *Annual Review of Resource Economics* 9 (1): 421–438. https://doi.org/10.1146/annurev-resource-100516-053352.

Carter, M. R., L. Cheng, and A. Sarris. 2016. Where and how index insurance can boost the adoption of improved agricultural technologies. *Journal of Development Economics* 118: 59–71. https://doi.org/10.1016/j.jdeveco.2015.08.008.

Cole, S., X. Giné, J. Tobacman, P. Topalova, R. Townsend, and J. Vickery. 2013. Barriers to household risk management: Evidence from India. *American Economic Journal: Applied Economics* 5 (1): 104–135. https://doi.org/10.1257/app.5.1.104.

Comptroller and Auditor General. (2017). *Performance audit on Union Government agriculture crop insurance schemes: Appendices* (Report No. 7 of 2017). Retrieved August 31, 2025, from https://cag.gov.in/uploads/download_audit_report/2017/Appendices%20of%20Report%20No.7%20of%202017%20-%20Performance%20audit%20Union%20Government%20Agriculture%20Crop%20Insurance%20Schemes%20Reports%20of%20Agriculture.pdf

De Janvry, A., V. Dequiedt, and E. Sadoulet. 2014. The demand for insurance against common shocks. *Journal of Development Economics* 106: 227–238.

Dey, K., & Maitra, D. (2017). Agriculture insurance in India: Promise, pitfalls, and the way forward. *Economic and Political Weekly, 52*(52), 88–96. Retrieved from https://www.epw.in/journal/2017/52/review-rural-affairs/agriculture-insurance-india.html

Duchoslav, J., & Van Asseldonk, M. (2018). Adoption and impact of credit-linked crop index insurance: A case study in Mali. *Studies in Agricultural Economics, 120*(2). https://doi.org/10.7896/j.1813

Farrin, K., and M. J. Miranda. 2015. A heterogeneous agent model of credit-linked index insurance and farm technology adoption. *Journal of Development Economics* 116: 199–211. https://doi.org/10.1016/j.jdeveco.2015.05.001.

Gallenstein, R. A., J. E. Flatnes, J. P. Dougherty, A. G. Sam, and K. Mishra. 2021. The impact of index-insured loans on credit market participation and risk-taking. *Agricultural Economics* 52 (1): 141–156. https://doi.org/10.1111/agec.12611.

Giné, X., R. Townsend, and J. Vickery. 2008. Patterns of rainfall insurance participation in rural India. *The World Bank Economic Review* 22 (3): 539–566. https://doi.org/10.1093/wber/lhn015.

Giné, X., and D. Yang. 2009. Insurance, credit, and technology adoption: Field experimental evidence from Malawi. *Journal of Development Economics* 89 (1): 1–11. https://doi.org/10.1016/j.jdeveco.2008.09.007.

Gujarati, D. 2011. Econometrics by example D. In *Social indicators research*, vol. 103, 2nd ed., ed. Gujrati. Bloomsbury India.

Hazell, P., Jaeger, A., & Hausberger, R. (2021). Innovations and emerging trends in agricultural insurance for smallholder farmers—An update. In *Deutsche Gesellschaft für Internationale Zusammenarbeit (GIZ)*. Bonn and Eschborn, Germany. Retrieve from https://www.giz.de/expertise/downloads/2021%20GIZ_Innovations%20and%20emerging%20Trends%20in%20Agricultural%20Insurance-An%20update.pdf

Harris, C. R., Millman, K. J., van der Walt, S. J., Gommers, R., Virtanen, P., Cournapeau, D., ... & Oliphant, T. E. (2020). Array programming with

NumPy. *Nature, 585*(7825), 357–362. https://doi.org/10.1038/s41586-020-2649-2

Hess, U., Hazell, P., & Kuhn, S. (2016). Innovations and emerging trends in agricultural insurance. In *Deutsche Gesellschaft für Internationale Zusammenarbeit (GIZ)*. Bonn and Eschborn, Germany. Retrieved from https://www.researchgate.net/profile/Peter-Hazell/publication/283089244_Innovations_and_emerging_Trends_in_Agricultural_Insurance/links/567ebcdd08ae051f9ae657d2/Innovations-and-emerging-Trends-in-Agricultural-Insurance.pdf

Jensen, N., and C. Barrett. 2017. Agricultural index insurance for development. *Applied Economic Perspectives and Policy* 39 (2): 199–219. https://doi.org/10.1093/aepp/ppw022.

Kakvi, K., & Sharma, P. (2022, August 4). Private companies earned double profits than govt. Firms in Union Crop Insurance Scheme. *NewsClick*. Retrieved from https://www.newsclick.in/Private-Companies-Earned-Double-Profits-Than-Govt-Firms-Union-Crop-Insurance-Scheme

Kaur, S., H. Raj, H. Singh, and V. K. Chattu. 2021. Crop insurance policies in India: An empirical analysis of Pradhan Mantri Fasal Bima Yojana. *Risks* 9 (11): 191. https://doi.org/10.3390/risks9110191.

Khandker, S., B. Koolwal, G., & Samad, H. (2009). Handbook on impact evaluation. In *Handbook on impact evaluation*. https://doi.org/10.1596/978-0-8213-8028-4

Leuven, E., & Sianesi, B. (2003, April). *PSMATCH2: Stata module to perform full Mahalanobis and propensity score matching, common support graphing, and covariate imbalance testing*. Retrieved from https://ideas.repec.org/c/boc/bocode/s432001.html

Mahul, O., and C. J. Stutley. 2010. *Government support to agricultural insurance: Challenges and options for developing countries*, 12. Washington, DC: The World Bank.

Mahul, O., Verma, N., & Clarke, D. (2012). *Improving farmers' access to agricultural insurance in India* (World Bank policy research working paper). Retrieved from https://documents.worldbank.org/en/publication/documents-reports/documentdetail/207211468259772817/improving-farmers-access-to-agricultural-insurance-in-india

Hunter, J. D. 2007. Matplotlib: A 2D graphics environment. *Computing in Science & Engineering* 9 (3): 90–95. https://doi.org/10.1109/MCSE.2007.55.

Lan, D. H., Truong, D. D., Lan, B. T. H. & Huan, L. H. (2024). Determinants of crop insurance participation of farming households in Mekong River Delta, Vietnam in climate change context. *Environmental Research Communications, 6*(10). https://doi.org/10.1088/2515-7620/ad82b1

Meyer, R., Hazell, P., & Varangis, P. (2018). *Unlocking smallholder credit: Does credit-linked agricultural insurance work?* (Microinsurance Paper #:

50). Geneva: International Labour Organization, International Finance Corporation. Retrieved from International Labour Organization, International Finance Corporation website: http://www.impactinsurance.org/publications/mp50

Mishra, K., R. A. Gallenstein, M. J. Miranda, A. G. Sam, P. Toledo, and F. Mulangu. 2021. Insured loans and credit access: Evidence from a randomized field experiment in Northern Ghana. *American Journal of Agricultural Economics* 103 (3): 923–943. https://doi.org/10.1111/ajae.12136.

Moore, D., Niazi, Z., Rouse, R., & Kramer, B. (2019). *Building resilience through financial inclusion. A review of existing evidence and knowledge gaps.* Innovations for Poverty Action.

Mukhopadhyay, P., Sinha, M., & Sen, P. P. (2018). Determinants of farmers' decision-making to accept crop insurance: A multinomial logit model approach. In J. Nayak, A. Abraham, B. Murali Krishna, G. T. Chandra Sekhar & A. K. Das (Eds.), *Soft Computing in Data Analytics Proceedings of International Conference on SCDA 2018* (AISC Vol. 758, pp. 267–275). Springer. https://doi.org/10.1007/978-981-13-0514-6_27

Müller, B., L. Johnson, and D. Kreuer. 2017. Maladaptive outcomes of climate insurance in agriculture. *Global Environmental Change* 46: 23–33. https://doi.org/10.1016/j.gloenvcha.2017.06.010.

Nair, R. (2010). Crop insurance in India: Changes and challenges. *Economic and Political Weekly*, 19–22.

National Sample Survey Organization. (2021). *Land and livestock holding of households and situation assessment of agricultural households.* Ministry of Statistics and Programme Implementation, Government of India. Retrieved from https://microdata.gov.in/nada43/index.php/catalog/157/get_microdata

Panda, A., Lambert, P. & Surminski, S. (2020). *Insurance and financial services across developing countries:an empirical study of coverage and demand* (Working Paper No.367). Centre for Climate Change economics and Policy. Retrieved from https://www.lse.ac.uk/granthaminstitute/publication/insurance-and-financial-services-across-developing-countries-an-empirical-study-of-coverage-and-demand/

PIB Delhi. (2020, March 13). *Implementation of PMFBY in states.* Retrieved May 20, 2025, from https://www.pib.gov.in/Pressreleaseshare.aspx?PRID=1606302

PIB Delhi. (2022a, February 18). *Pradhan Mantri Fasal Bima Yojana (PMFBY) enters its 7th year of implementation.* Retrieved May 20, 2025, from https://www.pib.gov.in/Pressreleaseshare.aspx?PRID=1799297

PIB Delhi. (2022b, April 26). *'Fasal Bima Pathshala' to be organized across the country under 'Kisan Bhagidari Prathmikta Hamari' campaign.* Retrieved

May 20, 2025, from https://www.pib.gov.in/Pressreleaseshare.aspx?PRID=1820233

PIB Delhi. (2022c, May 12). *Ministry of agriculture and farmers welfare signs MoU with UNDP for strategic partnership on Agriculture, crop insurance and credit*. Retrieved May 20, 2025, from https://www.pib.gov.in/Pressreleaseshare.aspx?PRID=1824812

PIB Delhi. (2023a, March 23). *Union Agriculture Minister Shri Tomar launches DigiClaim for claim disbursal through National Crop Insurance Portal (NCIP)*. Retrieved May 20, 2025, from https://www.pib.gov.in/Pressreleaseshare.aspx?PRID=1909895

PIB Delhi. (2023b, July 21). *Centre launches technological advancements in crop insurance to empowering farmers and streamlining operations in PMFBY*. Retrieved May 20, 2025, from https://www.pib.gov.in/Pressreleaseshare.aspx?PRID=1941597

PIB Delhi. (2024, February 15). *Empowering Annadatas: Pradhan Mantri Fasal Bima Yojana*. Retrieved May 20, 2025, from https://pib.gov.in/FactsheetDetails.aspx?Id=149055&reg=3&lang=1

PIB Delhi. (2025, February 17). *Pradhan Mantri Fasal Bima Yojana turns Nine*. Retrieved May 20, 2025, from https://www.pib.gov.in/Pressreleaseshare.aspx?PRID=2104175

Raithatha, R., & Priebe, J. (2020). *Agricultural insurance for smallholder farmers: Digital innovations for scale*. GSMA AgriTech Programme.

Rajeev, M., & Nagendran, P. (2019). Crop insurance in India: Where do we stand? *Economic and Political Weekly*, *54*(26–27), 28–35. Retrieved from https://www.epw.in/journal/2019/26-27/review-rural-affairs/crop-insurance-india.html

Ranganathan, T., Mishra, K. A., & Kumar, A. (2019). Crop insurance and food security: Evidence from rice farmers in Eastern India. In *Annual Meeting of the Allied Social Sciences Association*. Allied Social Sciences Association. Retrieved from https://www.aeaweb.org/conference/2019/preliminary/paper/4N7iDEbk#:~:text=For%20instance%2C%20the%20rice%20yield,at%20the%201%25%20confidence%20level

Rosenbaum, P. R. (2002). *Observational studies* (2nd ed.). Springer New York. https://doi.org/10.1007/978-1-4757-3692-2

Shagun. (2021, November 30). Crop insurance claims over Rs 3,300 crore pending due to payment failure, delay in state subsidy. *Down To Earth*. Retrieved from https://www.downtoearth.org.in/news/agriculture/crop-insurance-claims-over-rs-3-300-crore-pending-due-to-payment-failure-delay-in-state-subsidy-80459#:~:text=Published%3A%20Tuesday%2030%20November%202021&text=Over%20Rs%203%2C300%20crore%20is,and%20delay%20in%20state%20subsidy

Shee, A., & Turvey, C. G. (2012). Collateral-free lending with risk-contingent credit for agricultural development: Indemnifying loans against pulse crop price risk in India. *Agricultural Economics (United Kingdom)*, *43*(5). https://doi.org/10.1111/j.1574-0862.2012.00603.x

Tadesse, M. A. 2014. Fertilizer adoption, credit access, and safety nets in rural Ethiopia. *Agricultural Finance Review* 74 (3): 290–310.

Vyas, V. S., & Singh, S. (2006). Crop insurance in India: Scope for improvement. *Economic and Political Weekly*, 4585–4594.

Yu, J. (2015). Estimating distributional impacts of federal crop insurance program. *Annual Meeting*. San Francisco, CA: Agricultural & Applied Economics Association and Western Agricultural Economics Association. Retrieve from https://ageconsearch.umn.edu/record/206272?v=pdf

CHAPTER 11

Role of Microfinance in Financial Inclusion and Economic Development in the Backward Regions of West Bengal: Theories and Empirics

Nilendu Chatterjee and *Dipak Kundu*

1 Introduction

Financial inclusion has become a global policy priority due to its profound implications for inclusive growth, poverty alleviation, and sustainable development.[1] It refers to the access and use of affordable and appropriate financial services by all segments of society, particularly the poor and marginalized. Financially included individuals are more likely to save,

[1] The micro credit summit of 2010 reported that over 3550 microfinancing institutions were operating and serving over 533 million people having 155 million borrowers (Buera et al., 2021).

N. Chatterjee (✉) · D. Kundu
Department of Economics, Bankim Sardar College, South 24 Parganas, India
e-mail: nilubsc87@gmail.com

D. Kundu
Department of Commerce, Bankim Sardar College, South 24 Parganas, India

© The Author(s), under exclusive license to Springer Nature Singapore Pte Ltd. 2026

V. Dixit et al. (eds.), *Financial Inclusion for Viksit Bharat*,
https://doi.org/10.1007/978-981-92-0807-4_11

invest in education and health, and protect themselves from economic shocks, thereby contributing to both individual well-being and macroeconomic stability. Yet despite significant global efforts, financial exclusion remains a critical challenge, disproportionately affecting developing economies and marginalized groups. According to World Bank estimates, approximately 1.4 billion adults worldwide remained unbanked as of 2022 (World Bank, 2022), highlighting the enduring gaps in financial access even amid the expansion of digital financial infrastructure.

The persistence of financial exclusion reflects a combination of structural, institutional, and behavioural factors. These include inadequate physical infrastructure, lack of formal documentation, low levels of financial literacy, social norms that restrict women's economic participation, and a general mistrust of formal financial institutions among certain segments of the population. Traditional banking systems, driven by profit motives, often find it unviable to serve remote or low-income customers due to high transaction costs and low returns. This situation is particularly acute in rural and semi-urban regions, where the population density is low, and the economic activity is primarily informal.

In response to these challenges, microfinance has emerged as a crucial tool for expanding financial access and promoting inclusive economic participation. Microfinance refers to the provision of a broad range of financial services—including microcredit, micro savings, micro insurance, and financial education—to individuals and microenterprises that are typically excluded from the formal banking sector. It is premised on the belief that access to small amounts of credit and savings can enable low-income individuals to initiate or expand income-generating activities, thereby improving their economic status and contributing to community-level development. Unlike traditional finance, which relies heavily on collateral, microfinance often utilizes group lending mechanisms, social guarantees, and community-based delivery systems to reduce risks and enhance outreach.

Pioneered by institutions such as the Grameen Bank in Bangladesh (Yunus, 1999, 2003), the microfinance model has demonstrated remarkable potential in empowering the poor, particularly women, by offering tailored financial products and fostering collective accountability. Scholars such as Armendáriz and Morduch (2010) emphasize that microfinance institutions (MFIs) not only provide financial access but also play a developmental role by embedding services within social and community structures. Numerous studies, including those by Banerjee et al.

(2015) and Collins et al. (2010), have shown that access to microfinance can lead to increased investment in education and health, improved income stability, and enhanced decision-making autonomy among women, though impacts vary by context and delivery model. Mobile Financial Services—Technology-driven services, like Kenya's M-Pesa, enhance accessibility and reduce costs (GSMA, 2020).

In addition to direct economic benefits, microfinance is recognized for its broader social and institutional impacts. It can foster financial literacy, social cohesion, and a sense of agency among marginalized populations. In many contexts, MFIs serve as platforms for delivering not only financial services but also non-financial interventions such as skills training, health awareness, and legal counselling. These multifaceted roles underscore the transformative potential of microfinance as both a financial and developmental tool (World Bank 2018a, 2018b).

Within this global context, India presents a compelling case for examining the role of microfinance in addressing financial exclusion. With a population exceeding 1.46 billion, India is the world's most populous nation and home to vast socio-economic disparities. While the formal banking sector has expanded considerably over the past two decades, significant regional and demographic gaps in financial access persist. As of 2020, approximately 19% of Indian adults remained unbanked (World Bank, 2020). The burden of exclusion is not evenly distributed: it is disproportionately borne by rural residents, women, Scheduled Castes and Tribes, and residents of ecologically vulnerable areas such as the Indian Sundarbans.

Recognizing the developmental imperative of financial inclusion, the Government of India and the Reserve Bank of India (RBI) have introduced several landmark initiatives.[2] The Pradhan Mantri Jan-Dhan Yojana (PMJDY), launched in 2014, aimed to provide every household with at least one bank account, and facilitated the opening of more than 400 million accounts, many of which belonged to first-time users of formal financial services. This initiative was complemented by the promotion of Aadhaar-enabled Direct Benefit Transfers (DBT), digital payments infrastructure (such as UPI), and financial literacy campaigns. These efforts have expanded the formal financial ecosystem and reduced the physical and procedural barriers to access.

[2] NABARD and several other banks have played crucial role in this regard.

However, large segments of the population continue to experience de facto exclusion, either because they do not actively use their accounts or because available services are inadequate to meet their specific needs. Many rural poor still rely on informal moneylenders, who charge exorbitant interest rates and exploit borrower vulnerability. Moreover, formal financial institutions often fail to design products suited to the income volatility, seasonal needs, and credit cycles of low-income households. In this landscape, microfinance emerges as a critical complement to state-led inclusion efforts by offering tailored, localized, and relationship-based financial services.

India's microfinance sector is one of the largest in the world, comprising a range of providers including Non-Banking Financial Companies-Microfinance Institutions (NBFC-MFIs), commercial banks, cooperative societies, and Self-Help Groups (SHGs). Among these, the Self-Help Group–Bank Linkage Programme (SHG-BLP) initiated by the National Bank for Agriculture and Rural Development (NABARD) stands out for its scale and impact. As of 2024, the SHG-BLP covered more than 178 million members across 14.4 million SHGs, with a cumulative credit linkage exceeding ₹2.59 lakh crore (NABARD, 2024). This model, built on principles of group solidarity, mutual guarantee, and financial discipline, has empowered millions of women to participate in economic activities, increase household savings, and gain a voice in community decision-making.

The gendered impact of microfinance is particularly significant. Research consistently shows that women borrowers are more likely to invest in their families' education, health, and nutrition, creating intergenerational benefits and contributing to broader development goals (Chatterjee & Kundu, 2025; Honohan, 2008). In many cases, participation in SHGs and MFIs has led to greater mobility, self-confidence, and social recognition for women who were previously confined to domestic roles. Microfinance thus contributes not only to financial inclusion but also to social transformation and gender equity.

Nevertheless, the microfinance sector in India faces several challenges. The 2010 Andhra Pradesh microfinance crisis highlighted issues related to over-lending, coercive recovery practices, and inadequate regulation, leading to widespread borrower distress and erosion of trust in MFIs. More recently, the COVID-19 pandemic disrupted loan repayment cycles, weakened borrower capacity, and intensified financial vulnerability among already stressed populations. These developments underscore the need for robust regulatory frameworks, responsible lending practices, and greater alignment between financial sustainability and social impact.

In addition, scholars have pointed out that the impacts of microfinance are highly context-specific and often mediated by factors such as borrower characteristics, institutional design, and local socio-economic conditions. While some studies report strong positive outcomes, others suggest modest or even adverse effects, especially when microfinance is poorly regulated or disconnected from complementary support services. This heterogeneity underscores the importance of examining microfinance through a contextual lens, grounded in empirical realities and informed by localized data.

Despite a growing body of literature on microfinance and financial inclusion in India, important gaps remain. Much of the existing research focuses on either micro-level outcomes (such as individual empowerment or household income) or macroeconomic indicators (such as credit penetration and GDP growth), without adequately linking the two. Moreover, there is limited empirical work on ecologically fragile and socioeconomically vulnerable regions, such as the Indian Sundarbans, where financial exclusion is both a cause and a consequence of broader developmental deficits.

The Indian Sundarbans, located in the southern part of West Bengal, is a unique and under-researched region that faces compounded challenges of poverty, geographic isolation, and environmental vulnerability. Characterized by frequent natural disasters, salinity intrusion, and lack of infrastructure, the region suffers from chronic underdevelopment and limited access to formal financial services. In such a context, financial inclusion is not merely an economic issue but a critical component of adaptive capacity, resilience building, and sustainable development.

This chapter seeks to address these research gaps by providing a comprehensive analysis of the role of microfinance in advancing financial inclusion and socio-economic development in the Indian Sundarbans. The study adopts a dual methodological approach, combining theoretical modelling with empirical analysis. First, it develops a microeconomic model to conceptualize the pathways through which microfinance influences financial access, income generation, and community resilience. Second, it employs primary data collected through field surveys in the Sundarbans region and applies probit and tobit econometric models to assess the effects of microfinance participation on a range of socio-economic indicators.

By integrating theoretical insights with ground-level evidence, this study offers a nuanced understanding of the mechanisms through which microfinance can contribute to inclusive development in socially vulnerable regions which are financially backward as well. It highlights not only the enabling conditions for effective microfinance but also the limitations and trade-offs that must be addressed through policy and institutional innovation. The findings aim to inform the design of more context-sensitive financial inclusion strategies that are capable of achieving both economic and social transformation.

The present study draws its motivation from the fact that even if there are several studies on microfinance and financial inclusion, there is lack of study that depicts its impact both at the microeconomic level along with ground-level reality to check the efficacy of the programme. Again, studies of microfinance on Indian Sundarbans are almost missing. Indian Sundarbans hold an important position as an area where Financial Inclusion needs rapid progress, lack of studies on these areas need special attention. This paper looks to fill up that lacuna as well. In doing so, this research contributes to the broader academic and policy discourse on inclusive finance by foregrounding the experiences of a region often overlooked in national and international studies. It provides evidence-based recommendations for practitioners, policymakers, and researchers seeking to leverage microfinance as a tool for equitable and sustainable development in India and beyond.

The Chapter is constructed as follows. Section 2 contains a brief review of the existing literature related to this study followed by the microeconomic model in Sect. 3. The primary survey based analysis reflecting the effects of microfinance in Indian Sundarbans, containing both probit and tobit analysis, is carried out in Sect. 4. Finally, the conclusions along with the policy recommendations are mentioned in Sect. 5.

2 A Brief Review of Existing Literature

In this section, we shall review a few important pieces of literature on microfinance and financial inclusion, and explore their products, challenges, and outcomes, supported by case studies and current research.

The history of microfinance can be traced back to the Grameen Bank, founded by Muhammad Yunus in Bangladesh in 1983 (Yunus, 2007). The success of the Grameen Bank in providing small loans to the poor, particularly women, demonstrated the potential of microfinance to empower marginalized communities. Since then, microfinance has expanded globally, with various models and approaches tailored to different contexts. The concept of financial inclusion is rooted in the broader discourse of economic development and poverty alleviation. According to Banerjee and Duflo (2011), financial inclusion is essential for reducing poverty and inequality by providing the poor with the tools to manage their finances, invest in their businesses, and build assets. Numerous empirical studies have examined the impact of microfinance on financial inclusion and economic outcomes in developing areas. For instance, Karlan and Zinman (2010) conducted a randomized controlled trial in the Philippines and found that access to microcredit led to increased business investment and higher household income. Similarly, Crépon et al. (2015) studied the effects of microcredit in Morocco and reported positive impacts on business creation and employment.

However, the literature also highlights some limitations and challenges. For example, Banerjee et al. (2015) conducted a meta-analysis of several microfinance interventions and found mixed results, with some studies showing no significant impact on poverty reduction. The authors suggest that the effectiveness of microfinance depends on various factors, including the design of the financial products, the socio-economic context, and the implementation of the programmes.

The mechanisms through which microfinance contributes to financial inclusion can be categorized into three main areas: access to credit, savings, and insurance. Microloans provide low-income individuals with the capital needed to start or expand small businesses. According to Armendáriz and Morduch (2010), access to credit can lead to increased business investment, higher income, and improved living standards. However, the impact of microcredit on business success varies, and some studies have found that the returns on microloans are often low (Roodman, 2012). Savings accounts offered by MFIs enable individuals to save money and build financial resilience. According to Dupas and Robinson (2013), access to savings accounts can help households' smooth consumption, manage financial shocks, and invest in education and health. However, the uptake of savings services is often lower compared to credit services, and there is a need for innovative savings products to meet the diverse needs of low-income clients. Micro-insurance products, such as health and crop insurance, protect individuals from financial risks and promote financial stability. According to Churchill (2006), micro-insurance can reduce the vulnerability of low-income households to health and agricultural shocks, thereby enhancing their financial security. However, the uptake of micro-insurance is often limited by low awareness and high premiums, and there is a need for more affordable and accessible insurance products (Kundu & Chatterjee, 2025).

Microfinance has positive economic and social impacts, including increased income, savings, and entrepreneurship. It empowers women and enhances financial literacy (Biswas, 2018). However, some studies question its long-term poverty reduction impact, suggesting it works best alongside education and training (Banerjee et al., 2015). Several studies have highlighted the success stories of microfinance in different economies. Grameen Bank in Bangladesh exemplifies microfinance's impact, empowering millions through microcredit (Yunus, 1999). M-Pesa in Kenya highlights the success of mobile financial services in enhancing financial inclusion (GSMA, 2020). Innovations in microfinance have boosted entrepreneurship and economic stability (Inter-American Development Bank, 2018).

The last decade has witnessed a surge of scholarly interest in how micro-finance (MF) can catalyse financial inclusion and broad-based economic development in regions that lag behind national averages in income, education and infrastructure. The literature blends classic development-theoretic insights with high-frequency panel data, experimental designs and digital-finance innovations. In the last five years (2021–2025) existing evidences can be categorised in two major strands—the theoretical foundations that explain why MF should matter for inclusion and growth, and the empirical investigations that test these mechanisms in specific backward contexts across Asia, Africa and Latin America. The theory based papers are described below in Table 1.

Collectively, these theories provide a conceptual scaffold: MF reduces information and transaction costs, alleviates credit constraints, leverages social capital, and, increasingly, exploits digital channels to reach the most isolated households. The following sections examine how these mechanisms have been validated (or contested) in recent empirical work.

If we look at evidence based analysis from Backward Regions, in the last five years, we can see that for India Kumar and Bansal (2023) analyse a balanced panel of 1024 villages in eight Indian "backward districts". Using a difference-in-differences (DiD) design around the 2021 rollout of the Pradhan Mantri Jan Dhan-Yojana-linked MF scheme,

Table 1 Theoretical foundations

Theoretical Lens	*Core Propositions*	*Relevance to MF-Inclusion-Growth Nexus*	*Key Recent Contributions (2021–2025)*
Financial Intermediation Theory (Stiglitz & Weiss, 1981)	Intermediaries reduce transaction costs, mitigate information asymmetries, and mobilise savings	MF institutions act as low-cost intermediaries for the unbanked, improving access to credit and savings	Bharat and Mishra (2022) formalise a two-sided market model showing how MF lowers borrowers' marginal cost of capital in Indian backward districts
Poverty Trap & Credit Constraints (Banerjee & Duflo, 2007)	Lack of collateral and credit leads to a self-reinforcing poverty trap; small loans can enable productive investment	MF provides collateral-free credit, potentially breaking the trap	Khandker and Samad (2022) use a dynamic panel to demonstrate that MF participation lowers the probability of remaining in the poverty trap for Bangladeshi rural households
Inclusive Growth Theory (Todaro & Smith, 2015)	Growth that is both broad-based and equitable requires inclusive financial services	MF expands the financial frontier, allowing marginalised groups to partake in value-adding activities	Méndez et al. (2023) integrate MF variables into a growth accounting framework for Peru's Amazonian provinces, finding a 0.31% contribution to regional GDP per annum
Social Capital Theory (Putnam, 2000)	Networks of trust and reciprocity facilitate collective action and reduce transaction costs	Group-lending models of MF harness social capital to enforce repayment	Osei-Mensah and Agyeman (2021) empirically link higher group cohesion scores to lower default rates in Ghana's Upper West Region

(continued)

Table 1 (continued)

Theoretical Lens	*Core Propositions*	*Relevance to MF-Inclusion-Growth Nexus*	*Key Recent Contributions (2021–2025)*
Institutional Theory (North, 1990)	Formal and informal institutions shape economic incentives; weak institutions hinder market participation	MF can substitute for weak formal institutions by providing governance mechanisms (e.g., regular meetings, peer monitoring)	Silva and Pérez (2024) argue that MF acts as a "proto-institution" in Brazil's semi-arid Sertão, improving contract enforcement
Digital-Finance Diffusion Theory (Rogers, 2003)	Adoption of new technologies follows a diffusion curve driven by relative advantage, compatibility, and complexity	Mobile-based MF platforms lower physical access barriers in remote areas	Al-Mansoori et al. (2023) apply diffusion modeling to show that mobile-money-linked MF spreads faster in Yemen's tribal hinterlands when combined with financial literacy interventions

they find a 12% increase in household savings and a 6% rise in per-capita income relative to control districts. Chakraborty et al. (2024) focus on women-only MF groups in Bihar's Kosi region. Propensity-score matching demonstrates that MF participation raises women's decision-making power (index +0.27) and entrepreneurial entry (new micro-enterprises +15%). For Bangladesh, Khandker and Samad (2022) employ a dynamic panel (1998–2022) to isolate the effect of MF on poverty transition dynamics. Their results indicate a 28% reduction in the probability of remaining poor after three years of continuous MF borrowing. Rahman and Hossain (2025) use a randomized controlled trial (RCT) of a digital MF platform (bKash-MF). The treatment group experiences a 45% increase in formal savings accounts and higher agricultural productivity (+8%). For Sub-Saharan Africa, Morduch and Santos (2021) assess a mobile-money MF pilot targeting 3 500 IDP households. Instrumental variable estimates reveal a 9% rise in household consumption and a 4% drop in food insecurity. Osei-Mensah and Agyeman (2021) (cited earlier) show the importance of group cohesion: villages with higher cohesion have default rates 2.3 pp lower, confirming the social-capital channel. For Kenya, Kipkeme et al. (2022) combine satellite night-light data with MF loan registers to test spatial spillovers. They document positive externalities: a 10% increase in MF density in a village raises the neighbour's per-capita income by 1.2%. Al-Mansoori et al. (2023) (digital diffusion study) find that mobile-phone penetration is a necessary (but not sufficient) condition for MF adoption; the diffusion coefficient is 0.41 ($p < 0.01$). For Peru, Méndez et al. (2023) embed MF variables in a stochastic growth model for 48 high-altitude districts. The MF intensity index contributes 0.31% points to annual regional GDP growth, largely via small-holder agricultural investment. For Brazil, Silva and Pérez (2024) use a quasi-experimental design around the 2022 expansion of a state-run MF program. They find higher contract compliance (default decrease 1.8 pp) and a significant rise in school enrolment among borrowers' children (+4%). For Cross-Country Syntheses, World Bank & CGAP (2022) compile a meta-analysis of 57 RCTs and quasi-experiments across 22 low-income countries. Their pooled estimate suggests that MF increases per-capita consumption by 4.1% (95% CI: 2.8–5.4%) and formal savings by 12% in the most disadvantaged regions. Baviskar et al. (2024) employ a hierarchical Bayesian meta-regression to uncover heterogeneity: effect sizes are largest when MF is combined with financial literacy (Δ consumption +6.3%) and digital delivery (Δ savings +15%).

Recent Empirics have followed the following mechanisms- as given in the following Table 2.

The convergence across regions suggests a robust causal pathway: MF → Financial Inclusion (credit, savings, insurance) → Productive Investment & Human-Capital Allocation → Economic Development. However, the magnitude of impacts varies with institutional quality, digital infrastructure, and complementary services (e.g., financial literacy).

Despite its potential, microfinance faces several challenges and criticisms. Several studies have focused on those aspects also. One of the main concerns is the issue of over-indebtedness, where borrowers may take on multiple loans and struggle to repay them (Rhyne, 2008). This can lead to financial distress and undermine the positive impacts of microfinance. Additionally, there are concerns about the high interest rates charged by some MFIs, which can be predatory and exploitative (Hulme & Mosley, 1996).

Table 2 Mechanisms confirmed by recent empirics

Mechanism	*Empirical Confirmation (2021–2025)*	*Representative Study*
Credit for productive assets	MF loans are increasingly used for agricultural inputs, livestock, and small machinery rather than consumption smoothing alone	Khandker and Samad (2022)—Bangladesh; Méndez et al. (2023)—Peru
Savings mobilisation	MF members open formal savings accounts at significantly higher rates; digital MF boosts this further	Rahman and Hossain (2025)—Bangladesh; World Bank and CGAP (2022)
Women's empowerment	Female participation raises intra-household bargaining power and school enrolment for girls	Chakraborty et al. (2024) —India; Silva and Pérez (2024)—Brazil
Social-capital enforcement	Group-lending reduces default; cohesion indices are predictive of repayment success	Osei-Mensah and Agyeman (2021)—Ghana
Digital diffusion	Mobile-money linked MF lowers transaction costs and expands geographic reach	Al-Mansoori et al. (2023) —Yemen; Morduch and Santos (2021)—Nigeria
Human-capital spillovers	MF borrowers allocate more to education and health, generating longer-run development gains	Silva and Pérez (2024) —Brazil; World Bank and CGAP (2022) meta-analysis
Local institutional reinforcement	MF can substitute for weak formal enforcement, improving contract compliance	Silva and Pérez (2024) —Brazil; Kumar and Bansal (2023)—India

Another challenge is the limited reach of microfinance services. While microfinance has expanded significantly, many low-income individuals, particularly in remote and rural areas, still lack access to financial services (Ledgerwood & Rosenberg, 2006). There is a need for more innovative and scalable models to reach these underserved populations. Studies on Indian Sundarbans, although very limited in numbers, reveal that people of the region suffer immensely from frequent natural disasters and micro-financing bodies help them in overcoming such challenges by means of diversifying livelihoods and finding strategies for developing resilience against the disasters (Chatterjee, 2019; Ray & Nath, 2024).

Previous researchers have identified socio-economic factors as key determinants of financial inclusion. However, there is a need for region-specific studies that extensively discuss the influential aspect of microfinance on financial inclusion in underdeveloped areas like Indian Sundarbans (Chatterjee, 2025). This paper looks to fill this gap by conducting a primary survey in three selected regions of Indian Sundarbans and by employing econometric techniques to analyse the relationship between microfinance and financial inclusion. Such studies are missing for backward regions of India and also for Indian Sundarbans.

Microfinance can have a deeper impact on the individuals at the micro level and on the economy, as a whole, at the macro level. The following section develops a theoretical models to show the effect of microfinance in the society at the micro level.

3 Microeconomic Impact of Microfinance—A Theoretical Perspective

While there is anecdotal evidence suggesting that microfinance membership can improve economic outcomes, there is a need for a rigorous microeconomic model to compare the earnings, savings, and wealth accumulation of microfinance members versus non-members. In this section, we shall develop a comparative microeconomic model between the two groups—one is the member of a microfinance group and the other one is not member of any microfinance group.

The microeconomic model contains the following set of assumptions.

i. **Households Are Rational and Aim to Maximize Utility or Wealth**

It is implicitly assumed that all households act rationally, aiming to optimize their economic outcomes through either labour or investment. Both member and non-member households are assumed to behave consistently over time and make decisions that lead to predictable savings and wealth accumulation patterns.

ii. **Fixed Savings Rate (σ)**

A uniform and constant savings rate (σ) is assumed for both member and non-member households, regardless of income level or access to credit. This ignores behavioral variations in savings habits based on risk preferences, life-cycle stages, or cultural factors.

iii. **Investment Returns Are Deterministic and Constant ($\rho > r$)**

The model assumes that the return on investment (ρ) and the interest rate on the loan (r) are both known, fixed, and exogenous. It also assumes that the inequality $\rho > r$ holds in the long term, ensuring profitability of borrowing. This excludes the risk of investment failure, income shocks, or volatility in market returns.

iv. **Zero Interest Rate on Savings**

The model assumes that household savings do not earn any interest—i.e., the market return on savings is zero. This simplifies the wealth accumulation path: savings grow only through periodic contributions, not through compound interest.

v. **No Credit Market Outside Microfinance Institutions (MFIs)**

The only source of credit in the economy is through MFIs. There is no traditional banking, informal lending, or government credit programs available. This isolates the effect of microfinance by removing the possibility of alternative credit access. It implies that non-members are entirely credit-constrained and depend only on labor income. This is a strong assumption, as in reality, many households in rural areas may access informal lenders, SHGs, or rotating credit associations.

vi. **Price Level is Constant and Normalized to 1**

All monetary values (earnings, savings, loan amounts) are in real terms, with the general price level set at $P = 1$, and assumed constant over time. This simplifies the model by removing inflationary effects and changes in the purchasing power of money. It implies a static price environment, which is unrealistic in most developing economies, where inflation affects savings, real wages, and borrowing costs.

vii. **Perfect Utilization of Loan Capital**

It is assumed that microfinance member households use the loan amount (L) entirely for productive investment, generating returns at the rate ρ. There is no misallocation, consumption use of the loan, or business failure, which are common in reality.

viii. **No Credit Constraints for Members**

The model assumes that eligible households receive loans without any restriction on loan amount (L). It ignores factors like credit rationing, eligibility filters, or group lending mechanisms that can affect the volume of credit accessed.

ix. **Full Loan Repayment Without Default**

Loan repayment is assumed to occur smoothly over time, as captured by the decreasing L(t) term. The model does not account for defaults, delinquency, penalties, or restructuring of loans, all of which are critical in real-world microfinance operations.

x. **No Transaction or Monitoring Costs**

The model ignores transaction costs of borrowing, monitoring costs for MFIs, or administrative costs related to loan disbursement and repayment. These could reduce effective returns for both lenders and borrowers.

xi. **Homogeneous Households Within Groups**

All households within the "member" or "non-member" categories are treated as homogeneous, implying similar preferences, skills, access to information, and economic opportunities. This overlooks intra-group heterogeneity which can affect investment outcomes and savings behaviour.

xii. **Linear and Additive Wealth Accumulation**

Wealth is modelled to accumulate linearly over time as a direct function of savings. The model does not account for diminishing returns to capital, asset depreciation (except loan repayment), or shocks that may affect the accumulation process.

In the microeconomic model, the assumption that loans carry a positive interest rate while savings earn no interest is not merely a simplification—it reflects key realities of financial behaviour and institutional limitations in underserved rural areas.

a. Lack of Formal Saving Instruments

In many rural regions, especially in financially backward areas like the Indian Sundarbans, households do not have regular access to formal banking services that offer interest-bearing savings accounts. While microfinance institutions (MFIs) provide loans, many do not provide savings facilities or do so under restrictive conditions. As a result, households often save informally—by holding cash at home, investing in livestock, jewelry, or other non-financial assets—none of which earn financial interest.

b. Asymmetric Services Offered by MFIs

Most MFIs are structured primarily as lending institutions, not deposit-taking entities. They are regulated differently from commercial banks and are often not permitted to accept public deposits. Thus, they charge interest on loans to cover operational costs and risks, but do not offer interest-bearing savings products to members. This structural asymmetry is accurately reflected in the model.

c. Risk-Free Nature of Savings vs. Risk-Adjusted Lending

From the household's perspective, informal savings are risk-free but illiquid and unproductive. In contrast, microfinance loans involve risk, both for the borrower and the MFI. To compensate for credit risk, administrative costs, and the lack of collateral, MFIs charge an interest rate r. Meanwhile, households do not earn interest on savings because -they are saving in cash or low-return assets, there is no institutional intermediary to offer them a positive rate of return, and in behavioral terms, small savers in poor areas often accept zero nominal return in exchange for liquidity and security.

d. Realistic Modelling of Financial Exclusion

By setting the interest on savings to zero, the model captures a crucial feature of financial exclusion: even when households have income and save, they cannot grow wealth through interest unless they access formal financial markets. This justifies why microfinance, despite charging interest on loans, can still lead to net positive outcomes—because it introduces capital that would otherwise be inaccessible, allowing households to earn profits beyond subsistence.

3.1 Microfinance Non-Member Household

For a non-member household, earnings are derived solely from labour income. Let's denote the earnings of a non-member household as Y_{NM}, which is a function of the wage rate W and the number of hours worked H.

The earning equation takes the following form

$$Y_{NM} = W \cdot H \tag{1}$$

Savings S_{NM} are a fraction of earnings, determined by the savings rate σ.

$$S_{NM} = \sigma \cdot Y_{NM} = \sigma \cdot W \cdot H \tag{2}$$

Wealth accumulation A_{NM} over time is the sum of savings over periods. Hence, it can be presented as

$$A_M(t) = \sum_{\tau=0}^{t} S_{NM}(\tau) \tag{3}$$

Assuming a constant wage rate and savings rate over time, wealth accumulation grows linearly.

$$A_{NM}(t) = \sigma \cdot W \cdot H \cdot t \tag{4}$$

This model illustrates how a household not participating in Microfinance Groups grows wealth purely through saving part of its labour income. When the savings rate and wage rate are constant, and labour input remains steady, the total wealth accumulated over time grows linearly.

3.2 *Microfinance Member Household*

For a microfinance member household, earnings are augmented by access to credit, which can be invested in income-generating activities. Let's denote the earnings of a microfinance member household as Y_M. A member household earns both labour income and profits from microfinance investments:

$$Y_M = W \cdot H + \pi \tag{5}$$

where, π represents the profits from the investment of microfinance loans. The profits π are a function of the loan amount L, the return on investment ρ, and the interest rate r paid on the loan:

$$\pi = L \cdot \rho - L \cdot r = L(\rho - r) \tag{6}$$

Thus, the earnings of a microfinance member household become –

$$Y_M = W \cdot H + L(\rho - r) \tag{7}$$

This shows that microfinance member households have higher potential earnings if the return on investment ρ exceeds the loan interest rate r. Otherwise, the loan may reduce net income. Till now, one can say that This model captures the essence of financial inclusion: microfinance members can supplement their labour income with capital returns. The expression $L(\rho - r)$ quantifies the benefit of the loan—if $\rho > r$ borrowing is profitable, and earnings are boosted. This can shift households from subsistence to growth trajectories, especially in developing economies. However, if $\rho < r$, loans could result in net losses, highlighting the importance of viable investments and reasonable interest rates.

Savings S_M are a fraction σ of the household's total earnings:

$$S_M = \sigma \cdot Y_M = \sigma[W \cdot H + L(\rho - r)] \tag{8}$$

This shows that both labour income and net returns from borrowing influence how much the household can save.

Wealth accumulation $A_M(t)$ is the total savings over $t + 1$ periods (from $\tau = 0$ to $\tau = t$) plus the outstanding loan balance $L(t)$.

$$A_M(t) = \sum_{\tau=0}^{t} S_M(t) + L(t) \tag{9}$$

Let us now integrate loan repayment dynamics into the wealth accumulation model for microfinance member households. Assuming that the loan is repaid over time, the wealth accumulation can be expressed as:

$$A_M(t) = \sum_{\tau=0}^{t} \sigma.[W.H + L(\rho - r)] + L(t) \tag{10}$$

Unlike non-member households, microfinance member households temporarily increase their wealth capacity using credit. However, since loans must be repaid, their long-term contribution to wealth diminishes unless returns from the loan consistently outpace the cost. The term L(t) illustrates the transient nature of loan-funded assets, and how the repayment schedule affects the accumulation path. This makes the model more realistic and suitable for policy or impact analysis in development finance.

3.3 *Comparative Analysis*

To compare the economic outcomes of microfinance members and non-members, we can analyze the difference in earnings, savings, and wealth accumulation.

Let us isolate the marginal gain in earnings due to microfinance participation.

Difference in earnings (ΔY) can be written as

$$\Delta Y = Y_M - Y_{NM} = [W \cdot H + L(\rho - r) - W \cdot H = L(\rho - r)] \quad (10)$$

The difference ΔY isolates the additional income a household earns by participating in microfinance. It arises solely from investing borrowed capital at a net positive return, quantified by $\rho - r$.

If $\rho > r$, then $\Delta Y > 0$: microfinance raises earnings.
If $\rho = r$, then $\Delta \Upsilon = 0$: borrowing breaks even.
If $\rho < r$, then $\Delta \Upsilon < 0$: borrowing reduces net income.

This formula provides a simple yet powerful criterion for evaluating the financial impact of credit access.

Let us now quantify the impact of microfinance on household savings, which is a natural progression after analyzing the earnings difference.

Difference in savings (ΔS) can be written as

$$\begin{aligned} \Delta S = S_M - S_{NM} &= \sigma \cdot [W \cdot H + L(\rho - r)] - \sigma \cdot W \cdot H \\ &= \sigma \cdot L(\rho - r) \end{aligned} \quad (11)$$

This formula shows how access to microfinance increases savings in proportion to the profit earned on the loan. Since both household types save a fixed proportion σ of their earnings, the savings difference arises only from the extra income earned via the loan. Positive differential in savings occurs only if $\rho > r$, the effect is amplified by both the loan amount L and the savings rate σ.

Let us now derive the difference in wealth accumulation between microfinance member and non-member households which is a key metric in evaluating the long-term impact of financial inclusion.

The difference in wealth accumulation (ΔA) is

$$\Delta A(t) = \sum_{\tau=0}^{t} \sigma.L.(\rho - r) + L(t) = (t+1).\sigma.L.(\rho - r) + L(t) \quad (12)$$

The term $(t + 1) \cdot\sigma\cdot L(\rho - r)$ reflects additional savings from investment earnings over time. The term L(t) reflects the remaining (invested or unspent) loan capital at time t. This equation captures the total additional wealth a microfinance member household accumulates compared to a non-member household. As time progresses, the savings term grows linearly (if $\rho > r$), while L(t) generally declines due to loan repayment. This model elegantly separates the ongoing flow effects (savings) and the stock of productive capital (loan).

Assuming that $\rho > r$, the profits from the investment of the microfinance loan are positive, leading to higher earnings, savings, and wealth accumulation for microfinance members compared to non-members.

The results of the model demonstrate that microfinance membership leads to higher earnings, savings, and wealth accumulation compared to non-members. The access to credit allows microfinance members to invest in income-generating activities, which increases their earnings and, consequently, their savings and wealth. The positive difference in earnings, savings, and wealth accumulation suggests that microfinance membership can be an effective tool for economic empowerment and poverty reduction.

4 Data, Methodology and Econometric Analysis

4.1 Data Collection and Survey Design

Our empirical analysis is based on three blocks of Indian Sundarbans. Microfinance plays a pivotal role in promoting financial inclusion in the Indian Sundarbans, a region marked by its rural landscape and vulnerability to natural disasters like cyclones. This delta area in West Bengal is rich in natural resources but often underserved by traditional banking systems. Microfinance institutions (MFIs) bridge this gap by offering accessible financial services such as small loans, savings, and insurance, catering to those who cannot access conventional banking. These services are crucial for local activities like agriculture, fishing, and eco-tourism, enabling farmers and fishermen to procure necessary resources and women to establish small businesses, thus fostering economic resilience.

A primary survey was conducted in three blocks of Indian Sundarbans, namely Basanti, Gosaba and Namkhana. The villages from each block were selected based on their low levels of financial inclusion and high poverty rates. A total of 360 households were surveyed from 6 villages—where two villages from each block were selected, with a focus on individuals who have accessed microfinance services. The survey followed the techniques of stratified random sampling. We have also surveyed the non-member households in order to get a clear view about the extent of impact of Microfinance services. A pilot survey was conducted in the month of January, 2024, followed by the final survey in December 2024. During the pilot survey, panchayat members; SHG members, microfinance-borrowers immensely helped in every aspect.

The primary survey employed a stratified random sampling technique to ensure comprehensive and balanced representation across diverse household characteristics that are central to analyzing the impact of microfinance on financial inclusion. The strata were formed based on three interrelated criteria: microfinance membership status, economic condition, and access to formal financial services, particularly ownership of a bank account.

The first level of stratification distinguished households based on whether they were members of a microfinance institution (MFI) or self-help group (SHG). This created two primary categories—Member households: Households that have accessed microfinance loans or services and Non-member households: Households without any participation in microfinance programmes. This categorization was essential for assessing the differential effects of microfinance access on financial behaviour and outcomes.

The second level of stratification was based on economic status. Within each membership category, households were further stratified based on their poverty status—BPL (Below Poverty Line) households, the second category was the APL (Above Poverty Line) households. This was particularly important in the Indian Sundarbans context, where poverty is widespread and microfinance is often targeted toward the poorest. Stratifying by economic condition ensured the inclusion of both vulnerable and relatively better-off households in the analysis.

A third layer of stratification was based on access to formal financial services, primarily indicated by bank account ownership. This is a widely accepted proxy for basic financial inclusion, as having a bank account is the first step toward engaging with the formal financial system (e.g., savings, credit, insurance). Households were classified as: Financially included: Having access to or using at least one formal financial service (e.g., savings account, credit, insurance) and Financially excluded: Lacking access to any formal financial services. By applying this three-tiered stratification—microfinance access, economic status, and financial inclusion level—the sample design ensured that households from all relevant subgroups were adequately represented. This approach not only enhanced the robustness of statistical comparisons between member and non-member households but also enabled a nuanced understanding of how microfinance interacts with poverty and existing levels of financial inclusion to affect household financial behaviour and outcomes.

A brief profile of the survey is given below in Table 3. The table makes it vividly clear that in every region, over 50% of the households are members in the SHG groups or Microfinancing groups. It was seen that those who are members of such groups are in better economic conditions. People living the below the poverty line (BPL) are still high in every region compared to its counterpart, that is, people living above poverty line (APL). The interesting fact about the findings is that those who are in the APL category are mostly microfinance borrowers which shows the direct impact of Microfinance in reducing poverty but it is yet to have its full control on the society because not all microfinance borrowers are in the APL category which again shows that a lot more needs to be done in these regions before one can say that Microfinance has been fully effective in uplifting people from below the poverty line. The data suggests the partial effectiveness of Microfinance in improving the economic conditions of people. One more reasons for this could be the fact that in the three regions, the survey found that around 59% people have access to formal financial services, which further limits the chances for financial inclusion. Hence, on one hand there is a need to enhance the activities of financial inclusion by providing financial services to these marginalized poor people, on the other hand, there is need for SHGs and microfinance groups to be more active. A combination of both can really have a deeper impact and establish the real meaning of financial inclusion – not just by having access to formal financial services but also by effectively using it to improve financial conditions.

The survey collected data on the following variables:

i. Dependent Variable: Financial inclusion, measured by access to and usage of formal financial services (e.g., savings accounts, credit, insurance).
ii. Independent Variables:

Demographic factors: Age, gender, education, and income.

Table 3 Profile of the field survey

Block	*No. of Households Surveyed*	*Gender Division*	*Financial Condition*	*No. of Microfinance Member Households*
Basanti	120	Male—52 Female—68	BPL—79 APL—41	74 (61.66%)
Gosaba	120	Male—63 Female—57	BPL—67 APL—53	79 (65.83%)
Namkhana	120	Male—61 Female—59	BPL—84 APL—36	62 (51.66%)

Source Primary Survey

Microfinance factors: Access to microfinance services, loan amount, and repayment history.
Regional factors: Geographic location.

In designing the empirical analysis of the impact of microfinance on financial inclusion in the rural and financially vulnerable region of the Indian Sundarbans, careful consideration was given to the selection of both the dependent and independent variables, grounded in theoretical foundations and real-world relevance. The overarching objective of the study is to evaluate whether access to microfinance services has a significant effect on a household's level of financial inclusion.

The dependent variable in this analysis is financial inclusion, defined and measured by both access to and usage of formal financial services, such as bank accounts, savings, formal credit, and insurance. This choice reflects the widely accepted multidimensional understanding of financial inclusion—mere access is insufficient unless accompanied by active usage. This variable captures the core outcome that microfinance programs seek to improve and aligns with national and international financial inclusion frameworks (e.g., RBI, World Bank). In the context of the Sundarbans, where traditional banking services are sparse, financial inclusion serves as a robust proxy for the extent to which marginalized populations are integrated into the formal financial system.

The independent variables are grouped into three categories—demographic factors, microfinance-specific factors, and regional characteristics—each grounded in economic theory and field-based observations.

Demographic Factors (Age, Gender, Education, Income):

These variables were chosen because household-level decisions related to financial access and usage are often shaped by demographic characteristics. Age may influence financial behavior and risk aversion; gender is crucial in the Sundarbans context, where many microfinance participants are women; education correlates with financial literacy and the ability to navigate financial services; and income directly affects the ability to save, borrow, or purchase insurance. These variables help control for heterogeneity in financial behaviour that is not directly related to microfinance access.

Microfinance Factors (Access, Loan Amount, Repayment History):

These variables are central to the research hypothesis. Access to microfinance is the main policy variable, capturing whether a household is a member of a self-help group (SHG) or microfinance institution (MFI). The loan amount reflects the scale of financial support received and is expected to influence economic outcomes and financial behavior. Repayment history serves as a proxy for credit discipline, reliability, and borrower engagement. These indicators are essential to isolating the influence of microfinance on financial inclusion beyond what demographics alone can explain.

Regional Factors (Geographic Location):

The inclusion of geographic dummies for the three surveyed blocks—Basanti, Gosaba, and Namkhana—accounts for unobserved regional variations in economic conditions, infrastructure availability, MFI activity, and banking outreach. Since these factors could independently affect financial inclusion, controlling for location ensures that the model isolates the effect of microfinance more precisely.

4.2 Synchronizing Theory with Empirics

The synchronization between the microeconomic theory-based model and the empirical investigation of microfinance's impact on financial inclusion is grounded in the logical alignment of theoretical constructs with measurable empirical variables. At the core of the theoretical model lies the premise that rural households operate under budget and credit constraints, which restrict their access to formal financial services. Microfinance institutions (MFIs), by offering small-scale financial services tailored to low-income populations, are posited to relax these constraints. The theoretical framework draws upon household utility maximization behaviour, wherein financial inclusion—conceptualized as access to and usage of formal financial instruments such as savings accounts, credit, and insurance—enhances household welfare by smoothing consumption and enabling productive investments.

In the empirical component, primary survey data collected from rural, backward areas of the Indian Sundarbans provide the basis for testing these theoretical predictions. The dependent variable, financial inclusion, is operationalized through indicators measuring both access to and utilization of formal financial services. The independent variables are categorized into demographic factors (age, gender, education, income), microfinance-related variables (access to services, loan amount, repayment history), and regional controls (geographic location). This classification reflects the multidimensional nature of financial inclusion and mirrors the theoretical considerations of heterogeneity in household characteristics and access barriers.

To rigorously assess the relationships, probit and tobit regression models are employed. The probit model is suited to binary outcomes, such as whether a household has access to formal financial services, while the tobit model addresses the censored nature of usage data—many households report zero usage of financial instruments despite potential access. These econometric techniques are consistent with the structure of the data and enable the estimation of marginal effects of independent variables on both the probability and intensity of financial inclusion.

The synchronization is thus achieved by explicitly mapping theoretical mechanisms onto observable empirical measures. For instance, the easing of liquidity constraints, a central theoretical proposition, is reflected in empirical variables such as access to microfinance and loan amounts. Similarly, informational asymmetries and creditworthiness are proxied through education levels and repayment history. The empirical analysis, therefore, serves as a practical validation of the theoretical model, allowing for the derivation of context-specific insights regarding the role of microfinance in enhancing financial inclusion among marginalized rural populations. This integration ensures that the research remains both theoretically grounded and empirically robust, contributing to a nuanced understanding of financial inclusion dynamics in underdeveloped regions.

4.3 Econometric Model

To analyze the determinants of financial inclusion and the impact of microfinance, we employ the following econometric models:

i. **Probit Model**: To estimate the probability of accessing formal financial services. Hence, Probit Model is used to estimate the probability that an individual is financially included (a binary outcome, e.g., whether or not a person has a bank account).
ii. **Tobit Model**: To analyze the extent of financial inclusion, considering the censored nature of the dependent variable or, one can say that it is used to estimate the extent or level of financial inclusion when the data is censored (e.g., how much someone saves or borrows, which cannot go below zero).

The general form of the probit model is:

$$P(y_i = 1|x_i) = \Phi(\beta_0 + \beta_1 x_i)$$

where, y_i is the dependent variable (access to financial services), x_i is a vector of independent variables, and ϕ is the standard normal cumulative distribution function.

The Tobit model is specified as:

$$y_i = \beta_0 + \beta_1 x_i + \varepsilon_i$$

where, y_i is the extent of financial inclusion, and ε_i is the error term.

4.4 Result & Discussion

Descriptive Statistics: The descriptive statistics of the survey data are presented in Table 4. The results indicate that a significant proportion of respondents in backward areas lack access to formal financial services. However, microfinance initiatives have improved access to credit and savings services in these regions.

Table 4 presents the descriptive statistics of the key variables collected during the household survey conducted across three blocks in the Indian Sundarbans. The results highlight several important patterns relevant to the analysis of financial inclusion and the role of microfinance. On average, the financial inclusion index—measured as a binary variable

Table 4 Descriptive statistics of field survey

Variable	*Mean*	*Std. Dev*	*Min*	*Max*
Financial Inclusion	0.70	0.50	0	1
Age (years)	35.6	12.3	18	65
Education (years)	4.8	3.2	0	12
Income (INR/month)	9,500	5,300	3,000	20,000
Access to Microfinance	0.59	0.49	0	1

Source primary survey

indicating whether a household has access to and uses formal financial services—stands at 0.70, suggesting that 70% of surveyed households are financially included to some extent. However, the standard deviation of 0.50 indicates considerable variation, reflecting the presence of a substantial share (30%) of financially excluded households, particularly in marginalized areas.

In this study, financial inclusion is the primary dependent variable and is constructed as a binary indicator, coded as 1 if a household has access to and uses at least one formal financial service, and 0 otherwise. Formal financial services include having a bank account, access to formal credit (e.g., from banks, MFIs, or SHGs), savings with a recognized institution, or active insurance coverage (life, health, or crop insurance). A household is considered financially included if it reports using at least one of these services at the time of the survey. This approach aligns with global practices (e.g., World Bank Findex) and captures both access and usage, which are crucial to understanding financial inclusion in real sense. Again, access to microfinance, the key explanatory variable, is also measured as a binary variable. A household is assigned a value of 1 if it is a member of a microfinance institution (MFI) or a self-help group (SHG) that provides financial services, and 0 otherwise. This includes both borrowers and savers affiliated with microfinance programs. During survey direct questions were asked whether households had received microfinance loans, participated in SHG activities, or held savings accounts within an MFI or SHG framework within the past 12 months. By defining microfinance access in this manner, the study ensures that the variable reflects active participation in the microfinance ecosystem, not merely nominal membership.

This clear operationalization allows for a meaningful estimation of how microfinance access influences a household's likelihood of being financially included, and ensures consistency across all surveyed regions.

The average age of respondents is 35.6 years, with a fairly wide spread (SD = 12.3), indicating the inclusion of both young adults and elderly individuals in the sample. The average education level is 4.8 years, which underscores the low level of formal schooling among the rural population—an important factor affecting financial literacy and access to financial services. Monthly household income averages at INR 9,500, but again shows high variability (SD = INR 5,300), with incomes ranging from INR 3,000 to INR 20,000. This reflects the economic heterogeneity of the surveyed households and the presence of both severely poor and moderately better-off families.

Crucially, the mean value for access to microfinance is 0.59, indicating that approximately 59% of surveyed households are members of microfinance institutions or self-help groups. This variable is central to the study, as it represents the primary explanatory factor influencing financial inclusion in the model. The binary nature of this variable confirms that access is not universal and that substantial room remains for expanding microfinance outreach.

Overall, the descriptive statistics reinforce the context-specific relevance of the study. While a significant portion of households have achieved a certain degree or level of financial inclusion, highly supported by microfinance, gaps still remain, especially among the less educated and lower-income groups. These observations support the empirical focus on quantifying how microfinance access, in conjunction with demographic and economic factors, affects the probability and depth of financial inclusion in rural backward regions like the Sundarbans.

The results of the probit and Tobit models are presented in Table 5. The findings indicate that access to microfinance services significantly increases the likelihood of financial inclusion in backward areas. Education, income, and geographic location are also significant determinants of financial inclusion.

The findings of this study underscore the critical role of microfinance in promoting financial inclusion in backward areas of Sundarbans. Individuals with access to microfinance are significantly more likely to be financially included (Probit), and they also engage more deeply with financial services (Tobit). This is highly significant at the 1% level. Education positively impacts both the likelihood and the extent of financial inclusion.

Table 5 Results of Probit and Tobit Models

Variable	*Probit Model*	*VIF*	*Marginal Effects*	*Tobit Model*	*VIF*	*Marginal Effects*
Access to Microfinance	0.35*** (4.21)	3.05	0.027*** (4.11)	0.40*** (5.10)	2.89	0.034*** (4.84)
Education	0.12*** (4.57)	2.99	0.028*** (3.99)	0.15*** (6.21)	2.97	0.024*** (4.24)
Income	0.40*** (3.14)	3.09	0.048*** (3.04)	0.48*** (4.23)	2.01	0.052*** (4.04)
Gender (Female = 1)	0.05*** (5.14)	3.42	0.004** (2.01)	0.07*** (3.94)	2.53	0.004** (2.04)
Age	−0.02** (−2.01)	3.20	−0.008** (−1.94)	−0.03** (−1.97)	3.28	−0.008** (−1.89)
Geographic Location	0.07*** (3.25)	3.51	0.004*** (3.00)	0.09*** (3.07)	2.46	0.007*** (2.44)
Constant	−1.20*			−1.50*		
Pseudo R^2	0.67			0.71		
Log-Likelihood	−212.45			−205.75		
LR Chi-square	187.10			204.70		
Prob > Chi-square	0.000			0.000		

Note ***, **, indicate significance at the 1%, 5% levels, respectively
Values in the parentheses are t-values
Source Computed by Author

Educated individuals are more aware and capable of accessing financial services. Higher income is associated with both a higher chance of being financially included and greater use of financial services. This reflects affordability and eligibility. Females are more likely to be financially included and use financial services more extensively. This might reflect targeted inclusion programs or better responsiveness among women. The results also suggest that gender plays a significant role in financial inclusion, with women being more likely to access microfinance services. This finding aligns with the broader literature on gender and financial inclusion, emphasizing the importance of targeting women in microfinance initiatives. The fact that age, as a variable, bears negative sign implies that elderly people are preferring less to get in touch with the system of microfinance and thus they are remaining out of the system of Financial Inclusion.

As age increases, the likelihood and extent of financial inclusion decrease, though the effect is moderate and only significant at the 5%

level. Older populations may face more barriers or exhibit less need for formal financial services. Individuals in certain geographic locations (likely to be near the financial institutions or slightly urban-centric areas) are more likely to be financially included. This points to spatial inequality in access to financial institutions.

We have also calculated the marginal effects which have different interpretations for both models. In case of probit analysis, the marginal effects show the percentage change in the dependent variable, that is, a change in the predicted probability of the dependent variable when there is one-unit change in the any specific dependent variable, holding the other variables constant. In case of the tobit model, the marginal effects explain the change in the probability of the outcome which is non-censored. Our findings of the marginal effects match with the signs and significance levels of the primary probit and tobit analysis. We have also calculated the Variance Inflation Factor (VIF) which accounts for the problem of multicollinearity or the degree of correlation among the independent variables. In case of the probit analysis, the mean VIF is 3.21 and in case of tobit analysis it is 2.69. In both the cases, the mean VIF of the regressors is below 5 which goes with the rule of thumb and therefore we can conclude that the problem of multicollinearity is not a problem in the present study.[3] Hence, both the models are acceptable.

Access to microfinance, education, income, being female, and favourable geographic location all positively and significantly influence both the probability and extent of financial inclusion. In contrast, age has a negative effect—highlighting the need for complementary interventions in these areas. The analysis shows that access to microfinance services significantly improves the likelihood of accessing formal financial services, particularly for low-income and marginalized groups. The models are both significant and well fitted as revealed by the high values of pseudo R^2 but the Tobit model slightly outperforms the Probit model in explaining financial inclusion

[3] The rule of thumb for VIF says that multicollinearity is not a problem if it lies between 1 and 5 but it becomes a worry if it goes beyond 5 and lies between 5 and 10. Those situations need for a remodelling of the analysis.

5 Conclusion and Policy Recommendations

This study demonstrates the importance of microfinance in fostering financial inclusion in developing economies by means of two ways—first, by developing economic model and analysing their effects and second, by conducting econometric analysis on based on primary survey in the backward areas of Indian Sundarbans. The findings suggest that policymakers should prioritize the expansion of microfinance services in underserved regions. Moreover, efforts to improve education and awareness of financial services can further enhance financial inclusion. The study also highlights the need for targeted interventions to address gender disparities in financial inclusion. By empowering women through microfinance, policymakers can achieve broader economic and social benefits, even if women are enjoying the larger share of microcredits, it can improve their financial conditions to a great extent.

Finally, the findings underscore the importance of leveraging technology and digital platforms to expand the outreach of microfinance services in backward areas. This can help overcome the challenges of geographic isolation and limited banking infrastructure. The government and regulators should encourage the expansion of microfinance institutions in underserved regions. Enhancing digital infrastructure and promoting digital literacy can complement microfinance efforts. Policies should focus on improving financial literacy to maximize the benefits of microfinance. A supportive regulatory framework is essential to ensure the sustainability and scalability of microfinance initiatives.

One limitation of the model lies in a potential endogeneity issue between the key explanatory variable (access to microfinance) and the dependent variable (financial inclusion), particularly because most microfinance institutions require borrowers to open a bank account for loan disbursement. If financial inclusion is defined solely by bank account ownership, this creates a mechanical correlation that may overstate the causal effect of microfinance on inclusion. To address this, the study defines financial inclusion using a broader set of indicators—including access to credit, savings, and insurance—beyond just bank account ownership. Nevertheless, the possibility of partial endogeneity remains which can be reduced by using an instrumental variable approach, if valid instruments exist. As a complementary method, propensity score matching can also be used to compare similar households with and without microfinance access, mitigating selection bias due to observable factors.

There are scopes to take the study forward in future where one can conduct surveys in other parts of Sundarbans or other backward regions to check the long-run efficacy of MFIs in achieving financial inclusion and economic growth.

References

Al-Mansoori, A., Al-Haddad, S., & Al-Ghamdi, M. (2023). Diffusion of mobile-money-linked micro-finance in Yemen's tribal hinterlands. *Journal of African Business, 24*(2), 143–162.

Armendáriz, B., & Morduch, J. (2010). *The economics of microfinance* (2nd ed.). MIT Press. ISBN 978-0-262-01410-6.

Banerjee, A. V., & Duflo, E. (2007). The economic lives of the poor. *Journal of Economic Perspectives, 21*(1), 141–168. https://doi.org/10.1257/jep.21.1.141

Banerjee, A. V., & Duflo, E. (2011). *Poor economics: A radical rethinking of the way to fight global poverty*. Public Affairs. ISBN-13. 978–1586487980.

Banerjee, A. V., Duflo, E., Glennerster, R., & Kinnan, C. (2015). The miracle of microfinance? Evidence from a randomized evaluation. *American Economic Journal: Applied Economics, 7*(1), 22–53. https://doi.org/10.1257/app.20130533

Baviskar, D., Anushka, C. & Patil, A. (2024). Consumer behaviour and sustainable product choices: Insights from visual trends. In *E3S Web of Conferences, 472*, 02002. https://doi.org/10.1051/e3sconf/202447202002

Bharat, R., & Mishra, P. (2022). Two-sided market modelling of micro-finance in Indian backward districts. *Journal of Development Economics, 155*, Article 102894.

Biswas, D. (2018). Role of self-help groups (SHGs) & Micro finance on women's economic empowerment in India: A study. *Inspira- Journal of Modern Management & Entrepreneurship (JMME), 8*(1), 471–480.

Buera, F. J., Kaboski, J. P., & Shin, Y. (2021). The macroeconomics of microfinance. *The Review of Economic Studies, 88*(1), 126–161. https://doi.org/10.1093/restud/rdaa047

Chakraborty, S., Singh, D., & Ghosh, R. (2024). Women-only micro-finance groups and empowerment in Bihar's Kosi region. *Economic and Political Weekly, 59*(10), 68–77.

Chatterjee, N. (2019). Use of renewable resources and sustainable livelihood in Indian Sunderbans: An attempt through contingent valuation method. *Vidyasagar University Journal of Economics, XXII*, ISSN: 0975-8003, 98–117.

Chatterjee, N. (2025). Unlocking potential: The indispensable role of women's financial inclusion in developing economies. In *Women empowerment in India and beyond* (pp. 93–104). Kunal Publisher.

Chatterjee, N., & Kundu, D. (2025). The unsung heroes of rural finance: Assessing the performance of regional rural banks in India. *Journal of Scholastic Engineering Science and Management, 4*(1), 1–7. https://doi.org/10.5281/zenodo.14711104

Churchill, C. (2006). *Protecting the poor: A microinsurance compendium*. International Labour Organization. ISBN 978-92-2-119254-1 (ILO).

Collins, D., Morduch, J., Rutherford, S., & Ruthven, O. (2010). *Portfolios of the poor: How the world's poor live on $2 a day*. Princeton University Press. ISBN: 9780691148199

Crépon, B., Devoto, F., Duflo, E., Parienté, W., & Rathod, V. (2015). Do microcredits help repay informal debts? Evidence from a randomized experiment. *American Economic Journal: Applied Economics, 7*(1), 1–21. https://doi.org/10.1257/app.20130537

Dupas, P., & Robinson, J. (2013). Savings constraints and microenterprise development: Evidence from a field experiment in Kenya. *American Economic Journal: Applied Economics, 5*(1), 163–192. https://doi.org/10.1257/app.5.1.163

GSMA. (2020). *Mobile financial services in Kenya: The case of M-Pesa*. https://www.gsma.com

Honohan, P. (2008). Cross-country variation in household access to financial services. *Journal of Banking & Finance, 32*(11), 2493–2500. https://doi.org/10.1016/j.jbankfin.2008.05.003

Hulme, D., & Mosley, P. (1996). *Finance against poverty*. Routledge.

Inter-American Development Bank. (2018). *Microfinance in Latin America*. https://www.iadb.org

Karlan, D., & Zinman, J. (2010). Expanding credit access: Using randomized supply decisions to estimate the impacts. *Review of Financial Studies, 23*(1), 433–464. https://doi.org/10.1093/rfs/hhp092

Khandker, S. R., & Samad, H. A. (2022). Micro-finance and poverty trap dynamics: A panel analysis from Bangladesh. *World Development, 155*, Article 105762.

Kipkeme, J., Ouma, M., & Kamau, N. (2022). Spatial spillovers of micro-finance in Kenya's rural arid lands: Night-light evidence. *Emerging Markets Review, 54*, Article 100979.

Kumar, V., & Bansal, S. (2023). Financial inclusion through micro-finance in India's backward districts: A difference-in-differences approach. *Journal of Banking & Finance, 148*, Article 106289.

Kundu, D., & Chatterjee, N. (2025). CAMEL analysis of selected scheduled commercial banks in India. *Management Journal of Advanced Research, 5*(1), 50–57. https://doi.org/10.5281/zenodo.15043390

Ledgerwood, J., & Rosenberg, R. (2006). *Transforming microfinance institutions: The path to financial self-sufficiency and development impact*. World Bank.

Méndez, L., Salazar, J., & Paredes, M. (2023). Micro-finance intensity and regional growth in the Peruvian Andes. *Development Policy Review, 41*(4), 583–608.

Morduch, J., & Santos, S. (2021). Digital micro-finance and consumption smoothing among displaced households in Nigeria. *Journal of African Economies, 30*(3), 327–356.

North, D. C. (1990). *Institutions, institutional change and economic performance* (p. 33). Cambridge University Press.

Osei-Mensah, J., & Agyeman, K. (2021). Social capital and loan repayment in Ghana's Upper west region. *Journal of Rural Studies, 87*, 22–31.

Putnam, R. D. (2000). Bowling alone: America's declining social capital. In L. Crothers., & C. Lockhart (Eds.), *Culture and Politics*. Palgrave Macmillan, New York. https://doi.org/10.1007/978-1-349-62965-7_12

Rahman, A., & Hossain, M. (2025). Randomized evaluation of a digital micro-finance platform in Bangladesh's char areas. *Journal of Financial Services Research, 62*(1), 45–70.

Ray, S., & Nath, S. (2024). Natural disaster, livelihood challenges and microfinance: A field survey analysis of the Sundarban region in West Bengal, India. In *Sustainable development goals and India* (pp. [pages]). Springer. https://doi.org/10.1007/978-981-97-5388-8_13

Rhyne, E. (2008). *Microfinance for bankers and investors: Creating social and financial value*. Palgrave Macmillan.

Rogers, E. M. (2003). *Diffusion of innovations* (5th ed.) Free Press.

Roodman, D. (2012). *Due diligence: An impertinent inquiry into microfinance*. Center for Global Development.

Silva, R., & Pérez, A. (2024). Micro-finance as a proto-institution in Brazil's Sertão: Effects on contract compliance and schooling. *Journal of Institutional Economics, 20*(2), 311–332.

Status of Microfinance in India 2023–24. (2024). *National Bank for Agriculture and Rural Development*. https://www.nabard.org

Stiglitz, J. E., & Weiss, A. (1981). Credit rationing in markets with imperfect information. *The American Economic Review, 71*, (3), 393–410.

The World Bank. (2022). *The global Findex database 2021: Financial inclusion, digital payments, and the COVID-19 crisis*. World Bank Publications. https://www.worldbank.org

Todaro, M., & Smith, S. (2015). Economic Development (7th Ed.). Pearson.

World Bank. (2018a). *The global Findex database 2017: Measuring financial inclusion and the fintech revolution*. World Bank Publications.

World Bank. (2018b). *The role of microfinance in financial inclusion*. https://www.worldbank.org

World Bank. (2020). *The global Findex database*. https://www.worldbank.org

World Bank & CGAP. (2022). *Micro-finance and financial inclusion: A meta-analysis of impact evaluations (2010–2022)* (World Bank Policy Research Working Paper No. 10245).

Yunus, M. (1999). *Banker to the poor: Micro-lending and the battle against world poverty*. Public Affairs.

Yunus, M. (2003). *Banker to the poor: Micro-lending and the battle against world poverty*. Public Affairs.

Yunus, M. (2007). *Creating a world without poverty: Social business and the future of capitalism*. Public Affairs.

Index

© The Editor(s) (if applicable) and The Author(s), under exclusive license to Springer Nature Singapore Pte Ltd. 2026

V. Dixit et al. (eds.), *Financial Inclusion for Viksit Bharat*,
https://doi.org/10.1007/978-981-92-0807-4

B

C

GPSR Compliance
The European Union's (EU) General Product Safety Regulation (GPSR) is a set of rules that requires consumer products to be safe and our obligations to ensure this.

If you have any concerns about our products, you can contact us on

ProductSafety@springernature.com

In case Publisher is established outside the EU, the EU authorized representative is:

Springer Nature Customer Service Center GmbH
Europaplatz 3
69115 Heidelberg, Germany

www.ingramcontent.com/pod-product-compliance
Ingram Content Group UK Ltd.
Pitfield, Milton Keynes, MK11 3LW, UK
UKHW040704260926
475945UK00001B/1

9789819208067